AMERICA IS INDIAN COUNTRY

Opinions and Perspectives from

INDIAN COUNTRY
TODAY

Edited by José Barreiro and Tim Johnson

Fulcrum Publishing
Golden, CO

Library of Congress Cataloging-in-Publication Data
America is Indian country : opinions and perspectives from Indian country today / edited by José Barreiro and Tim Johnson.
    p. cm.
  Includes index.
ISBN 1-55591-537-X (pbk.)
1. Indians of North America--Politics and government. 2. Indians of North America--Government relations. 3. Indians of North America--Tribal citizenship. 4. Federally recognized Indian tribes--United States. 5. Self-determination, National--United States. 6. United States--Race relations. 7. United States--Politics and government. I. Barreiro, José. II. Johnson, Tim, 1947-
  E98.T77A43 2005
  320.1'5'08997--dc22
                                                        2005019746
ISBN10 1-55591-537-X ISBN13 978-1-55591-537-7

Printed in the United States of America
0 9 8 7 6 5 4 3 2 1

Editorial: Sam Scinta, Katie Raymond
Cover image and design: Jack Lenzo
Back cover image courtesy of Michael and Kathryn Walton

Fulcrum Publishing
16100 Table Mountain Parkway, Suite 300
Golden, Colorado 80403
(800) 992-2908 o (303) 277-1623
www.fulcrum-books.com

DEDICATION

For the Voices

This book is for all those who have raised their voices on behalf of American Indian tribal nations' right to survive and prosper on these American lands. America is Indian country; the seed is in the memory, the roots are in the land. Our audience—the core intellectual and community-oriented tribal networks and peoples and their circles of activist allies in the world—is a most demanding circle, always pressuring us to hold the line on Indian rights. We treasure the challenge. The covenant is to uphold the recognition that Indian country is part and parcel of the central formative and original fiber of America and to assert that Native America has deep roots in the land and in the places of origin. Everything else flows from there.

CONTENTS

FOREWORD
CAMP CRIERS SPEAKING ACROSS THE GENERATIONS

Native peoples have rich traditions of spreading the news and documenting our time. Our ancestors recorded their ideas, visions, events, and feats in oral histories, songs, and myriad other documentary forms: winter counts on hides, pictographs on rocks and trees, weavings of reeds and hair, beaded bandoleers, wampum belts, ledger drawings, and messages carved in stone, shell, wood, and metal.

Through these forms of communication and the print and broadcast media we chronicle experiences, interpret meanings, provide instructions, and prophesy the future.

In many Native traditions, those who report and analyze news are called camp criers. They are esteemed persons who are chosen for their credibility, judgment, memory, and voice, but mostly for their ability to get the story right and to get it to the people.

Camp criers walk or run or ride from person to person, home to home, until everyone knows the news. In modern cultural or social settings, they may tell the people about a ceremony that is starting, a person who is being honored, or a guest who is entering the grounds.

In the days when most Native peoples lived lives on the run, the camp criers carried life-and-death news: "Bluecoats on horses on the horizon! Break camp now! Can only take babies!" It was the job of the camp criers to remind the people of emergency plans and point them in the direction of safety. The wisest ones in the late 1400s warned, "Destruction by land and sea."

Camp criers also perform lifesaving duties in today's camps, where they sometimes have to alert the people to the dangers of tornadoes or water moccasins or tourists.

The most aware in the early 2000s sound the alarms of present danger: "governors coming to tax you to death" or "scientists coming for your bones."

From "the buffalo are running from the east" to "Kevin Costner is shooting at noon," the camp criers are concise and accurate. They headline their information with the precise words in Native languages for different kinds of news. The prefatory word for news about the time for dinner is a far cry from "the meat will make you sick" or "the summer clans will prepare the death feast."

There is big-deal news and news you can use and news about what's happening now. There is up-to-the-minute news and commentary on old news. In some Native languages, there are phrases for "pre-news" that translate roughly as "news growing from gossip" or "this is the saying, but is it really so?"

Two Mohawk words for news have subtle distinctions in meaning: *ori:wase*, which means "new matters or information," and *karihwanakere*, "news or information in this area."

The Yurok language has separate words for "good news," *skuhson*, and "bad news," *kimsook*.

News in Karuk, *ikxaareehi*, means "to be news."

In Hoopa, *k'iniwh* and *k'iniwh 'a:dilchwe* mean "(S)He hears about it." and "(S)He makes him/herself hear the news."

Among dozens of words for news in the Navajo (Diné) language, the basic one is *hani'*.

In the language of the Yakama Nation, *taymu* and *tamun* mean "to tell." In Yakama meetings, people announce that they have *timash*, "big newspaper" or "important documents."

In the Muscogee (Creek) language, the most common words for news are *opunvk'v-mucvse*, which means "new word," and *opunv'k'vsan*, "news." The root word means "voice" too. The Muscogee words with the closest ties to those for news mean "report" and "text" but also "parable" and "slander." *Opunv'kv-sarv* is a "news carrier" or "news messenger," as well as a runner or angel.

In the Tsistsistas (Cheyenne) language, *tseve-he'nov'e* means "the news" or "sayings" and *nixhotahaovsx tseve-he'nov'e* means "tell me the news" or "tell me what the sayings are."

There is a word in Tsistsistas for "crier-paper" or "newspaper," *hoo?xeva-voxe?estoo?o*.

Indian Country Today is a crier-paper, blending the traditions of documenting and telling the news. The people who write editorials and opinion pieces for the crier-paper are informing and communicating with the people today, but they are also speaking across the generations. Relatives in a distant time can read them and learn what we were doing and, perhaps as importantly, what we thought we were doing.

There is a canon of construction in federal Indian law that requires treaties and other legal instruments to be interpreted in accordance with what the Indians at the time believed and understood. The volume of laws and treaty adjustments increases yearly and each has an accompanying legislative history, case background, or administrative record. Much of this is based on testimony and news accounts of what the Indians wanted.

This rule of interpretation not only has legal consequences, but the matter of what the Indians thought at the time of their actions reverberates through history and shapes Native nations and individuals. It has been of critical importance to those of us who are descendants of treaty makers to know what our ancestors thought they were providing for their coming generations and for the land and water and creatures beyond their time.

Our descendants will want to know our intentions as we engage in the development of laws and policies. The crier-paper documents what we worry and dream about, what we agree and disagree with, and what we meant to do.

Welcome, readers of this time, but especially our most distant future relatives, to the news of camp criers in the first years of the new century.

—Suzan Shown Harjo

Editors' note: Suzan Shown Harjo (Cheyenne and Hodulgee Muscogee) is president of The Morning Star Institute in Washington, D.C., and a columnist for *Indian Country Today*. The following researchers also contributed to this piece: Dr. Manley A. Begay Jr. (Navajo), Carol Craig (Yakama), Dr. Henri Mann (Cheyenne), Frank Miller (Six Nations Mohawk), Lois J. Risling (Hoopa, Yurok, and Karuk), and Robert W. Trepp (Muscogee and Cherokee).

THE VALUE OF RESPECT

The old Indian way encouraged a circle of opinion, not only debate, as a way to arrive at the truth of a thing. Only then was it possible to do what was best for the people. Three elements were required in seeking and providing thinking for all major decisions: integrity, intelligence, and respect.

This is what many of us in leadership circles among Native peoples and within national institutions such as the U.S. Senate have seen emerging at *Indian Country Today*. Week by week, we receive it and can appreciate the depth and clarity of its content and production. There is truth seeking going on at *Indian Country Today* that I think is an important development for Indian nations and indeed for the country.

Indian country has needed good, serious journalism, one backed by intelligent curiosity, always with tough, penetrating questions and yet always, too, consciously respectful in the handling of people and information. We all benefit from professional reporting and crisp analysis. We all benefit when information is accurate and timely, when the editorial attitude is reflective, inclusive. We now have a national newspaper of record on par with any of the leading newspapers of our times, a historical timepiece useful today and useful for the generations.

I am happy to welcome such an open-ended vehicle for communications among and by opinion leaders in Indian country. We may not always agree on a given issue, but we can agree that we are all human beings in it together. It appears to me that this is a valued principle at *Indian Country Today*. I believe that the country at large, the United States of America, will always benefit greatly from upholding such a principle. Sitting in the great tipi that is America, looking at the circle of faces, each adding their own important log to the central fire, we learn best by appreciating our common destiny.

Congratulations to the editors on this book of editorials and other commentaries from the first several years of the new century. I truly hope this edition will be the first of many that will document American Indian views and currents over the next few decades.

—Senator Ben Nighthorse Campbell

Editors' note: Former senator Ben Nighthorse Campbell, R-Colo., served as chairman of the Senate Committee on Indian Affairs. He is a member of the Northern Cheyenne Tribe and Council of 44 Chiefs.

ACKNOWLEDGMENTS

Many people—who collectively have hundreds of years of experience in Indian country—contributed to this book. To all, I humbly express my highest appreciation and admiration.

Through the course of many experiences in the workplace and in the field, in North America, Central America, and the Caribbean, I have prized my partnership and collaborations with José Barreiro. I am thankful for Barreiro's wide-ranging thirty-plus years of active experience within the Native world of the Americas and for his highly perceptive and poignant writings that constitute valuable contributions to the national discourse on American Indian issues. From his early service at *Akwasasne Notes* in the 1970s and early 1980s to his substantial hemispheric contribution from his twenty-year perch at Cornell University, I have followed Barreiro's fascinating communications and community-development projects, collaborating in not a few of them. In the past five years of journalistic endeavor, I have been highly pleased to have him as chief editorialist and senior editor in the first circle of advisors and contributors to *Indian Country Today*.

From that circle as well, Dr. Jim Adams, associate editor of *Indian Country Today*, gifted us with his precision and accuracy of reporting and with his principled defense of American Indian life and land. I express my heartfelt gratitude to this journalist of exceptional range and skill, honed by many assignments including thirteen years at *The Wall Street Journal*. In his work with *Indian Country Today*, Jim consistently exhibited intellectual enthusiasm for the modern Indian movement. In addition to writing hundreds of outstanding news reports, he informed and influenced the newspaper's editorial knowledge on numerous critically important topics, including the history and culture of European government, American history, and the banking and finance industries. He played an essential role as a trusted advisor to the newspaper for the past five years.

As senior editors, we are joined by a growing editorial think tank featuring several national columnists who offer their unique perspectives. Among these are Suzan Shown Harjo, veteran journalist and top-shelf American Indian commentator. Seriously experienced, Harjo is as good as they come in gathering, thinking through, and delivering a piece of analytical commentary, sometimes with humor and sometimes with bite, but always with insight.

Dr. John Mohawk, an intellectual powerhouse whose oratorical skills make him one of the most significant Indian communicators of any era, lent his considerable genius to our pages. It is always a privilege to work with and learn from Dr. Mohawk, who has introduced myriad wonderful ideas and concepts to Indian country readership.

Rebecca Adamson, who runs her own community economic-development institute and is a leader in Native American philanthropy, has also graced the perspectives pages of *Indian Country Today* with her own brand of culturally appropriate business and social commentary.

Steve Newcomb, indigenous law research coordinator at Kumeyaay Community College, exhibited a tireless spirit in seeking out and revealing the truth of issues that some wished to bury quickly within the footnotes of history. The complex story of the attempted theft of Western Shoshone lands emerges as paramount among his many research-and-reporting achievements.

Our deep gratitude is also expressed to Marty Two Bulls, Oglala Lakota from Pine Ridge, the editorial cartoonist whose work graces the pages of this book. Two Bulls, an exceptional artist whose talents led him to graphic reporting and commentary for several newspapers throughout his career, has published many memorable cartoons on the editorial pages of *Indian Country Today*. His images often draw out the irony, poignancy, contradiction, or humor of a particular issue. At other times, he presents inspirational portraits of American Indian leaders or artistic studies of historical events or editorial concepts. Like our national commentators, Two Bulls carries within him a solid reservoir of community-based experience. This greatly stimulates his creativity and aids him in arriving at the nugget of the idea for each cartoon. On his enjoyment in working with *Indian Country Today*, Two Bulls recently said, "The quality of their editorial commentary has been a great inspiration to my cartoons." Well, the feeling is mutual; his entertaining and informative work has also inspired the newspaper's editors and readers.

Others on the et al roster include former senator Ben Nighthorse Campbell, Katsi Cook, Kevin Gover, Maurice Lyons, Carey N. Vicenti, Pete Homer, John Guevremont, Charles E. Trimble, David E. Wilkins, Harold A. Monteau, Steven Paul McSloy, and Rachel Attituq Qitsualik. We thank them all, as we thank the many more who have strengthened our circle since the relaunch of the newspaper.

I also appreciate the early support for our work provided by philanthropic organizations such as Lannan Foundation, the John D. and Catherine

T. MacArthur Foundation, and Ford Foundation, which see the need for varieties of cultural and ethnic voices to emerge in public media. I also express my gratitude to Buffalo State College for many years of collaboration and ongoing innovation in the field of American Indian communication.

We profoundly appreciate Four Directions Media, Inc., owned by the Oneida Nation of New York. The solid suppport of the Four Directions leadership for First Amendment rights and toward the important independent work of Native journalism is significant. We have welcomed the understanding of the Oneida leadership that *Indian Country Today*'s credibility and impact—the measure of our quality—are founded on the newspaper's independence and ability to range intellectually free and ethically sound by fairly applying its resources to the concerns and needs of American Indian peoples east to west, north to south. Even when the Nation and the newspaper have been at odds over issues, editorial and journalistic acumen have prevailed. In particular, newspaper executives Ray Halbritter and Peter Golia are recognized for their advocacy of the newspaper's historic value, intellectual content, and its contributions to American Indian journalism.

INTRODUCTION

For American Indians, the beginning of the twenty-first century was considerably different from the year 1900, when Indian nations were still literally under the gun in various regions of America.

In the pages of this book are found editorials, commentaries, and editorial cartoons reflecting a reemerging American Indian world, one where financial resources generated by gaming and other business activities began enabling tribes to rebuild their communities and nations. Indeed, against dire predictions, even traditional cultures—always resilient—are seeing benefits of the new economic clout. In the future, this current era may well be seen as a time of reassertion in which American Indian peoples increasingly fought to secure their rightful places in their own lands.

Indian Country Today was rededicated on January 1, 2000. New owners and editors committed themselves to a task predicated upon the belief and mutual agreement that Indian country deserved a national newspaper that could communicate to its readership with the highest standards of editorial excellence. This group, which I was privileged to chair, believed that it was possible to stand side by side with the dominant American newspapers of the day and not only compete effectively and genuinely with original reporting and commentary, but, particularly, to establish a respected and credible forum for the analysis of issues that affected tribal communities.

The new editorial team also believed that the newspaper could establish an identity that focused not on the personalities of its editors, but on the issues that mattered most. From the very start of the newspaper's conceptual overhaul, a commitment was made to focus on the most crucial events and issues and to draw perspectives from the leading American Indian figures of our times. We were keenly aware that the editorial concept and practice over this work was to be independent and self-driven to uphold the highest journalistic standards for fair and accurate coverage. The significant role for *Indian Country Today* was not only documenting this fascinating era, at the dawn of a new century, but also in providing commentary and perspective, always with an eye toward the future, toward our children's grandchildren. This book, a selection of American Indian editorial essays and perspectives from the pages of *Indian Country Today* from the years 2000 through 2004, is the manifestation of a conceptual intention that was envisioned at the time the newspaper was rededicated.

In calling upon the most experienced and expressive minds in Indian country, it was necessary that there be a foundation to which the op-ed section was anchored for the long term. After all, the high-quality contributors we wanted to attract to the newspaper needed to possess substantial experience in the Native world, both at the community level and at the level of national policy. It is always easy to render opinion, but depth and power are added to viewpoint when real-world experience underlies the delivery of informed opinion. If we were to elevate the newspaper's standing and reputation, we believed that experience combined with maturity was needed to make the difference in providing a high-quality thinking-and-information vehicle for Indian country.

As a result, the depth of experience of our editorial staff and contributors who possess Indian-country policy experience has increased dramatically. We needed to ask the questions for ourselves and for others: Why participate if just another exercise in American Indian publishing? Why write if our words were only to have a fleeting purpose, filling column inches on newsprint and pasting electrons on the Internet? Why devote significant time to yet another project unless it could help to elevate the art, to inform, share, shape, and activate the minds of those making differences at all levels of American Indian policy, from education, health, or housing workshops to meetings and conferences; from cultural events and ceremonial gatherings to hearings and deliberations of tribal governments; from the Bureau of Indian Affairs (BIA) to the Senate Committee on Indian Affairs, and even the Internal Revenue Service? We believed, therefore, that the rebirth of *Indian Country Today* was a noble pursuit and a worthwhile endeavor. Thus in the editorials and perspectives of our leading national newspaper I believe a reader will find lessons in American Indian success and failure, initiative and dysfunction, honor and dishonor. We committed to the proposition that American Indians can still shape and influence not only their own communities, but also their broader national societies.

Among those very impressive editors and contributors who have joined us on this fascinating journey—those who have been there, who themselves have made substantial contributions to the American Indian world, and who remain impressively vigilant about protecting the inherent sovereign powers and authorities of our peoples—there exists a shared understanding of the strategic importance of a publication such as *Indian Country Today*.

As writers and editors have coalesced around *Indian Country Today* during these years, we have been fortunate to add a great list of names to the underlying purpose of the newspaper. The result has been a steady production of some great opinion pieces, most written on the hoof, within the weekly heartbeat of political time, and by experienced Native journalists and national thinkers and writers of the highest caliber. The result, which we begin to conceptualize and contextualize within these pages, is not only a record of the first years of a new American Indian century and millennium; it is a teaching tool that provides a dynamic interpretation of national events, legal and legislative trends, and how they influence and shape Indian country.

I invite the reader to engage in necessary thinking about Indian country predicated on the idea that American Indians—our families, peoples, and nations—hold in common principles of community and tribal ways and have many jurisdictional matters to defend. These are concerns that deserve the clearest of thinking. They also deserve a wide-ranging discussion, where all well-argued positions are considered openly and respectfully. We believe that our points of view must rightfully range and sometimes clash, tribally and nationally. This must be possible without destructive approaches. The widest reporting and deepest debate are exactly the recipe needed to establish the kind of solutions-oriented discussions that make achievement possible. I don't propose that the following editorials and columns are always right, but they always make a point: they inform and teach and they always represent a sincere effort or quest toward reaching appropriate awareness, understanding, and belief. We believe that the quality of dialogue improves when elevated to the real issues and trying to locate truthful, integrative perception, rather than offensive, adversarial, wantonly combative approaches. This is very important in trying to avoid situations that result in conflict with no resolution. Firm reporting and perspectives, yes; insults, no. These pieces teach because the voices that articulate them express sound human themes centered on political, economic, and cultural interests.

From our first years of publishing in the new century, I extend my deepest appreciation to a dear friend and colleague of some twenty years, Dr. José Barreiro.

Dr. Barreiro, of Taino base and spirit and a Cornell scholar for two decades, applied his considerable intellect and prolific creative and perceptive knowledge of contemporary American Indian issues and realities. His weekly editorial essays helped conceptualize and fashion the broad range and elegant tone of *Indian Country Today*'s editorial pages. Week by week I requested his editorial advice, insight, and prose, and he constantly gave it, generously and always with earnest, intellectual enthusiasm. Together we discussed and determined our editorial topics, seeking out principled opinions and positions that were inclusive of both intellect and spirit. Dr.

Barreiro contributed most of the original editorial writing; I reworked these pieces, respecting their original bent and style but adding paragraphs and additional fact-pattern to hone the newspaper's position.

What has made Dr. Barreiro's and my recent collaboration on *Indian Country Today* so uniquely interesting and enjoyable to me is that we are challenged to reach a mutual position on matters upon which we don't always agree. This is not necessarily definable within the liberal-conservative spectrum, but often we work antithetical opinions in order to arrive at a position of truthful intent. My distinguished colleague perhaps leans toward more radical-liberal (*radical* as in "going to the root," *liberal* as in "liberty") predilections, while I tilt toward more moderate-conservative ones. Neither of us, however, fits squarely into any labeled ideology, and sometimes these roles reverse. The intent is deeper philosophic and contemplative perception. On our commentary on the Iraq War, for example, our early ruminations were considerate of the full range of public debate while encouraging the United States to lead for peace. When, however, the facts revealed great and deliberate lapses in American intelligence combined with poor foreign-policy judgments, it became clear that our original admonition was and remains the best course for America abroad and at home. Where we have most often found common ground has been in our shared search for the pragmatic and for committing to solutions that seek what is best for American Indians based on what is realistic and workable and, always, within what maintains the strongest possible sovereign posture.

My welcome role as first editor was to encourage and help Barreiro craft pieces toward the greatest and broadest sense of a consistent American Indian opinion, reaching out for additional knowledge, experience, and strategic perspective by incorporating the best business and professional as well as culturally and traditionally applied minds. In this manner, *Indian Country Today*'s editorials, which are published weekly as the "Editors' Report," are direct fruit of this collaboration to reflect the braided thinking of dozens of experienced people who help all of us deepen our understanding of these issues on an ongoing basis.

The consistent high-level work demanded by the weekly national Indian publication became possible by the collective vision of Native people who have experienced the highs and lows of the American Indian experience. From direct lived experience, the generation that refashioned this newspaper carries in its memory those times when poverty was endemic and, even worse, when most governments responded to Indian demands with police or military action. Little hope prevailed. Within this generation, disadvantage has begun to turn toward advantage. So it is that we all shared and respected the vision that a high-quality national American

Indian newspaper must be of benefit to all Indian peoples, each of whom can learn from each other's experiences. The editorial content of the newspaper is consistent with proper journalistic standards for fair play, accuracy, and intelligence. We understand the scale of coverage required of the primary national American Indian newspaper, where thousands of other tribal voices from hundreds of nations must be heard and considered for coverage. As professional integrity is both the essence and definition of the quality of the product, the importance of understanding the nature of the journalistic ethic is always paramount.

This book is a limited selection of *Indian Country Today*'s editorials, memorable columns, and editorial cartoons from the beginning of a new American Indian century. A complete record would be too voluminous for one book, but this covers a substantial piece of the era. We believe anyone with an interest in American Indian affairs will find it useful as a reference source of evolving American Indian policy and of American Indian opinion rendered on history at the time of its making. It may serve as a guide to Indian leadership perspectives and provides talking points on a broad range of issues.

In these years, we find American Indians actively engaged in a number of issues, projecting a surprising level of influence. For example, American elections dominated the year 2004, as they did in the first year covered in this volume. At the turn of the century, it can truly be said that American Indians became highly visible in America. In politics, business, education, and entertainment—in all fields of endeavor—the American Indian presence was seen, heard, and felt. Perhaps nowhere was this more evident than with the opening of the National Museum of the American Indian on the National Mall in Washington, D.C., in September 2004. Tens of thousands of American Indians from throughout the Western Hemisphere converged in a historic gathering that revealed the power of culture and the importance of identity.

In what may become an obscure historical footnote, the role played four years earlier by Winona LaDuke, an American Indian woman whose 2000 vice-presidential candidacy along with her presidential running mate, Ralph Nader, on the Green Party ticket, helped throw the whole of American presidential politics into disarray. The Green Party drew thousands of votes from the Democratic Party in Florida, enabling George W. Bush to become competitive there and set the stage for his ultimate Supreme Court victory in George W. Bush, et al, Petitioners vs. Albert Gore Jr., et al. That decision enabled his ascendancy to the presidency of the United States.

These are but two examples in a book filled with interesting and intriguing analysis and commentary about American Indian issues. What could it mean, for instance, for tribes to increasingly work together on political and economic initiatives? Where else will you find pieces that document the climate observations of tribal elders and caution about the dangers of the international community's lack of consensus to curtail global warming? Just as fitting has been the examination of the impacts of the U.S. drug and anti-terror wars on tribes whose territories straddle the border with Mexico. Our editors tracked the trends of increased voter organization by Indian constituencies within Latin American democracies and forecasted potential breakthroughs. We reviewed the records of Assistant Secretaries of the Interior Kevin Gover (during the Clinton administration) and Gale Norton (during the Bush administration). Gover's historic speech on the occasion of the 175th anniversary of the BIA made headlines when he apologized for the U.S. government's "legacy of racism and inhumanity." *Indian Country Today* has encouraged proper discussion of the increased presence of American Indian nations in the country's body politic and tracked myriad occurrences and commentaries, now amply preserved within these pages.

While this book is not a comprehensive volume of every major American Indian event that had national ramifications in the years 2000 through 2004, it does provide readers with a contextual view, framed by American Indian editors, of events and ideas that shaped American Indian opinion at the beginning of a new century.

Indian country leadership, including the whole range of opinion leaders in all walks of life, read *Indian Country Today*. Active with an influential subscriber base and an exponentially expanding group of Internet readers, the newspaper has built a solid international audience. This is a network and the core of an American Indian media initiative that continues to grow. It includes thousands of educators and teachers and thousands of policy makers and government workers. Most of all, the record of these years at *Indian Country Today* portends that American Indians must have an informing, opining, newspaper-driven, media-savvy information network founded upon integrity, intelligence, and respect. It is a way of educating our peoples faster across tribal boundaries. And for those with whom we must contend, the message resolutely conveyed is that Indian sovereignty is good for America.

—Tim Johnson

CHAPTER ONE
INDIAN SOVEREIGNTY IS GOOD FOR AMERICA

The reality of American Indian survival—as tribes of human families with common cultural and legal bases—takes many American citizens by surprise, even in these modern times. Unjustly dispossessed and persecuted in their own ancient lands, even into the twentieth century, Native American tribal nations have survived, decade by decade, throughout the long history of the United States, contributing many wonderful values, structures, and bioriches to American life and striving to build economic enclaves of self-governed communities with their own distinct federal-to-tribal relationships. Realities of Indian life and culture underlie the many myths about tribal America as great tensions over land claims, political and economic sovereignty and diversity, cultural distinctiveness, and tribal recognition issues persist.

Indian Sovereignty Is Good for America
March 29, 2000

At the dawn of the twenty-first century, the United States has a unique opportunity to make good on the country's accumulated debt to American Indian Nations—on whose land and resources American progress was built.

As we start the new millennium, American Indian nations are asserting tribal sovereignty, and, in good measure through the fruition of gaming revenues and other economic initiatives, are poised to rebuild the prosperity of their peoples. This is good for American Indians and it is good for America.

The dispossession of American Indian nations from lands and resources and the directed repression of ecologically successful indigenous cultures inflicted almost irreparable damage to American Indian peoples.

However, the anticipated "vanishing" of Native peoples at the start of the twentieth century did not occur. In fact, after a century of survival and the endurance of abject poverty and destitution, progressive gains in political rights and economic-base building have prepared American Indian nations for a time of restrengthening, a time of realigning the best of our cultural past with a well-trained young population that can generate a viable future for our cultures and nations.

The end of the second millennium finds American Indian nations in a reinvigorated political and economic position, even if still sometimes mired in bureaucratic dysfunction. The legal cases that confirmed jurisdictional and treaty rights won throughout the 1970s and 1980s—added to the great efforts made in all fields of endeavor by Indian educators—have solidified the concept and practice of sovereignty.

Jurisdictional rights and taxation exemptions to tribal bases, rights re-won in court cases, now generate capital-building enterprises of significant volume. While it is only in the past decade that, for the first time ever, Native American nations have gained the opportunity to rebuild economic bases, this is perhaps enough of a stimulator to place more and more communities on the path to financial self-sufficiency. With good strategic planning, calling upon the best of our community-building traditions, Native nations could parlay the present financial gains into long-term prosperity.

While some condemn the gaming industry that has been developing in Indian country, easily fostering a troubling anti-Indian sovereignty movement, many more understand that as Native nations work to stabilize their governments and improve their strategic planning, gaming revenues can provide the financial base necessary for the support of community services and the development of a sound, diversified business base.

In 1998, the Indian gaming industry generated some $7.5 billion. It not only signals a financial revolution in Indian country, it already provides major revenues for many municipal, county, state, and federal governments. We believe this is not only good for Indians; it is also good for America.

In California, for instance, the Indian gaming industry generated $1.4 billion in 1997. Yet, according to a 1998 study (Analysis Group/Economic, Inc.), this Indian industry annually contributes $120 million in state and local tax receipts. The Indian casinos employ nearly 15,000 Californians, 90 percent non-Indians. This employment, in areas of high-rate unemployment and low per-capita income, is estimated also to have reduced California's Aid to Families with Dependent Children payments by $50 million.

Additional revenues generated from gaming patrons' expenditures in noncasino local businesses amounted to $273 million. This adds up to a total contribution by the Indian tribes to the state's economy of more than $450 million. And this is without counting nearly 34,000 additional jobs supported through "subsequent spending" by employees and vendors.

A similar study conducted in Washington state concluded that twenty-seven federally recognized tribes contribute $1 billion annually to that state's economy, including $865.8 million for vendor supplies and services. The tribes employ 14,375 Washington state residents.

In Minnesota, Indian industries sustain a combined payroll of $185 million and support the state's tax base by more than $15 million. Indian gaming is Minnesota's seventh largest employer, creating more than 12,000 jobs. Wisconsin, Michigan, Arizona, New Mexico, Mississippi, Connecticut, New Hampshire, New York, and other states report similar economic realities. Indian gaming is not only a stimulus for tribal economies; it stimulates local-regional business and contributes in substantial ways to the economic well-being of the country at large.

In Connecticut, a single Indian gaming establishment is the state's largest revenue provider. The Pequot enterprise in Connecticut has also expanded into a magnificent new museum and teaching facility on Native culture in the region.

As humankind begins a new chapter in the post–Cold War era, America has a unique opportunity to understand the Native peoples within their borders. And rather than destroy or obstruct their opportunity to construct successful futures, America should respect and protect these long-held Indian rights to water, land, distinct culture and language, legal territorial jurisdiction, and power of taxation.

These very specific cases of justice making represent one important and perhaps fundamental healing element required for the American Republic to move forward into the new century and make good on its eternal need to carry the goodwill of the Native peoples upon whose land, blood, and resources the country was built.

Let's Learn about Sovereignty
December 13, 2000

The proper understanding of tribal and indeed any type of sovereignty is lost to most of the American public. Indeed, even among Native people there is a wide variety of definitions on what constitutes sovereignty. By all accounts, there is a great deal of education needed on this subject.

We want to invite all nations and all Native opinion leaders, young, old, from any persuasion and walk of life, to help us discuss and define over the next few months the significance of sovereignty in our lives. What are the bases of the Indian argument for tribal sovereignty considering the realities of living in a modern North American society?

Respect for national and even local and other sovereignties is an established methodology of international law. But for this type of inherent respect, what would keep any government, or all governments, from constantly overrunning and/or taxing one another? Thus, on national, state or provincial, tribal, and municipal levels, various ranges of sovereign jurisdiction have been and continue to be exercised by varieties of political entities.

Sovereignty, we would offer by way of a start, is completely inherent in the concept of self-government, both within U.S. democracy and in the language of United Nations covenants. American Indian peoples have maintained sovereignty based on legal and daily factual realities. But Indian nations, like all small nations, are more or less dependent on the larger nations to, more or less, keep the covenants upon which they rely well polished and alive.

In this respect Native nations are just like all small nations. Often in the Americas, the more recent nation-states completely surround tribal nations, but nevertheless, the tribal nations exist and persist in sustaining their sovereignty and self-government. The right of federally recognized U.S. tribes to tribal sovereignty is an established, if always contested, part of the nation-to-nation concept within the United States.

In every way possible we know states will seek to impose their laws on tribal territories, seeking to diminish sovereign rights tribes maintain are inherent. Worcester vs. Georgia (1832) is invoked for establishing this principle early on. This important case cites the "extraterritorial status" of tribes, their "preexisting sovereignty," and the supremacy of treaties in U.S. law that affirmed the independent nature of tribal people.

Beyond the early recognition of the tribes' "right of occupancy," both the Articles of Confederation and the U.S. Constitution recognized the distinctiveness of Indian tribes. The federal government early on established sole claim to both make treaties and to "regulate" relations with tribes.

While states have extended their jurisdiction into tribal matters behind a number of court cases and legislative campaigns, tribes can always do the worst damage to their own sovereignty by consenting to the application of state laws on Indian reservations. Native tribal settlements that give in to state law are troublesome developments that most always reappear in unforeseen ways.

In the Maine and other cases of eastern Indian land claims and federal tribal recognition, the drive by some attorneys for early, if only partial, victories on occasion led to trade-offs on aspects of sovereignty that tend to come back with negative force. The line that guards tribal jurisdiction from local towns and counties and from the state must be continually upheld. In all cases, tribes must always ask: what are our inherent sovereign powers and authorities?

We invite Native opinion leaders to share with us your understandings of tribal sovereignty. In your estimation, what are the main pillars of tribal sovereignty? What should every Native student graduating from high school know about the basis and uses of tribal sovereignty in the twenty-first century? A lively discussion within Indian country on the meanings and fundamentals of tribal sovereignty can only help at this time.

In the final analysis we believe we may all realize American Indian sovereignty is actually quite simple. It has only been obscured and made seemingly complicated by a tangled history of U.S. imposition and intervention, by organized obfuscation, and through historically negotiated giveaways of our inherent powers and authorities.

American Indian Sovereignty and Taxes
August 7, 2001

"The power to tax involves the power to destroy." This bedrock maxim of the U.S. Supreme Court was first pronounced by Chief Justice John Marshall in the 1819 case McCulloch vs. Maryland. It should be a foundation of Indian legal strategy toward the court's shifty interpretation of tribal sovereignty.

In this ruling Marshall was talking about a sovereignty based on

European political theory. Tribal sovereignty has an older base. Probably no idea has broader support in Indian country, because at its heart it says, "We were here first. We survive and we have the inherent right to keep surviving."

Tribal rights to territory and self-government predate the U.S. Constitution and all Anglo-American law and there are some who insist the new arrivals are irrelevant. But in practical life, in dealing with mainstream commerce and politics, the preservation of tribal sovereignty comes in the courts of the dominant government. The goal is to compel the U.S. Supreme Court to recognize the rights of the tribes based on its own logic.

Tax cases are crucial to this campaign and this is why, even though the Navajo Nation recently lost a big one, in Atkinson Trading Company vs. Shirley, the misstep is not necessarily fatal. Taxation to Marshall was crucial in defining the boundaries between sovereign powers. If you have sovereign power over someone, you have the right to impose a tax. If not, no way can you tax them. As he put it: "All subjects over which the sovereign power of a state extends are objects of taxation. Those over which it does not extend are, upon the soundest principles, exempt from taxation. This proposition may almost be pronounced self-evident."

Specifically, Maryland was trying to tax an institution of the U.S. government, a national bank, in a way that could drive it out of business within the state. If one government had a right to build something up, Marshall said, no other government had a right to tear it down. Although the case pitted the rights of the national government against a lesser state government, Marshall made a more general argument. "Would the people of any one state trust those of another with a power to control the most insignificant operations of their state government? We know they would not."

The same principle applies to tribal government, which Marshall repeatedly declared were not subordinate to states. Later courts confused the issue, letting Congress snip away at tribal power. A later Justice Marshall—Thurgood—even wrote that Congress had plenary power over tribal sovereignty, dismissing inherent rights as a "Platonic" delusion. So tribal lawyers have a serious job ahead to revive John Marshall's logic.

The Navaho's Atkinson case was a loss and maybe a blunder, but there may be good in it because it was a loss based on John Marshall's logic. The Navajo Nation was trying to uphold a hotel occupancy tax on the Cameron Trading Post, a modern resort based on an Indian trader's outpost set up in 1916. In 1934, the Navajo Reservation was enlarged so that its boundaries surrounded the post, which, however, remained non-Indian fee land. Could the Navaho Nation tax non-Indian activity on non-Indian fee land, even if surrounded by the reservation? Chief Justice Rehnquist, for a unanimous court, said no.

What's remarkable is that the Navajo case prevailed in lower courts based on loopholes in other decisions that expanded tribal authority. Tribes might be able to regulate "through taxation, licensing, or other means" nonmembers in a "consensual relationship." Rehnquist denied this exception applied to the paying guests at the Cameron Trading Post who were taxed through their bills, but he left open the possibility of a direct tax on the owners of the hotel who voluntarily sought a license as an "Indian trader."

And there is no barrier for demanding, or paying, fees for specific services. These are more in-line with a business contract. But the court rejected the general extension of tribal civil authority.

The flip side of this argument, however, is that state and local governments have no right to tax Indian-generated economic activity on Indian land. Basic as this principle is, a lot of people need reminding of it. The towns surrounding the Mashantucket Pequots are asking if the tribe will pay taxes on the modest amount of land it wants to add to its reservation. They ought to receive a resounding no. The Defense Department is ending a long-standing practice of deducting state taxes from paychecks of servicemen with a reservation home address, but it took years of complaints and Congressional pressure.

We won't even go into the long and bloody history of state government drives for tax compacts on gasoline and cigarette sales. The Indians in New York state won this battle hands down four years ago, and two court decisions in recent months have confirmed the victory. No tribe anywhere should feel compelled to make tax concessions, even for the richest of gaming compacts.

Coming months will bring even more activity on the tax front. The tribal lobby in Congress is focusing on tax exemption this year, to see that tribes win the same status as state governments in a range of laws. The Internal Revenue Service is encouraging Indian country to explore financing by tax-exempt municipal bonds. These are a powerful means of cutting construction costs and they derive directly from the powers of sovereignty outlined in McCulloch vs. Maryland.

John Marshall was one of the deepest thinkers on the status of the tribes in the new U.S. government. There are many ambiguities in his legacy and massive failures to live up even to his rulings. But his logic can be a powerful weapon for sovereign rights, if the Nations use it clearly.

American Indian Contributions and the Lie of Savagery
April 19, 2002

A large contribution by the Oneida Nation of New York to the National Museum of the American Indian (NMAI) was announced last week: ten million dollars to help build the Smithsonian Institution's fifteenth and likely last major museum on the Washington Mall. The announcement gave evidence that the impulse to contribute is alive and well in Indian country.

The Oneidas' is the third such hefty contribution by Indian nations to the up-and-coming national museum. Added to the earlier donations by the Mashantucket Pequot Tribal Nation and the Mohegan Tribal Nation of Connecticut, the Oneida contribution bolstered this critically important national project that will provide a permanent presence for Indian cultural representations at the center of America's political geography.

More than a museum, the NMAI is a tremendous cultural endeavor. A century after the heyday of anthropology and the "other-directed" study of Indian people, here arrives an academic institution directed and substantially advised by American Indian culture-bearers, academics, writers, artists, and other professionals. By its own definition it is, "an institution of living cultures dedicated to the preservation, study, and exhibition of the life, languages, literature, history, and arts of the Native people of the Western Hemisphere." It holds a monumental collection of Native cultural artifacts, family and tribal treasures spanning thousands of years, and Native cultures from throughout the Americas.

We find it particularly appropriate that American Indian nations that manage successful enterprises, such as the Oneidas, the Mohegans and the Pequots, donate to such a major source of academically based yet community-connected scientific knowledge. Such strategic donations represent a profoundly useful way of sharing the wealth to push back one of this country's major misconceptions: that Native peoples of the Americas had no appreciable culture prior to contact with Europeans.

The Oneida donation coincided with the arrival in the mail of a new book, *Encyclopedia of American Indian Contributions to the World: Fifteen Thousand Years of Inventions and Innovations*, that deserves our acknowledgement and appreciation. Published by Facts on File, Inc., and edited by Emory Dean Keoke and Kay Marie Porterfield, the new encyclopedia is a treasure trove of information about the large range of technologies and productions of American Indian peoples throughout the past history of known inhabitation of the Western Hemisphere. Although certainly not intended as an exhaustive study, this is indeed the most comprehensive compilation of American Indian inventions and contributions to date. It is most worthwhile and should be on the bookshelves of every library and home in America.

As the editors point out, during the very early contact period, early adventurers, including Christopher Columbus, wrote many accounts that marveled at the many accomplishments they found in their travels among American Indian nations. Most spectacular to the early Spanish were the large, well-regulated, and supplied cities of the Aztecs, Mayas, and Incas. The Andean road system, for instance, was more sophisticated than that of Rome. The Aztec capital, Tenochtitlan, before its destruction by the conquistador Hernan Cortes, was home to more than 250,000 people, as large as any major European city of the time.

These were truly magnificent urban centers and featured guilds and professions of very learned people, which provided medical and other services quite at par if not more complex than those found in Europe at the time. Surgical techniques were practiced by the Mesoamericans that were not yet known in the Old World. The Aztecs conducted cesarean sections and also procedures to remove cataracts from eyes using thin pieces of obsidian flint as scalpels. The Aztecs also used anesthetics and antibiotic medicines (sap from maguey) to combat infections and balsam as a disinfectant. They performed amputations (blood vessels were cauterized with heated stones) and constructed prosthetic limbs. Bone doctors were common and are still found in Latin American Indian communities. In South America, brain surgery was performed and medical anthropologists who have studied human remains of these patients report a survival rate of 83 to 90 percent.

But making the most impact on European minds (and palates) was the variety of agricultural production, including medicines and foodstuffs available throughout the Americas. Of course, the pharmacology of American indigenous peoples was (and is) truly prodigious. According to the editors, "North American Indians had medicinal uses for 2,564 species of plants." They extracted medicines from some 10 percent of the "flora available to them." More than 200 of American Indians' many discoveries are today part of the U.S. pharmacopoeia. Seventy-five percent of the 120 drugs made from plant extracts today originate in traditional indigenous medicine.

Of the many contributions of American Indians to the agriculture and nutritional base of the world, much has been written. The editors go over this in fine detail. Most people know about corn, potatoes, and beans. There is much more: cocoa, manioc, papaya, avocado, cashew, all manner of peanuts, chilies, artichokes, pineapples, pumpkin, tomatoes, squash, tobacco—enough to say that today's world would be quite a deprived place without these American Indian gifts.

We could add long lists of items in many areas: cropping systems, architecture, astronomy, dentistry, dyes, varieties of clothing and footwear, fiber, stimulants, containers, transportation, embalming, distillation, etc. Indian life and the traditions of invention sought the simple and the functional or useful. It used almost exclusively local or regional materials; it tended to work with rather than in opposition to natural cycles and characteristics of elements.

The trouble was that not long after recording their marvelous first impressions, conquistadors and other colonists began the long and intense process of denigrating the capacity of American Indian peoples. The brutality of colonization, the intent to take the Indian peoples' possessions, land, natural resources, and labor had to be justified. In the public record of the colonial period then, American Indians became "brutes," "beasts that talk," "a race incapable of civilization." The so-called discoverers even speculated widely about other potential origins for some of these accomplishments, such as a "lost tribe of Israelites," or as Erich Van Daniken asserted into the 1970s, extraterrestrials.

The implication has been that American Indians could not possibly have produced the wonderful feats of engineering required for the pyramids of Meso and South America; the Mounds of Cahokia, near present-day St. Louis; or any of the many wonderful constructions and innovations listed in this wonderful encyclopedia. The early use of terms such as "savages" and "heathens" helped to dehumanize Native people and equate them to animals. It set the stage for hundreds of years of denial that is still being fought and overcome today.

The NMAI, a major scientific center within the aegis of the Smithsonian Institution, managed and now generously financed by Native professionals and intensely counseled by traditional elders from throughout the hemisphere, is a major bulwark of that struggle to bring out the truth about the histories and cultures of our peoples. That financially successful Indian nations, such as the Oneida Indian Nation of New York and the Mohegan and Mashantucket Pequot Nations of Connecticut, see fit to contribute such substantial gifts to its construction and growth is a clear sign that the spirit of contribution and the wish to set the record straight is alive and well in Indian country.

Building the Pillars of Freedom
July 20, 2004

In all cultures and peoples, those from within (members) must often engage, and most importantly, educate those from without (strangers). This is an area of great tension throughout the world. In some places, people are killing each other, daily, over such in-group/out-group tensions—horrible brutalities that must repulse any decent human being. Of course, at the same time, great and sincere and mutually supportive relationships develop between peoples of different ethnic and cultural groups. It's all in how we go about it, how we choose to remember our histories, and whether we prefer to emphasize the negative or the positive in our strategies for improving our communities, both from within and from without.

American Indian tribes—leadership and membership—cope with this issue every day. Particularly among tribes with growing organizations and enterprises, large numbers of nonmember professionals and other employees and partners now often cut through the influence and decision-making circles. Perhaps it has always been so, but nowadays this condition is much more prevalent. This is a hugely important and yet difficult topic and we must find good ways to discuss the issue. We are urged to seek fair ways to arrive at good solutions that will ensure Indian control of Indian institutions and Indian assets into the seventh generation yet to come. At the same time, we must fully understand that all team members deserve and must have respect, a sense of mission, and a feeling of belonging. This is the basis of long-term loyalty and true understanding.

The capacity of non-Natives and nonmembers within tribal systems to be increasingly educated on fundamental tribal strategies of self-governance, growth, and prosperity should be a dominant quotient in the new enterprises being built across Indian country. Cultural sensibility and loyalty to tribal self-governance, tribal well-being, and prosperity are qualities to be exalted among tribal members and team members.

It makes a huge difference in the interweaving of new people into Native systems to properly orient everyone, and particularly non-Native peoples, on the fundamentals of tribal affairs. Tribal elders and leaders who can supply good superlatives or principles from their cultures and traditions for how to impartially conduct and manage enterprises are at a premium. Good, well-trained management needs to reconceptualize and impart these messages and these unifying concepts. Not nearly enough thought and education is presently going into this particular dynamic and many are the tales from tribal organizations and enterprises where tension, power cliques, and outright dysfunction emerge that traumatize and can even paralyze tribal operations.

Finding the right balance is as precious as it is difficult. Tribal members everywhere will complain that they are not hired or are being passed over for strangers. In fact, there are many cases where Indians are pushed out by fear among coworkers of a rising star. But tribal members can also be notoriously troublesome in taking direction from nontribal management, with fault cutting both ways. Tribal leadership that pays attention to the education and socialization of tribal members is also of essence everywhere. Only the strength of understanding and the resistance provided by robust thinking and action can sustain the national Indian recovery.

This is a very important issue, as a great deal of potential strength is lost in the proliferation of conflicts and attitudes that weaken trust and diminish the efficiency of any operation.

Presently there are numerous enterprises in Indian country employing tens of thousands of people. Through these operations pass tens of millions of people every year. Yet very little still is being done to educate these folks on the fundamental principles of American Indian cultures and legal foundations. The opportunity that is lost is irrecoverable; it passes each time but once. American Indian nations need to forcefully and substantially reach out to the American public and make it aware of the present and historical bases for the rebuilding of Indian country. Indian nations cannot afford to employ people who do not learn about these principles and bases. Indian nations cannot afford to miss any opportunity to educate the American public, and what better opportunity than to do so with hotel patrons, with restaurant patrons, with even the gaming clientele, which, in subtle ways, can become aware of the Indian realities, as the participation in an Indian casino has a social benefit. We understand that there are many gaming patrons who could care less about Native issues and the intention is not to detract them from their particular entertainment pursuit—but, nevertheless, Indian nations cannot afford to miss the opportunity to reach as many among the American mainstream base as possible over the next few years.

Nor can Native leaders afford to let other management styles (management contracts) and/or prerogatives deter their outreach on this level. In every Indian hotel or lodge there should be a copy of an Indian newspaper available—any Indian newspaper. Each season choose a book that explains well the basis of Indian rights. There are some that are quite easy to read. Have it available in every room. Of the tens of millions of people who pass through Indian enterprises each year, if just 100,000 will positively consider where tribal governments and peoples sit within the American fabric of Indian country, the gains in understanding will be great. Get creative:

posters, video clips, and designs of many kinds—these all can be used to educate in a light, palatable, and yet impressive, long-lasting way. Remember: the court of public opinion is the main line of defense of American Indian freedoms.

Sovereignty and Intellectual Property Rights

March 2, 2002

Rebecca Adamson, *Indian Country Today*

Native peoples around the world have been fighting to affirm their sovereignty and cultural identity on a number of fronts in recent years.

But what tools are being used? What battles are being fought? I believe that all such individual battles are important. A single tribal fight won in one location anywhere in the world reinforces the efforts and power of indigenous peoples everywhere. In turn, individual struggles attract support from other tribes and organizations, individuals of goodwill, and international agencies.

The battle over intellectual property rights has become a key one in asserting and reclaiming tribal sovereignty for cultural identity and economic development. An important international support agency is the World Intellectual Property Organization, responsible for the promotion of intellectual property rights. This United Nations agency broadly defines intellectual property issues to include genetic resources, traditional knowledge, and folklore. These issues have emerged in a wide variety of policy areas, including food and agriculture, biological diversity and the environment, human rights, cultural policy, and trade and economic development.

Here are some examples of individual battles being fought that are attracting international support for indigenous peoples around the globe.

A good example of genetic resources intellectual property is the controversy over blood, skin, and hair samples taken from the Yanomami Tribe in Venezuela and Brazil during the 1960s and 1970s. The story is documented in the Fall/Winter 2001 issue of *Native Americas*.

Tribal leaders thought the blood samples were being taken for promised clinical help for their increasingly serious health situation. Instead of help, the Yanomami got thirty years of silence. Only recently did the tribe learn that the samples they provided in good faith had been used as the control group in experiments on the effects of radiation. The Yanomami were more shocked to learn that some remaining samples had been turned over to scientists in the Human Genome Project and others are in storage at Pennsylvania State University.

The fact that the blood of dead relatives is still in storage is a moral and cultural affront given the important role that blood and mortuary taboos play in Yanomami ritual life. The Yanomami destroy everything that belongs to a deceased person; they cremate the body and the relatives never mention his or her name again. The Yanomami are demanding answers.

In New Zealand, the Maori are very much concerned about the misrepresentation of their culture perpetuated by the Danish company Lego. The Maori want Lego to stop using Maori words for their high-tech toys. In this case, Maori complaints have garnered positive results. Lego has agreed not to use offending words in future launches of its Bionicle game. In addition, Lego has sent a representative to New Zealand to consult with Maori leaders over setting up a code of conduct for the use of traditional knowledge in the manufacture of toys.

A final example comes from Alaska, where King Island Native Community members are fighting for the proprietary rights to their name, cultural heritage, and related tribal resources and intellectual property. Their story is one that Native peoples find all too familiar.

The King Island Record Company of New York has been selling musical recordings and related products over the Internet using the name King Island. The lyrics use names and refer to biographical episodes of community members and refer to stories, imagery, and cultural property that belong to King Island Native Community, King Island Native Corporation, and the King Island people themselves.

The author of the lyrics to the recorded songs tried to get King Island permission to use such cultural and intellectual property. Record company material implied that such permission had both been given or was not necessary if it had not been given. In fact, the King Island Community had refused such permission.

Of course, the King Island people are offended that the recording company has engaged in these activities without their knowledge or prior informed consent. They are even more offended that the recording company has attempted to obtain intellectual property rights in the form of copyright and other registrations of their name and integral components of their traditional heritage and knowledge, as well as of their personal publicity rights and an unwarranted invasion of their personal lives. As if this isn't bad enough, King Island people, who have seen the lyrics and the musical production upon which they are based, contend that the content is based on inaccurate portrayals of real people and historical events and are of the opinion that the recording is denigrating, offensive, and racist.

As these examples indicate, indigenous peoples continue to fight back against misuse of their cultural property with various tools, including international networks, governmental agencies, alliances of tribes, and the growing network of socially responsible companies, such as Lego. Progress is slow, but it is occurring round the world.

During the March 2001 international roundtable on "Intangible Cultural Heritage," United Nations Educational, Scientific and Cultural Organization Director-General Koichiro Mastura told the delegates that: "Intangible cultural heritage is gaining increasing recognition worldwide for the fundamental role it plays in our lives in the maintenance and enhancement of cultural identity and diversity. [It] urgently requires increasing protection due to the vulnerable aspects of living culture and tradition."

Indigenous communities are fighting singly and together against the offensive use of our sacred images, ways, and symbols—even of our blood. We are not alone.

Three Indian Contributions to Western Civilization
May 2, 2003

John Mohawk, *Indian Country Today*

When Roger Williams first arrived in New England, he set about the task of converting the heathen Indians to Christianity. He was one of the authors of the American tradition of freedom of religion and founder of Rhode Island; his life is instructive of what "freedom of religion" really means. Williams had ideas about freedom of religion before he left England and his views about the rights of the Indians to their property were not popular among the English. He also was strongly against forced conversion of the Indians to Christianity. Williams is thought to be the first Euro-American to advocate complete freedom of conscience and complete separation of church and state. This latter advocacy resulted in his banishment from the Massachusetts Bay Colony and that in turn led to the foundation of Providence, which welcomed the first Jewish synagogue.

Shortly after his arrival, Williams found some Indians, learned their language, and taught them his version of Christianity. The Indians were receptive and proceeded to embrace the new teachings. Shortly after this triumph, however, Williams discovered that while his new converts were practicing Christianity, they were also practicing their ancient religion as well. Williams hastened to explain to them that they had to choose one or the other, that Christianity was to be the religion to the exclusion of all others.

America is the birthplace of a single contribution to world philosophy: pragmatism. Its roots extend into the Indian cultures of the Americas. Pragmatism relies not on an ideology about how the world ought to be, but rather on thinking about what the outcome should be. It is characterized by

Sitting Bull's admonition about putting minds together to create a world for our children, an admonition to work for a desirable outcome. Those who know of the Iroquois Great Law will recognize this impulse in the admonition that the chiefs should weigh their actions against the impact it will have on seven generations into the future. Williams had wandered into a set of cultures that embraced outcome-oriented thinking.

When Williams insisted that the Indians set aside all their beliefs and follow the one true religion, some Indians would have summoned him to a sidebar conversation. "Mr. Williams," one would have said, "we do not insist that people believe this or that. We are relatively small in number and it is very important that we maintain peace and harmony in our world. If we told people what to believe, there would be nothing but discord and disharmony. People would spend all their time arguing about religion. The more insistent we became, the more discord and disharmony. In the end, we would be a society that did nothing but argue about things that no one knows for sure. And we don't do that, like some people we have heard about.

"Among us, some people believe things that other people do not believe. Some people believe that the otter, for example, has the power to cure disease. They have called upon the otter spirit when they were sick, they were administered medicine, and they became well. Now they believe in the otter spirit's power to cure. Surely it cured them. But there are others who would be very skeptical. So we have a custom. The people who believe in the otter form a 'secret society.' Those who seek cures from the otter, if they live, join that society. But it has rules. It is a secret society. People can't tell what they know about it. You cannot proselytize. When it comes to religion, we leave people to their own conscience."

Williams seems to have gotten the message. He also understood the nature of the European government and he felt it was important to protect religion from the corrosive force of the state. Williams spent years living with the Naraggansett Indians and wrote the first book about their language and customs. He seems to have had an inclination to defend the rights of individuals against the coercive powers of the state and this was reinforced by his time with Indians whose society lacked even a notion of the coercive state. This was but the first of three areas of impact of Native American culture on relationships within Western civilization.

Other Europeans, especially members of the British military, noted that women were often present at peace negotiations. These were considered men's affairs and Indian men did do most of the talking, but there was a definite female presence. As they came to know each other better, Europeans realized that women had a far greater role in Indian society than in white society. In European society of the early-contact years, a woman had no right to property, divorce, or even personal safety from her husband. Indian women of the northeast woodlands enjoyed all of these. When young English women were captured or otherwise came to join Indian societies, they were treated with respect. Quite often, when offered repatriation with English society, they declined and chose to stay instead with their adopted Indian families. Although the English found Indian customs of women's rights peculiar, the Indians might have pointed out that European practices excluding women were in fact impractical and rendered half of the society as marginally productive and deprived society of the wisdom of half its people.

A third area involved treatment of children. Early Jesuit missionaries were exasperated that their new converts did not beat or otherwise force their children to their will. A book on the subject, *Chain Her by One Foot*, recounts how Jesuits browbeat their charges to do something because a young woman insisted on seeing a young pagan male. English customs of the time favored using the rod as an instrument of discipline. It was not a practice based on class. Even children at exclusive boarding schools, such as Eaton, were beaten with such force that were a headmaster to do so today, he or she would be arrested and charged with felony child battering.

These were three ideas from the Americas that must be forever vigilantly guarded. Freedom of religion encompasses ideas of freedom of speech and freedom of association. Women's rights are the key to solving problems of the world's poor and dispossessed. And children's rights involve those of the most powerless in society. On reflection, Western civilization has adopted ideas from the Americas that render the common thinking in most Western societies around these three issues much more like the thinking of the Indians than like the thinking of seventeenth-century Europeans. Good thing.

The Growing Power of Tribal Economic Diversification
September 9, 2003

Maurice Lyons, Morongo Band of Mission Indians

Indian gaming may have made the majority of headlines over the past decade, but there is an important economic trend with Indian tribes that should not be overlooked, and that is the significant evolution of nongaming businesses.

Tribal government gaming has never been an end to itself. It was always intended as a means of tribal economic development. Congress, in establishing the Indian Gaming Regulatory Act of 1988, intended that gaming "provide a means of promoting tribal economic development, self-sufficiency, and strong tribal government."

Morongo's 32,000-acre reservation is one of the largest in California. We have used the land for fruit farming and cattle ranching. In later years, land was leased for sand- and gravel-mining operations or to various utilities, water districts, and rail lines. But it was never enough to fully support our tribal community.

With the advent of tribal gaming, the Morongo Tribe made an important strategic decision to utilize gaming revenue as a catalyst to establish a diversified tribal economy.

Morongo is fortunate to be located in one of the fastest-growing counties in the United States. The tribe's developable land is located on both sides of a major transportation route with excellent freeway visibility. The reservation's location combines both freeway access and proximity to population centers.

With gaming revenue we moved to diversify. In 1997, Morongo opened one of the largest Shell gasoline stations in the country. In 1999, it was joined by an A&W drive-in restaurant nearly twice the size of the national prototype. The restaurant is one of the most successful A&W franchises in existence. Also in 1999, Morongo opened the first Coco's restaurant ever owned by an American Indian tribe. The tribe then acquired Hadley Fruit Orchards' three retail stores and mail-order operations. This year, a $26 million Arrowhead Mountain Spring Water bottling plant was opened on the Morongo Indian Reservation.

On another front, Morongo is exploring how to provide clean, reliable, and low-cost energy to its businesses, tenants, and tribal members. The tribe's goal is to become energy self-sufficient, create yet another income stream, and to maintain its traditional role as a steward of the environment.

With its diversification into nongaming businesses, the tribe has become the largest private-sector employer in the Pass Area and is a major contributor to the regional economy. Morongo now employs close to 2,000 people and has an annual payroll that exceeds $25 million. The tribe generates millions more in payroll taxes, unemployment benefits, employee benefits, and health programs.

A recent economic-impact analysis conducted by economist Dr. John Husing estimated that jobs directly or indirectly attributable to all of the economic operations of Morongo will rise from approximately 1,726 jobs in 2002 to approximately 5,800 in 2008. Total economic impact brought to the Inland Empire area during this period will be $2.8 billion including the creation of more than 4,000 new jobs and $1.4 billion in new goods and services purchased.

It is important to note that communities that are nearby tribal economic ventures gain the most number of newly created jobs. Why? Because tribal memberships, in many cases decimated over the past century, cannot now accommodate the employment requirements of tribal gaming and nongaming ventures. In California, nearly two-thirds of the jobs created by tribal government are held by residents of nearby communities.

In addition to job creation, tribes also impact the economy with their purchase of goods and services. Morongo spends an estimated $20 million per year for goods and services purchased from about 1,200 outside vendors. (About 25 percent of these businesses are minority owned and operated.)

This does not include the sale of goods and services generated by patrons visiting the area or services and merchandise purchased by tribal employees. The U.S. Department of Commerce research estimates that forty-two jobs are created for every $1 million spent on goods and services.

An excellent role model for tribal economic diversification has been the Mississippi Band of Choctaw Indians, which owns and operates a diversified portfolio of manufacturing, service, retail, and tourism enterprises. Throughout Mississippi, the Southeast, and even into Mexico, the Choctaw provide more than 8,000 permanent full-time jobs for tribal members and others—more than 65 percent of its workforce is non-Indian. With an annual payroll of more than $123.7 million, the Choctaw is one of the ten largest employers in Mississippi. In addition, tribal revenues have helped the Choctaw to reinvest more than $210 million in economic-development projects in Mississippi.

In the last decade, according to the U.S. Commerce Department's Census Bureau, the number of American Indian–owned businesses increased 93 percent from 52,980 in 1987 to 102,234 in 1992. Receipts for these businesses increased by 115 percent from $3.7 to $8.1 billion. The next census will reflect even more growth.

Last fall, the National Summit for Emerging Tribal Economies announced its goal of creating 100,000 jobs in Indian country by 2008 and establishing new sustainable, market-driven tribal economies by 2020 in a wide range of industry areas, such as fossil and renewable energy, manufacturing, agriculture, utilities and telecommunications, hospitality and tourism, aerospace, health care, construction, media, and finance.

According to the Virginia-based Falmouth Institute, "Native American businesses are emerging—from oyster farmers in the Northwest to Everglades tour operators in Florida. Lodging has seen a boom, particularly in the Southwest."

In California, tribal nongaming economic development has included RV parks and mobile-home development at Chemehuevi and Pechanga; retail stores and gas stations at Morongo and Pechanga; energy recovery and recycling programs at Cabazon; and banking ventures by the Agua Caliente and the Viejas Tribe. Other tribes operate agribusinesses including alfalfa, citrus, avocado farming; fisheries and forestry operations; sand and gravel businesses; golf courses and real-estate investments.

The National Indian Gaming Commission reports that 330 tribal casinos in the United States generated $14.4 billion in revenues last year. That revenue is being dedicated at a growing rate to investment and development of nongaming businesses. In short, economic diversification is a smart bet for tribal governments and a long-term boon for surrounding communities as well.

Job Creation Should Be Indian Country's Top Priority
September 9, 2003

Pete Homer, National Indian Business Association

In Indian country in this day in age, we find teenagers who believe that a job at a fast-food restaurant is all they are capable of getting. This shouldn't be. These teenagers need to realize that there are bigger and better jobs available to them in their future. In the Palm Springs area, Native American teenagers can't even get a job at a fast-food restaurant if they don't speak Spanish. It's time that Indian country stop relying on others for employment opportunities and create their own. Economic-development planning for tribes seems to be lagging in one area: job creation.

When you think in terms of unemployment rates and poverty lines in which American Indians find themselves, consider this: "With more than a quarter of Indian people living in poverty, and unemployment rates of reservations more than double the population at large—13.6 percent on average, and over 80 percent in some communities—there is no group of people with a more urgent economic crisis than American Indians." (National Congress of American Indians, Weaving Our Future: A Proposal for Economic Stimulus in Indian Country, February 2003)

With that in mind, how should tribes go about lessening the gap? One way is through long-range economic-development planning. Not very often do we see a comprehensive long-range tribal economic development plan that has the underlying theme of job creation throughout each department, whether it is in the areas of tribal government, environmental, health, human resources, social services, justice, or education. If there were more out there, then perhaps there would be better guidance and understanding between tribal governments and the federal government regarding a tribe's economic stimulus.

An excellent source of job creation is through entrepreneurial enterprises. Why not teach these teenagers as well as other members in their communities the value of going into business themselves? Tribal leaders need to encourage their members to create their own businesses by offering to them the capital needed or direct them to the means necessary in order to start a small business. Not only is a venture such as this beneficial to the business owner, but it also benefits the economic stability of the tribal economy by bringing in dollars and creating jobs. Ultimately, this could only aid the goal of becoming a self-sustaining entity and in developing a strong economy.

One invaluable resource can be found at the U.S. Small Business Administration's (SBA) Office of Native American Affairs, headed by Ms. Thelma Stiffarm (Gros Ventre Tribe). As the assistant administrator, her job is to outreach to tribal colleges and universities and to tribal leaders. Her main focus is to get the SBA Office of Native Americans more exposure and to provide more information to Native-owned businesses throughout the United States.

Let's not stop there. Why don't we start educating our youth at the Head Start level about business? Even at that age, they are very aware about the value of a dollar and how much candy it can buy them. They already know about trading their peanut butter and jelly sandwich for a bag of chips at lunchtime. At this age, they are already acting as businessmen and businesswomen. Why not use this analogy to teach them about the business world as it pertains to real life and the global economy? This is where we need to reach these children and get them to start thinking about the opportunities off the reservation and creating opportunities on the reservation. Getting our future business leaders to start thinking as business leaders is where our economic development needs to begin.

In Washington, D.C., there are numerous national Indian organizations creating legislation left and right, but they are failing to include the job creation perspective in all aspects. Take, for example, a new piece of legislation that is going to provide new housing initiatives on reservations. It's a good thing that there will be new houses for families who need them, but who is building these houses for them? Is it yet another non-Native contractor who swoops in to get the bag full of money? The construction workers who are painstakingly pounding each nail, who are they? Do they really care about the houses they are building and who these houses are meant for? If a Native-owned contractor accepted the proposal to build these houses, this means that the money is going back to the community and, most likely, construction workers would be hired straight from that community. This means dollars going back into the tribal economy. Now this is a good thing.

This is just one example of how even at the policy-making level, job creation is forgotten. Ideally, this is where it should start.

If you are the head of one of these programs or departments, think about how you can use those federally funded dollars to create jobs after the money has run out or is running low. Think about the teenager who is looking for a job, a job that isn't there. Think about the new graduates out of college and university who spent the years and dollars they didn't have in order to help their tribe succeed in the future. It doesn't matter what department you are working for—there is always room for job creation!

©2003 Marty Two Bulls

CHAPTER TWO
NATION BUILDING IS KEY

After centuries of loss and dispossession, tribal Americans emerged in the last quarter of the twentieth century with Indian leadership striving for unity to challenge American bureaucratic power over Indian peoples. A dual challenge engages Native leadership as families and communities are still rebuilding—socially and culturally—after long histories of assault. Yet ancient human and community values and consistent ceremonial spiritual practices have been a reliable basis upon which to rebuild Native nations, languages, land bases, schools, health systems, ceremonial houses and grounds, and economic and educational initiatives. From "Vanishing American" in the 1890s to "emergent protagonist" at the beginning of the twenty-first century, American Indian self-determination, trailed by charges of corruption and challenged by the controversial rise of megarich tribes in the midst of severe Indian country poverty, nevertheless continues on the upswing. Reasserting toward a larger and more proper role for their ancient nations in modern society, tribal peoples struggle and adapt to new relations with other sovereign nations and other peoples.

Rocky Paths to Unity

April 5, 2000

What do Oklahoma Kickapoos, Pine Ridge Oglalas, Akwesasne Mohawks, San Carlos Apaches, and so many other Indian peoples have in common? They have all experienced internal conflicts so severe they felt they needed outside intervention to help settle conflicts in their internal relations.

It is a lamentable state of affairs that so much of conflict and governmental crisis in Indian country is handed over for resolution to outside courts and agencies. Too often this lack of clear choice is detrimental to tribal sovereignties.

Tribal and inter-tribal court systems, conciliation, and conflict-resolution boards might offer better pathways and help keep tribes from fighting internal battles in state and federal courts. But the problem is often fundamental, rooted in governmental structures that do not fit the mold and do not do the job, formalizing rather than resolving internal community conflicts.

It should be understandable, if regrettable, that mediation so often requires outside intervention, given that most tribal governmental problems stem from flawed constitutions and other continuous external meddling in Indian tribal life by the Interior Department and other federal agencies and bureaus.

Most tribal constitutions are modeled on the boilerplate legal foundations mandated for tribal governments by the Indian Reorganization Act of 1934 (IRA). The Indian complaint has always been that these constitutions did not take into account accustomed patterns of tribal leadership and governance.

With more than 550 recognized Indian nations plus perhaps another 150 unrecognized ones, the level of Native cultural and governmental diversity is obvious. A process of sorting out the specific cultural needs of each tribe was clearly called for but never implemented.

Amendments and reconsiderations of the tribal constitutions might have been the follow-up, if U.S. Indian policy had been rational for more than a few years at a time. But it was (and is) not; and certainly, the federal bureaucracy, for nearly sixty years, obstructed and slowed all procedures and applications by the tribes to amend or update their constitutions.

Tribes who tried often waited four and more years to hear back on reform initiatives, crucial delays that destroyed momentum for reform within the tribes. Only since 1988, when Congress amended the IRA to impose more strict timelines on the ratification process by the Bureau of

Indian Affairs (BIA), have tribes had a better option for amending their constitutions or adopting new ones. And still, the BIA is characteristically slow, and admits it, in responding to tribal attempts to reform their governments.

Constitutional change is not at all easy. Mucking with the elemental basis for tribal unity, the tribal constitution, can destabilize a Native nation. The Akwesasne Mohawks at St. Regis have been saddled with two governments over the same elective system since a hair-splitting election vote, close but not decisive, was accepted to change the constitution. The contending sides have dug in and show no sign of give-and-take toward a united system. Meanwhile, first the BIA and then non-Indian courts bat Mohawk governmental legitimacy back and forth.

Takeovers of tribal councils are currently reported in half a dozen situations. In all, there are real complaints and many have to do with process and governmental structure and accountability. Some charges are groundless, but all the situations need clear and adequate paths to resolution.

In the recent rash of takeovers, raw force has been kept at minimum and, thankfully, intense violence has not erupted. But deadly violence is in the history of intra-tribal strife and extreme care must be taken that violence be contained.

Clearly, takeovers, while sometimes necessary for breaking open the problems of the body politic, are extremely limited as long-term managerial strategy. The change needed is in a process of generating the long-term agreement about the type and amount of government a people must have to improve and prosper.

Unity of process and clear, respectful incorporation of ideas must be main goals. How do the people best organize themselves and their children to produce income, food, economic life? What is the unified basic culture that each child will need and should know? How is our style and structure of government best to represent that?

The type of thinking required is not abundant these days, but it is available and needs to emerge and be utilized for a proper constitutional process to be possible. Such a process would need to be completely inclusive. Community involvement must be on a home-by-home, workplace-by-workplace basis. It would need to represent all districts and factions.

A new constitution, even reform of an existing government, is possible and can be the beginning of rational government and community prosperity, but not in a simple referendum or election. The initiative must necessarily involve a painstaking, comprehensive process that includes active participation by the most loved and respected members of the whole community.

The discussion of points and principles must be deep, translatable to the home language. Finally, a vast majority of all members ultimately must understand and sign on to the final draft. In many corners of Indian country, such a process is long overdue.

Unity is a precursor to effective governance. But it requires intricate preparation of the people, and the strongest possible commitment to the future generations.

Strength to the Tribal Colleges, Native Higher Education
August 30, 2000

The founding of tribal colleges was a tremendous idea. The goal of American Indians in higher education, particularly in a context of cultural awareness, underlies the potential for tribal growth and prosperity into the twenty-first century. At the end of the present century, Native peoples are fielding an ever-larger number of professionals in all fields of endeavor and significantly in governance and in private-sector enterprises, all due primarily to the great strides of the past two decades in tribal education.

Since 1968, with the founding of the Navajo Diné Community College in Tsaile, Arizona, the first ever controlled by a tribe, thirty other tribal colleges have been established. There are also more than a hundred Native studies programs at county, state, and private colleges and universities, and dozens of other institutions that matriculate Native students. More than 130,000 tribal students are enrolled in colleges and universities nationally any given year, of which more than 25,000 attend tribal colleges.

Arguably, the basis of tribal survival and recovery throughout the twentieth century has been the vanguard of students who sought and gained an education. What started at the turn of the last century as a network of twenty-six boarding schools, where the prevailing philosophy was to pressure and force the culture out of Indian youngsters, did not quite work out that way. At the end of the twentieth century, the vast majority of American Indian college students reject any identity, American or Canadian, that would supersede their own tribal identity, according to a Cornell University survey. The assimilationist model has not been embraced by the new generation and today the sense of identity with the tribal nations is strong. What is needed is education and the economic opportunity to use it to build those home bases.

The tribal colleges are geared to the specific situations in communities. Many are two-year (three are four-year programs) where instruction is offered in a variety of opportunities to upgrade skills. Tribal colleges are well recognized for their facilitation of transfers into other colleges. As a group, the tribal colleges offer more than 350 degree programs and 179 certificate-granting vocational programs. Seventy percent of tribal college students are female and more than 50 percent are single parents with an average of 2.8 dependents. Some 85 percent of tribal college students come out of poverty situations.

In October of 1994, the tribal colleges achieved land-grant status through a rider in the education law, providing a $23 million endowment. With Bureau of Indian Affairs grants to nearly 18,000 Native students and the American Indian College Fund raising some $8 million annually, other foundations have also come onboard in recent years. Lilly Endowment earlier this year put up a fund for $10 million to upgrade worn-out facilities in tribal colleges and the Kellogg Foundation has provided millions of dollars in programs and infrastructure development.

Across the country, in addition to the tribal colleges, more than a hundred colleges and universities with Native studies programs are promoting a wide range of skills training and lines of research and activity that can be a great positive development for tribes.

We salute the tribal colleges and other programs of American Indian higher education. We stand ready to support all manner of tribal educational institutions and initiatives, from Head Start programs to high school precollege mentoring, to solid programs of counseling and retention at the university level. The tribal college movement is a great rotor for meeting the whole range of higher educational goals across the widest possible spectrum of Native communities. Meaningful partnerships across the many circles of Native education—leading to an explosion of national scholarship and fellowship programs for Native students from tribal, foundation, and federal coffers—is the call of the moment.

The concept of full circle or community involvement for Native students is widely accepted. The seventh generation starts with our very own children.

Large, Land-Based Tribes Reprise Need for Unity
December 20, 2000

The effort by large, land-based tribes from the Middle Western states— all too often bypassed in recent years—to unite and create a common front for their concerns and interests can be a welcome sign.

While the activist and lobbying presence of Indian people in Washington, D.C., expanded during the 1990s, often the most prominent profiles have been of those tribes with successful gaming operations. By and large, these are located near urban centers.

Compared to tribes in the northern Great Plains and the Southwest, some with millions of acres in rangeland and forest, many relatively small tribes from the Eastern states and urbanized California have done well with gaming. Most, though not all, have relatively small reservations and some have very small populations. These get their share of publicity when per-capita payments get exorbitant.

Clearly, all people benefit from alliances that stem out of common interests. Led by the Montana-Wyoming Tribal Leaders Council and the Great Plains tribes, the initiative recently traveled to the Navajo Nation, where the largest and most populous Native nation was asked to join. The objective, says Cheyenne River Sioux Chairman Gregg Bourland, was "to form a powerful alliance and coalition, one the federal government will have to contend with."

Anytime American Indian tribes can coalesce among important issues for their specific communities, there is something to be gained. All of these tribes have suffered greatly from federal cutbacks in services in the past two decades.

While under President Bill Clinton, Indian tribes in general secured access to a more open administration and found support for sovereignty-protected enterprise, and even while the recent budget shows a marked increase in funding for Indian country over the past several years, nevertheless there is a great deal of poverty and misery in many of the western reservations.

Economic conditions are very difficult across the board. Hunger is not uncommon. Navajo President Kelsey Begaye noted the appalling "crisis conditions" in health care delivery services for his people. Education facilities and staffing and upgrades on roads are also among major issues. Begaye pointed out the importance of passable roads to the many removed homesteads and communities on the large reservations, a huge problem for rural Indians, but an issue, he noted, that more urbanized eastern tribes, such as the Pequot, might not need to address.

These leaders have complained that major national Indian organizations, particularly the National Congress of American Indians, have not paid enough attention to their issues. Getting past the complaint, however, they have certainly identified issues and potentials for unity in their range of important issues and that emerging determination certainly will make them stronger and more likely to prevail in their effort to exert political power.

The hopeful message and careful language reported from one recent meeting of the emerging coalition in the Navajo Nation was particularly resonant. While their main complaint is duly registered and they press it firmly, the group stresses overall Indian unity and speaks proactively rather than negatively.

As Fort Peck Councilwoman Patt Iron Cloud put it: "We need each other. Our tribes will flourish with help from one another."

The impulse by large, land-based tribes to band together appears fueled by the national organizations' concentration during the past decade on the issues of the more visible gaming tribes. But while it appears a reality that the big lands tribes' particular issues were sidetracked, certainly the fierce lobbying campaigns led by the National Congress of American Indians and other such organizations and tribes in recent congresses against anti-Indian sovereignty bills have benefited all of Indian country and deserve respect.

At the same time, the new coalition might be seen as a wake-up call by both the national organizations and by the successful gaming tribes, a good signal to realize that Indian country needs leadership in deploying more interrelated and sophisticated development strategies. No one should be left behind.

Common cause on Indian sovereignties and jurisdictional issues are completely tied up in economic empowerment issues. Much of Indian country needs help. Tribes who have truly benefited from the Indian economic expansion of the last decade are wise to consider investing in the rest of Indian country.

A "Buy Indian" campaign under way is promoting efforts to support each other's Indian businesses. Very importantly, ways of exercising philanthropy as enterprise development and as economic empowerment are available with strategic planning through such groups as the First Nations Development Institute and other development and investment programs.

Something akin to a Marshall Plan is needed for the economic and social betterment of Indian country. As capital bases grow among the more fortunate tribes, the rest of Indian country rightly wonders if some of these funds might not be channeled toward development opportunities for all. It's an idea whose time certainly needs to arrive.

Strategic Communications Called for in Indian Country
October 18, 2001

If there is a covenant with Indian country that perhaps overrides all others, it is that the U.S. government has for more than thirty years generally supported a commitment to tribal self-government. And it is no accident that because of this sometimes-faltering but nevertheless steady and progressing policy, current American Indian nations in North America have achieved a measure of economic success and political power in the past two decades.

American Indian nations have carried the message of self-government to Congress again and again, for as long as the country is old. Along the line, they achieved a changing of the terms of the collaboration between tribal governments and the other sovereign entities that surround them. In recognizing tribal sovereignty in ways both de facto and de jure, the U.S. federal courts, as well as legislative and bureaucratic systems, have provided the opportunity for the tribes to improve their social and economic conditions under federal status within American society.

This social contract is the guarantee and guarantor of a sense of proper dealing between the American federal government and the Native nations of the United States. This complex system, by and large, for all its foibles, has worked. For all its contentions, a measure of peace and collaboration has been possible, even for peoples who were cheated and overrun, who survived great adversities, and only later were increasingly recognized to have survived and retained some footings in federal law.

Around the country, tribal leaders are planning for the continuous survival of their peoples while looking to guard the prosperity of their respective enterprises and institutions that best serve their communities. At the same time, many are offering effective analysis of threatening trends to better defend those American Indian rights that are so essentially required for the survival of their future generations.

We respect and commend the recent call by Navajo Tribal President Kelsey Begaye for all tribes to unite their thoughts and perspectives upon some fundamental issues of national importance. Begaye warned the tribes about serious erosion of the recognition of American Indian sovereignty by the U.S. Supreme Court. Begaye is not alone in that thought. Many native leaders have expressed it for years. But the trend by the current justices, as he identified it, is arching to diminish tribal powers and authorities.

To quote Begaye, "The concept of sovereignty is the foundation of federal Indian law and is embodied in the principle of self-determination." He challenged the tribes to develop strategies of assertion to self-government "to halt the court's attempt to erode tribal sovereignty." And he announced that the Navajo Nation would seek to fully reaffirm its rights as a tribal government. Begaye stated, "Without these two very important principles, it will be difficult for individual Indian nations to fully address these issues." He stressed the "need for a united front by the Indian nations." Navajo Nation strategists are encouraging a national Native strategy to reaffirm congressional recognition of tribal sovereignty and jurisdiction.

Major senators from both parties hold the American Indian policy portfolio. These include Republicans such as Arizona's John McCain and Colorado's Ben Nighthorse Campbell. One major Democrat, Senator Daniel

K. Inouye, D-Hawaii, chairman of the Senate Committee on Indian Affairs, recently reexpressed his support for tribal sovereignty, reasserting that, "no one on Capitol Hill [can] tell the tribes what to do or how to do it."

Inouye is absolutely correct. So, too, is Begaye. The Navajo Tribal President's initiative is encouraging and completely necessary. All tribal nations, more than ever, need to elicit the best possible thinking and action around positive self-government and what constitutes successful community building. Whether through enterprise, educational, cultural, and governmental institutions, the human face of Indian country needs to be visible to a much larger swath of the American public, particularly policy makers. A major new campaign by each and every Indian nation to develop and deploy well-documented, quality-produced materials telling the positive, most fundamental, and important parts of their tribal realities is required.

This was also the theme and call of another meeting, the recently organized State-Tribal Relations Day event in Montana. Indian leaders there strongly recommended the intense education of non-Indians about cultural and sovereignty issues as a prime component of successfully expanding reservation economies. Education and collaboration to build trust and confidence among their own people and with outsiders was stressed as a major requirement.

The U.S. Supreme courts of the 1970s and 1980s, which regularly contemplated well-reasoned tribal arguments, are no more. But what made reasonable decisions possible on Indian cases even then was the general perception that at least a measure of national political will was being applied toward a justice-oriented resolution to Indian issues.

The political will is not lacking in Congress to sustain the basis of Indian self-governance and jurisdictional rights. But it must be given serious and consistent attention. It must be constantly energized. Collectively, tribes must generate and guide their most extended networks of people, including their own membership, employees, students, families, societies, meeting houses, and churches to guard this most basic pillar. Creative approaches by Native media that can effectively make the case for sustained government-to-government relations within American law are very much encouraged.

More than ever, in these perilous times, it is most important for all tribal nations to project their own most positive images. Reasoned discussion on what constitutes unity of purpose for communities and peoples is much in order. Converging on a national initiative to educate each and every member of the U.S. Congress more diligently on tribal self-governance and its fundamental role in forging strong Native communities is a crucial focus for Indian country.

Pointing to the need "to address the fear that nonmembers will not be accorded due process and equal protection as guaranteed in non-Indian courts," Begaye asked that, "Indian nations must provide constitutional protections for nonmembers and non-Indians" who fall within their jurisdictions.

We salute the Navajo Nation and all those who encourage American Indian nations to unite as one, to speak with one voice on those universally held principles, to advocate for true recognition of inherent sovereignty by the U.S. Supreme Court and Congress.

Those are all positions we can strongly support.

Education Resources and Indian Education Futures
January 14, 2002

John Trudell, the poet laureate of American Indian activism, had it right when he said in 1996 that Indian education had changed much for the better in the past generation. American systems of education went from indoctrinating young Indians against their own cultures ("education was there to beat you down," Trudell put it) to an attitude of more respect, even celebration of Indian cultures and identities. Additionally, many schools these days are managed by communities themselves and now directly teach a more positive, value-oriented attitude to the new generations.

A principal element in institutionalizing and strengthening the Native cultural base has been the tribal community colleges, now numbering thirty-three and growing. The advent of the tribal community colleges in North America, dating from the founding of Navajo Community College in 1968, signaled a huge change in potentials for American Indian students and their communities. It began the building of an indispensable higher-education base within communities and created the opportunity for severely disadvantaged young people who clearly have wanted to pursue an education to achieve increasing degrees of success.

As Assiniboine educator James Shanley has said, "Tribal colleges promised to help individual tribal members become able to survive economically in the modern world and to help our tribes develop the economic base needed to allow the tribe to survive as a people on their own land in their own way."

The record of the tribal colleges is impressive. Enrollments are high, more than 25,000 annually from 250 tribes, and levels of every type of achievement are higher among tribal college graduates. A year 2000 survey released by the Institute for Higher Education Policy (IHEP) (Creating Role

Models for Change: A Survey of Tribal College Graduates) showed that "91 percent of 1998 tribal college and university grads are working or attending college one year after graduating." The same survey conducted by the IHEP in collaboration with the American Indian Higher Education Consortium and the Sally Mae Education Institute revealed that nearly three-fourths of tribal college graduates are female and that most of those attending tribal college are from first-generation college-bound families.

Among a population saddled with endemic poverty over generations, the tribal colleges have made it possible for tens of thousands of young people, particularly single women with children, to overcome poverty and the limitations of living in remote communities to embark on a path of useful instruction and successful careers. Sixteen percent of graduates go into health care fields; 13 percent into teaching; 24 percent go on to management or entry-level administrative/clerk positions. Forty-eight percent go on to further education, with more than 80 percent pursuing the bachelor's degree. Of those, about 40 percent pursue business management and computer science fields.

Thus, the news that the Shakopee Mdewankanton Sioux Community had donated nearly $1 million to the American Indian College Fund strikes us as a great signal to all of Indian country to support the growing strength of Indian education. If there is one area upon which tribal philanthropy (such as it is) should focus, it is education. It is the single most important nation-building element. Reach and hold your young people through a pleasant and instructive educational experience, guide them into serious study habits, and help them develop clear thinking about their professional potentials—the nations will grow. Attach to a sound, modern education the central principle of sustaining Native language and language appreciation curricula through middle school; revitalize and teach the cultural, historical, and legal base of tribal sovereignty—the nations will certainly deepen.

Education was a major issue in the presidential campaign of 2000, when both candidates endorsed serious new expenditures for infrastructure building and more Native teachers in Indian country. Finding good middle ground with the new Republican administration on education issues, Indian country leadership later emphasized education's priority importance to Indian communities during congressional hearings and information sessions in the spring of 2001. The tribes, of course, strongly supported current trends to tribal control and self-administration of education.

However, given the slump in the economy and shifting global priorities, the education of American Indian generations could potentially recede in importance at the federal level. Indian country leadership must remain vigilant in this respect. In each instance, there needs to be a commitment to sustain the necessary institutional support for the educational initiative that is greatly helping Indian country to fulfill its potentials. While not every tribe benefited from the relative affluence and business opportunities of the 1990s, generally, for Native college-bound students, opportunities have grown. This is an area of major promise, as surveys show that large percentages of Native college students would opt to take their training and talents home to settle and work in their communities.

Not that tribal colleges are alone in the pursuit of higher educational profiles for Native peoples. The self-determination trend has touched everywhere, including Bureau of Indian Affairs (BIA) schools. The Office of Indian Affairs at the BIA operates 185 schools in twenty-three states, serving 55,000 students from sixty-three reservations. It funds programs that impact upward of 400,000 Native students of all ages. Yet of their 185 schools, about two-thirds are tribally controlled and operated. It was mostly these schools, which certainly can use the infrastructure support, that the administration has sought to fund.

All efforts to upgrade the educational opportunities of Native youth are welcome and need support. This season we welcome the example of the $900,000 gift to the American Indian College Fund from the Shakopee Mdewankanton Sioux Community, put up as a three-year challenge to other financially strong Indian communities. This effort resonates and deserves ongoing attention. It signals not only generosity of spirit; it serves as a teaching on philanthropic strategy. This season, tribes seeking a good project to support might consider meeting this worthy challenge on behalf of the American Indian College Fund, which distributes scholarships to Indian students going to the tribal colleges.

Tribal colleges hold tremendous promise right now for a great range of talented Native students only asking for the opportunity to get on their way. To all those who can, we say: support the tribal colleges, individually or via your tribal institutions, organizations, and national networks. This timely initiative signaled by the Mdewankanton deserves to be kept strong.

Hail Cecilia Fire Thunder: A Voice for Women and the Indian Family
November 12, 2004

There are too many places, in and out of Indian country, where the lot of women has fallen tragically to the brawn and will of men and the ravishes of an alcohol-infested existence. Such has happened in too many communities on too many reservations, and in Pine Ridge, South Dakota, it has become as well a pitiful and traumatic fact of life.

Thus, we hail the decisive election victory of Cecilia Fire Thunder as the new president of the Oglala Sioux Tribe (OST) of South Dakota. She defeated Russell Means by more than 600 votes in her first attempt and his third to seek the tribal presidency. Both Fire Thunder and Means agree that the women's vote put the first woman president of the OST over the top. Fire Thunder asserts the vote represents the women's power coming to bear on Pine Ridge. The tribe's first woman president was quoted last week saying: "The women have played an integral role in keeping things going. Going to school, getting degrees, working, taking care of the family (and winning the election), that's the value of the Lakota woman re-elevated back to where it belongs." (KOTA News)

Fire Thunder has dedicated much of her adult life to the defense of the Indian family and the struggle against abuse of Indian women and children. She is an advocate of the rescue and use of the Lakota language by the younger generation. Marjene Ambler, in *Tribal College Journal*, wrote, "Lakota language advocate Cecilia Fire Thunder uses healing ceremonies to free the tongues of people too ashamed to 'remember' their Native language. In many cases, these feelings toward the language have led to hating their own skin color." *Indian Country Today* columnist Suzan Shown Harjo wrote on our Web site edition recently about Fire Thunder's work "to educate Lakota people about Lakota traditions of gender balance and the sacredness of children and elders." Harjo pointed out that Fire Thunder's Lakota name means "Good Hearted Woman." A practical nurse, Fire Thunder established an organization, Sacred Circle, to address domestic violence. Her career stands as testimony of the effort to help rebuild the self-esteem of women in her community and nationally. She is just the kind of courageous and outgoing woman leader that a people wanting to restrengthen their nation from the ground up, family by family and *tiospaye* by *tiospaye*, could appeal to for understanding and assistance.

The election of a woman to the nation's highest office is a first for the Oglala people and we hope it signals a new volition to confront the issue of respect and rebuilding of families for that embattled community. Pine Ridge is not alone as a community, not by a long shot, to be in the quagmire and tragedy of family violence. However, it could be the place where the body politic begins to heal itself, from the women outward. The election of Cecilia Fire Thunder—a grassroots advocate to properly challenge even Russell Means—represents just this kind of potential new mandate by the voting community.

We congratulate Cecilia in her victory and wish the outstanding woman leader all the perseverance and support she deserves. If the Oglala families—including the strong family men—get behind their new leader and work with her to build coalitions for political power and development, much could be accomplished. Not only from the federal government but also from foundations and private donors, Cecilia is well suited, as a woman leader heading up a new administration, to bring home important benefits in response to the aspirations of the Oglala communities.

Most importantly, Cecilia Fire Thunder will be an inspiration to young women to reach for leadership and pursue the path of self-esteem and self-dignity. From consideration as sacred and as centrally important to the nations, Indian women have too often been denigrated and abused. This is the conclusion of the Family Violence and American Indians/Alaska Natives: A Report to the Indian Health Service Office of Women's Health, a compendium produced in October 2002 by Dr. Laura Williams, et al. Sexual assault against Indian women is more than double that among blacks and three times that of whites. Forty-six percent of violence and 70 percent of crime is alcohol related. Acquaintances (38 percent) and strangers (46 percent) have the highest rates as perpetrators against Indian women. Family and intimates account for around 10 percent. In domestic violence, poverty and alcohol are the major factors.

We commend Cecilia for focusing immediately on the economic and financial transparency situation at the tribe. She notes it is her first mandate and has been the sore point about the Oglala Sioux Tribe for her whole base of supporters. The Pine Ridge Reservation suffers from extreme unemployment—a severe lack of any work opportunity for most of the tribal youth and membership. Yet, specific business and *tiospaye*-building initiatives are growing in capacity and are important pieces of the nation-rebuilding puzzle. These are essential building blocks of any new campaign to tackle the serious problems of Indian country. We urge the foundation world and the NGO community to pay attention to Pine Ridge, its issues, and problems; to support the work of both government but also of independent organizations as they confront the problems of their people. More importantly, we urge Indian country itself to identify ways it can create or stimulate employment opportunities for the Oglala Sioux Tribe and South Dakota's other tribal communities. It is time to end the despair and restore opportunity.

Again, congratulations to Cecilia Fire Thunder and to the children, women, and men of the Oglala Sioux Oyate. May your path be well guided on the Red Road to peace and prosperity.

Whither the Wealth of Indian Nations?

December 2, 2004

The enclaves of knowledge where people take a quality professional approach to economic and financial matters continue to grow in Indian country. This is all to the good. Tribal peoples have been severely marginalized across the hemisphere, but particularly in North America, where the gap between modern industrial wealth and dispossession and poverty is so stark the thought of financial power being exercised by Indian people seemed almost a contradiction.

As an extended circle of related tribal nations, Indian people had not moved in powerful economic currents in this country since the ancestors first defended sizeable pieces of territory and natural resources. We know, of course, how by hook and by crook, by two-tongued pen, and by the cold steel of death, 90 percent of all that physical manifestation was lost, along with much of the cultural life and the political will of our peoples.

Cohesion as kindred peoples, not always cordial or even politically functional, still sustains among most tribal nations; this is the source. It has endured huge indignity and catastrophe and is the primary fountain of strength by which a more modern-day skilled and educated Indian population could really cement ancient and established rights in a consistent growth toward just and prosperous futures.

As always in rapidly changing times, new skills are needed, are being commanded, and put to work. Just as the 1950s and 1960s saw a new crop of Indian educators and social workers come along, and the 1970s witnessed the growth of a core group of Indian lawyers who could litigate from the inside, so the 1990s ushered in more formal training in the business and managerial professions. The trend was visible even in the early 1980s, but accelerated explosively with the advent of the gaming revolution.

Even now, nearly two decades later, the Indian financial revolution is only in its adolescence. It requires more than ever a great boost of recognition and attention—not preferably in conflictive ways, but in cooperative (i.e., mutually beneficial) approaches—where the values of the fundamental culture can always be guaranteed a central guiding place among the core principles of appropriate business and community development for tribal peoples.

It was good to see this approach to principles emerge at a couple of recent Indian finance and business conferences, amidst many wide-ranging, recognizably intelligent strategic conceptions and proposals.

One, the Inaugural Tribal Wealth Management Conference gathered the go-getters among tribal financial officers and representatives of the broader financial industry. It was held at the Seminole Hard Rock Hotel and Casino (Florida) and networked through the United South and Eastern Tribes.

Consider these guideposts:

- Preservation of new-found wealth for the future generations
- Encouraging financial firms to advance Indian employees, deepening the range of skills available generally to Indian country
- Adopting the major potentials and documented successes of the Community Development Financial Institutions, which are designed to foster small business and home ownership
- Practically, to create an organization focused on finance and economics, much as the American Indian Science and Engineering Society now functions for science and engineering

Another conference, the National Indian Business Association Annual Conference and Trade Show, held in September but that still reverberates, concentrated on identifying keys to success in the financial world. Excellently reported for our pages by Washington correspondent Jerry Reynolds, it features in part the prescriptions of Chuck Johnson of the Johnson Strategy Group, who outlined some important markers.

Key to success in accessing capital from the private-equity sector, Johnson taught, require quality people and strategy in:

- Big-picture economic planning, as well as entrepreneurial initiatives, for the tribe
- Incorporating a "tribal investment portfolio" approach
- Demanding due-diligence processes for business deals; overlapping with the tribal wealth conference, where casino executive Hugh Lordon stressed the importance of: 'Knowing your potential partner. Who are you dealing with? What are they up to?"

Tribal ventures—in cases, joint tribal ventures—now reach beyond reservation territories, even into the global economy.

Or, of utmost importance:

- Creating a crosswalk between tribal sovereignty planning for the governmental operations and the type of extremely detailed operational planning needed for business success
- Committing to more detailed operational-enterprise planning

Pechanga Band of Luiseño Chairman Mark Macarro, among other

enlightened leaders, is calling for a "national economy for Indian country." We thoroughly agree with this concept and will continue to endorse it in these pages.

There exists great and wise counsel in this range of advice. No doubt, business has its own, primary, efficiency-toward-profit logic, but this must be adaptable to the overall building and rebuilding of our peoples, not only to a "business class," not only to a "purchasing agent class," not only to a "millionaire class," not only to a "leadership class." Clearly, this approach will not come automatically, even if the Native cultures by and large prescribe it.

It fell to Oneida ambassador Keller George, who tirelessly contributed to the building of United South and Eastern Tribes, Inc., and is the organization's elder conscience, to gently admonish the various publics in that audience. The tribal sovereignty economic revolution is "not about accumulating wealth," George reminded everyone, to considerable reception. "We are doing this for unborn generations, still beneath the ground."

For the upcoming crop of Native college students, we say this: if initially business language is alien to you, you are not alone. Many Native professionals and activists have had to catch up, having been brought up to distrust business, as earlier they were right to distrust education and religious institutions. We are convinced here, however, that our peoples must fully accommodate in the common intelligence a magnified understanding of the complex world of business and high finance. The new dimension, as fraught with conflictive pitfalls as it is, excites for its promise and potentials: it is absolutely necessary to the capacity of any people in today's world to be able to handle major economic affairs.

To assess the tragic loss of billions of dollars in American Indian life-enhancing assets to federal corruption and mismanagement, we need go no further than the Cobell class action suit. Maybe there was nothing in that 100-plus-year-old process that anyone could have stopped, but now we (as a collective of distinct peoples) are at the helm in many places of serious opportunity to recapture a solid piece of what is ours, truly, for the seventh generation to come. It's serious business indeed, business that offers so much potential, provided American Indian wealth is retained under Indian control and used wisely.

Vampire Policy Is Bleeding Us Dry—Blood Quantums Be Gone!
February 14, 2001

Suzan Shown Harjo, *Indian Country Today*

Native peoples have the traditions, openness, and patience that come from measuring time and possibilities against the entirety of our ancient cultural continuum. That's why we, collectively, have gotten so many things right— we have tried things out for myriad generations, incorporating those that work and discarding those that do not.

We like to observe something new from a distance and circle around it for a while. We don't hate or love the new thing—we just show it respect. It could be dangerous, such as a rifle, a tool of destruction, and of providence. It could be charming, such as cut-glass beads, a good way of sharing a vision.

We may want to admire it from afar and we may want to invite it to our camp, either to stay as family or to come and go as a friend.

Oftentimes, decisions about societal incorporation have been forced upon us. Our ancestors did not get to make a leisurely decision about "civilization," for example. From 1880 to 1936, the federal government banned our traditional religions and made outlaws of our spiritual leaders. While American Indians were starving and eating rancid rations, the coffers of Christian denominations were fattened by annual congressional appropriations for civilizing the Indian. Children were taken to prison schools, parents were held hostage at home, and no one had a choice in this new thing.

This new thing was a way for the white man to keep Indian land without keeping treaty promises. Some white men had a theory that went roughly this way: savages could be tamed and taught to be God fearing and English speaking at the government schools and their allegiances to their families and tribes would diminish. Cross-tribal and non-Indian alliances should be encouraged until Indians value pan-Indianness and white values.

The federal government calculated it would take three generations for American Indians to breed themselves out as tribal people. By 1900, the terms "full-bloods" and "half-breeds" were commonly used on reservations and in popular culture.

Eligibility for most federal Indian programs was made dependent on a quarter-degree Indian-blood-quantum requirement. The idea was that the

United States would continue to uphold treaty promises for health, education, land protection, and the like, but only until the Indians were down to one-quarter Indian blood. At that point, the government could stop paying for their new lands, water, gold, and silver.

In the 1930s, the Bureau of Indian Affairs forced many tribes to codify this slow genocide policy in tribal constitutions, declaring that once their people were down to a certain level of tribal blood, they would cease being tribal citizens and Indian people. In the 1940s, the BIA made lists of those tribes whose people had low tribal blood quantums and few cultural attributes, who could be sent sailing down the mainstream; and of those whose people spoke their tribal language and practiced their traditional ways, who still needed the government to take care of them.

Congress, in the 1950s, started terminating ties with tribes whose people were the most decultured. Some tribes even raised their blood-quantum requirements to one-half to escape being targeted for termination.

Now the blood-quantum requirements are having exactly the pernicious effect on many Native peoples they were intended to have. Lots of children and grandchildren of tribal citizens do not qualify for enrollment because their parents and older ancestors married outside their nation. We are not talking about the pseudo-Indians who have zero Native ancestors or cultural ties. These are real Indian kids and many of them speak their language, practice their traditional religion, contribute to their nation, and in fact are the future of their nation.

So what federal laws are forcing us to keep these blood-quantum requirements? None.

In the mid-1970s, the Supreme Court ruled that no federal agency or any entity except an Indian tribe could determine who its people are. For even longer, the high court has held that Indian nationhood and tribal citizenry are political, not racial, matters. If we cling to these blood standards, which are solely about race, some clever neo-terminationist is going to try to unravel the Indian political status doctrine by using the fixation on and fiction of tribal blood. (The BIA Draculas make us particularly vulnerable in this regard by their continuing use of CDIBs—certificates of degree of Indian blood.)

For the past twenty-five years, we have been free from any federally imposed standards for tribal citizenship. While some nations dropped the blood-quantum nonsense, most have not. This is an excellent (and sad) example of internalized oppression. We don't need the federal government to breed us out of existence—we are doing it ourselves.

I talked with some tribal leaders this year who do not know that tribes have had the power for a quarter of a century to drive a stake in our constitutions' vampire clauses. Some want to do it, but are worried about fakes flooding the tribal rolls and siphoning off precious tribal monies and benefits.

Native peoples have traditional ways of defining citizenship, ways that worked for millennia before there were any non-Natives or pseudo-Indians in our countries. Those ways begin with family. If one or both parents are tribal citizens, frauds are automatically eliminated.

For those leaders whose nations have lost their traditional ways of deciding citizenship, there are more than 560 Native nations today with governmental relations with the United States. Ask a leader of one of those what kind of citizenship standards they have. Shop around—compare tribal citizenship requirements to those of France, India, China, Zimbabwe, South Africa, Mexico, or the United States.

Blood quantums are not new things and they are not our things. We have circled them and been surrounded by them for more than a century, easily long enough to know that we do not respect them, need them, or want them. Doing something about this is almost as easy as one, two, three—blood quantum, begone!

Charting a New Course in Indian Health Care
January 24, 2003

Senator Ben Nighthorse Campbell, United States Government,
Northern Cheyenne Tribe

America is the richest and most powerful country the world has ever known. We are indeed fortunate to be citizens of this great nation, but we must also recognize that most Indians live in abject poverty and that much needs to be done.

In my years on the Senate Committee on Indian Affairs, Congress has enacted bills to reform Indian education, increase housing stock, strengthen tribal economies, settle an array of land and water settlements, and protect Native sacred places.

Poor health has properly been called the "twin sister of poverty" and, unfortunately, Indian people know these siblings all too well. Year after year, Congress debates the President's budget request for Indian health and argues about whether it is sufficient to meet current needs and whether it is properly targeted.

We can choose to do this again this year or we can take a different route—one that may in the long run be more beneficial to Indian people.

The time has come to tackle the fundamental and systemic problems and improve the health of American Indians. We have this opportunity with the reauthorization of the Indian Health Care Improvement Act of 1976.

We can do this by taking a comprehensive review of the facts on the ground and then deciding how to best spend limited Federal resources. Let's start with the facts.

1. Indian population growth. According to the 2000 Census, the Native population soared to more than 4 million from 2.2 million in 1990. Continuing a trend begun years ago, only 34 percent of the Native population now lives on-reservation, compared with 66 percent living in urban or suburban settings.

What do these trends mean for how the Indian health system is structured and funded? Well, right out of the box it tells me that more focus must be paid to the urban Indian health system, both structurally and financially. Figures clearly show that spending has not tracked these demographic changes and federal funding for urban health is a fraction of total health spending.

2. Health disparities continue. Similar to a lot of Americans, I am encouraged that incoming Senate Majority Leader Bill Frist has indicated that eliminating disparities in health care is one of his main priorities for the 108th Congress.

We should all be alarmed when the Indian death rate for diabetes mellitus is 249 percent higher than rest of the American population; when the pneumonia and influenza death rate is 71 percent higher; when the tuberculosis death rate is 533 percent higher; and when the Indian death rate from alcoholism is 627 percent higher.

3. The current health care system results in Indian health problems being treated, not prevented. When I return to Lame Deer, Montana—home of the Northern Cheyenne Tribe—I see the consequences of a "treatment only" health care system: growing obesity in young Cheyennes, a daily regimen of McDonald's and cigarettes, eight-hour round-trips to Billings for dialysis therapy, and amputations for those lucky enough to grow old.

To make the kind of sea change required in Indian health care, we must shift the "Band-Aid strategy" of responding to symptoms rather than attacking the root causes of these health problems and planting the seeds for a healthier Native population in future years.

Nowhere is this more important than with our Indian youngsters. In the 107th Congress, I held hearings on the many problems facing Indian youth and Indian elders across the country. The hearings pointed up the need to teach Indian youngsters that a good diet, physical activity, and positive lifestyle can prevent the fate that meets far too many of their elders:

diabetes, amputations, emphysema, and shortened lives due to alcohol and tobacco use.

Just last December, Congress took a step in this direction by expanding the Special Diabetes Program for Indians to include $100 million to tribes and tribal organizations for diabetes treatment, research, and prevention.

Because every dollar of diabetes funding is precious, I believe the major hospitals and research facilities that engage in Native diabetes research—in New Mexico, Colorado, Georgia, Alaska, and Hawaii—can, at a minimum, share their results and encourage the use of "best practices" guides by the Indian Health Service (IHS), tribal, and urban health providers.

Evolving technology must be a part of the answer to better health care. Large swaths of Native America are rural, out-of-the-way places, far from urban areas. Native Alaska offers probably the best example of a thin but widely dispersed population that is highly susceptible to tele-medicine and state-of-the-art technologies. For example, the technology now exists to allow a physician sitting in Anchorage to download and analyze an X-ray, mammogram, or blood work-up sent from a clinic in the bush country of Alaska. This can provide significant reductions in the cost of providing treatment to rural Native communities and ought to be expanded.

We must maximize dollars dedicated to Indian health. In time of scarce Federal dollars and our nation preparing to fight a war abroad, the reality is that there will not be huge increases in discretionary funds for Fiscal Year 2004. The key will be on how to use the significant funding that already exists in the most productive way.

Since the enactment of the Indian Self Determination and Education Assistance Act in 1975, tribes and tribal organizations have provided quantitatively and qualitatively better health services than the IHS using the same core funding.

I am a strong supporter of contracting and compacting and am proud to have sponsored the Indian Tribal Self-Governance Amendments, enacted in 2000, that made self-governance in Indian health permanent. The trend toward greater tribal contracting and compacting continues: the IHS now contracts and compacts out to tribes and tribal organizations more than 50 percent of its $2.2 billion budget. It is my hope that more tribes will enter self-governance in the years ahead.

As we enter the 108th Congress, I believe that a health care effort that focuses on these core elements will advance the cause of improving Native health for years to come.

Editors' note: Among other key committee assignments, former senator Campbell, R-Colo., was the vice chairman of the Senate Committee on Indian Affairs and a member of the Senate Energy and Natural Resources Committee.

Land Rich and Dirt Poor, the Story of Native Assets

September 8, 2003

Rebecca Adamson, *Indian Country Today*

The assets of American Indian and Alaska Native tribes would make anyone else in the world wealthy. Their landholdings of almost 100 million
acres, if aggregated, would form a land base larger than all states except
Alaska, Texas, and California. And these lands are rich in resources, with
timber, range, and cropland, oil and gas reserves, uranium deposits and
water reserves, and a host of other tangible assets.

Yet, tribes are the single poorest population group in the United
States, justifying the unique title "land rich, dirt poor."

The problem is that tribes do not control tribal assets. To the contrary,
federal policy toward Native peoples in America has always put others in
control of tribal assets. Whether these others are colonial agents of usurpation, or agency superintendents, or businessmen sizing up an Indian deal,
or corporations seeking advantage, or state governments demanding tribute
from "their" tribes—they have all found ways to gain from tribal assets
while the Native owners go without.

Whether in small towns or corporate boardrooms, government offices
or legislative assemblies or courtrooms, these mostly sordid gains depend
on the same underpinning: the majority of assets still owned by tribes are
by law held "in trust" for them by the Department of Interior through its
subordinate agency, the Bureau of Indian Affairs.

True enough, not every tribe since the outset of the reservation era
has been qualified at all times to manage its own affairs in a cash economy.
But this became a self-fulfilling critique as Native peoples in America were
habitually discouraged from managing their own affairs—this set the stage
for the ongoing transfer of tribal assets into other hands. It is the trust status of tribal assets that has enabled our trustee, the federal government,
and its delegates to concentrate the levers of dispossession in judicial, legislative, and administrative venues.

In judicial settings, tribes regularly prove that the greatest wrongs have
been committed against them—but tribes generally haven't been at the table
when the laws were drafted, leading to what one Alaska Native leader has
called "weasel-worded disclaimer language" that leaves tribes without recourse
in the courts. The latest decision to demonstrate this crippling weakness of
our legal system is the Supreme Court's ruling in March that without specific statutory language in place, tribes cannot hold the trustee accountable
for its clear and knowing participation in the miscarriage of justice for tribes.

What's more, on those occasions when evidence of historical mismanagement (that would stagger an ox) is proved to even a courtroom's satisfaction, settlement almost never includes lost interest or earnings from lost revenues.

In legislative settings, tribes simply cannot count on Congress for the dollar-for-dollar restitution of our losses or often for correction of the laws that facilitate these losses. The current Cobell litigation over the Individual Indian Monies accounts is a classic example: after fifteen years of effort on all sides, Congress passed a reform law in 1994 that may be another fifteen years or more in implementation. And just you watch: Congress will not risk bankrupting the country to recompense our losses, but will rather come up with a settlement that falls far short of the dollar-for-dollar obligation other errant trustees must meet.

But perhaps most wrongful of all to tribes is the administrative setting—here, over years, government agents have agreed with corporate interests on the valuation of tribal assets for leasing, almost always to the detriment of tribes compared with private-sector lessees. Land is leased at below-market rates in a clearly codependent lowball "bargaining" arrangement that benefits underfunded federal agencies and corporations, but not Native beneficiaries. Oil prices are suggested by companies and accepted by federal agents in negotiations not involving Indian beneficiaries. Royalties are under-collected on the administrative watch of government-indemnified careerists who bite off a solid paycheck while Indians settle for scraps and (often) resign themselves to thinking they've got it good.

Where is the safeguard against conflict of interest, de rigueur for other trust administrators? Everywhere else where law abides under the authority of the Securities Exchange Commission, it is well-known that a trustee must conduct client affairs with an undivided interest—conflicted interests are forbidden. Under the duty of care, a trustee is required to execute transactions with prudence and in the manner most favorable to the beneficiary.

One example of how the government's neglect of these standards works together against Indians should be presented in detail. Until 1962, Interior held it to be illegal, a violation of trust, for tribes to develop their own mineral properties. Similar to the owners of many other asset classes in Indian country, tribes were simply leaseholders. Negotiations took place, if they took place at all, between government delegates and business interests, an exclusive club that did not admit Indians. The law, the court system, and administrative practice kept it thus for generations. The result is that instead of enjoying a fair share of the nation's $280 billion a year power industry, tribes owning 10 percent of the resources that fuel it received less than 1 percent of power-industry revenues in 1999. Although improvement since must be noted, that is the kind of legacy we are up against.

Who in their right mind would want the BIA as an asset manager? But without the right to hire or fire the asset manager, much less to seek a demonstrably more qualified replacement, tribes have watched as probably billions of dollars of natural resource assets have been mismanaged, or rather managed for the benefit of non-Native interests.

Tribal control of trust assets must be the theme of tribal activities and of federal policy going forward.

Red, Black, and Bruised
October 21, 2003

David Wilkins, University of Minnesota

A specter is haunting Indian country—the specter of First Nation–African American relations. Unlike communism, however, which has seen better days in Europe and elsewhere, this particular specter, one of many that continues to bedevil Native nations, continues to fester and poses increasing problems for a number of tribal nations, African Americans, mixed-blood black Indians, and the federal government as well.

This volatile issue was recently discussed by Brent Staples, an African American columnist, in an editorial column in *The New York Times* titled "When Racial Discrimination is Not Just Black and White."

After giving a short history lesson in which he accurately recounted the not insignificant amount of intermarriage between Africans and permanently settled African Americans and the darker reality that some Native communities held African Americans as slaves, he arrived at the gist of his argument.

While noting that some whites were finally confronting their own mixed-race heritage that includes black-white connections, after generations of denial, he then argued that "the attitudes of some Native Americans have not evolved in the same way. Both the Seminole and the Cherokee tribes have employed discriminatory policies to prevent black members from receiving tribal benefits and to strip them of the right to vote in tribal elections."

For Staples, this type of Native discrimination against African Americans is particularly egregious, given the history of colonialism, slavery, and discrimination members of both these groups have endured and continue to endure at the hands of Euro-Americans and policy makers and given the reality of close indigenous and African American relations in many parts of the country.

The bulk of the column then focused on the historically, legally, and culturally complicated situation of the Seminole, Creek, and Cherokee nations in present-day Oklahoma, each of which allowed the enslavement of African Americans until the Civil War.

The Cherokee, however, by an act of their National Council in 1863, had already abolished slavery and involuntary servitude, but as a result of the participation of some of their nation's members on the side of the Confederacy, federal officials forced them in their 1866 treaty to reaffirm their pledge never to enslave African Americans and to extend to their former slaves and their descendants "all the rights of Native Cherokees."

Former slaves under the Creek's 1866 treaty were also entitled to similar rights, "including an equal interest in the soil and national funds, and the laws of the said nation shall be equally binding upon and give equal protection to all such persons ... "

The 1866 treaties were, it is important to note, coercive documents forced upon the Five Tribes by the victorious federal government and they contain a number of punitive and detrimental provisions—the loss of thousands of acres of their reserved lands, lands that would thereafter be unavailable to both the freedmen and other members of these nations among them—that wreaked havoc on the Indian communities, including black freedmen.

The subsequent allotment years for the Five Tribes (and all allotted Indians) in the 1890s and beyond were even more trying and led to additional federal impositions on the tribal nations: the ultimate one being the loss of additional vast swaths of communal and individually held lands and the construction, by the federal government, of membership rolls for the allotted nations that, as Staples correctly pointed out, were segregated, with "Indians by blood" on one roll and the black "freedmen" on another.

Staples maintains that these segregated rolls have poisoned indigenous and African American relations and that the tribes "have used them time and again to argue that black Native Americans are not tribal members at all." In fact, he goes so far as to say that "the Freedmen sometimes had clearer Native American bloodlines than non-black brethren on the Blood Rolls." Precisely what Staples means by "clearer" bloodlines is, unfortunately, not clear.

As David Chang, a historian, has noted, a person whose mother was enrolled as a "full-blood" Creek and whose father was enrolled as a "Negro Freedman" would be enrolled as a "Negro Freedman," although Creeks are matrilineal. More interestingly, a person with significant Euro-American ancestry and very little Creek ancestry "by blood" would be enrolled as Creek "by blood." That is, of course, as long as those individuals had no known African ancestry.

The interracial and intergovernmental tension today in Oklahoma between the Seminole and the Cherokee, enrolled and disenrolled African Americans, and the BIA, is palpable, frustrating, and will not be easily resolved.

This prickly situation is not, however, limited to Oklahoma. The real and perceived relationship between indigenous communities and African Americans has also affected the inherent rights and status of the Mashantucket Pequot and other Northwest tribal groups who have been embroiled in controversy because of commentators such as Jeff Benedict and his controversial work, *Without Reservation*.

It has also affected the efforts of tribes such as my own, the Lumbee of North Carolina, and other southeastern tribes in their quest for federal recognition. Some federal lawmakers and other recognized tribes have made the specious argument that due solely to their perception that Lumbees had historically intermixed or intermarried with African Americans, that this had somehow diminished their tribal consciousness or identity.

Interestingly, for those groups petitioning for federal recognition who have a real or perceived mixture of English, French, or German blood, the same argument is generally not used to deny them political or cultural status as a bona fide First Nation.

I am convinced that the specter of indigenous and African American relations, and the situation of those mixed-blood individuals who consider themselves African Indians, will continue to haunt Native communities, cloud our relationship with African Americans and those of African American/indigenous ancestry, and will continue to be wielded by some in positions of political, economic, and media power as a means to deny or discredit those being challenged.

I disagree with Mr. Staples' comparison of tribal governments who have or are in the process of disenfranchising their African American citizens with southern states' rights' political officials in the mid-twentieth century who winked and looked the other way when African Americans were being hanged, beaten, and harassed for trying to vote, looking to be seated in restaurants and movie theaters, or desiring nothing more than to be allowed to sit in any open seat on buses or trains. But his urging that African American citizens of tribal nations should and must be treated fairly by both tribal and federal officials is unassailable.

A key point not mentioned by Staples in his discussion of the Seminole situation is that black members who can trace lineal descent through their mother's line to a Seminole ancestor are considered full members of the nation.

Tribal nations are, by definition, sovereign nations and do indeed have the right to determine their own citizenry. That said, federal officials have at times acted to interfere or override tribal decisions on who can legally and politically belong to a tribal nation. Cultural and kinship connection in a tribal nation is an altogether different creature, however, than legal affiliation, and I hope that tribal membership or citizenship deliberations on this crucial and complicated issue will take full stock of the wide range of historical and social developments and interpersonal relationships that have shaped and determined each First Nation's unique population and social character today.

As one writer put it, "if we don't form history, history will surely form us." Let us then, as First Nations, form a realistic understanding and appreciation of our respective and diverse tribal histories that draws from rather than shirks or denies any aspect or component of our cultural, genetic, political, or legal past or present. Let us choose not to act from bigotry and racism. There is enough of that still being leveled on us psychologically, emotionally, and structurally by the larger state and society.

Hey wait a minute, we're disappearing!

Chapter Three
Tribal Nations and American Justice

Justice is not easy for Indians to attain, given the fundamental rationale that allows the theft of one's property because one is not Christian. Nevertheless, Indian tribal sovereignty resides in the law, internal to the tribes and in the precedents of court cases through two centuries. States and tribes are historical antagonists. Tribes deal with the federal government via Congress and the bureaucracy. The bureaucracy has been consistently incompetent— charged with protecting but seriously diminishing the tribal bases. In one major case, the bureaucracy stands accused of stealing or mismanaging hundreds of millions of dollars of Indian monies for which the federal government had taken responsibility. Courts follow the national trends, as always too willing to dispossess tribal nations of their treaty-guaranteed lands (i.e., Western Shoshone), justified in the obviously discriminatory Christian-can-steal-from-Native invented myth of the American legal system. Bitter thought? Perhaps. But consider the Doctrine of Discovery, often cited by the High Court in Indian cases. There is no doubt that the concept of "chosen peoples" deserves scrutiny.

EDITORIALS

Working for Justice in Indian Country
October 25, 2001

In 1968, the American Indian Movement (AIM) exploded into existence
primarily to confront issues of racial injustice. The immediate cases
involved police harassment and brutality suffered by urban Indians in
Minneapolis, a pattern easily identified in many urban centers, from Gallup
and Albuquerque to Rapid City, from Los Angeles to Philadelphia. It was
not long, however, before the AIM patrols that came together to monitor
treatment of Indians in the streets became the impetus for a much wider
modern discussion by Native activists on the meanings of justice for their
peoples in North America.

Issues of sovereignty, questions of jurisdiction, of tribal authority over
their territories and membership, and about the myriad complex relations
with non-Indian neighbors, quickly surfaced. The reality of aboriginal existence, of retention of a political identity, of inherent rights to self-governance, of legal title to still-held lands as well as claims on lands corruptly
taken, became apparent to an ever-widening movement of people. Outrage
at the many historical layers of injustice that perched over tribal existence—
particularly as administered by the Bureau of Indian Affairs and the
Department of the Interior—spilled into a decade of militant confrontations, takeovers of buildings, and other protests designed to bring attention
to the obvious suffering. While the protests brought a measure of change in
Indian country, they also spawned further injustice, unleashing a massive
persecution that targeted Native activists and produced conditions that led
to further violence. We believe it was this severe federal reaction that pre-
cipitated the unfortunate 1975 shoot-out at the Jumping Bull ranch on the
Pine Ridge Reservation, which made Leonard Peltier a target and victim of
the campaign designed to scare the emerging Indian bases into submission.

There are many manifestations of injustice. Some are in the communities, in the streets and prisons; others occur at higher levels, even in the
courts. In South Dakota, the setting for much of the action during the
intense protest years, the question of selected justice toward Indians charged
in criminal court is still highly contested. South Dakota is again at the forefront in large part because of the case of Robert Many Horses, a Lakota
youth whose death, after being beaten and stuffed into a trash can upside
down, resulted in initial charges against white suspects that were later dismissed by a local magistrate. There have been many such cases in the

Dakotas—of white culprits, charged in violent crimes against Indians, given exceedingly light sentences or never brought to trial. There is also the suspicion by many families that Indian defendants tend to get heavier sentences than whites for similar crimes.

We are hopeful that a South Dakota study presently under way to gauge racial disparities within the criminal justice system, due for release soon, will shed reasonable light on the subject. Although public forums to discuss the study brought out few people, we suspect this is more the result of so many decades of inaction, which have produced a sense of hopelessness about the criminal justice situation. The study is expected to help establish a protocol for tracking the state's justice system, which will hopefully bring a measure of equity for Native people.

Even worse injustices, however, particularly for the long-term, are found in the higher chambers of government. Certainly, the intent by American Indian nations to uphold the widest possible measure of sovereignty and its practical applications has met many obstacles. In this context, tribes are shuffled and must shuffle themselves, strategically, between the High Court and the U.S. Congress. This ping-pong of Indian policy goes back two centuries and is likely to continue ad infinitum.

There is near despair these days at the U.S. Supreme Court. Several of its recent decisions, which went against the concept and practice of tribal jurisdiction, have Native leaders wondering if it is at all possible to turn to the High Court for any kind of justice. In Nevada vs. Hicks, the current court reversed a lower court ruling that upheld tribal rights to civil claims against nonmembers for actions on tribal land. While three justices expressed apprehension that the "majority's sweeping opinion ... undermines the authority of tribes to make their own laws and be ruled by them," the decision worked to firm up the notion that, "an Indian reservation is considered part of the territory of the State."

The Supreme Court's erosion of tribal sovereignties vs. state sovereignties has an active history. In a crucial case, Seminole Tribe vs. Florida, decided in March 27, 1996, the Court declared that a state cannot be sued by a tribe in federal court. This highly controversial decision was later applied "in its opposite' by the tribe, which used it to base an argument that its own tribal sovereignty could not, conversely, be sued by the state. But in the final analysis, both in the Seminole case and in other decisions, the Court's direction of fortifying states' sovereignty at the expense of tribal or even federal sovereignties has been very much in evidence.

Two important lessons: first, internal tribal justice systems need support and improvements. Where customary tradition continues to hold the social agreement and can be strengthened or improved as a basis of tribal governance, it should be. But whatever legal system they may choose to adapt, all tribes can only benefit by ever more efficient, transparent (to members and counterpart authorities), and fair justice systems. Second, tribes must intensely search for the common markers of unity they all benefit from and go out and make their case loud and clear. The main line of defense is to build the most knowledgeable base possible—among tribal members, among local, regional, and national publics, and at all levels of public communication.

These days, once again, Congress is the court of last resort for tribes, which are well advised to work the congressional field of action (and the media) intensely. The U.S. Congress has come a relatively long way in understanding the bases of tribal existence since it passed Public Law 280 in 1953, which extended state criminal jurisdiction over Indian reservations. Through the disputed Plenary Power Doctrine, it still enjoys virtually unlimited power over Indian people. In fact, the High Court almost never holds any of its laws affecting Indians to be "unconstitutional."

Especially at this critical historical moment, when the national terrorism crisis takes precedence over most strategies, tribes cannot afford to by lulled into inaction on their bottom-line issues. The legal-political field is brimming with immediate dangers to long-term survival. Serious problems, internal or external, require serious solutions. In the long track of point-counterpoint represented in the histories of both federal statutes and case law, one reality is clear: the survival and enhancement of tribal sovereign powers and authorities, which are fundamental to the ongoing quest for justice by American Indians, will require the highest vigilance, diligence, and commitment.

Fate of Indian Trust Fund and Other Cases
November 5, 2001

One must wonder about the direction of the federal Indian agency toward tribal nations at this time of war footing in America. Will it be able to defend the tribal bases? As America streamlines all its systems to confront the terrorist emergency, what might be lost or imperiled in the widespread apparatus of American Indian rights?

Where might go the focus on trust reform, for example, particularly the recovery of resources for the Indian trust accounts? This is seriously stalled, because of the lack of fundamental accounting.

Monitors appointed by the courts speak of a trust reform process "on the verge of failure." Does this mean that the Bureau of Indian Affairs

(BIA) does not know how to fix a problem of such magnitude? On this issue, which has faltered for years, is the BIA's incompetence of such long standing that it is nearly impossible for anyone to penetrate it, to command enough resources to fix it? Is this the issue that so clearly shows the country's continuing process of rapaciously eating up the resources of American Indian peoples?

The case of billions lost to Indian family and tribal accounts is the story of a major federal boondoggle going back a century. It needs huge attention, and to the thousands of families who might be better off right now but for the extremely mismanaged if not corrupt federal oversight, it is a crucial issue. It is a question of whether fundamental justice can be done.

So far, every study and court action appears to castigate the Indian agency. That is the current. On this issue, the bureau is inconsistent with its information, has not moved with any efficiency to clean up the system or to make proper accounting procedures come to bear. The court's special master on the case, Alan Balaran, in pursuit of missing and intentionally destroyed documents, continues to rap Gale Norton for falling "short of the requisite diligence and good faith necessary."

So were rapped soundly Kevin Gover, Secretary of the Treasury Robert Rubin and former interior secretary Bruce Babbitt in the previous administration—all charged with contempt for "failing to comply" to court orders to produce records in a timely manner. A recent report to the court points to "widespread mismanagement" by senior officials who failed or refused to conduct a proper historical accounting, "covered up their mismanagement," and "all the while providing this court with ... misleading assessments ... "

The court's report excoriated both BIA and Interior "career executive service managers" for failing to solve the problem, although they "have had the time." Secretary Norton has asked for more extra time to solve the severe standstill. She appeared close to being next on that contempt line up, at least until September 11.

But, are all bets are off after September 11, as the focus on combating terror attacks dislocates internal justice issues from their normal place of attention? Unfortunately, this is after half a decade of repugnant federal foot dragging on the more than 100-year-old process.

Democrats and Republicans alike, as well as Indian and non-Indian bureaucrats alike, have utterly failed at this important question of whether the U.S. Interior Department, charged with the safeguarding of the most ripped-off and destitute peoples within its nation, can halt this ongoing dishonor.

In respect for the people who have suffered destitution and despair as a result of this continuous injustice, we hope this case will not be disregarded now, as the country moves to other priorities. On the contrary, congressional forces, as they take up regular business, should demand an independent task force, a "receiver" worth its salt, armed with the necessary skill sets, to completely tackle this thorny problem.

We express our deepest appreciation and a strong salute to those who have worked to hold Interior's feet to the fire on this issue and who act from virtuous motives.

We urge your important network not to desist now in seeking justice for Indian people but to keep pressing, respectfully and in spirit of collaboration and efficiency, for this, and, indeed, for the whole range of extremely important Indian country issues. To sustain the continuous process of community betterment; to strengthen the struggle to improve our social, economic, and cultural conditions; to seek a sense of proper justice that will balance the mind and improve the body—these are excellent goals for Native peoples, now and always.

For ourselves, we clearly understand that the American leadership must seek to hold accountable the perpetrators of such a horrible and clearly directed crime as occurred on September 11. But, while many might think of this time in history only in terms of war, reality tells us that the other side of this unfolding time is the duty to pursue life, liberty, and happiness in all of our necessary goals and activities.

In the sacrifice of seeking justice, it is reassuring and reaffirming to see justice done.

Indians and Court Unite to Tongue-Lash Interior
December 21, 2001

A "daylong tongue-lashing" from tribal leaders is the way the papers described Interior Department's first consultation on its plan for fixing the massive Indian trust funds debacle. Simultaneously, a federal judge was no less caustic in denouncing the Department for its interpretation of his recent order to Interior to protect the accounts from Internet hacking.

The Indian leaders were responding to Interior's surprise proposal to remove management of Indian trust money from the Bureau of Indian Affairs (BIA) and thus create a new Bureau of Indian Trust Assets Management, also within the Department of Interior. This highly controversial decision, legally tendered to the court as solution to grievances, is considered widely by American Indian leadership as debasement of Indian standing and a severe departure from the expected government-to-government consultation structures that had become expected from the federal bureaucracy.

In Albuquerque, about 500 Indians faced Secretary Gale Norton and Assistant Secretary Neal McCaleb in the first of a series of seven after-the-fact consultations. More than fifty tribal leaders, including all nineteen Pueblos, the Navajo president, and many others, spoke to the embattled officials. Their unanimous answer was an unmistakable "No." The sense of insult expressed was palpable and genuine. Norton expressed the wish to take their recommendations but asserted that the basic plan as presented to the federal court cannot be pulled back now.

Meanwhile, as tragic comedy turned to farce, the Interior's leadership apparently and seriously overreacted to the order by Judge Royce Lamberth to "disconnect" the trust account computer systems. The judge, as reported nationally all last week, was responding to the latest set of errors, after his court-ordered hacker walked anonymously all over the Bureau's system. The hacker proved that the Indian trust accounts were completely assailable from any outside phone line. Disconnect it from the Internet, said the judge.

But the judge did not mean for the Secretary to shut down the whole of Interior's systems' connections to the Internet, which she did, wreaking substantial havoc on all kinds of ongoing and necessary work by a variety of federal agencies. The precipitous shutdown further punished Indian trust account holders all over again by holding up perhaps as much as $15 million in some 43,000 accounts two weeks before the most expensive family season of the year. Interior's 70,000 employees got paid by faxing or mailing in handwritten statements.

The federal lawyers accused Interior of misunderstanding the order. Judge Lamberth could hardly hide his suspicion when he said, "I don't know why you decided to disconnect all your systems." To be sure, Interior jumped through the hoop the other way quickly enough, seeking injunctions to open up communications with affected agencies such as the U.S. Geological Survey and the Nation Fire Information Center, although at press time individual account holders had not received their payments.

So it goes with Interior. From where we sit, both tongue-lashings were entirely justified. Hounded by an Indian trust system in collision course with the federal courts, Secretary Norton lashed out at the tribes. She seems intent on playing hardball with Indian country. The down-your-throat approach to splitting the BIA, with its disrespectful consultation-as-afterthought, was clearly a way to channel the pain, similar to saying, "You wanted a change, well, here it is!"

Then to misread a simple order clearly focused on protecting the security of trust accounts to mean a complete institutional disconnect; this seems another way of turning the blame on the court. Again, similar to saying, "See, now they are making you suffer by making me do this."

Either way, it is bureaucratic hardball of the most callous type. The moment is past when such attitudes can pass for Indian policy. The Indian population may appear irrelevant to some, but it is increasingly well tuned to political maneuverings and doubletalk whose obvious goal is obfuscation. The national leadership is often fractious with each other on internal issues but, increasingly, questions of national impact are impeccably analyzed and addressed. Then, too, these days, national Indian leaders are in constant touch with each other, via several important networks and organizations.

A fuller understanding of potentials and imperatives of Indian country needs to permeate the top echelon of the federal Indian policy group. Norton, McCaleb, and now, again, Ross Swimmer, among others, need to seriously work to align with Indian country thinking and not be so presumptuous of their proposals or antagonistic to comment and critique. Somehow a true dialogue must be established. If policy makers would only explore the realities behind the Indian leadership's opinions, they would welcome Indian country's vibrant trajectory—its recuperation and re-empowerment—which, if sustained and encouraged, could be a shining example to the world.

The human spirit is vitalized by the promise of justice attainable. This is the resilient quest of America and springboard of its numerous and complex powers. Good, wise signals are called for at this moment in history, and, most importantly, on Indian affairs. How America treats its first governments and peoples is of utmost significance to the whole wide world. Rather than confusion and obtuseness, rather than the current game of poke and smile, Republican Indian affairs managers should set the moral tone for the country's dealings with its most impoverished and dispossessed group. In fact, they should work to show the world at large that tribal cultural and economic success is as American as turkey, corn, and pumpkin pie.

Last Stand for Western Shoshone; It Might Look Legal, but It Stinks
September 26, 2002

At Shoshone, they called it cattle theft. That's last week's description, after a massive, gun-toting raid by federal authorities to confiscate Indian cattle. This week's Senate version of the same issue is more clearly land theft. Just days after the raid by Bureau of Land Management (BLM) agents intended to destroy the economic life of Western Shoshone horse and cattle ranchers, the Senate Committee on Indian Affairs approved the distribution of money-for-land-title payments to Western Shoshone tribal members. The distribution plan, now slated to become law, effectively destroys the Shoshone claim to their aboriginal lands under the Treaty of Ruby Valley.

In an effort to continue a process that has otherwise been thoroughly discredited by any and all accurate historical accountings, the U.S. government has moved mightily to conclude, in the twenty-first century, a massive land swindle that has been some 140 years in the making. The federal government has a growing number of people deeply troubled by its actions in this case. And they should be troubled. Among the affected, a large minority of the tribe, including the Dann sisters, a pair of grandmother-ranchers who have tenaciously upheld the assertion that their people never gave up title to their aboriginal lands. The United States asserts it that it seized the land by encroachment starting as early as the 1860s.

Under the bill introduced by Senator Harry Reid, D-Nev., those who are at least one-quarter Shoshone from around 6,600 tribal members living mainly in Nevada, California, Idaho, and Utah would share the bulk of a $138 million fund. The bill now moves to the full Senate. Reid, who sits on the Senate Indian Affairs Committee, is expecting Senate passage this year.

This massive land swindle has the appearance of legality, but it still stinks. In particular, there is no just cause for what Interior Secretary Gale Norton's BLM agents and enforcers are doing to the Dann sisters, Carrie and Mary, and other Western Shoshone ranchers. Its an outright shame that legitimate Indian farmers, Western Shoshone grandmothers in this case, have to undergo SWAT–type raids from the federal government for living and working on their ancestral lands. With guns at the ready, under cover of darkness, and with roads blocked, the forty-agent federal attack came, and more than 200 head of prime, locally adapted cattle were confiscated, hauled away to be auctioned in penalty for fines.

The issue is of long standing. Shoshone ranchers and many other ranchers have traditionally used the vast Nevada rangeland to feed their beef cattle. In the case of the Shoshones, traditional elders rely on the Treaty of Ruby Valley, which they claim did not relinquish title to their homelands. While the government claims the Shoshone lost title because of "gradual encroachment," even today, as Carrie Dann points out, "If they took it by gradual encroachment, where are all those people who encroached?" Of her Nevada homeland, she says, "The only people living out here are Indians."

As reported by *Indian Country Today* Southwest Bureau Chief, Valerie Taliman, in this edition, the Danns and other Shoshone ranchers pasture their cattle on the contested ranges, for which they are fined exorbitantly by the BLM, with the intent of breaking them financially. The raids are mounted to enforce the heavy penalties. The Dann sisters and Western Shoshone traditionalists maintain that their tribe never legally ceded their rangelands. For this perspective, which has much legal precedent and a supportive international ruling, they are treated like criminals. The federal raids are clearly aimed at causing demoralization and economic damage to the more politically astute traditional families.

Coming just days before the U.S. Senate Indian Affairs Committee "marked up" Reid's bill to finally extinguish Western Shoshone territory, the raid stoked the sense in Indian country that federal agencies are once again playing in-your-face hardball, rather than searching for some other type of compromise over very deeply disputed Indian country lands.

As Taliman reports, a recent report by the Inter-American commission on Human Rights of the Organization of American States (OAS), of which the United States is a member, found that the United States is violating the human and civil rights of Western Shoshone people. The report accused the United States of using illegitimate means to claim ownership and control of Western Shoshone land and resources. The OAS commission recommended a remedy that will respect the Western Shoshone's rights to the land. This interesting development is a good reminder that federal Indian policy can be scrutinized by international bodies even though it remains to be seen whether the United States will respect the OAS report.

Nevertheless, the long-standing issue comes to a head as Interior ponders the privatization of huge sectors of rangeland. Extinguishment of Shoshone land ownership has been very high on the agenda and lawyers representing Western Shoshone opponents of the payout point out that Reid's bill is part of a drive to open the land to lucrative, private gold mining. In a statement, they said it provided 15 cents an acre for land encompassing the Carlin gold trend, "with a mined value of $20 billion dollars and rising."

The white ranchers, too, are feeling the pinch of the BLM. The intensity of persecution against the Dann sisters at this moment has all the earmarks of an early sweep of the field. Consider that Nevada Senator Harry Reid has two bills in Congress. Senate bill 958 would pay off the Shoshones 15 cents an acre to "settle" their claim to the land. The other, Senate bill 719, opens the land for privatization, selling the land to the highest bidders. Expectedly, these will be for multinational gold-mining companies and other powerful interests. *Indian Country Today* will closely follow these developments.

The Nevada LivesStock Association, feeling the threat to their own lifestyles, also came out in defense of the Indian ranchers. Chairman David Holmgren and his wife, who were on the scene of the raid, called it, "unlawful seizures" and "cattle rustling" by the BLM. Holmgren stated on behalf of the statewide association: "Grand larceny of the Dann cattle is being committed and the right to due process of law is a joke right now. We plan to stand against this threat to our liberty with the Western Shoshone people."

This is an eyewitness description of the attack provided by the Nevada Livestock Association:

"The Bureau of Land Management (BLM) attacked the Dann Sisters from Crescent Valley, Nevada, early Sunday morning September 22, 2002, in the Pine Valley area of Eureka County. They impounded an unknown amount of cattle (BLM estimates of 200 head), with the help of Greg Cook of Vernal, Utah, and his hired rustlers as well as from fifty to 100 BLM and federal personnel.

"Helicopters and surveillance airplanes roamed the skies. The BLM deployed and established a lockdown of a great portion of Eureka County with armed quasi-militarized BLM enforcement officers as well as other federal agents. All access by roads, including the road from Carlin, Nevada, and county access roads, were blocked by BLM with assistance on state highways from the Nevada Highway Patrol.

"BLM set up the evening before the attack in Pine Valley. A large base camp with helipad, command-post trailers, and up to 100 personnel, the majority of which were armed. Various types of weaponry, camouflage, military paraphernalia, night vision scopes, flack vests, as well as some special-operations type personnel. Manned four-wheel drive pickups and special camo-green ATVs were deployed throughout the area."

No, this wasn't Afghanistan. This was Western Shoshone Territory, within Nevada.

The national media needs to take a good look at this crisis. It is a classic case of land dispossession and business corruption under the guise of old mining laws and one of the most egregious sleight-of-hand Supreme Court decisions in history. Callous and heavy-handed federal bureaucratic injustice now adds the weight of post–9-11 law enforcement against regular ranching people. It is urgent that the Interior Secretary forcefully review this dangerous policy of conducting paramilitary raids of enforced cattle rustling against productive and peaceful Indian families who are only trying to reclaim their proper land rights and to sustain a way of life.

To be fair, a majority of Western Shoshones did vote to accept the money-for-land-rights offer, but clearly out of economic desperation and necessity, a position to which they were pushed and cajoled by the United States even after a century of staunch assertion of continued possession of their lands. History will properly judge this powerful country for this unjust deed. The truth of the Shoshone claim is self-evident, even if their power has been curtailed by historical forces. Again, in 2002, and as always with Indian property, the land dispossession is being made legal, but it still stinks.

Governance Initiative Would Temper
U.S. Supreme Court on Erosion of Tribal Powers

October 11, 2002

First last June, and then this past week, federal agents busted up traditional Indian ranchers pressing for recognition of land rights. In both instances, the pressure was on Western Shoshone people, whose land claims case provides an example of how the U.S. Supreme court can decide on the incidentals of an Indian issue rather than deal fairly with the central sequence of history, which in this situation does not equate to the court's legal assertion.

The harshest criticism is due the High Court for their decision on Western Shoshone land rights. That decision denied a fair hearing to the question whether Western Shoshone lands had been, in fact, "taken over" by U.S. jurisdiction, when and if such condition as "encroachment" constitutes legal basis for usurpation of commonly held tribal lands, loss of title, loss of right to ever claim such lands again. Transfer of title was never determined but the federal government argued it and the Supreme Court affirmed it. While for many years the Western Shoshone would not accept a money settlement from the Indian Claims Commission, Interior Department accepted it on their behalf. This legal but dishonest maneuver that the U.S. Supreme Court chose to uphold in 1985 was made to pass for "acceptance" of the Claims Commission pay out. That case was brought by Western Shoshone sisters Mary and Carrie Dann, whose cattle was confiscated and auctioned last week by the Bureau of Land Management. It saw the U.S. Supreme Court rule that the tribe lost judicial recourse when the Secretary of Interior accepted the money for them. However, no one ever affirmed that title over the lands in question had transferred; it was simply assumed.

The trend in U.S. Supreme Court decisions negatively affecting tribal sovereignty has become obvious in the past fifteen years. Last week, a coalition of lawyers and student and tribal governments took their challenge public, right to the steps of the Supreme Court building, to question the legal definitions and biased positions assumed by the Supreme Court in recent years.

While the legislative and certainly the executive branches of government have made serious strides in affirming, accepting, and even championing the obvious historic reality and practice of tribal sovereignty, the judicial branch has been tilting negative since court appointments began moving toward more fundamentalist conservative ideology under President Ronald Reagan. However, even Reagan himself could not have foreseen or agreed with the consequences. Consider his own statement on Indian policy on January 24, 1983: "Despite the Indian Self-Determination Act, major tribal government functions enforcing tribal laws, developing and managing tribal resources, providing health and social services, educating children are frequently still carried on by Federal employees. The Federal Government must move away from this surrogate role which undermines the concept of self-government."

The proposal presented to Indian country and the nation this week (published in *Indian Country Today*), by American Indian tribal leaders Tex Hall (president, National Congress of American Indians) and Kelsey Begaye (president, Navajo Nation) and the very active Native attorneys, John Echohawk (executive director, Native American Rights Fund), and Susan Williams (partner, Williams and Works, Corrales, New Mexico), deserves serious attention, reflection, and action by all who support the inherent sovereignty of Indian governments. The four coauthored a concept paper and legislative initiative, which responds to two recent decisions that "severely diminished tribal authority to govern Indian country."

One decision they cite is Atkinson Trading Company vs. Shirley, where "the Supreme Court held that the Navajo Nation hotel occupancy tax could not be applied to a hotel on non-Indian land within the boundaries of the Navajo Nation even though the Navajo Nation tribal government was providing police and fire protection services to the hotel." This ruling deserves further scrutiny in that it has also been used, extensively, to Indian advantage in the Montana Supreme Court taxation case Flat Center Farms, Inc., vs. State of Montana, Department of Revenue. The converse also applied that the state could not tax Indian businesses for public "benefits."

The other is Nevada vs. Hicks, where the Supreme Court denied the Fallon Paiute-Shoshone Tribal Court's jurisdiction over a state game warden who violated the civil rights and damaged the property of a tribal member on tribal land. These decisions created a "governance crisis" by seriously damaging tribal authority over non-Indians in Indian country, claim the four coauthors, who also are at the forefront of a national movement, the Tribal Sovereignty Protection Initiative, cochaired by Hall and Begaye, with a Legislative Options Committee cochaired by Echohawk and Williams.

The initiative emerges from a fateful September 11, 2001, Washington, D.C., meeting by tribal leaders responding actively to the court decisions. The right to have control over Indians as well as non-Indians in Indian country was considered by tribal leaders a crucially important principle to sustain. This is particularly relevant because "non-Indians commit 70 percent of the violent crimes experienced by American Indians." The leaders formed and called for the launching of the pro-Tribal Sovereignty initiative. Principal objective: pass congressional legislation that will reaffirm "inherent tribal governance authority over all people and all places within Indian country." International events superceded the Indian jurisdictional discussion for a time but it is back with full force as a national "Sovereignty Run" just ended its marathon jog across the United States.

The Initiative's concept paper calls for federal legislation to "reaffirm the inherent authority of tribes to govern all people and all places within Indian country and recognize tribal governments as the primary governments in Indian country." The authors write, "Should tribal governments only have authority over Indians in Indian country or should tribal governments have authority over all people and all places within Indian country?"

Standing on this principle, which has been firmly articulated by presidents since John F. Kennedy and quite refreshingly since Richard Nixon's introduction of tribal self-determination as federal Indian policy in 1975, and including the many clear executive pronouncements affirming American Indian sovereignty by presidents Carter, Reagan, Bush I, Clinton, and Bush II, the four distinguished "initiators" of the Sovereignty Protection Initiative offer a well-reasoned position that does and should command much interest and support. They accuse the Supreme Court with "breaking from the established legal framework set by Congress and previous judicial opinions." Court decisions "threaten and [limit] tribal governance and economic progress in Indian country."

The great variety represented by 562 tribes is specified in the Concept Paper, which intends to provide flexibility, including "the option of accepting as much civil jurisdiction and misdemeanor criminal jurisdiction over all people and all places within Indian country as they choose to exercise." They also call for funds to "enhance tribal institutions, such as tribal courts, that are exercising the jurisdiction that they opt to take under this legislation."

The concept paper cites non-Indians' fears of mistreatment by tribal courts. Separating fact from myth is important in this context. An overwhelming reality is that many tribal court decisions involving non-Indians are now unreviewable in federal courts. This causes serious political problems by limiting jurisdiction for tribes.

In response, the concept paper describes the "problems faced by tribes as a result of the recent Supreme Court decisions and the need for Congress to address these problems in its constitutional role of forging federal Indian policy." The paper, which provides a succinct overview of Indian jurisdictional issues, proposes that those tribes who choose to exercise any of this broad jurisdiction over non-Indians also agree to "limited federal court review of their tribal court decisions affecting civil rights and other questions of federal law." However, tribal court decisions "involving internal tribal matters like tribal elections and tribal enrollment would not be subject to federal court review." For states obliged to provide services in Indian country, the concept paper prescribes payments from federal government in lieu of taxes.

During the fall election campaigns, tribal leaders will lobby congressional and state candidates and other congressional and state leaders to seek support for and comments on this concept paper.

This is an excellent public-policy issue for leaders, both Indian and non-Indian, to fully study, analyze, and sharpen. Going to Congress now with concrete and substantial sovereignty-affirming legislation is an important effort. The Supreme Court, left to its own devices, divorced from the broader context of congressional and executive branch policy, and now extensive history of affirming the powers of Indian governments, is a recipe for further dismay.

Anna Mae, the Beginning of Clarity
April 15, 2003

The case of Anna Mae Pictou-Aquash, the American Indian Movement activist murdered during the winter of 1975–76 on Pine Ridge, South Dakota, broke to the surface again as two men were indicted (one arrested) for her murder last week. An unrelenting cop's decades-long record of pursuit and newly compelling grand jury testimony has apparently started prosecution on the twenty-eight-year-old case. Since Aquash's body was found in a remote ravine by a local rancher, and was later desecrated by the FBI, who cut off her hands to send to Washington, many stories and many different layers of interpretation have shaded the truth of that unfortunate time. Most everyone would agree that the murder of Anna Mae Pictou-Aquash marked a low point in the activist Indian era of the mid-1970s.

The two men indicted, Arlo Looking Cloud, forty-nine, and John Graham (aka John Boy Patton), were charged with first degree murder in the death of Aquash. In 1975, they were young security people and soldiers on the fringes of the American Indian Movement. Presumably and allegedly, higher ups in the movement ordered the two men to execute Anna Mae.

There are various layers of accusations in all of this. Many blame the FBI for fostering the climate of intimidation that was prevalent in Pine Ridge during those years. We are grateful for the diligent work of Denver police detective Abe Alonzo, who has dedicated ten years to digging out the first set of facts in the case.

The birth of the activist Indian movement, particularly its first fiery years, created situations of intense pressure. The confrontation with the federal government that ensued after the seventy-one-day occupation of the Hamlet of Wounded Knee, in 1973, gave every appearance of a hit-and-run war and campaign of attrition against any rising Native leadership. The Indian rebellion of that time, while many will disagree with its tactics and even over its actual achievements, nevertheless delivered a major message to the new Indian generation and to the world at large. It declared the Indian independence of thought and action to be alive and well and willing to tangle with the system, if the system did not listen to Indian perspectives and demands.

The mid-1970s was a time when hundreds of Indian warriors—men and women—could descend on a town and stage major protests that could shut down and besiege places such as Custer and Rapid City, South Dakota, or Gordon, Nebraska. It was a time when large gatherings in the prairies actually heard from ancient chief's councils and from elderly matrons—clan mothers and family headwomen—who spoke of a pride in the precious center of tribal cultures and who challenged the new leaders to "act like men" in taking on corruption and nepotism in tribal government and in federal bureaus.

Academic and professional careers went out the window as many young, talented people took up the cause of the movement, which was fluid and passionate and mobile, and ultimately splintered in several directions. Rooted in confrontation, its leadership grew out of prison life as well as community indignation. With federal repression increasingly organized (to violence), defense and resistance also organized, most often from the traditional grassroots. But it also took a violent turn. By the summer and fall of 1975–76, several Midwestern reservations, but most notably Pine Ridge, South Dakota, were awash in armed confrontations, shoot-outs, and beatings that had political factions attached. Helicopter raids by federal agents armed with machine guns were all too common. All too often the violence followed a deep cycle of social recrimination.

A Mi'kmaq from Nova Scotia, Anna Mae Pictou-Aquash was a newcomer to the currents and crosscurrents of the American Indian Movement. By all accounts, though, she was bright and agile and many liked her dearly. Anna Mae is even memorialized in the prize announced in her name annually by the international organization, Indigenous Women's Network. But, obviously, some did not like her at all and the going theory is that she was suspected by a core of movement leadership of being an FBI informant. The FBI had a way of arresting Anna Mae in major sweeps of AIM activists, then letting her go before others similarly arrested.

This pattern, allegedly deliberate, tended to arouse suspicion. Following the heat of the Movement, Anna Mae was far away from her home base. Her path intersected with people capable of violence in moments very turbulent. She paid the price, shot in the head execution style—allegedly shot by young Indians following orders. The indicted men are allegedly these young Indians—young at the time of their alleged act of execution.

Not a few people have theorized on the complexities and peculiarities of the murder of the young mother and activist, who has been mourned by Indian family and publics since her death. Conspiracy theories abound already (sometimes the game is called: accuse your enemy of having something to do with it). For the sake of truth and justice, however, this issue should be focused on its main historical players.

Those who know about these things say that from the grave, Anna Mae's spirit has called for justice all of these years; the truth is profoundly wanting in this case. We are gratified that the tragic murder of a young woman, beyond three decades of rumor, has now reached the light of the courtroom. The indicted men, if they are, indeed, guilty, would not have acted on their own. The best thing about this moment is that a clear pattern of fact-finding is in the record. Perhaps a broadening of the investigation can finally move forward. Clarity, long trampled on this history, begins to regain strength. Clearly, the one or ones who gave the order should be nervous. We congratulate the law-enforcement investigators who have kept digging into this case. They are the best hope we have of seeing justice done.

The American Pathology
September 10, 2004

Behold in these pages this week an interesting and perhaps uniquely Indian discussion: perspectives on the roots of the American conquest of mythology—seeking to understand the origins of the particular American belief that continues to justify the destruction of Native cultures and the taking of Native peoples' assets, particularly lands and political rights to independent cultural and economic self-governance.

This might be heresy to the "true believers" in America, but among Indian thinkers these days, as has been the case for many generations, the question of what drives the voracious American appetite to own the Indian world has always been an honorable one. As Indian cultures have their own creation stories and subsequent cultural and legal histories, so the fundamental culture of the American mainstream requires study and understanding.

Every new Indian generation, believe it, will examine these questions in the ongoing search for understanding of the justifications for the theft of their lands, resources, freedoms, and even identities, and in their continued quest for actual justice. The perspective of Oglala Chief Red Cloud, who said in the 1890s, "They made us many promises, but they only kept but one: they promised to take our land and they took it," remains a topic of discussion. (Consider, too, David Monongwe, Hopi elder, at the United Nations in 1977: "They say they took our land, but where did they take it?")

The old raiding cultures are somewhat understandable, where what might be called "theft" was conceived as part of honored traditions, depending on what is being taken and from whom. But the complete theft of possession or use of land and resources, the many brutal wars of contact and conquest, the forced abuse of people's labor, the usurpation of Native leadership in long-standing traditional communities—we submit that a piece of present-day America continues to believe and propagate the myth that great crimes committed against American Indians were and are somehow justifiable.

Question: how is it that courts and certain fundamental political opinion can justify the theft inherent in the usurpation of Indian properties?

For Native nations who still hold lands and are working to hold onto their sovereign territories and add new parcels of land to their peoples' destinies, this is always a good discussion. Tribal peoples rarely forget any unjust loss of lands or resources that once were properly owned and managed by their own people. The more unjust the theft or taking of the resource, the more it is remembered and often continually claimed throughout history.

We highly recommend these pages this week as a good historical foundation to ponder. American policy makers, tribal leaders, legal and historical scholars, high school and college students, Indian opinion leaders, indeed, all of our readers, please take it for the weekend and deepen your historical and cultural understanding of the deeply ingrained and presumably religious justifications of the dispossession of American Indian peoples.

Prominent *Indian Country Today* columnist Steven Newcomb, a primary researcher in this area, leads the way by examining the metaphors that have been prevalent in forming America's perspective of the Indian world. Newcomb cites research by Steven L. Winter that "the mind functions largely by means of metaphors." The question that Newcomb follows through is the extent to which these metaphors have led to thoughts and, this is critically important, behaviors that exhibit dehumanizing and pathological tendencies. Writes Newcomb: "Cognitive theory posits that how we conceive (think) of something predetermines how we will behave toward that thing. Thus, the imaginative American conception of Indians as 'beasts of prey' led to very specific kinds of pathological behavior consistent with that mental image (thought, or idea)." Such behavior was demonstrated in the abuse and killing of Indians while compulsively stealing massive amounts of their lands and resources, writes Newcomb. Remarkably, the irrational thinking that enabled such injustices to occur still serves as the foundation of federal law dealing with American Indians.

Preeminent scholar of world cultural history and American Indian philosopher John Mohawk points us to the "peculiarly American version of Christianity," which induced the self-identification of early Americans as new Israelites, "a Chosen people," entitled by virtue of discovery to "all the riches of the world." Mohawk links this belief to the version of American nationalism currently constructed by the neoconservative wing in America. Mohawk: "Here you find the roots of America's go-it-alone, treaty-breaking, empire-building, xenophobic, us-against-them psychology." Most Americans don't believe the mythical credo of manifest destiny, says Mohawk, but the much louder true-believer minority is always ready to take the reins of power. These intimidate the media who do not analyze whether things are true or not, as much as whether they reinforce the mythical claim of American "infallibility." Mohawk warns that while the most Americans, who are capable of thinking through such issues, "Rational America" as he describes them, are nonetheless "dangerously tolerant of it."

Other contributors land on the "Doctrine of Discovery," which emerges from the concept of "the chosen people" gaining title to lands and resources by right of claiming it from the "heathen" or non-Christian peoples. This, amazingly, is the doctrine that defines the fundamental American legal policy with American Indians known as American Indian Law. "The entire Western Hemisphere was deemed to be terra nullus—'vacant land,'" according to contributing columnist Steven McSloy. McSloy writes, "Americans thought themselves, "the 'chosen people,' with a 'Manifest Destiny' to own the continent." Christian sects and religions diversified and warred among each other, confounding everything even more. From a traditional Indian spiritual perspective, one complaint is central: fundamentalist Christians will claim that only through Jesus can a human being be "saved"—i.e., have spiritual life, after death. This denies the direct Creator or Creation-driven belief systems, prayers, and practices of traditional non-Christian ceremonies, which are very seriously prescribed and practiced in Indian country.

This discussion might seem dull to some, but Indian leaders call for it because the fundamentals of the thinking that has historically been arrayed against Native peoples is formidable and remains active. We can only educate ourselves if we aspire to accurately communicate with those who deny our histories, cultures, and identities. We hope it is also refreshing to those Americans who in recent years have felt beaten over the head by the loud and nationally prominent Christian political missionary movement. There are a lot of assumptions worth challenging in the Christian-based argumentation aimed at Indian circles. A humble step back from arrogance of Western cultural beliefs in these matters, not to mention the intellectual chasm that renders these beliefs groundless, remains a welcome gesture.

President Bush, Not His Father's Son on Indian Policy
November 22, 2001

Harold Monteau, Monteau and Peebles, LLP

Under President George W. Bush's father (George Herbert Walker Bush), tribes experienced enactment of the Indian Gaming Regulatory Act (IGRA), expansion of tribal Self-Governance, Self-Determination, and other economically driven policies originally advanced during the Republican administrations of Richard Millhouse Nixon and Ronald Reagan.

In those days, the Grand Old Party approached the advancement of Indian policy through the concepts of creating greater economic development on Indian lands as well as allowing tribes to exercise greater autonomy over their governmental decisions and business operations.

When it came to Indian country, the canons of GOP politics were intact—economic stimulus and local government control reigned supreme over paternalistic concepts such as social-service handouts and increased federal government intervention.

So what's up with President George W. Bush? Did he skip the course given by his Republican predecessors on Indian policy? It seems so. And it also seems as though the rules are changing dramatically when it comes to Republican Indian policy being formulated under the current George W. Bush administration.

Since January of 2001, tribes have been faced with a series of Bush administration decisions that are in direct conflict with former GOP policy toward Indian country.

We have seen the reversal of a scope of gaming rule that was considered a prerequisite to the use of IGRA alternative compacting procedures authority by the secretary of the Interior, which gives the secretary authority to approve Class III tribal gaming when a state refuses to negotiate in good faith.

Moreover, there is no incentive for this administration to even consider utilizing the alternative procedures under the IGRA. Tribal gaming has been the most successful form of economic development ever implemented in Indian country, even with federal, state, and tribal government regulatory requirements equaling ten times the regulatory oversight of what comparable non-Indian gaming is subjected.

We have also seen a reversal of several tribal recognition decisions, tearing at the soul of tribal sovereignty and the dreams of self-sufficiency that those Indian nations thought they had finally achieved. The promise of this administration to immediately begin developing an economic-development plan for Indian country, including a comprehensive domestic energy policy, is nowhere to be found, especially in the enacted FY2002 budget for federal Indian programs.

Yet this administration continues to tout Indian economic development as its primary goal when publicly addressing Indian affairs issues.

This administration is doing no better than the previous administration when it comes to trust-funds mismanagement. The federal courts said it best in threatening contempt charges against the secretary for blatant disregard to the court's orders to provide a plan for reconciliation of those accounts.

All of this after many bipartisan backed plans for "fixing" the trust-funds mismanagement situation has been submitted to the Interior secretary. Some of these plans included additional ways to develop a revolving loan fund for tribes to utilize in creating economic-development opportunities on Indian lands.

Instead of considering any of those solutions, however, the department has decided to strip the Bureau of Indian Affairs of its authority over these accounts, vesting it instead within the Bureau of Indian Trust Assets Management (BITAM).

Not only were tribes not consulted on the secretary's decision to create this new bureaucratic entity, there has been no clear or encouraging information offered by the secretary on how BITAM will improve the reconciliation of tribal trust accounts.

And now we have the assistant secretary for Indian affairs withdrawing a revised set of regulations on taking lands into trust for tribes from final promulgation because this administration feels states and local governments do not have enough opportunities under the proposed rule to influence the decision-making process in their favor.

If I remember the legislative history behind the Indian Reorganization Act, states and local governments were never intended to have a significant voice in the fee-to-trust application process.

Tribes worked hand-in-glove with the former administration for more than two years to develop the proposed rule, which included a compromise by tribes to allow additional advantages to states that are not part of the current fee-to-trust process.

It is truly a sad day in Indian country when the "trustee" for Indian tribes is less interested in what is justifiably right for tribal governments and instead more interested in what the states and local governments want to have provided to them under the fee-to-trust process.

It seems this administration is more concerned with undoing everything the former administration has done instead of moving ahead with its own agenda. Is this because they do not have an agenda, or is their agenda that "anti-Indian?"

It is painfully obvious that Bush II is taking a completely different course of action than previous Republican administrations when it comes to strengthening the economic base of tribal governments and allowing our people to move away from the federal dependency that has hurt us over the years.

This administration is seemingly unwilling to protect and strengthen our sovereign rights as Indian nations the way its Republican forefathers sought to do. President Bush should explain to our Indian people why he chooses to allow such decisions to be made that weaken our ability to take care of ourselves.

If this administration wants to polarize all of Indian country to the Democratic Party, its current course of action will achieve that goal. This administration is playing a dangerous game in promoting an "anti-Indian" policy. This attitude merely emboldens our attitude to annihilate our enemies. In the mid-twentieth century, such tactics led to the termination era and an outright attack on our basic human rights as indigenous peoples.

As a child of that era, I remember vividly the horrors Indian people suffered, including our children and our elders, at the hands of an uncaring federal government, and at the hands of city, county, and state governments when our Indian people were forced to relocate to find the means to feed their families.

President Bush, do not forget the rights created for American Indians under the Constitution and treaties of the United States. Do not forget the atrocities committed against the First Americans stemming from cultural differences, racism, discrimination, and the chain of broken treaties committed by the federal government over the past three centuries.

Do not forget the contributions and sacrifices our Indian people make to this country's freedoms and liberties each and every day in spite of the history between our governments. If you forget these things, we all will suffer from a mutual disrespect for which forgiveness and positive relations can never be nurtured.

First Nations and States, Contesting Polities

May 22, 2003

David Wilkins, University of Minnesota

The U.S. Supreme Court in a historic case in 1886, U.S. vs. Kagama, which devastated tribal sovereignty by affirming the legality of the 1885 Major Crimes Act that problematically extended federal criminal jurisdiction over "all" Indians for seven major crimes—murder, manslaughter, rape, etc., (today that number has increased to fourteen crimes)—more accurately declared in that same case that state governments could be characterized as the "deadliest enemies" of indigenous nations.

This has been the case ever since the beginning of the American republic. State officials have represented ever-expanding non-indigenous populations that have always clamored for more Indian lands and resources, and which have constantly sought to extend their authority over tribal peoples and their territories. States have consistently clamored for rule over Indian nations despite existing safeguards that deny them such authority—treaties, federal supremacy over the nations' Indian policy (not over Indian peoples), the trust doctrine, and, finally, state constitutional disclaimer clauses. I'll return to discuss the disclaimers momentarily.

Today, as state governments flail away in an ever-deepening economic crisis of their own construction—and denied help from a supposedly states' rights oriented Bush administration and Republican Congress—the clamoring has expanded to outlandish attempts by state governors and legislatures to compel Indian tribes with successful gaming operations to pay more of their hard-earned proceeds to state coffers to help with their self-inflicted deficit burdens.

Governor Gray Davis of California is currently seeking an additional 1.5 billion in annual revenues from tribes; Governor James Doyle of Wisconsin recently forced six of the eleven tribal nations to sign new compacts that will net the state some $200 million over the next two years, a steep increase from the $24 million the tribes had paid the previous year. Other states are contemplating their own squeeze plays on tribal government revenues.

States have been emboldened to extract these additional monies in part because a series of U.S. Supreme Court decisions since the early 1990s have elevated the questionable notions of states' rights and state sovereign immunity to levels not seen since the 1890s. Furthermore, states have been more audacious in their efforts to pressure tribal nations to surrender more of their revenues because Congress has failed to aggressively respond to the judiciary's usurpation of congressional authority over the field of federal Indian policy. Congressional lawmakers have also failed to respond partly because they, too, benefit from tribal resources and because they enacted the law, the Indian Gaming Regulatory Act in 1988, that actually created the conditions that gave states a heretofore unheard of economic inroad to Indian economic-development decisions by requiring tribal leaders to negotiate compacts with states before they could enter the lucrative gaming industry.

This was a critically demeaning requirement thrust upon tribal government leaders by their federal trustee—that tribes be required to negotiate compacts with their oftentimes "deadliest enemies." After all, state governments have never been similarly required to negotiate compacts with tribes for their economic decisions, much less be expected to pay ever-escalating percentages of their revenues to tribal nations should Indians fall upon hard economic times (which has been their perpetual status from the late 1800s to the advent of Indian gaming).

States, you see, especially the eleven Western states (Alaska, Arizona, Idaho, Montana, New Mexico, North Dakota, Oklahoma, South Dakota, Utah, Washington, and Wyoming) home to more than 80 percent of the indigenous nations and a majority of the 278 reservations and trust areas, have no inherent constitutional authority to exercise jurisdiction or any taxation power whatsoever over Indian lands or peoples, absent express tribal and federal consent.

In fact, each of these states have in their constitutions explicit Indian disclaimer clauses that were required by the federal government before the territories could be admitted to statehood. These disclaimer clauses, dating from Wisconsin's territorial disclaimer of 1836, to Alaska's constitutional clause of 1959, explicitly declare that these territories—later states—are not allowed to extend their authority inside Indian country.

While there is some variation in the language of these clauses, they generally contain unequivocal language designed to assure both indigenous nations and the federal government that the territory or state would never, without federal consent and/or a treaty modification, interfere in the internal affairs of indigenous nations.

Arizona's disclaimer clause, for example, lodged in Article 20 of the state's Constitution of 1912, reads as follows:

> The people inhabiting this State do agree and declare that they
> forever disclaim all right and title to the unappropriated and
> ungranted lands, public lands, lying within the boundaries
> thereof and to all lands lying within said boundaries owned or
> held by any Indian or Indian tribes, the right or title to which
> shall have been acquired through or from the United States or

any prior sovereignty, and that, until the title of such Indian or Indian tribes shall have been extinguished, the same shall be, and remain, subject to the disposition and under the absolute jurisdiction and control of the Congress of the United States ... and no taxes shall be imposed by this State on any lands or other property within an Indian Reservation owned or held by any Indian.

The inclusion of such clauses serve to reiterate that the federal government has exclusive authority over the nation's Indian policy, to reaffirm tribal sovereignty vis-a-vis states, and to remind the states that their quasi-sovereign status in the federal system does not extend into Indian country, absent express federal law, tribal consent, and the expunging of extant disclaimer clauses.

Since these states lack the inherent authority to impose their jurisdictional or taxation authority over Native nations or properties without express approval, why do they now act as if they have the right to demand additional percentages of Indian gaming proceeds? Although the states' demands are technically not a "tax" on gaming proceeds, the effect of the states extractive attempts amounts to the same thing. More critically, we must ask why the federal government, the Indians' supposed trust agent and treaty partner, has not stifled the states constant cries for what is nothing short of the legalized extortion of tribal revenues.

I find it both detestable and ironic that the very peoples, indigenous nations, who for several generations were falsely accused of being economic drains on state welfare and social-service systems are now enduring unrelenting pressure from a number of states to share ever-greater percentages of their gaming profits, at the same time that several of these same states are seeking to expand their own gaming programs, which will only further diminish tribal gaming revenues, the one consistent form of economic development that has enabled a number of tribes to significantly raise their economic, political, and social standards.

Even as these crass developments are intensifying, tribal nations and states, in some respects, have improved their relationship over the years and cooperation between the two unequal polities occasionally breaks out in areas such as cross-deputization of law-enforcement personnel, environmental regulation, taxation, etc. But the general thrust of tribal/state relations continues to be far more contentious than cooperative.

In fact, John McCain, the conservative Republican senator from Arizona, accurately summed up the states typical stance vis-a-vis tribes when it comes to gaming and intergovernmental relations: "The state and gaming industry have always come to the bargaining table with the position

that what is theirs is theirs and what the Tribes has is negotiable." Until
this attitude changes, and unless the federal government renews its pledge
to support American Indian self-determination, the tribal/state relationship
will continue to be a profound set of problems in search of an elusive set of
equally profound solutions.

Law and Politics in Indian Country
June 13, 2003

John Mohawk, *Indian Country Today*

There is no question that indigenous peoples enjoyed sovereignty. They
made their own laws and rules and they had power to enforce those laws.
Although there are hundreds of cultures and each did things in a distinct
way, it is certain that each of them developed a way to settle disputes
among their members. The widespread adoption of confederations across
North America is evidence that there were ways of settling disputes among
and between different nations as well. By all accounts, indigenous laws and
customs as they existed in 1492 and from time immemorial were sophisticated, complex, and honorably practiced.

The ancient Indian governments derived their powers from the people
of their nation and occasionally from spiritual sources. Some Indian nations
had constitutions, others carried their rules in oral traditions, and most had
unlimited power to rule within their own territories and over their own
people. To the extent that a government is defined by the laws and customs
of its own culture and traditions and is able to enjoy freedom to make
rules and settle disputes among its own people, and to make agreements
and conduct relations with other peoples, it is a true indigenous government.

Of course, there are those who would lead us to believe that there are
very few such governments within the boundaries of the United States and
Canada. Both the United States and Canada have a long history of efforts
to purposefully erode or diminish indigenous sovereignty and especially
jurisdiction over their lands and peoples. Indigenous laws and customs do
not give the United States or Canada the right or the power to interfere in
the internal affairs of the indigenous nations, and international law gives
no such rights or powers, but both countries have assumed absolute power
to do so. The United States has even arrogated to itself the power to termi-
nate or extinguish the legal and physical existence of Indian nations. Indian
nations have, therefore, survived under a cloud of subjugation, and sometimes oppression, wherein their interests have been ignored and subsumed

under the interests of the United States.

It hasn't always been this way. When the United States was first established, Congress promised that "(t)he utmost good faith shall always be observed toward the Indians; their lands and property shall never be taken from them without their consent, and in their property, rights, and liberty, they never shall be invaded or disturbed ... " Some of the states never honored these words. In Georgia and New York, Indians were arrested for crimes in Indian country and were subjected to vigilante justice—which had a color of state law. These executions were later recognized as illegal and the federal government eventually stepped in to stop them.

Some Indian nations agreed in treaties that some crimes committed by Indians against whites in Indian country could be adjudicated under federal law, and by 1817, the U.S. Congress passed the General Crimes Act, which extended this law to tribes that had not agreed to this kind of transferred jurisdiction. A landmark case that was a serious blow to Indian sovereignty came six years later in Johnson and Graham's Lessee vs. McIntosh, in which the Supreme Court decided that no matter how illegal or immoral a claim by the U.S. government to Indian land may be, the court could not question it. This was the beginning of the "political question doctrine" in Indian law, and it was a license to steal.

By 1831, the state of Georgia was intent on destroying the Cherokee Nation in violation of treaties with the United States. When the Cherokee Nation sued (Cherokee Nation vs. Georgia), the Supreme Court opined that only a foreign state could bring such a suit and the framers of the constitution did not view Indian nations as foreign states in this sense. This decision, as are many decisions of the Supreme Court in Indian cases, states not the law, but the political position of the United States. It was the political position of the United States that they could take Indian land without due cause or just compensation, and they took it, and the courts raised no objections. In this case, when a state was doing this, the Supreme Court decided that federal law did not protect Indian rights and the United States had no honor.

By 1846, Chief Justice Taney, in United States vs. Rogers, was arguing that Indian nations were not regarded as nations at all, nor "regarded as owners of the territories they respectively occupied." In other words, the Indian nations had no rights as nations, and no rights to protection of property. But despite such rulings, the federal courts moved to keep power over the Indians away from the states and in 1866, the Supreme Court decided that Kansas had no right to tax Indians. In 1870, the Supreme Court, in The Cherokee Tobacco Case, decided that the federal government could tax Indian territory.

There are far too many aspects of the federal law in Indian country to address in a column, but the racialization of Indian membership in federal law deserves mention. In America, race is socially constructed by law in ways that limit and restrict the rights and possibilities of the subjects. Indians have been treated more as a racial category than as separate nations, and membership in Indian nations is determined by racial markers such as blood quantum and not by the standards of nations such as where a person is born and what laws they follow, their language, and their allegiances. It is possible to be born in England to English parents and to spend a life there, never seeing an Indian, but to be Indian by law because of the existence of some long-forgotten Indian ancestor. And it is possible to be born in Indian country to two Indian parents, fully conversant in the language and customs of the people, but to be left off any "tribal roll."

Membership in Indian nations has been largely determined by racial ideas that are now obsolete everywhere but have been internalized in Indian country. In some of Indian country, where blood quantum prevails, the long-term prospects are that the numbers eligible for membership in the Indian nation will decline over time. In others, the membership will increasingly be people who have little or no connection to Indian country, the culture, or the people.

This is, in broad strokes, how laws that were not based on the traditions and customs of the Indian nations threaten to continue to erode the cultures and peoples and sovereignty of Indian country. This, it seems to me, is consistent with Justice Taney's intent.

A Bird's-Eye View of American Indian Law and Its Future
September 26, 2003

Steven Paul McSloy, Hughes Hubbard & Reed, LLP

American Indian law is often metaphorical. As Supreme Court Chief Justice John Marshall wrote in 1831, the relationship between American Indian nations and the United States is like "that of a ward to his guardian." The classic Indian law metaphor, however, is the "miner's canary." As Felix Cohen, the dean of American Indian law studies, wrote in 1953, the year he died:

> [T]he Indian plays much the same role in our American society
> that the Jews played in Germany. Like the miner's canary, the
> Indian marks the shifts from fresh air to poison gas in our political

atmosphere; and our treatment of Indians, even more than our treatment of other minorities, reflects the rise and fall in our democratic faith.

Cohen was right, of course, but we must remember what he was writing about: Federal Indian Law. He was writing as an observer, looking at Indian law from a sympathetic perspective, but, nonetheless, he was wearing the miner's headlamp, looking at the canary. The canary, or the Indian, on the other hand, is similar to the protagonist in the Talking Heads song who is asking himself, "Well, how did I get here?" The answer, of course, is that the canary is brought down into the coal mine, just as the Indians were, as scholars have politely put it, "incorporated" into the United States. Indian nations were at first just pushed westward, but then gold was discovered in California and settlement leapfrogged the Indians, locking them in the middle—in the coal mine, if you will.

And what sort of place was that? A constitutional federalist republic, split along two major axes, as per Federalist No. 51: The state/federal axis and the separation of powers axis. Indians have been constantly buffeted along these dimensions ever since. Professor David Getches has described Indian law as the "crucible for forging a larger agenda important to majorities of the Court." Similarly, Professor Richard Monette has called tribes "federalism['s] football." But I think the canary metaphor goes the furthest. Remember, the miners did not just plunk the canary down somewhere; they carried it around to explore new areas—to test them, to find the seams and fissures, the dangerous places, the safe harbors. Indians, despite the good arguments by some scholars, are not really part of the federalist design. They are an instrument of federalism, a means by which the dominant society has explored the boundaries between state and federal power and among executive, legislative, and judicial power.

A cursory review of the Supreme Court's major Indian cases reveals this dynamic. First, Cherokee Nation vs. Georgia: in 1831, an Indian nation challenged the power of the State of Georgia to apply its law in Indian territory. This was an easy result to forecast—the state won. Second, Worcester vs. Georgia: the same case, one year later, but Indians were not parties. A Vermont Yankee who was a federal employee living in Indian country was imprisoned by a southern state demanding he take a loyalty oath. Georgia lost on the ground that its laws were "repugnant to the Constitution, laws, and treaties of the United States." In order for the Supreme Court to reach this federalism result, the Cherokees won a ringing endorsement of their sovereignty, yet they were not parties in the case.

The 1871 Act that ended treaty making with Indian tribes also was not about Indians. Instead, it reflected a separation-of-powers fight. The House became tired of appropriating money for treaties that only the Senate had a role in ratifying, so the two houses struck a constitutional (or unconstitutional) compromise—ending treaty making and replacing it with the regular congressional legislative process. Indians were the subject of the Act, but they were bystanders to its passage.

Another example is the 1883 Crow Dog case. By the 1870s, Indians were no longer a frontier concern but rather an "Interior" matter, and the BIA was feeling fettered in its efforts to control them. The Commerce Clause, the power constitutionally delegated to the federal government regarding Indians, did not authorize things such as criminal laws. To change this, the BIA created a sham case—one it wanted to lose—after Spotted Tail, a chief popular in the East, was murdered by another Indian, Crow Dog. As Professor Sidney Harring's book uncovered, the BIA actually paid Crow Dog's legal bills to get the case to the Supreme Court, where it was held that tribal justice was the only applicable jurisdiction, and Crow Dog would not hang under federal law. The federal government lost the case, but, as predicted, the ensuing outrage about "Red Man's Justice" led to the passage of the Major Crimes Act shortly thereafter—the first direct application of federal criminal law to inter-Indian crimes and the BIA's long-sought goal. The next year, in the Kagama case, also an inter-Indian murder case, the BIA received the decision it wanted. The Supreme Court held that the federal government had the power to pass laws over Indians even if such power was not authorized by the Constitution—even if the power had never been delegated to the federal government by the states or by the people.

On the strength of this holding, Congress passed the General Allotment Act the next year, resulting in the loss of 80 percent of the remaining Indian-held lands and completing the settlement of America. Commentators frequently call Kagama an "extra-constitutional" case, but in reality it was a "supraconstitutional" case, as it increased federal power beyond the federalist design. Crow Dog and Kagama involved only two dead Indians and their Indian murderers, yet they were used to create the basis for federal plenary power over the Indians and the loss of huge portions of the continent to settlement by states.

Another example of Indians being caught in a federalism firefight is the 1968 Indian Civil Rights Act, which at first blush seems a noble enterprise, applying the Bill of Rights statutorily to Indian tribes. Yet, Indians did not lobby for it; it was a states' rights issue. It was introduced by Sam Ervin, Senator from North Carolina, to take the heat off civil rights violations by southern states by pointing at tribal governments as allegedly more egregious violators. In the words of author Donald Burnett, "In the angry clash of black and white, North and South, Indian law was made."

The 1978 Indian Child Welfare Act is another seemingly noble statute, one for which Indians did lobby. States had acted inappropriately in removing Indian children to non-Indian foster homes, and the tribes successfully lobbied Congress to uphold their jurisdiction over their children. In the 1989 Holyfield case, a state court challenged tribal court jurisdiction over adoption matters and lost—but why? The state lost because the federal law was clear in preferring tribal court jurisdiction, and thus it was a supremacy issue. However, had the case involved inherent tribal authority, as opposed to federal power, the result would have been much different, as it was in the recent Strate, Atkinson, and Hicks cases, all of which went against the Indian parties.

It is the same story with Indian land claims. The text of the 1790 Non-Intercourse Act is clear—no state can buy Indian land. Thus, 200 years later, the Supreme Court held that a state could not have ignored such a clear federal command grounded in the Commerce Clause of the Constitution, even if the case was not filed for two centuries. If, however, a federal command was not so clearly grounded in constitutional bedrock and sought to subject a state to federal court jurisdiction, you get Seminole Tribe vs. Florida and an opposite result. In enacting the Indian Gaming Regulatory Act, Congress was explicit in subjecting recalcitrant states to federal court jurisdiction to resolve disputes about gaming, but the Supreme Court in Seminole held that such jurisdiction violated state sovereignty.

Justices Rehnquist, Brennan, and Scalia all have (or had) their miner's headlamps on, dragging the canary hither and yon in search of doctrine, testing the boundaries of the federal/state relationship and the interrelationships among the three branches, including their own. The usual result, however, is that the bird dies.

So what are Indian nations to do? Avoid being a canary. Stay out of the Supreme Court. Taking Indian cases to the Supreme Court has been prima facie malpractice for the last twenty years.

Indian nations should particularly stay away from state/tribal conflicts, and, if they are unavoidable, settle them. Couldn't somebody have just paid Floyd Hicks for his damaged stuffed sheep heads rather than let it go all the way to the Supreme Court? (The genesis of the dispute was alleged damage to Mr. Hicks' stuffed sheep heads in a warrant search executed by Nevada state officials on tribal land.) The only time an Indian nation should take a state to court is if the federal government is strongly and soundly on the Indian nation's side, thus changing the federalism calculus. For example, in the Oneida, Mohawk, and Cayuga land claims, the courts have dismissed all suits against private land owners, saying there can be a complete recovery from the state. This would be problematic but for the fact that the federal government has strongly intervened in all of the cases. If an Indian nation feels the need to sue somebody, it should sue the federal government—it at least has a trust responsibility of some sort.

In general, Indian nations should stay out of court. Cases force a decision—they put the tribe in the coal mine. Bringing a case means that someone else is doing the deciding. After Justice Rehnquist became ascendant, the courts were no longer the answer. Maybe it is my corporate-lawyer bias, but what tribes should do is do deals. Compacts and quasi-treaties have been made about water, roads, taxes, gaming, cross-deputizations, full faith and credit agreements, and even land claims. Indian nations should engage other governments and be proactive, not just sit around and then sue when some action is taken against them. Indian nations need to be practical sovereigns—not all-or-nothing litigants.

The United States is the most powerful nation on Earth. Small nations, not just Indian tribes, get caught up in its wheels. Similar to the canary, they get used by the United States as it experiments in its ongoing journey of self-discovery about its society and federalist structure. So, Indian nations should do what small countries do—make deals. If you have a strong suit, such as oil or water, play it. If you have a weak hand, at least market what you do have. Indian gaming, for example, is not a recent idea. Look at Monaco, a principality smaller than many reservations and more controlled by France than Indian tribes are by the United States. The Grimaldi princes, however, realized they were just sovereign enough to legalize gambling when France and Italy banned it. Up in the Pyrenees, Spanish and French people today flock to tiny Andorra to buy cigarettes, just as people in the United States do when they drive out to the reservations.

Indian nations should get out of the sovereignty talk, get out of the rights talk, and get out of the constitutional talk, because it is not going to work before the current Supreme Court. Litigation is only one weapon in the arsenal of tribal sovereignty—it should not be a tribal way of life. The best way for the canary to survive is to stay out of the mine.

The Fundamental President

December 30, 2003

John Mohawk, *Indian Country Today*

Religion, and specifically Southern Protestant Fundamentalism, is the dominant cultural reality in the Bush White House and in the process that has led to war. Although George W. Bush is nominally a Methodist, he has pandered shamelessly to the religious right and many of his views are consistent with those of Protestant Fundamentalist extremists. He has confirmed such views more than once and is on record stating his belief that non-Christians can never go to heaven. This is a statement with enormous implications that he is not president to all Americans but to a minority, albeit a sizeable minority. The religious culture he comes from is even more narrow than that, defining only born-again Christians as true to the faith and therefore eligible for admission to heaven.

Mr. Bush is steeped in the culture of West Texas, a culture with many of the characteristics of the Old South. It is tinged with a history of racism, has a strong anti-environmentalist ethos, wallows in crony capitalism, exalts in jingoistic militarism, and has an anti-public education and anti-welfare bias. The president has discovered that it is not productive to embrace all these ideologies publicly, but he has set into motion an agenda that makes the radical religious right as happy as it has been in generations.

It is not difficult to understand how the Old South came to be the way it is. In the nineteenth century, America was alone among industrialized nations to tolerate slavery. In the South, slave labor not only drove agricultural profits prior to the industrial revolution in agriculture, it also set the tone of the culture. People who depend on beatings and other forms of torture to keep their laborers in line and who casually rape and abuse the women they "own" have good reason to sleep with a gun under their pillow for fear that their "property" might rise from their hovels and kill them in their sleep. It helps to explain America's love affair with firearms. Although slavery was outlawed in 1863, significant elements of the culture that spawned it are thriving.

The South is the most militaristic area of the country and a higher percentage of its population is in the military than any other population in the country. The United States has never entered a war that the South didn't like, including the War of 1812, the Mexican War, numerous Indian wars, their part of the Civil War, the preemptive Philippines War, and so forth. Southern white Protestant males are the most violent population in America and possess the highest murder rate. Despite intense religiosity and lots of rhetoric around "family values," that population also has the highest divorce rate in the country.

Mr. Bush began his "walk," the embrace of Fundamentalism, as he turned forty and resolved to stop drinking. Instead of turning to Alcoholics Anonymous, he joined Community Bible Study (CBS) and became an ardent member of this bible study group. Although he has made fundamentalist conservatism a cornerstone of his political life, he appears to be a genuine convert and he seems determined to use the lessons of his faith to transform American society and drive the destiny of the world. These are grandiose and dangerous impulses that utilize ideas of good and evil to support dismissal of anyone who disagrees as either ignorant of the difference or willfully in favor of evil.

The isolationism of George W. Bush is not driven by a Henry Kissinger-like Machiavellianism, but is inspired by writings of somewhat obscure religious philosophers such as Oswald Chambers (whose books Mr. Bush reads for inspiration) and the spiritual descendants of such men as Jonathan Edwards. All of this adds up to a remarkable but unavoidable conclusion: the President of the United States is living an ideology that has its roots in the Great Awakening of the eighteenth century.

If all this information is reliable, it could explain a lot. The Awakening launched a discussion about individual salvation that tends to explain fundamentalism's hostility toward federal programs intended to help poor people because it urges that the individual must take responsibility for their own well-being. Indeed, there is some resistance here to the idea that society should try to solve society's problems, unless those problems are cast in terms of recruiting the irreligious to the fold. The idea of "compassionate conservatism" is linked to faith-based initiatives in ways that are not transparent to people who are not involved in the conversations of the religious right.

More alarming perhaps are the implications of the mix of religion and war. President Bush is clever enough to avoid using the language of religion too loudly in the rhetoric of war (he had to back off shortly after 9/11 when he used the word "crusade" to describe the war he was planning), but he has had trouble finding an alternative explanation for the attack on Iraq. At first, he said Saddam had weapons of mass destruction, but he and all his men couldn't put together credible proof of that, so the explanation shifted to an accusation that Saddam was involved with al-Qaida, an accusation that was also never proven.

But proof wasn't necessary because George W. Bush believes Saddam and the Iraqi regime is evil and that's enough to lead a religious man to initiate a faith-based war that leaders of most of the Christian denominations believe has failed the requirements of Just Warfare, and which is difficult, at best, to defend under international law.

Just what else he believes, the world seems destined to discover.

Editors' Note: This commentary first appeared in the Spring 2003 edition of *Native Americas Journal* (Volume 20, Number 1), the independent policy quarterly of hemispheric indigenous issues.

Justice Thomas and Federal Indian Law—Hitting His Stride?
April 29, 2004

David Wilkins, University of Minnesota

Since the ascension of the Rehnquist-led conservative majority on the Supreme Court, indigenous nations have been assaulted by a tsunami of rulings that, with a few rare exceptions, have significantly undermined, or, in some cases, flagrantly denied the essential sovereign nature of First Nations.

As the court, the political branches, and the country, for that matter, turned more conservative in the 1990s, as the very nature of federalism was redefined to support the resurrection of a powerful states' rights agenda, and as the court inexorably whittled away the basic governing rights of First Nations, Native peoples, both collectively and individually, sustained devastating losses in cases involving non-Indians, conflicts with state officials, and federal power vis-a-vis tribal governments.

All of which makes the Supreme Court's recent decision, United States vs. Lara, handed down April 19, a most exciting and yet still deeply distressing decision. It was exciting because the court, by a seven-to-two verdict, held that tribal courts have the inherent sovereign power to criminally prosecute nonmember Indians, in this case, one Billy Jo Lara, a Turtle Mountain Chippewa who had married a Spirit Lake Sioux woman, for crimes committed on the Spirit Lake Reservation.

And since a tribes' criminal jurisdiction over tribal members and members of other tribes, though not over non-Indians, derives from their inherent sovereignty and is not a delegated federal authority, the U.S. Constitution's Fifth Amendment Double Jeopardy clause, which protects individuals from being tried twice for the same offense, did not apply because the clause does not prevent successive prosecutions by "separate" or "dual" sovereigns.

The court's explicit recognition of First Nations' inherent power to prosecute nonmember Indians, which had been denied by a similarly manned court fourteen years ago in Duro vs. Reina, but was quickly restored by Congress less than a year later in 1991, is being touted by many as an important counterweight to much of the court's recent litigation that dramatically stresses that tribal nations may only exercise those powers specifically retained in ratified treaties or that have been statutorily delegated to them in express congressional acts.

It was also exciting because Associate Justices John Stevens and Clarence Thomas, who concurred with the finding of the majority but gave different reasons why in their separate rulings, raised several important dimensions that warrant further examination. Stevens, for his part, correctly reminded everyone that there was nothing unusual about the acknowledgment of the inherent sovereignty of tribes. He noted that this power of self-governance has "a historical basis," while most states, by contrast, "were never actually independent sovereigns, and those that were enjoyed that independent status for only a few years."

But it was Justice Thomas, the lone African American, whose voting record on Indian cases is more anti-Indian than even Rehnquist or Scalia, who, in his concurring opinion, made several critical points that were most telling. Thomas will never be mistaken for Thurgood Marshall, who wrote several affirmative Indian law rulings, and his intention in crafting his opinion in this case was almost certainly not meant to be transparently supportive of tribal sovereignty. Yet, he identified several enigmas in law and policy that, if acted upon by tribal, state, and federal policy makers, might lead to a clearer status for indigenous rights and a reduction or outright termination of the still virtually absolute, or plenary, power still wielded by the Congress over tribes.

Thomas surprisingly and accurately identified and discussed six major issues:

1) the Court should reexamine the core premises and logic of cases dealing with tribal sovereignty because current precedent both recognizes its existence but simultaneously also denies its force;
2) the U.S. Constitution, through the Treaty and Commerce clauses, does not authorize the Congress to wield plenary (read: absolute) power over the meaning and scope of tribal sovereignty;
3) the 1871 congressional law that purported to end treaty making with tribal nations is "constitutionally suspect;"
4) tribal nations continue as extraconstitutional bodies whose sovereignty is not guaranteed or protected by the U.S. Constitution;
5) federal Indian policy is "to say the least, schizophrenic," and this fact necessarily colors federal Indian law, and finally
6) Thomas concluded that since tribes continue as preconstitu-

tional and extraconstitutional polities "the federal government cannot regulate the tribes through ordinary domestic legislation" since neither the Treaty or Commerce clauses give the Congress the power to modify tribal sovereignty.

The logical conclusion Thomas should have then reached but never quite articulated was that the treaty relationship should be renewed since it is evident that diplomatic accords authorized and overseen by the president and carried out with the leadership of First Nations are the only legitimate means by which the United States was recognized as a polity, gained title to lands it now claims, and formed lasting political relationships with many Indian peoples.

Thomas, of course, would probably deny that he was even hinting at the revival of the treaty process—one that has long been called for by Vine Deloria Jr. and by Indian activists since the Trail of Broken Treaties in 1973—since he said earlier in his opinion that "it is at least arguable" that tribes were no longer recognized as sovereigns once their treaty-making days were stifled by the 1871 statute, although many agreements, often described as treaties, continued to be negotiated and ratified by the Congress long after that date.

Thomas' concurrence seems to indicate, unlike his previous Indian law opinions, that he at least has attained an uncluttered understanding of the actual basis on which the U.S. government forged its distinctly political relationship with tribes, and he astutely notes that neither the Treaty nor Commerce clauses empower the Congress to wield absolute plenary power over tribes. These are trenchant observations from a justice not normally associated with such searching ideas, especially in this area of law.

Lara, however, despite its recognition of inherent tribal sovereignty, is also a troubling ruling because, as Thomas rightly opined, the majority opinion, written by Justice Breyer, reaffirms congressional plenary (read: virtually absolute) power in relation to tribes by declaring that Congress retains the power under the Treaty and Commerce clauses to either relax or restrict a tribes' inherent sovereignty. But, as Thomas noted, and as a close reading of Indian treaties and the Commerce clause reveals, these two powers do not explicitly or even implicitly extend to the Congress such paramount, or I should say, antidemocratic, authority, since treaty making forged diplomatic relations while commerce decisions cemented economic alliances.

Second, and equally as unsettling as their reinvigoration of the plenary power doctrine, the majority never satisfactorily explains why tribal nations have inherent authority to try and punish their own citizens and nonmember Indians but are denied that same fundamental right over non-Indians who live on or traverse tribal lands. This racial and political disparity is unfair to those tribal nations who have treaty provisions guaranteeing them such authority over all those who come onto their lands, and who also have the requisite institutions of governance necessary to administer justice to all parties within their borders. That's what sovereign governments do.

Finally, and almost as peculiar as Thomas' surprising concurrence, was the strange pairing in the dissent of the court's most conservative ideologue, Justice Antonin Scalia, with arguably the most liberal justice, David Souter, at least in so far as Indian law goes. Souter's opinion, joined by Scalia, griped that as "dependent" peoples, tribal nations had been shorn of the power to try those outside their membership. And since Congress, in Souter's words, had effectively "delegated" to tribes the power to punish nonmember Indians in 1991, this, in effect, meant that Lara had the right to invoke the Double Jeopardy clause.

First Nations, given the overwhelming preponderance of anti-Indian cases in the last decade (and before), are entitled to feel a palpable sense of relief that Lara was decided the way it was. It very easily could have been seven-to-two against the tribes, or even nine-to-zero. Native leaders and their legal analysts should not, however, allow their rapture over this single decision to cause them to believe that the court has permanently turned an ideological corner and is now prepared to embark on a series of cases more supportive of tribal self-governance. This would seriously misconstrue the ongoing reality that indigenous political and legal status remains fundamentally unstable and that, whether we like it or not, our governments, resources, and rights are still largely subject to the attitudes and policies of federal, corporate, and, increasingly, state officials.

Don't Buy into the Red-States, Blue-States Myth
November 26, 2004

Suzan Shown Harjo, *Indian Country Today*

How can the red-states, blue-states division of America be a myth? Everyone has seen the maps on every newscast in every newspaper. There it is, as plain as day for all the world to see—a United States that is etched in blue along the Pacific and Atlantic Oceans and Great Lakes, but is red from south to southwest and in the middle.

Behold the graphic equivalent of what President George W. Bush calls his mandate.

Well, let's take a look at that mandate. The president won more votes—more than 59 million—than any other presidential candidate in a U.S. election.

Do you know who won the second highest number of votes in U.S. history? That would be Senator John F. Kerry, with more than 55 million votes.

That's a difference of 3.5 million votes, or less than one-half of the 8 million people who live in New York City and fewer than the 4 million in Los Angeles.

The election came down to Ohio, which went for Bush by some 134,000 of the votes counted (such as they were or may be), including that magic jurisdiction where 600 registered voters gave Bush 4,000 votes. If Kerry had gotten 68,000 more votes in Ohio, he would be president.

The margin of difference between who won and who did not was 67,000 votes. That's what is known as a narrow margin. That is not a mandate.

In most states, the margin between being tinted red or blue was quite thin, and the states really should be a mix of dots in red, blue, and colors in between for the cities, towns, and rural areas next to each other that went with the Democrats and Republicans.

Almost no place in America voted as clearly as did the District of Columbia, which, by way of comparison, has more people (570,000) than Vice President Dick Cheney's Wyoming (500,000). Among the closest neighbors to the Congress, White House and Supreme Court, nine out of ten voted for Kerry.

In whose interest is it to keep the blue and the gray—oops, I mean the blue and the red—divided? With the mythology of the red and blue states, the Republicans get to keep running the country by promoting us against them, both abroad and at home, and keeping a list of political enemies that is longer than the no-fly list of suspected terrorists.

The Democrats get to keep subjecting basic rights to test votes designed to lose, but to show how bad the Republicans are. Lobbyists and politicians get to keep shaking down Indians and making the rules of the House. Indians get to settle old scores with new money.

In the red-state/blue-state configuration, the party in power has to protect the heartland—the inner white Christian child in America's womb— against those states with too many multicultural cities and ports of entry for too many nonwhite immigrants.

And what of the southern border? Let's build a 2,000-mile-long security barrier and some duck blinds and shoot anyone who makes it past the razor wire.

Speaking of that wall, a Republican congressman from southern California got the House to agree to build San Diego's part of it over the bodies of dead Indians and live eagles, notwithstanding any other provision of law. It was squirreled away in that foot-high bill not one member of Congress read before lurching toward lawmaking after the national election.

Senator Kerry was done in by his own Catholic church, which admonished the faithful in Arizona, New Mexico, Ohio, and South Dakota that he was an "abomination" for his pro-choice beliefs and that it was a sin to vote for a sinner. That plus Senator Pete Domenici's hand-over-fist voter turnout tactics changed just enough votes from the Kerry column to Bush's to make a difference in New Mexico.

In Oklahoma, voters put aside their "moral values" and voted a man into the Senate who had sterilized women without their consent. That should have alienated both pro-life and pro-choice advocates, but it didn't. That's how much they didn't want to elect the Cherokee candidate.

The successful Defeat Daschle campaign in South Dakota played on anti-Indian sentiments that are never far below the surface. Senator George Allen of Virginia, who spearheaded the GOP's Senate campaign and picked up four new seats, pandered to the worst race-baiting instincts of his minions, even instructing them that saving Indian sports mascots was a Republican mission.

President Bush was put over the top by radical Christians in the South and Midwest, who include in their numbers those who may not be willing to die for their beliefs, but who have proven ready to kill doctors and women who don't share them. The Republican campaign strategists have unloosened some wing nuts and the Bush administration will have a hard time governing without the whole apparatus coming unhinged.

Native people should not depend on the goodwill of either the red or blue states. Even before the election, the governors of two of the so-called blue states, California and Minnesota, began behaving like extortionists, demanding their "fair share" of tribal gambling profits.

When did any states or non-Indians gain an entitlement to any Indian property? This notion of white privilege and Manifest Destiny was articulated by President Ronald Reagan in this way: there was enough land here for everybody, but the Indians were greedy and didn't want to share.

This sense of entitlement is evident in the various efforts to wipe out the trust funds case by imposing a penny-on-the-hundred-dollar settlement on Indians whose property—actual cash, in this instance—has been withheld and used by the same federal government that has a duty to protect it and use it to benefit Native people.

The young people of the country are to be congratulated for turning out to vote in higher numbers than ever in U.S. history. The young and first-time voters as well as the majority of Native, African-American, and

Hispanic voters almost elected Kerry. Many might be discouraged that their candidate did not prevail.

They should be encouraged that they were nearly successful, enough so to try it again in two years when the House and Senate majorities will be decided and in four years when the White House will await a new first family.

Justice is blind

©2003 Marty Two Bulls

Chapter Four

Tribal Nations in the Body Politic

Presidential politics kick off a new century and signal a meaner political season for North American Indians. Indians become involved in the national contest even as politics led by religious fervor begins to infringe on the future of tribal identities. As populations and tribal incomes grow and develop, protagonism increases among tribal leadership. Tribal nations and their individual citizens take positions of influence, both regionally and nationally. Democrats and Republicans vie for Indian alliances and Indian votes, which can become decisive in several states and have sent at least one senator to Washington. The long-term spiritual center of Indian country extended to encompass many points of view. As right-wing slander politics targets tribes, Republican attachments suffer. Indian self-governance and sovereign rights are a rallying cry in all contexts.

An American Indian Protagonism
September 27, 2000

At the turn of the twentieth century, American Indians and Alaskan Natives are growing faster and are better educated and more prominent in regional and national life than at any time since early contact with Europeans.

In ten states, American Indian, Eskimo, and Aleut people comprise a large enough percentage of the population that their voting preferences could significantly affect political elections.

With percentages of population listed, the states where the Native American swing vote could prove impactful are: Alaska (16 percent), New Mexico (9.5 percent), South Dakota (8.2 percent), Oklahoma (7.8 percent), Montana (6.5 percent), Arizona (5.5 percent), North Dakota (4.8 percent), Wyoming (2.3 percent), Washington (1.8 percent), and Nevada (1.8 percent). Other states with large Native populations but with lower proportionality include California, Texas, North Carolina, New York, and Florida.

In what the Census calls "Indian Tribal Groupings: 2000," the government counts the population of the ten largest "groupings." The figures here include mixed and only Indian combined in each grouping: Cherokee are largest, with 729,533; Navajo second, with 298,197; then Latin American Indian, 180,940; Choctaw, 158,774; Sioux, 153,360; Chippewa, 149,669; Apache, 96,833; Blackfeet, 85,750; Iroquois, 80,882; and Pueblo, 74,085.

Cities with the largest Indian populations were New York City (87,241) and Los Angeles (53,092). Cities with overall populations greater than 100,000 with the highest percentage of Indians or Alaska Natives were Anchorage, Alabama (10.4 percent); Tulsa, Oklahoma (7.7 percent); Oklahoma City (5.7 percent); Albuquerque, New Mexico (4.9 percent); Green Bay, Wisconsin (4.1 percent); Tacoma, Washington (3.6 percent); Minneapolis, Minnesota (3.3 percent); Tucson, Arizona (3.2 percent); Spokane, Washington (3 percent), and Sacramento, California (2.8 percent).

The majority of Indians, 43 percent, live in the West. According to the Census, 31 percent live in the South, 17 percent in the Midwest, and 9 percent in the Northeast. The highest percentages are in the Southwest, with majorities in many counties around the Four Corners area that designates the boundaries of Utah, Arizona, New Mexico, and Colorado. In Utah, the Indian population grew from 24,283 in 1990 to 40,445 a decade later.

The recognized Native population of 2.4 million remains around 1 percent of the U.S. total, but its unique history and growing entrepreneurial vigor give it influence beyond its numbers. During the decade of the 1990s, Native Americans grew at a rate of 16 percent, while the national growth rate was 9.7 percent. Native American median age is 27.6 years old, a full eight years younger than the national median.

The figures from the 2000 Census again show that the American Indian population is increasing at a faster rate than the overall U.S. population. American Indians make up the majority of the population in many counties. In nineteen states, the American Indian population exceeds the U.S. average of 1.5 percent.

People identifying themselves solely as American Indian increased 26 percent, twice the rate of the nation as a whole. People reporting American Indian lineage combined with at least one other race or ethnicity rose by 110 percent. The total U.S. population grew by 13 percent from 248.7 million in 1990 to 281.4 million in 2000.

Recently released projections from the Census Bureau: of 750,000 recognized American Indian, Eskimo, and Aleut households (averaging 3.59 people per family), nearly three-quarters are family homes. Married couples maintained 65 percent while 27 percent were headed by women and 9 percent by men. While one-third of those were under the poverty line, the rate of increase in business starts for Native tribes between 1987 and 1992 was 93 percent.

The number of businesses owned by American Indians, Eskimos, and Aleuts increased 93 percent between 1987 and 1992, from 52,980 to 102,271 firms. The rate of increase for all U.S firms was 26 percent. During the same five-year period, Indian business income grew at a rate of 48 percent faster than that of U.S. firms overall. Considering the explosive growth since 1992, there are likely nearly 150,000 Native- owned businesses operating across the United States today.

While it is true that serious problems continue to plague Indian country, these figures reinforce the general notion that Native people are growing in force. A Native protagonism now emerges that coalesces a series of important elements: a base of common culture that treasures distinctiveness; a youthful, increasingly educated population; a rising economic base that should increasingly capitalize tribal and personal initiatives, and a shared political identity built upon American Indian sovereignty that shows signs of being able to go on the offensive.

Nader/LaDuke: Good Challenge, Wasted Vote

November 1, 2000

One week before the presidential Election Day, the contest between Democrat Al Gore and Republican George W. Bush remains at a dead heat.

As the race goes down to the wire, the likelihood increases that the five to six percentage points Green Party candidates Ralph Nader and Winona LaDuke have garnered in several states could make a crucial difference. Since the Green Party support comes from left-leaning or progressive voters, it appears its success will be at Democrat Al Gore's expense, and could hand the presidency to Republican George W. Bush.

Eight states are in the balance—Oregon, Washington, Nevada, New Mexico, Wisconsin, Michigan, Minnesota, Maine—with a combined seventy electoral votes, and where the percentages of votes going to Nader/ LaDuke could tip the balance to Bush.

This makes for a difficult voting decision in many minds. A lot of American Indians are partial to the Nader/LaDuke ticket (26 percent according to our American Indian opinion survey). Not only is LaDuke an Anishinabe from Minnesota, the Greens' platform and general approaches to Native peoples' issues are keenly supportive of the retention of Native sovereign rights and of the range of environmental and economic initiatives of tribes and Native activists.

Nader/LaDuke are the quintessential activists. Involved in myriad causes over forty and twenty years, respectively, they have gathered the sympathies of social-change activists across the color spectrum. Nader, in particular, has been both symbol and example of the Spartan, low-key, incorruptible, and bulldogged champion of the oppressed, the downtrodden, and the hoodwinked.

Nader deserves tremendous respect for his great effort over a long and illustrious career to hold government agencies and private corporations accountable for bad deeds. From auto safety to environmental law to basic human rights, Nader has organized, canvassed, litigated, negotiated on hundreds of cases. Nader's Raiders, the Public Interest Research Groups that he generated on the landscape of inner cities and university campuses, deserve more gratitude and recognition than they have gotten. The country's quotient of real democracy, we believe, has been improved as a result of Ralph Nader.

LaDuke has been also been a whirlwind of political activism. Her anticorporate stance on behalf of environmental issues in Indian country have brought resources and a measure of clout to many isolated and poor groups faced with huge pressures from large companies and agencies. Ably organizing musicians such as Indigenous, Bonnie Raitt, Jackson Browne, the Indigo Girls, Ulali, and others into the benefit concert series "Honor The Earth," she has been instrumental in raising awareness of Indian environmental issues throughout the country.

But they are not real contenders in this presidential contest. They cannot win; they can only challenge. In fact, they could be huge spoilers.

Because there are important differences between the two major candidates on many issues. Particularly on issues important to American Indians, clearly the recent Democratic administration's approach to tribal sovereignty, land claims, current economic initiatives, and open recognition of government-to-government relations is difficult to dismiss.

This year we endorse Democratic candidate Al Gore. We understand the sympathy of Indian people for the ideas and positions of Nader/LaDuke, but such would be a misspent vote in an election that will set the tone for the beginning of a new century.

And while American Indians have important champions and great friends within the Republican fold, not to see the threats and initiatives emerging against tribal sovereignty from within Republican constituencies and governors' offices (so prominently behind Bush) would be a naive and grave mistake.

It is unmistakable that a vote for Nader/LaDuke this year is a vote wasted in a contest that means a great deal to American Indians and to the regular people of America.

Remembering Proposition Five as an Act of Self-Determination
November 12, 2002

Some moments of history are too good to forget. They need to be savored and studied and understood. This happens to a degree with old history. Dozens of books have been written, for example, detailing every minute and every perspective of the Battle of Little Big Horn and of the massacre at Wounded Knee. However, recent history, certainly within the past twenty years or so, is often ignored. Happenings of great importance to the contemporary reality are thus obscured by time and discarded into uselessness.

Such could happen to the 1998 California referendum initiative, Proposition 5, which successfully forced California to meet its obligations and negotiate fairly with the state's Indian tribes for their gaming compacts. The California Proposition 5 initiative was probably the single most substantial victory ever engineered by a coalition of Native nations.

Even though the referendum was later voided by a decision of the

California Supreme Court, the political momentum of the tribes' public win in a statewide election carried the issue to a successful breakthrough.

California tribes had been held back and largely ignored by then-governor Pete Wilson, Republican, who stalled negotiations over gaming compacts with the state's tribes for several years. Instead, Governor Wilson had engineered negotiations with nongaming tribes, attempting to end-run the majority of the state's Native nations. The governor's obfuscation forced Indian strategists to analyze the pros and cons of going to the public with their issue.

The tribal leadership decided to explore fully what their chances were of scoring a major victory with California voters in the face of a very well funded opposition. Putting up a public referendum, they found out, was risky indeed. First off, they had a formidable array of strange-bedfellow enemies. Not only was the governor against them, the racing industry and card clubs, the religious right and other antigambling organizations, and, most importantly, the Nevada gaming conglomerates were investing heavily against successful Indian gaming in California. The tribes were also starting with low positive public support for Native gaming. All presented serious obstacles.

However, the initiative challenge, issued by then Morongo Mission Band chairwoman Mary Ann Martin Andreas and chaired by Ken Ramirez, San Manuel Band of Mission Indians, achieved an overwhelming victory. How it did this is worth reviewing.

One, it rallied the tribes, initially gathering thirty and ultimately eighty-eight tribes into the campaign. Unity was key to be able to convince voters that most Indians (96 percent of reservation residents, the campaign could claim) were in favor. The tribes made sure they were right, then put up the needed resources to do the job. More than $100 million was spent overall on the proposition.

Two, the tribes scientifically gathered the needed information; they did their research on voter opinion. They found out that there was marginal public interest but not opposition to gaming per se. However, there was considerable voter sympathy for Indians doing what was needed on their own reservations.

Three, the tribes designed the proper approach. Worthy of great note: they picked the right enemy, focusing their case on the most assailable opposition, the Nevada gaming conglomerates. According to Richard Maullin, a Democratic pollster and consultant who has analyzed the initiative, this move alone gave the tribes an early defense against potential negative messages. It fixed in voters' minds a clearly identifiable but very unsimpatico opposition.

Four, the tribal initiative put forth the best position by framing the issue as one of Indian nation building and self-reliance, with a strong dosage of the American ethic of self-determination. To accomplish this, they put forth their best voice, Mark Macarro, chairman of the Pechanga Band of Luiseno Mission Indians. Flanked by elders and other reasonable, likeable Indian people, Macarro projected wonderfully with compellingly reasonable but emotional approach. Macarro became a well-accepted spokesperson, recognized statewide.

Five, the tribes prepared a smart and quick-response campaign, ready to counterattack the opposition's ads within forty-eight hours. Whether to respond or to ignore the opposition's attack needs pondering. There are for and against reasons for each. In the California initiative, they felt it was necessary. But these were presented almost always in the form of positive testimonials from tribal members and others telling their stories of how the gaming initiatives had improved their lives. The tribal initiative conducted much direct work with journalists, editorial boards, and public figures.

Many predicted the campaign's defeat but because of clear goals, excellent strategy, and smart tactics, it won a resounding victory of 67 percent to 37 percent. It was a great moment in American Indian public engagement.

The way of this 1998 victory—others come to mind as well, such as the defeat of Indian sovereignty archenemy Slade Gorton in 2000—merits study and reflection by Native leaders everywhere. A concise and pertinent article by political consultant Richard Maullin (Campaigns and Elections, February, 1999) recounts the successful tribally run campaign. The topic would make a great Masters or Ph.D. thesis for public-policy and communications students. When we find our points of unity and put jealousies and egos aside, Indian people can do wonders. When we believe in ourselves and work hard together we can change the world.

Beyond Right and Left, the Spiritual Center
July 7, 2003

The basis of American Indian tribal rights goes beyond the left and right of the political spectrum. The protection of our peoples and communities, the assertion of sovereign jurisdiction over our lands, and the cultural values that uphold our existence as tribal peoples—these are not issues that can ever be carried completely under Republican or Democratic banners.

Of whatever political persuasion, Native opinion leaders might always consider the fundamental Indian bases for protection of lands and social contract with the state and federal governments. The constancy of the government-to-government relationship spans the whole history of tribal

America, evident even in the darkest days of termination. This constancy is paramount. Perhaps you lean toward a conservative approach: strong family and self-responsibility, anti big government yet for a strong military; or perhaps you lean toward a liberal persuasion: strong social services, cooperative international approach, likely also very pro family. Either way, we believe we can and should always get together on the fundamental issues that support tribal sovereignties within American society.

We encourage all Indian people to exercise their best talents within any or all fields of endeavor, in whatever jurisdiction of their choosing. We encourage American Indian Republicans as well as American Indian Democrats, Indian Independents as well as Indian workers and entrepreneurs. We believe that Indian people must, in fact, join every issue and we encourage Indian opinions from every angle. Just remember to keep in mind the inherited bases upon which Indian country is retained; we should all agree to defend, within any camp, the rights of tribal nations of the hemisphere to their own cultures and languages, to their own self-determined governments and land-based jurisdictions, to the full opportunity to exercise those rights to establish sustainable and prosperous economies and societies for their peoples.

Everything else we can argue and even negotiate about; but we cannot negotiate our right to exist as distinct peoples and governments of the world, nor ever give up our right to our own viewpoints, based on our particular histories, philosophies, and worldviews. This is very important and provides us an interesting and unique vantage point. Thus, we are able to work from the truth of our own tribal histories and philosophies. Thus, beyond the left and the right, we can hold on to the spiritual center in our perspective, the one that often can see from the heart of the land, from a language that understands and best describes the place where we stand.

This is not to pretend that there are "perfect" cultures, or that Native viewpoints are always necessarily correct. There is faulty reasoning in every culture and every people and in every individual. But this is to say we are committed to looking for the best of Indian country, for all that is being done well.

The superlatives in Native cultures are always worth noting, documenting, and teaching. There are excellent values that can provide guides to life and behavior. No one can claim we are nearly at our best in upholding these values, but we are lucky to have them in our tribal knowledge, and this is great food for ongoing improvement. Our cultures assign a spiritual (not necessarily religious) underpinning to all existence, which can be the greatest of foundations for our young people; there is always, too, the commitment to social contract between leaders and their communities; a celebration of life and new children; a deep understanding of the importance of family, *tiospaye*, band, clan, and tribe; a commitment to the essential relations that form the core of identity: the idea of helping the people.

Within a great diversity of perspectives, Native peoples bring a unique point of view to American life and the world. We can provide a unique critique, not always based on point-counterpoint, but just as often based in the circular or multidimensional way of arriving at a full view of reality. Beyond the denial of anything positive in those who disagree, this method can seek truth and instruction even in the thoughts and words of an adversary.

Public discourse today in America is quickly erasing all traces of humility and respect. Radio and now television demagogues control the public mindset. The dumbing down of America through vitriolic argumentation began in earnest with Rush Limbaugh's hours-long harangues on national radio. Limbaugh got away with brush painting "liberals" as effeminate, unpatriotic traitors. A nauseous invective befalls now on anyone who disagrees with these "superpatriots."

Indian country should not fall into this kind of discourse, nor lose its ability to tolerate varieties of points of view. At a time in history when greed and distortion of values are the dominant game, Indian country has its own set of values and must continually polish and repolish them. Indian country, if true to itself, can assist America to achieve a much better sense of itself and of the world.

No doubt, we are in an age of secrecy, on a warlike footing. But beyond terrorist acts, the quality of life in America for the working-class is about to get severely squeezed. Fears and paranoia are manipulated easily in a fattened people as class warfare intensifies. We are in a time not of compassionate conservatism but of stern greed, when the most affluent are quite content to take advantage of the moment. The recent tax cut amounts to affirmative action for the wealthiest in America, where the demographics reveal a compelling story indeed. The socially pervasive European fable that eulogizes the pauper who would be prince does not hold a fixation within American Indian tradition. We contend that, culturally, leadership must be valued on how their actions benefit those most in need, on how well they share. Within a community context, would we distribute more of our resources to those chieftains who need it the least?

Increasingly, American Indians and many within American society are questioning whether the connection between money and patronage has taken over American politics. Tax policies that clearly benefit the wealthy are returned in kind. A growing national budget deficit that may well be passed off to our children. A social safety net increasingly in danger. We are in a critical time, when national leaders—corporate and political—

mistreat the facts, fudge the numbers, and willingly corrupt basic information. This is not good. The challenges to maintain and advance appropriate social values are no less important today in some parts of Indian country where resources are growing and accumulating rapidly. Would American Indians become like the rest of America? In democratic societies, good intelligence, contemplated open-mindedly, needs to form the basis of public policy. Corruption of this type leaves the country and the world with serious doubt; it leaves the people adrift within a value system American Indians should neither recognize nor support.

Indian country, for all its problems and contradictions, is still the soul of America. It contains and sustains primordial human values that can cut through the veils of confusion, and which could yet guide a much-needed reawakening in humanity. A recovering Indian country, growing stronger each generation, might need to contribute, in healing its own peoples, a healing for the heart of America itself.

Tight Presidential Race Yields to Indian Voice
August 13, 2004

With both presidential candidates answering Indian questions at the recent UNITY Convention in Washington, D.C., and the subsequent visit by Kerry to Navajo land while Republican ads ran in the Diné language, you just have to know this election is going to be awfully close. The candidates are going all-out to canvass for anything even remotely whispered to be a "swing" vote. Indians are just such an item this year in several states, and so this is a great moment to shout loudly and clearly about Indian rights, sovereignty, and the pursuit of inherent freedom.

Native journalist Mark Trahant's request that President Bush define Indian sovereignty we thought right on the button: "What do you think tribal sovereignty means in the twenty-first century and how do we resolve conflicts between tribes and the federal and the state governments?"

Expectedly and to some uncomfortable guffawing from the audience, Bush stumbled to answer the question—yet his simple, repetitive response registers. We think it needs be used, over and over, until the whole Republican Party has it memorized.

"Tribal sovereignty means that, it's sovereign. You are a—you've been given sovereignty and you are viewed as a sovereignty (sic). And therefore the relationship between the federal government and tribes is one between sovereign entities."

Duly criticized later for the "you've been given" portion of his recognition of sovereignty—as we all must acknowledge that American Indians are the first self-governing peoples of this land—Bush's somewhat stark assertion of respect for tribal sovereignty is nevertheless welcome. Additionally, the president noted that, "the federal government has got a responsibility on matters like education, security ... and health care ... on the promising area ... of economic development ... small business ... encouraging capital flows ... " He ended the response to applause by claiming to have spent "$1.1 billion in the reconstruction of Native American schools." Pity that Trahant did not pursue the sovereignty issue on his follow-up question to the president, but again, the simple sovereignty-recognizing words of the president's response are good to remember.

Ditto for presidential contender Senator John Kerry's presentation at UNITY. Kerry is clearly more articulate about his relations with Indian tribes. In fact, he has a decent record in his home state and in congressional support for Indian causes, while Bush as governor unleashed his attorney general against the Texas tribes' sovereignty. It fell to Lori Edmo-Suppah, editor of the *Sho-Ban News* on the Shoshone-Bannock Reservation in Idaho, to question Kerry. Edmo-Suppah pointed out that tribes now have to go through states or counties to share in antiterrorism and preparedness funds.

"I think some of the funds need to go directly to tribes," Kerry said. "I think there are law enforcement, jurisdictional difficulties right now in the dealings with many of the tribal jurisdictions, and we need to work those through, particularly in the Southwest. I'm prepared to do that."

While Bush was assertive if tongue-tied, Kerry was characteristically deliberate and sedate. Answering Edmo-Suppah's follow-up about the No Child Left Behind Act, again the intelligent detail droned rather than sparkled. Perhaps more than anything, this issue of style is before the mainstream media, but in Indian country, no doubt acuity and persistence will get the attention and the support. Throughout last week, Kerry persevered. On his campaign train trek through the Southwest, Kerry made it a point to touch base with tribal communities.

Under the blazing sun of early August, before an immense red rock, a Navajo elder fanned off Kerry and his wife, Teresa Heinz Kerry, before 4,000 Native participants at the annual Zuni Navajo inter-tribal pow wow. With photography disallowed by the officiating medicine man, the Kerry campaign won't get the popular value of such a moment, but Kerry the man and candidate certainly continues to gain in Indian country. Speaking with tribal leaders at the eighty-third annual Gallup Inter-Tribal Ceremonial in Gallup, New Mexico, Kerry hit several welcomed chords on health care and on Indian representation in high government office while consistently and loudly committing himself to tribal self-governance. Kerry pledged to name a Native American office in the White House to be "directly responsible for our relationship working with all of the tribes and all of Indian country in America." Before the Kerry train had left Southwest Indian country, the Democrats had organized a "Native Americans for Kerry-Edwards" advisory group. "When I take the oath of office as president of the United States, I will swear to uphold the Constitution of the United States and that means to uphold the treaties we have made with Native Americans," Kerry said.

It wasn't lost on Indian leaders that Kerry is the first presidential candidate to visit the inter-tribal Indian ceremonial since Dwight D. Eisenhower, according to organizers. It wasn't lost on local newspapers that Indians represent 9.5 percent of the state of New Mexico's 5.2 million residents, a decisive vote in the tight balloting expected for November 2. Of course, South and North Dakota, Oregon, Washington state, Nevada, and Arizona all can be expected to feature the importance of the Indian vote.

The Indian vote usually breaks Democratic, but not always. With proper understanding and sincere, consistent follow-through, Republicans could yet appeal to tribal publics. The upcoming Republican Party Nominating Convention in New York City will reveal if the Bush team will include credible and capable Indian advisors and if such inclusion will enhance and deepen the President's tribal sovereignty message at UNITY. So far, since the President's short answer on sovereignty at UNITY in Washington, the Republican message has not clearly amplified for Indian country.

For American Indians, this is a perfect season to inject every approachable candidate with a sound dose of knowledge about Indian treaties and self-governance while seeking their strongest endorsements for tribal political and economic freedoms. We must continually educate both political parties and their leading lights that Indian tribal rights predate the formation of the United States, are recognized in the U.S. Constitution, and are well-entrenched in any accurate reading of the history of the country. American Indian tribal rights to an adequate defense against state covetousness and cultural destruction are as American as Thanksgiving, motherhood, and that Sacred Eagle that flies overhead in vigilance of our national unity.

"Swift Lies" Besmirch Democracy

August 27, 2004

Once again, in the dirty-tricks department, right-wing extremists rule.
What passed for "paranoia" in Nixon's time has become the banal routine
for how to treat your political opponents. Clearly, the torture excesses of
Abu Ghraib and the squalid mad-dog attitude and gutter morals of today's
political strategists have a common source in the murky days of political
burglaries and government underhanded intrusion into the civil discourse
of the country.

The right-wing orchestrated campaign to besmirch the honorable combat service record of a decorated soldier such as Senator John F. Kerry is,
we feel, despicable and seriously anti-American. Kerry, who as a volunteer
soldier and officer won a roster of combat medals and came home to wage
a vigorous campaign for early peace in Vietnam, is now slandered by a
political hound pack created in the Nixon White House and resurrected by
the Bush campaign team. The tactic is obvious, but the way the mainstream
media and the many right-wing propagandists on network television have
played it has in fact dominated the much-needed national discussion on
issues for which the current White House has not produced coherent and
workable answers.

A presidential campaign should not be a slander fest. Once again, this
climate of seething hatred is right-wing driven, a gift to the president from
his most visceral sector. Now confirmed to be directly connected to the
Bush team, we believe the president clearly must bear responsibility for the
lies and the smear campaign. We lean to the view, as many now contend,
that this is the Bush way to dumb down enough regular folks so that they
can pillage the economy and wantonly eviscerate the workable international consensus of fifty years.

The "Swift Boat" slander campaign is part and parcel of the type of
thinking that has permeated the Bush presidency. This is an attitude that
predates the crimes of September 11, 2001. An attitude of disregard for
truthful discussion permeates this White House. Naked power-grabbing
under dubious and now-discredited pretenses has proved the death of
nearly a thousand Americans, the maiming of thousands more, and perhaps
20,000 to 30,000 Iraqis killed and injured. We honor those who are serving; we hope they are always respected for their selfless sacrifice regardless
of what attitude or perspective they bring back from their time in the the-
ater of military operations.

From all indications, the Swift Boat accusers are twisting facts and
telling lies. The good news is that a major portion of the serious media is

beginning to increasingly denounce the tactic. *The Chicago Tribune, New York Times, Los Angeles Times*, and many others have studied the evidence and found it to be invalid, the result of "fabrications" and "false assertions." Neither are many people buying the cover story that Bush does not approve of the misleading ads. The connection to the president's inner circle is undeniable. *The Washington Post* last week revealed that Benjamin L. Ginsberg, chief outside counsel to the Bush campaign, has closely advised the brazenly misnamed slanderous group Swift Boat Veterans for Truth. The authors of *Unfit for Command*, the signal book to lead the attack, are longtime GOP operatives John O'Neill and Jerome Corsi. O'Neill is the hateful main spokesman, originally launched against Kerry by the Nixon Dirty Tricks White House. O'Neill's former wife was appointed to the Texas State Court of Appeals by then-governor George W. Bush. The connections go on and on. Coauthor Corsi, by the way, is an avowed racist and hate-monger whose bigoted opinions on Semitic peoples are already a source of embarrassment. His rantings should shock and alarm every good and decent American.

We hope the world can see this tactic for what it is—a dirty campaign of obfuscation and deceit that demeans the office of the commander in chief of the United States Armed Forces. When such a campaign is wantonly directed against a record of honorable military service by a sitting president, something very wrong is afoot in an administration representing the United States in the world arena.

The willingness to amplify the use of big lies and vicious slander in public life is evidence of a willingness to manipulate the American public. This is inherent in the method, when employed as primary strategy.

The mainstream media has serious problems in tackling the issue of slander in public life because it feeds on juicy controversies no matter how ludicrous. The excuse is that if a "source" merely mentions an issue or makes an unfounded accusation, then media is duty bound to "question" it. Problem is, most media, including established figures such as Judy Woodruff, don't question it, they besmirch along with it, trotting out the most confused and hate-obsessed individuals to be found, to be carelessly launched as credible spokespeople. Yell about something enough times and you will get an audience. What an indecent way with which to manage a nation's forum! Yet it works, most all of the time, as media too often become willing allies to those seeking to create a false version of events without any seeming concern for reasonably documented truth.

We disagree with the shameless approach of the Bush team. And we wonder about a president who would allow the use of outright lies in dealing with the American public, as has now clearly become the pattern. The tradition of dirty tricks is prominent currently among his evangelical core. Building on misinformation and lies to achieve objectives, as in the case for the Iraq War and the ongoing military occupation of Iraq, is a dangerous method. Until moderate (read wiser) conservatives come forward, the GOP and its current political neocon thinkers are bent on collision with the reality of the world. This is as true in Indian country as it is America's relationship with most of the world. If the target of big lies can be a distinguished veteran today, it can well be Indian country tomorrow.

More than anyone in this country, combat veterans - who know about the fog of combat and the controlled chaos of war - have earned the right to voice their most honest and incisive opinions on the execution and rationales for the war in which they fought honorably.

This tradition of respect and honor of veterans is particularly visible in Indian country, where on a per-capita basis, more of its finest have served in the American armed forces than any other group. As a result, we lean here toward the judgment that the Bush team's false claims against an honorable veteran who actually served and who also spoke clearly and honestly about the faulty rationales for the Vietnam War should disqualify him (Bush) for the presidency.

Mean is not the same as tough. Any nation must be tough in defense of its interests. If a nation genuinely identifies its self-interest in the pursuit of global peace and stability, then it will be honest and diligent in the pursuit of justice. Since all justice begins in fairness, and all fairness is based in the accurate assessment of the credible information available, we would hope this would be so.

The current slander campaign by the president's men stinks to high heaven. The sacred trust customarily accorded combat veterans should not be betrayed, particularly by those operatives serving a president and vice president who themselves never fought and sacrificed in war. How disgraceful. The country cannot afford to easily break such covenants. It becomes inconceivable to support such a style of government. America deserves better.

Weak Economy Hurting American Indian Families
September 23, 2004

The shift in the American economy is edging toward the obvious. The working sectors that supported manufacturing are left hanging out to dry, as "American" companies scramble to employ cheaply and without much environmental concern in countries from Mexico to India to China.

The point is that now that they are no longer needed, American jobs, meaning American working people, are increasingly becoming expendable.

In the midst of the wealthiest country on Earth, poverty keeps rising. According to the U.S. Census Bureau, the number of Americans living in poverty is now 35.9 million, up 1.3 million from last year, while people without health insurance rose to 45 million. It was the third straight annual increase in both areas. Democrats now can claim that 5 million have lost health insurance over the past five years. These are serious losses, reflecting only the tip of the iceberg of growing anxiety about where America's economic values are heading.

There is fear of the international situation; there is great anxiety among many families about the state of an economy that grows strong while reducing jobs and pay scales. In Iraq, more and more die for an occupation process that grows more violent, unstable, and complicated by the week. What the wiser group of GOP heads avoided under Bush the father, namely, the occupation of Iraq, knowing full well the political and military costs would be long-term and unbearable, the younger generation from Texas went off in a cavalry charge into the sandy quagmire of Arabia. The perception is spreading among many Americans, perhaps too late for this election, that after all, the Iraq war was unnecessary and avoidable. The steep cost will likely become unbearable as that realization grows. And, what can be the support, ultimately, for a president who sends soldiers to war unnecessarily?

International turmoil can also churn domestic anxiety. Economically, the country is out of step, in huge debt, paying through enormous sums to a mammoth military budget that saps the vitality out of economic life. Household incomes are down for a third straight year. Low pay, low-benefit jobs, diminishing scale is the name of the new economy. Nationally, this is one of the issues that actually matters to the American people. It matters greatly to Indian communities, just now barely reconstructing from more than a century of theft and misappropriation and bureaucratic mismanagement.

Rising poverty and stagnant economic waters still plague most of Indian country. The new census data tells us that an average of 23 percent of single-race Native families live in poverty. That Indian rate is almost twice the national average of 12 percent.

Income levels stayed flat nationwide. "The median income over the past three years for single-race Native households was $33,024, a drop of 1.6 percent. Nationally, income levels fell 0.6 percent to a median of $43,527."

These statistics are contained in a new report, "Income, Poverty, and Health Insurance Coverage in the United States: 2003." They reflect a troubling picture. Nearly 28 percent of single-race American Indians and Alaska Natives are without any health insurance at the present time. This rate is almost twice the national average of 15.1 percent.

The national doubt about the economy comes from both conservatives and liberals. It focuses on the huge debt the present administration has generated. Wrote Nelson P. Valdes (July 21, article, "The Worst That Can Happen," "Revista Rebelion, Mexico): "The United States has the greatest economy in the world; its Gross Domestic Product is slightly more than $13 trillion dollars"—yet—"The accumulated total United States federal and state debt is $7.2 trillion. Since September of 2003 the U.S. debt grew $1.7 billion per day. This means that the debts of the federal and state governments represent $24,619.86 per capita. (The GDP per capita is $37, 800). Consequently, the accumulated federal debt represents 65 percent of the mean national income."

These numbers should be taken seriously.

Corporate sectors are often protected, but not the workers. Consider the oil industry as a whole. Here is a sector that has consistently manipulated and eviscerated the American consumer and the American people time and time again. America's reliance on the oil economy as blind faith is decided by the very people who now drive the oil economy.

John Kerry has many important issues to raise, not the least of which is the state of the economy for working Americans. He has been right to cite higher costs for gasoline, college tuition, health insurance, and prescription drugs, along with "dramatic and startling" new figures on declining wages and several other negative economic indicators.

With only six weeks left before the election, the presidential campaign is sorely in need of focus on both international and economic security issues.

Waking up to Republican Hegemony
November 5, 2004

It was a huge turn out for the American electorate, but the predictions of such a trend signaling Democratic victory turned out wrong, seriously wrong. No doubt Senator John Kerry ran a clear and commendable race— stayed on message, brought out his base—but the bulk of the high turn out actually emerged for Bush. America, George W. Bush can now rightfully claim, went for the Republican ticket.

By significant numbers Indian country had favored Kerry. This paper endorsed that general mandate and pointed out our own severe differences of opinion with the present administration, particularly over the Iraq War and the bungled peace strategy, as well as over the skyrocketing national debt and the encroachment of church matters into public policy. Those opinions remain, firmly held yet always open to be evaluated and further developed as the events of our time evolve.

Indian Country Today congratulates George W. Bush in his victory and for his courage to undertake, once again, the life-and-death, make-or-break burdens of the American presidency. Given the squeaky, nationally unsatisfying year-2000 victory, this decisive election must be welcomed by the president, who also solidified his base in Congress.

For American Indian peoples, communities, and nations, it is a good moment to reflect on the directions of American politics. Where now is Indian country in the new, clearly solid Republican term, if not era? Where now the direction of Indian leadership? What are the principal Indian messages, nationally, that America's political leadership, regardless of party, must hear and understand? What is the best way to approach political power and policy decision-making in America?

The call for a time of reevaluation is hereby put forth. While Native America voted overwhelmingly and in record numbers for John Kerry, caution about joining too intensely in the ongoing American political vendetta is in order. For some, the pain of loss might seem too traumatic, but the reality is more important. Fix the broken tire, don't curse it. America can move in either of two directions right now. It can polarize even more severely or it can emphasize those issues upon which it agrees. When America polarizes, Native communities can be completely drawn into the battle rather than focusing on the prize—advocating on behalf of tribal cultural, political, and economic rights. Engaging a process of political education should involve tribal leadership and all prominent tribal members across the country. Native leadership might consider examining their relationships with their Republican allies and leaders of their regions. Tribal leadership is advised to strategize on every possible way to get to know and educate and engage—amicably—those people, organizations, and projects on the right, as well as on the left.

The Bush reelection brings up another analogy. In the past, some historians compared the father-son team to John Adams and John Quincy Adams of Massachusetts, two generations of one-term presidents. But the Bushes make a closer fit to the Pitts of eighteenth-century England. Prime Minister William Pitt led England to a sweeping victory in what it called the "French and Indian War" and lost his job in the next election. William Pitt the younger, then a lightly regarded twenty-four-year-old, took the premiership by the narrowest of margins at the end of the American Revolution in 1783 and held on during a grinding foreign war to become one of the country's longest-serving leaders. Perhaps media pundits need to look beyond the Northeast and the West Coast to understand both history and the country.

America's political process reflects an ongoing dilemma. Evenly and deeply divided, America has developed a bipolar public policy mind. The two-minded good and evil characters of some traditional stories loom large over the land. Not even remotely consensual at the moment, these two public minds treat each other like a long-married but estranged couple finally locked into visceral antagonism, all yelling and screaming of accusations. Such has become the state of mainstream cable news media and talk radio. But as the shrill voices crackle, many Americans also wonder just who is minding the family, the entire family. It is incumbent upon the president and the Republican Party, now that they have gained solid control over the executive, legislative, and, some would argue, judicial branches of government, to genuinely work toward unification of the people. The president in his gracious victory speech expressed as much. Perhaps the participation of tribal leaders could even play an increased role in alleviating this situation of utmost hostility between the parties.

Our contention always has been that Indian country must know, understand, and engage both the left and the right of America's political spectrum—yet be owned by neither. For the Native peoples of the land, we believe, the place to hold is the spiritual center, with both feet planted firmly on the land and informed by the superlative lessons from some of the most ancient of human traditions. Holding this particular place for American Indian peoples, among ourselves as we share those things that are particularly Indian and in the way we approach the American conscience, is crucial.

Despite our basis for unity—not always sought but always present—Indian activists and professionals will work in every part and for every concept of the political and economic spectrum. This need not be a disunifying weakness, but can be rather a great source of strength. American Indians' deployment in many walks of life, religions or political parties, has been as necessary as it has been formative of the current strength of tribal peoples. The intercultural human bridge has been a source of resources and assistance for the tribal communities. Perhaps naive to state but ultimately true, extensions of the tribal peoples, the whole web of relations belong to the spiritual center, where we hold our families, as prescribed in our traditions, to be sacred; where we too have valued—if not always practice—open democracy, freedom of expression, freedom of movement, freedom of sovereign self-government.

Probably the political issue most skillfully exploited by the Republican election team is the question of cultural values. The Republican base in this context is overwhelmingly Christian-evangelical—but interestingly, the family issues projected resonate with a majority of the people, who are engaged in building, repairing, and otherwise working to maintain their families as viable and healthy institutions. This is no less true in Indian country, where strengthening family ties is a primary objective for anyone seriously engaged in helping their communities. What are tribes and kinship nations but huge extended families of relatives who still have a formal way of relating to each other? More than most Americans, Indian peoples maintain strong relations across generations, through language, and sometimes even over international borders that actually divide their nations.

While there exists much common ground in matters of personal and collective spiritual belief among various people and cultures, some institutions as well as some who are institutionalized can be prone to excess. One inappropriate religious impact found an immediate echo in the victory statement from House Majority Leader Tom DeLay, architect of the Texas redistricting that ousted four Democratic incumbents. Ignoring the warning of St. Augustine, he told his cheering throng, "We are going to bring God into the public square." St. Augustine, the great indigenous North African Christian of the fifth century, said in "The City of God" that it wasn't fitting to discuss theology in the marketplace. This mixture is a recipe for hypocrisy and it might explode in the face of the ethically challenged DeLay, who has already been admonished by the House Ethics Committee and whose aides are under Grand Jury investigation for fund-raising violations. His name figures prominently in the Abramoff/Scanlon tribal lobbying scandal. The new House might not have the stomach to probe deeply, but it might heed the example of another powerful Texas congressional leader. House Speaker Jim Wright was forced to resign in 1989 after his heavy-handed protection of crooked financiers helped produce the megabillion dollar savings and loan debacle.

No doubt, Native America is riddled with all the social ills of the rest of America, yet traditional values—the ideal among Indian people—are quite conservative, sober, chaste, and seriously respectful of relations between the genders and between generations. Concurrently, American Indian people are also characterized by their generosity and tolerance. As tribes achieve economic prosperity, fiscal objectives surface that parallel the urge for self-sufficiency and for fiscal responsibility that is also a central traditional value. We could go on, Indian country is very rich this way—the point being that an effort to continue to educate and influence other publics in America begins and ends with sharing our values, dreams, and aspirations, to go out and meet the folks, to represent and to gain a piece of their intelligence, their point of view, and hopefully their goodwill. For the good of the people, this includes Greens and Democrats; for the good of the people, this includes Conservatives and Independents and Republicans.

The time is now for Indian leadership to be truly and strategically open-minded, that you may always know, always engage, always influence and prevail for the good of the people. Following the 2004 election results, a recommended first step is to begin by focusing attention on that with which American Indians, the president, and the Republican Party firmly agree, that tribal sovereignty and tribal self-determination and the federal government's long-standing commitment to government-to-government relations is to be respected and honored.

Until January 3, the Cry Is "Slade Lost!"
December 3, 2000

Suzan Shown Harjo, *Indian Country Today*

The news spread like wildfire December 1, when Representative Maria Cantwell, D-Wash., was finally declared the victor over Senator Slade Gorton, R-Wash., for the seat he has held for eighteen years.

Washingtonians split their 2.5 million votes so evenly that an automatic recount was ordered and no official winner was named until nearly one month after the national election. When the counting was done, the challenger was elected by a mere 2,229 votes over the incumbent, who quickly conceded.

Age and money were contextual issues in the campaign. She was new-economy. He was old-guard. She had fresh ideas. He had long experience.

At seventy-two, Gorton is senior to Cantwell by thirty years. Both are millionaires. His money is from the family fish business in Massachusetts. Hers is from stock options from a dot-com company in Seattle. He did not run on any of his own money. She spent $10 million of hers, some 25 percent of her RealNetworks fortune.

Voters in Washington elected Gorton to three terms as attorney general and sent him to the Senate three times, first in 1980. His campaign coffers were filled by the paper, energy, mining, airlines, and other industries most affected by his influential committee positions. Cantwell served as a state legislator for six years and as a U.S. House member from 1993–1995. Her bid for senatorial office was bolstered by Native Americans, environmentalists, women's rights advocates, and others Gorton had alienated over the decades.

"Maria won," Democrats cheered. Cantwell's victory makes the party split in the Senate an even fifty-fifty going into the 107th Congress. She will be the thirteenth woman in the Senate and Washington will be the third state, after California and Maine, to be represented by two women senators.

But, for most Native people, it was "Slade lost," said more in disbelief than in jubilation.

Tribal leaders and business owners started raising money for Dump Slade 2000 last year, before Cantwell was even a contender. They viewed the campaign as a very long shot, but necessary. Gorton's track record on Native rights earned him the name Slade the Blade. Millions of tribal dollars had been spent since the 1970s fighting Gorton's persistent attempts to end tribal rights and treaties, and the fights were not getting easier.

As attorney general, Gorton advanced arguments that were the white-glove equivalent of the anti-Indian agenda of local and national hate groups, geared toward abolishing tribal sovereignty and Indian group rights. In 1979, he suffered a sharp blow when the U.S. Supreme Court held in favor of Indian treaty fishing rights and chastised Washington for its recalcitrance in honoring them.

Fresh from defeat by the high court, Gorton entered the Senate and immediately tried to achieve legislatively what he had failed to do through litigation. His early burn-and-slash efforts were rebuffed by senior senators, including some who agreed with him on the substance, but objected to his trampling on committee turf and protocol.

Over time, Gorton settled into the style of the Senate, where tone trumps content most days of the week. He began using the scalpel more than the machete, but was ever-focused on his task: undercutting federal Indian law.

He was gaining surgical precision, along with seniority and clout on key committees for energy and natural resources, budget and commerce, science and transportation.

After the 1996 election, Senator John McCain, R-Ariz., announced that he would step down as chair of the Senate's select committee on Indian affairs. Gorton was next in line for the job. The sound of alarm from Indian country was loud and effective. Majority Leader Trent Lott, R-Miss., interceded and Gorton withdrew in favor of Senator Ben Nighthorse Campbell, R-Colo., who became the first Native American to head the Indian panel.

The senator from Washington assumed the reigns of the appropriations subcommittee that controls most of the federal Indian budget. He backed funding for Indian health, education, jobs, and museum programs. Why? Because, in his view, these serve the interests of Indian people, whose individual needs he supports as civil rights of American citizens.

At the same time, he used his positions to undermine and even punish tribal governments, whose group interests he opposes as those of "super citizens." He also seldom missed a chance to champion the cause of white folks who lived on reservations, but objected to tribal laws and authority.

Gorton, whose manner is composed and courtly, wonders why his help to Indian people is not recognized. He rejects the view he has been mean-spirited, an Indian fighter, or a racist to the state's twenty-seven tribes and 100,000 adult tribal citizens.

Indian group rights were anathema to the senator and organized groups of Indians may have put him right out of office.

Soon, Native peoples will say, "Maria won!" But, until January 3, Gorton's last day in the Senate, it will be "Slade lost!"

A Party of Choice: Voting by American Indians

September 16, 2002

Carey Vicenti, *Indian Country Today*

Voting in the United States for Indian people is a paradox. No other right in the American legal system is more symbolic of a Native person's "inclusion" into the political body of the United States of America. But that's the source of the paradox: as members of Indian tribes, we owe our allegiance first to our tribes, our clans, our societies, our relatives, our friends, and our ancestors. You can be certain that our ancestors would be wondering about our newly claimed allegiance to America.

The drafters of the U.S. Constitution never contemplated including us in the newly formed Union. We were always intended to be "outside" in a political sense even though we were "inside" in a geographical sense. And even when the Nation reunified at the end of the Civil War, when the Thirteenth and Fourteenth Amendments to the Constitution were adopted, the latter making "persons" born within the States into citizens, there was no intent to make Indians into citizens.

Our path to citizenship was opened in part by the bravery of young Indian men and women who filed off to war during the First World War. They were aided by a growing movement of non-Indian political activists, emerging anthropologists, and wealthy "do-gooders" who felt that the right to vote was the only appropriate reward for service and heroism. But that was merely a revised form of assimilationist theory, whereby "inclusion" took the place of "assimilation" as an imperial term of art. The Congress of 1924 was convinced of the merits of the liberal argument and so they passed the Citizenship Act: we became citizens of the United States.

The "Indian Citizenship Act," as we came to call it, was not passed upon any sound legal basis. Nothing in the U.S. Constitution granted to Congress the power to annex the souls of Native peoples. Contrary to the popular American philosophy of "government by consent," the U.S. brought us in without any effort to gain our consent.

The twentieth-century history of Federal-Indian relations, however, has manufactured that consent. It has done so in legal, cultural, and social ways. After 1934, for instance, as hundreds of tribes were offered the option to reorganize as constitutional governments under the Indian Reorganization Act, many did so by adopting a boilerplate document that vowed to uphold U.S. laws and committed tribal actions to the approval of the Secretary of the Interior. Our children have been schooled in State or Bureau of Indian Affairs schools and taught a history that purposefully omitted the true history of our loss of lands and independence. We've been made to believe that every affront to the United States is an insult to Native America, meriting even a military response.

And even though we had a right to vote, at least on federal paper, as we learned in the Bush vs. Gore case, it was still up to the states to determine the particulars about elections. Indians were kept from the polls by one means or another. It wasn't until the Indian veterans of World War II challenged state elections law that the right to vote took on any meaning. Thirty years after the vote was granted, Native peoples finally made actual political choices, in theory, at least.

Over the past several decades, it has become almost customary for Native peoples to select membership in the Democratic Party. It has been as difficult to find an Indian Republican as it is to find an Indian vegetarian. When one appears, he or she makes pretenses at bravery or innovation while supporting nothing more than a xenophobic American conservatism. Tribal leaders endorse candidates in hopes of creating a block vote only to offend the pseudo-independent tribal voter. Most Indian voters do not vote at all. Ironically, the freedom of choice created by the right to vote has not been exercised wisely. What good is choice if one either does not vote or does not demand the highest standard in candidates or parties?

But back to the paradox: what party or candidate is actually on the side of Native peoples? The Democratic and Republican Parties are similar to a pair of twins who argue between themselves about their differences. The two-party system itself has no grounding in the U.S. Constitution either. Both of the major parties serve the interests of wealth, corporate expansion, and a kind of globalism that eats up tribal peoples. Neither party has ever offered a principled political solution to our desires for independence and cultural integrity.

At heart, whether we like it or not, politically we are "Tribalists" and the clothing of American politics rarely, if ever, fits us well. The urges toward "self-determination" and "sovereignty" do not conform to Democratic or Republican visions of their America. So when our leaders do get consolation from the parties, it isn't because the parties have evolved philosophically, it's because in the opportunism to prevail over the errant twin party, they see Native votes as up for grabs—it's mere political greed. And all too often, the Natives who endorse the parties are engaged in the same sort of opportunism: we learn all too well sometimes.

This is not to say that the Green, the Libertarian, the Socialist, or the Communist Parties are any different. Every party wants to reconfigure the United States as a nation-state built by their standards, but none of them have transcended the limitations of Western political philosophies that recognize no political place for tribal thinking. They do not truly appreciate cultural diversity, linguistic survival, repatriation, sovereignty, self-determination, tribal religious freedom, and the many other interests that are the distinguishing characteristics of the "Tribalist" political agenda.

Maybe some of us are veterans, and maybe some of us are modern warriors of a different kind, but it appears that we must, as previous Native warriors have done, take the right to vote to a different level. Our "Tribalism" should be openly admitted as a political philosophy. Voting ought to be a universal ethic of tribal peoples. Block voting should be openly discussed in general meetings of the tribal membership. Indian scholars and politicians should be engaged in a dialog to define the tolerable limits to the concessions we may make to American party politics or perhaps to demand principled, articulated, and tangible concessions of all of the parties of choice.

Attention Party Indians and Other Native American Voters: Ranking the "Modern" U.S. Presidents
October 31, 2002

Suzan Shown Harjo, *Indian Country Today*

With the November 5 Election Day fast approaching, seasoned vote counters say dozens of congressional races are too close to call and party leadership of the Senate and House is up for grabs.

In some states, both Democrats and Republicans are in a mad scramble for Indian votes and cash. In South Dakota, Indians often provide the margin of victory in congressional races, usually for Democrats, and Republicans are watching Indian voter registration like hawks.

South Dakota's high-volume charges of voter fraud in reservations are not helping Senator Tim Johnson, D-S.D., who has a good Indian policy record and deserves Indian votes returning him to the Senate.

The scandal also could hand the state's only House seat to Governor William J. Janklow, (R), who deserves to be retired from his long career of disservice to Native peoples and denied the opportunity to promote anti-Indian legislation in Congress.

Republicans in South Dakota say Indians there vote blindly for Democrats, irrespective of what's best for them. Democrats and a voter-rights lawsuit say many Indians are discouraged from voting at all. In this year's congressional races, it is in the Indian interest to vote for the Democrats, sending Johnson back to the Senate and Stephanie Herseth (D), rather than Janklow, to the House.

Party politics are nothing new to Indian politicos. One of the most strategic was the late Reuben A. Snake Jr., Winnebago/Sioux, a kindly leader who played hardball to better the lives of his people in Nebraska. In the 1980s, they suffered injuries and indignities under the regime of an entrenched local sheriff he dubbed "Small in the Saddle."

Snake convinced the Winnebago Democrats to switch parties and vote for the sheriff's opponent in the contest for the GOP nomination. The new Republican Winnebagos block voted "Saddle" out in the primary and then counted coup by electing the Democrat in the general election.

The rule of thumb used to be that Indians would work on property rights when the Republicans were in and poverty programs under the Democrats. A more deadly political axiom was that Republicans exterminated and Democrats terminated. In fact, Indian genocides and slow-genocidal policies were carried out by leaders of all parties in power in the Capitol and White House, and the same holds true for efforts to reverse those destructive policies.

Now that some Indian nations have money, office seekers and campaign fund-raisers fawn over tribal leaders and shake the Indian money tree, even in places where coffers are full, seats are safe, and Indians haven't lived for a century or two.

Democrats raised a bundle of Indian money in the 1990s, offering breakfasts and photo ops with President William Jefferson Clinton for $150,000 per tribal leader. There was even a fire sale: three leaders of different nations could put on the feed bag for $50,000 each.

Presidents courting Indians is nothing new. General George Washington recruited Indian nations to help win the Revolutionary War. As president, he maintained federal relations with the Indian allies, hedging against conflicts with foreign countries and the powerful states.

President Abraham Lincoln courted chiefs from the Great and Southern Plains in an 1863 meeting in the White House, where he asked for and received their neutrality in the Civil War. They likely did not know that one year earlier, he signed the death order for thirty-eight Dakota men at Mankato, Minnesota. Most Great Lakes Indians are Democrats, in no small part because Lincoln was Republican.

President Andrew Jackson didn't court Indians; he killed Indians, mostly Muscogees (Creeks). He carried the campaign to Congress, where three Indian-fighting comrades chaired the Indian affairs committees before and during his presidency, greasing the way for Indian removal legislation. Cherokees, Chickasaws, Choctaws, Muscogees, and Seminoles were marched at gunpoint to Indian Territory, and tens of thousands died on those Trails of Tears. Most citizens of these nations are Republicans, because Jackson was a Democrat.

Early in his presidency, Clinton stated publicly that Jackson was his favorite president. This appalled Muscogee Second Chief Shelly Stubbs Crow, a nurse on the First Lady's health task force, and she told the president so. Crow reported to other Muscogees that Clinton was shocked to learn of Jackson's Indian history.

A few Indian Republicans say the Clinton administration was the most dangerous of all time for Native peoples. This is no truer or less laughable than the claim of some Clinton Indians that theirs was the best of all administrations for Indians.

These same Indian Republicans claim the current administration is the best ever for Indians. No kidding. They actually say this out loud, usually during brownnosing meetings with administration officials, but to other Indians, too, so they might believe it.

This claim is, at best, premature. Taking the optimistic view, President George W. Bush's administration hasn't had enough time to do much of anything for Indians. At worst, the claim is preposterous, given the record as it stands now, what with the Interior secretary being held in contempt of court in the trust funds case and all.

Which administrations and parties have been the best and worst and what have modern presidents done for and to Native peoples? I have ranked the presidents who served between 1963 and 2000 in terms of tangible, substantive, far-reaching accomplishments, considering also how they used the bully pulpit, how long they were in office, and what else they did with their time.

President Jimmy Carter is tops in my book. I confess bias (but not error), because I am a former political appointee in the Carter administration and an unabashed fan of the former president. He made serious campaign promises to Indians and, amazingly, kept them. I fault him only for listening to campaigners who advised putting off Indian actions that might cost votes until the second term.

The top two administrations in this ranking, Carter and Bush Forty-one, never got second terms and served only four years each. The last two, Clinton and Reagan, are the only ones with eight years in office. Ford's ranks just above those and had the shortest tenure, two years and five months. The administrations in third and fourth place, Nixon and Johnson, each served a little over five years.

It could be said that credit for certain accomplishments attributed to one president really should go to another—that President Richard M, Nixon laid the policy foundation for the self-determination act, even though President Gerald R. Ford signed the law, or President Lyndon B.

Johnson ended terminations, even though Nixon signed the first untermination law—but, both credit and blame even out rather neatly from each administration to the next.

The presidents' Indian policy rankings, from best to worst:

First: Jimmy Carter (D/1977–1981). Signed the groundbreaking child welfare, religious freedom, and tribal colleges' laws. Personally involved in Eastern Indian land claims and signed the first settlement (Rhode Island) and the largest (Maine). Approved the first Indian water rights settlement and acts restoring, recognizing, and/or returning land to fifteen Native nations. Appointed the first Indians to serve as Interior assistant secretary and associate solicitor for Indian affairs. Advocated Pacific Northwest treaty fishing, tribal inclusions in international fisheries treaties, and Alaska Native whaling and subsistence rights. Overruled his attorney general to advocate high standards of federal trust duties in legal and policy decisions and conduct of programs. Recognized Indian self-determination and human rights as international rights.

Second: George H. W. Bush (R/1989–1993). Approved acts authorizing the national Indian museum, mandating the Smithsonian to return Native remains and property, and requiring nationwide repatriation and graves protection. Signed laws establishing the Indian memorial at the Little Bighorn monument (and dropping the name of Custer from its title), strengthening Native languages, promoting authenticity in Indian arts and crafts, providing Native Hawaiian health care, protecting Indian children, and preventing family violence. Approved measures for Indian law-enforcement reform and economic development and technology-related education, as well as three tribal restorations and settlements and two demonstration projects for employment and training services and for tribal self-governance programs.

Third: Richard M. Nixon (R/1969–1974). Signed the Indian Financing Act, the Navajo college and Indian education acts, the Alaska Native claims settlement, and the first law reversing a federal termination and restoring the Menominee Tribe. Returned Mount Adams to Yakama Nation (by executive order), Blue Lake to Taos Pueblo, and lands to Warm Springs and Payson Yavapai-Apache. Established environmental protection nationally, but did not recognize tribal governmental or jurisdictional rights. Myriad Indian people were placed under surveillance for advocating tribal sovereignty and Indian rights.

Fourth: Lyndon B. Johnson (D/1963–1969). Included Indians in the "Great Society" and "War on Poverty" laws and programs of general applicability for economic development, education, elders, housing, jobs, legal services, and youth. Recognized tribes as service providers and community developers. Set up Indian desks in agencies and created the national council on Indian opportunity. Appointed the first Indian in nearly a century as Indian-affairs commissioner. Advocated an end to federal terminations of tribes and signed the Indian Civil Rights Act.

Fifth: Gerald R. Ford (R/1974–1977). Signed two of the most sweeping federal Indian policies, the Indian Health Care Improvement Act and the Indian Self-Determination and Educational Assistance Act, which promoted an end to federal paternalism in conducting Indian programs and changed the relationship between tribes and federal agencies. Approved the Indian Crimes Act, as well as legislation returning land to the Havasupai Tribe, and making surplus federal property and submarginal lands available to Indian tribes.

Sixth: William Jefferson Clinton (D/1993–2001). Signed the law for Indian religious use of peyote and an executive order on Indian sacred sites, but opposed substantive legal protections for sacred places and failed to even threaten to veto the desecration of Mount Graham. Issued orders on tribal consultation and Indian education, established the Office of Tribal Justice in the Justice Department, and approved tribal justice and arts and crafts enforcement acts. Used the bully pulpit for positive statements about and images of Indians. Signed the Indian trust management reform act, under which his Interior and Treasury secretaries were sued and became the highest ranking cabinet officers ever held in contempt of court. Tried to unrecognize "nonhistoric" tribes (two or more tribes the United States had placed on reservations), forcing an unnecessary congressional clarification. Approved land settlements and conveyances for six Native nations.

Seventh: Ronald Reagan (R/1981–1989). Signed laws regulating tribal gaming, mineral development, and housing, as well as preventing and treating Indian alcohol and substance abuse and settling Indian old-age assistance claims. Approved laws returning a sacred place to Zuni Pueblo and restoring, recognizing, and/or settling claims of a dozen tribes. Tried to turn over Indian education to the states, but was stopped by Congress and eventually signed Indian education and tribally controlled schools acts. Tried to subject Michigan treaty fishing to state jurisdiction, but was stopped by the courts. Tried unsuccessfully for six years to cut one-third of the annual federal Indian budget. Used the bully pulpit in Moscow to deride federal Indian policy, saying the United States should not have "humored" Indians by putting them on reservations.

Why a Republican Federal Government Is Good for Indians
November 10, 2002

John Guevremont, Mashantucket Pequot Tribal Nation

The Republican's victory on November 5, 2002, is not only historic, but also poses some interesting propositions for the way Indian country sees its participation on the national political stage. As a Republican, I welcome my party's success in this election, but as an American Indian, should I have cause for concern?

I am concerned, but not about Republican control. I am concerned about the inherent skepticism the Democratic-leaning American Indian community has for Republican leaders. Every statement made by a Republican is (often) overly scrutinized with suspicion, but invariably the conclusions, drawn in a climate of defensiveness and distrust, lead to bad decisions and political dead-ends. Ultimately, Indian country is the loser, due to its pursuit of a self-defeating national policy born of inaccurate perceptions.

Case in point: While campaigning for the 2000 presidential election in upstate New York, Governor George Bush made a remark to the effect: " ... in tribal-state relations, the states have precedence ... " This quote has been oft repeated throughout Indian country. Unfortunately, that statement may dog many American Indians' perceptions of the President and his intentions for the remainder of his term.

However, then–governor George Bush made up for his New York remarks in a widely circulated (but largely ignored) August 18, 2000, letter to tribal leaders, in which he emphatically supported the federal government-to-government relationship with the tribes. On November 1 of this year, President Bush, in declaring National American Indian Heritage Month, again stressed that Indian nations are self-governing, self-supporting, and self-reliant. Furthermore, the Republican National Platform for the 2000 Election serves as yet another indicator for judging presidential "intent." President Bush clearly and enthusiastically adopted the Platform as his own. His campaign repeatedly stressed the commitments made to the American people during the 2000 Philadelphia convention. The 2000 Platform stated that, "tribal governments are best situated to gauge the needs of their communities, while self-determination and economic self-sufficiency are the twin pillars of an effective Indian policy."

There is a wide gulf between deliberate conduct to suppress Indian country's rightful aspirations and missteps arising from an incomplete understanding of the tribes' rights. Emotionally engendered attacks, even if fueled by righteous indignation, are not conducive to either effective negotiation or objective achievement.

Support for self-governing, self-supporting, and self-reliant tribes is the official Republican position. Will it be adhered to by 100 percent of its candidates? Probably not, but not because there is intentional duplicity. This platform acts as a beacon by which the national leadership steers itself, occasionally straying off course, but always guiding itself back. Indian country and its leaders can help in this process by acting as the foghorn that calls attention to necessary course corrections.

The awareness and momentum at the federal level for Indian issues grows day by day. The Native American Caucus has increased to approximately 104 members, with many new additions coming from Republican ranks. Republicans in both houses have stood up in great numbers to defend Indian country from unfair attack (from both Republican and Democratic colleagues), while pro-Indian bills outpace anti-Indian legislation. Each legislative victory experienced by American Indians has come about through stalwart leadership and participation by Republicans in both the House and Senate.

Support for Indian country transcends the Congress. The White House has stepped up and energized its outreach to Indian country through both its executive departments as well as the Office of Intergovernmental Affairs. The RNC Chairman, Governor Marc Racicot, has established an Indian outreach office, clearly recognizing American Indian contributions and impacts on the national political process. Let us also not forget that Tom Cole, newly elected to the House from Oklahoma's fourth district, is also an enrolled member of the Chickasaw Nation. Tom recently served as both executive director of the National Republican Congressional Committee and chief of staff of the Republican National Committee.

How can we, as American Indians, deal with the new Republican reality? An effective strategy is based on a willingness to engage in productive dialog and mutual compromise. Indian country must maintain and grow its relationship with the federal government, the Congress, Executive branch, and regulatory agencies. Second, it must enhance internal cooperation between the various tribes and their representatives in Washington, including the various associations, offices, and political lobbying law firms. Innumerable divergent interests dissipate the focus on our core issue:

self-governance preservation and enhancement. By focusing on a few, but critical, collective interests, Indian country can provide support, structure, and leadership to their representatives' efforts.

Lastly, bipartisan political outreach, communication, and education efforts in Washington help increase the number of supporters within the congressional ranks and within the administration. Fund-raising activities, briefings, conferences, and seminars support friends and reach out to members who otherwise would have little knowledge or interest in Indian matters. An informed legislative body is the best protection for the tribes' unique status, rights, and liberties.

Only through engagement with Republican leadership can Indian country plant the seeds that will grow into understanding for our priorities. It is through this government-to-government relationship that specific legislation to increase Indian program funding, enhance education, provide economic development incentives, and reinforce tribal self-governance can be, and has been, accomplished. There is no conceivable reason why the 2002 election results would fundamentally change this dynamic for anything but the better.

The American Indian Vote Comes of Age
November 15, 2002

Kevin Gover, *Indian Country Today*

There was a lot of good news in the November 5 election results for American Indians. Indian gaming referenda were passed in Arizona and Idaho. Seven Indians were elected to the Montana state legislature. A governor very friendly to tribal interests was elected in New Mexico (former Congressman and Energy Secretary Bill Richardson), and it appears another respecter of tribal sovereignty was elected governor in Arizona (former U.S. Attorney Janet Napolitano). And longtime friend of the tribes Tim Johnson was reelected to the Senate from South Dakota.

Beneath these results, though, lies the greatest news of all: Indian votes count. And in a close election in the right state, Indian votes can be the difference between the election of a friend and the election of an adversary.

In the late 1980s, I worked for several New Mexico tribes that decided it would help their cause to get more involved in the political process and began effective efforts to register tribal members to vote in state and federal elections. While this was not a new idea, it marked the beginning of aggressive and organized political involvement among the tribes. There had always been a few kingpin tribal leaders whose endorsements were sought by candidates for public office, but there were few if any broad and systematic efforts to register Indians to vote.

Activists in other states, uniformly Democrats, began Indian voter-registration efforts in their states as well, and by the time the 1992 presidential election rolled around, there seemed to be a national effort by the Democrats to register Indian voters and turn them out to support then–governor Clinton. The appearance, frankly, was deceiving to some degree. While there were Indian activists working on behalf of the Democrats in several states, these efforts could not truly be characterized as a national initiative. Nevertheless, appearances meaning so much in politics, it appeared that there was an organized national effort.

Two states stood out in the 1992 election. In New Mexico, the state Democratic Party made a concentrated effort to involve tribal leaders in the Clinton campaign. These efforts resulted in all of the state's twenty-three tribal leaders endorsing Clinton, and a Democrat carried the state in a presidential election for the first time since 1968. Thirty thousand votes were cast from Indian precincts, the most ever, and 90 percent of those votes went to Clinton. Clinton won in New Mexico by 45,000 votes; more than half of that margin came from the reservations.

The results in Montana were even more dramatic. Clinton won in Montana, carrying all of the state's cities. In the rural counties, though, he was beaten badly, except in those counties where Indian reservations were located. He won in those counties, and turnouts of 80 and 90 percent were reported on the reservations. Montana's Indian Democratic activists clearly carried the state for Clinton.

The potential of the Indian vote to make the difference in close elections was thus established, and politicians of both parties became more serious in seeking Indian support. In 1994, Republican gubernatorial candidate Gary Johnson turned to New Mexico's gaming tribes for their support. The gaming tribes, all Pueblo and Apache, supported Johnson against antigambling Democrat Bruce King, and provided tens of thousands of dollars to Johnson's campaign.

When the votes were counted, though, the Indian precincts had cast 65 percent of their votes for King. Navajo voters apparently could not bring themselves to vote against the Democrat. Still, losing 65 percent of the Indian vote is much better than losing 90 percent. Moreover, the high visibility of the tribal leaders who supported the Republican candidate created the perception that the Indian vote had been a key factor in the defeat of the Democratic incumbent.

The Indian vote in New Mexico had matured into a potent force by the 1996 presidential campaign. All but one of the state's tribal leaders endorsed President Clinton, and Clinton again captured 90 percent of the Indian vote. The Indian vote was not decisive in Clinton's landslide win, but one impressive statistic stood out for Indian activists. Although only 11 percent of the state's voting-age population was Native American, Indians cast 15 percent of the vote in New Mexico in 1996. This means that Indian turnout, traditionally very low, was actually higher than the turnout for the state as a whole. Now that's Indian voting power.

By the 2000 election, federal and statewide candidates in New Mexico and elsewhere were fully aware of the strength of the Indian vote, and candidates Bush and Gore openly courted tribal leaders for their support. Despite earnest appeals from the Republican candidates, the tribes stayed true to their Democratic tradition and voted overwhelmingly for Vice President Gore. Gore won New Mexico by only a few hundred votes. Tens of thousands of Indian votes clearly provided the margin of victory.

In the state of Washington in 2000, the tribes set out to defeat Republican Senator Slade Gorton, and they did so. The impact of the Indian vote is difficult to tally, because Indians represent a relatively small percentage of Washington voters. Nevertheless, the tribes made themselves a key part of the coalition that eked out a narrow victory.

Indian Democrats like me had been touting to the party the wisdom of developing the party's strength among Indian voters, pointing out that, in several Western states, Indians could provide the margin of victory in close elections. In states such as Arizona, New Mexico, Alaska, and South Dakota, Indian voters could be extremely important parts of winning Democratic coalitions. Indeed, without Indian votes, Democratic candidates stood very little chance of winning.

Some of this was hype, frankly. The numbers were real enough, but it still was not clear that a targeted voter registration and get-out-the-vote effort could succeed in a place such as South Dakota, where Indians register and vote only in small numbers. It is easy to understand why. Given the dire poverty of the South Dakota Indian population, many Indians believed that their votes were meaningless; potential Indian voters lacked hope and had no confidence whatsoever in the political process.

But a remarkable thing happened. Indian Democrats, with strong support from the state Democratic Party and the campaign of Senator Tim Johnson, set out to prove that the Indian vote could be decisive in South Dakota. And did they ever! Although Indian voters have long been part of the winning coalition of Senator Tom Daschle and Senator Johnson, never before have Indian voters been so visible in South Dakota, and never before so decisive a factor in the outcome. Turnout on the reservations hit record levels everywhere in South Dakota, and those votes clearly carried Senator Johnson to victory over John Thune, the man recruited by President Bush to run against Johnson. While Democrats elsewhere were losing tight elections in states where President Bush campaigned hard for Republicans, the record Indian vote stemmed the tide in South Dakota.

Meanwhile, Arizona tribes were also registering and turning out their voters in support of Proposition 202, a tribal gaming initiative sponsored by a coalition of seventeen tribes. The initiative appears likely to pass by a margin of 20- to 30,000 votes, a fine win for the tribes under difficult circumstances. But along with their votes for Proposition 202, the early returns indicate that Indian voters also supported Democratic gubernatorial candidate Janet Napolitano. Absentee and early votes are still being counted at this writing, and if Napolitano wins, her margin of victory likely will have been provided by Indian voters.

These ventures into the electoral process required courage and commitment from both the leadership and the general membership of the tribes. In South Dakota especially, new Indian voters were subjected to intimidation in the form of Republican threats to pursue allegations of vote fraud on the reservations. Thankfully, these bold ventures to turn out the Indian vote were met with success in Arizona and South Dakota. The Indian voters in those states now know for sure that their votes can make a difference in the outcome of close races. Congratulations to the activists and visionaries who made it happen.

In the political system today, tribes have two ways to make their mark. One is money, and the other is votes. Small tribes in large states such as California cannot influence the process with their votes, so they use their wealth to do so. We shouldn't fault that, but neither should we mistake the influence that money can buy for the kind of power that comes from votes. Money can win you access and the occasional favor. But putting your votes behind someone who needs them wins a supporter for life.

The tribes won some important races both for themselves and for some important friends last November 5. More importantly, they have served notice that the Indian vote has come of age. The Indian vote must continue to grow stronger, and it can. In a country where less than two-thirds of the eligible citizens vote in presidential elections, even a small minority can have a disproportionate impact on elections if they get out and vote in larger numbers than the public at large.

When we become known as people who protect our interests aggressively at the ballot box, we gain the respect of those who make decisions affecting our lives. Politicians of both parties already are competing for money from the tribes, and we should doubt seriously the sincerity of elected officials and their parties when they do so. Now, though, they have begun competing for our votes, and the question becomes not what we can do for them, but what they are going to do for us.

Indigenous Voices and American Politics
August 20, 2004

David Wilkins, University of Minnesota

As a polarized American electorate uneasily traverses the time between the recently concluded Democratic National Convention and the pending Republican bash, one small yet extremely diversified segment of the American electorate—the 562 federally recognized American Indian and Alaskan Native nations—find that their governments and their citizens may play an important, if minor, role in the 2004 presidential election.

This despite the fact that Native nations are not an integral part of the U.S. constitutional order since that document only addresses the federal and state governments and mentions Indian tribes only tangentially. Interestingly, since tribes were not involved in the U.S. Constitution's creation, they are generally exempt from its major provisions and also are denied the protections that states enjoy. Stranger still, individual tribal citizens were unilaterally enfranchised by federal law in 1924, and, the same as other Americans, enjoy basic constitutional rights and privileges.

In recent days, in fact, American Indians have been prominently mentioned by both Senator John Kerry and President Bush. Kerry, in a speech on Indian health care on August 8 before 5,000 people in Gallup, New Mexico, pledged that as president he would "uphold the law of the land, and that includes treaties and the special relationship that exists between the United States and the Indian nations."

President Bush, in a convoluted response to a question on the meaning of tribal sovereignty (essentially the inherent right of indigenous nations to self-governance) posed by a minority journalist on August 6, told the 7,500 assembled journalists that "tribal sovereignty means that it's sovereign. You're a—you've been given sovereignty and you're viewed as a sovereign entity. And therefore the relationship between the federal government and tribes is one between sovereign entities."

Native nations, in reality, have existed in the Western Hemisphere for millennia and were never "given" sovereignty, certainly not by governments that are themselves less than three centuries old.

Nevertheless, these two statements by the leading presidential candidates are big deals for Indian nations. They provide a measure of overt national political recognition for several of the most potent symbols, doctrines, and historical realities that affirm the unique status of Native nations—recognition of the value of tribal sovereignty, acknowledgment of the importance of ratified treaties, reassurance of the unique trust relationship. The United States and tribal nations have a unique moral relationship, with the United States acting as a protector of Native lands, resources, and essential rights—and an implicit nod toward the permanence of tribal territories (a.k.a. "reservations").

Tribal sovereignty, treaties, trust, and territory, or the four "Ts" if you will, underscore the distinctive qualities of indigenous nations that fundamentally separate them from other racial and ethnic groups.

For Native peoples, the four "Ts" are sufficient to warrant express recognition and political and economic action by their junior sovereign partners, the United States and state governments, who, as the latter-day governments lack the moral or lawful authority that tribes have based on their longevity on the hemisphere and in explicit recognition in hundreds of ratified treaties and agreements.

But tribal leaders are keenly aware that while these forces have been in evidence for the better part of two centuries, it was not until the advent of the Indian gaming phenomenon, which has spawned a much more politically active Indian electorate, that indigenous peoples and their distinctive and shared issues began to attract the concentrated attention of state and federal officials vying for their votes and campaign dollars.

The Indian vote, even when gaming is not a defining factor, was critical in the defeat of Senator Slade Gorton of Washington in 2000. Native voters also figured prominently in Tim Johnson's 2002 defeat of Representative John Thune for one of the Senate seats in South Dakota. Tom Daschle, the Senate Minority leader, is also in a close reelection campaign and is spending a fair amount of time in Indian country. The Indian vote may also prove to be important in state and national elections in Arizona and New Mexico as well.

Of course, a number of state legislatures and governors are trying to squeeze additional gaming revenue from tribal governments, claiming that they are entitled to an increased share of Indian proceeds, when, in fact, there is nothing in the 1988 federal law that established the programmatic context for Indian gaming that gives the state, or the federal government, for that matter, any authority to claim a greater share of what is, after all, Indian money.

Tribal nations today find themselves situated in a unique, if precarious, position vis-a-vis the state and federal governments. It is unique in that tribes and their citizens are being wooed in ways never seen before, and they have opportunities to more fully engage in American electoral politics in an effort to effect positive changes for their citizens, who also happen to be American citizens.

It is precarious, however, because Native nations are still not an organic part of the U.S. constitutional system and their reserved treaty rights, trust opportunities, and separate territorial homelands may still be vanquished or circumscribed at virtually any time by state or federal policies that take advantage of the extraconstitutional character of Native nations.

While the number of Indian voters in non-Indian elections continues to ratchet up, with many tribal leaders expressing the view that the only way to protect their remaining sovereign powers is to become more actively engaged in state and national elections, some commentators wonder what the long-term impact of such electoral participation will be on tribal sovereignty.

If tribal peoples continue to insist on functioning in this manner, then they should at least be more demanding of both national political parties regarding what it is they expect in return for their votes and tribal dollars.

Instead of vague homilies about tribal sovereignty, the sanctity of Indian treaties, and the "unique" relationship between tribal nations and the United States, Native leaders should instead call for, at a minimum, a four-pronged constitutional amendment that would 1) entrench ratified treaty rights and authorize a new round of treaties with tribal nations; 2) provide explicit language to tribal governments that, similar to states in the U.S. constitution, they, too, have a "guaranteed" right to exist and to be protected from unlawful and unwarranted intrusions by federal or state officials without tribal consent; 3) would formally disavow the doctrine of congressional "plenary" power that allows the Congress or its delegates to act largely without restraint insofar as tribal lands or rights are concerned; and 4) would send notice to state governments that under the Constitution they have limited powers inside Indian country since the relationship between the United States and Native nations was federalized from the birth of the nation.

If the presidential candidates would agree to back such an amendment, and if U.S. and state officials would then seriously engage in the hard discussions and actions that might culminate in such an amendment, then Native nations would have a genuine reason to even more actively participate in the American political process. This level of participation would be about much more than merely protecting the at-risk tribal gaming operations from avaricious state lawmakers. It would indicate that the United States had fully returned to the more cooperative period of diplomacy and multicultural democracy that was sometimes evident in the early years of Native/white relations.

California Dreaming!

Gale Norton finally succeeds in uniting the tribes!

CHAPTER FIVE
IN THE MEDIA EYE

Journalism gets meaner as tribal governments emerge onto the economic scene. Tone of attack on tribal rights goes negative as anti-Indian forces practice derivative journalism to diminish Native standing in the public mind. Pundits with ideological motives and little grounding in Indian country realities put forth skewed coverage that media generally begin to follow. A major challenge for tribal voices is the proper engagement of media opportunities and the strategic intelligence to communicate consistently and positively to regional and national audiences. Pervasive stereotype is vicious. Negative metaphors emerge. Media and public perception very often leads to public policy, for good or evil, that impacts generations.

Indian Journalism Is Good for Sovereignty

March 29, 2000

It is important that American Indian journalism lead by example. We should strive to provide accurate coverage of events as well as to search out the best thinking on the range of important issues facing Indian communities and nations. Open and trustworthy information channels are needed in Indian country. As we relaunch *Indian Country Today* this week with a new design and new thematic sections, it is appropriate to rededicate the foundation principles of our editorial mission.

Indian Country Today intends to research and report to our readership on the important stories, trends, and opinion and power circles that can impact American Indian communities and nations. We follow stories from North American Indian perspectives but also with keen interest in Central and South America, the Caribbean, and even global indigenous affairs.

We agree with the editorial entitled "Indian Sovereignty Is Good for America." We believe a relevant American Indian journalism necessarily reflects the fundamental concept framework of Indian sovereignty, always in its broadest interpretation. It should champion the protection and enhancement of American Indian rights, and assist their projection and understanding, in national and world affairs.

Very importantly, Indian journalism should champion common-cause thinking among Indian tribes, nations, and communities.

Indian unity is extremely important. However, our commitment and loyalty are just as rooted in the principles of integrity, fairness, and accuracy. Journalism cannot be less. These principles need apply everywhere, internally and externally, to the coverage of the nations.

Honest government, broad and clear thinking, the search and welcome of "good mind," are all necessary bases to hold up as guide posts. We look for good solutions to common problems; we intend to profile the quiet leaders of superlative projects and enterprises everywhere in Indian country: the solution makers.

We believe in an Indian journalism that defends the totality of activity and pushing of frontiers by Native people anywhere. We respect the cultural messages that tell our people about our relationship with the natural world; we are strong supporters of an ethic of respect for Mother Earth.

Our peoples always do well to explore, sustain, and reapply their ancient traditions. Yet, we must be able to report and explain the rapid pace of change in all fields of endeavor, as this is the reality of our present generations. The tremendous growth of business enterprise in Indian country requires special support in the communications field, as well as rigorous attention.

Ethical practice in business, as in all areas of endeavor, is required, and a watchdog journalism can provide important touchstones on those paths.

Indian journalism should always strive to help the nations generate the most beauty, pride, and production possible from the daily practice of Indian sovereignty.

Destroying Journalism
November 22, 2000

Perhaps Rush Limbaugh is not the only one, but he certainly is the best at it. One could even say he embodies it: that he is master of the journalism of intolerance.

For all of the injustice in American history—the continual social violence, the outright theft of land and other resources; the slavery of whole peoples and the dismemberment of entire cultures—the power of a reasonably objective free media has always made it possible for minority viewpoints to survive, sometimes even to prevail.

When in 1973, during President Nixon's administration, the U.S. Army was massing troops outside the hamlet of Wounded Knee, in anticipation of launching an outright attack, it appears clear that the national media attention, along with a poll that showed 51 percent of American people sympathetic to the Wounded Knee defenders, kept the assault from happening.

Throughout the political turmoil of the '60s and '70s, media reporting and commentary—mostly moderate but professional—gave the American people a measure of truth about the world. People argued and fought, sometimes virulently, but in the national media world, the general agreement was that professionalism dictated a sense of fairness; that journalism required a dedication to balance.

That kind of journalism is disappearing. It began rapidly shrinking with the advent of Rush Limbaugh's style of talk-show commentary. Acidic, masterful in the use of the straw man, the caricature of the opponent, as a primary tool, the new wave of right-wing commentary is driven by a voice of disdain and complete demonizing.

Arousing large audiences for several hours each day, the attitude never leaves room for compromise, training its audience, slowly and comprehensively, toward a zealotry of perception and expression that can only tolerate confrontation. The opponent, after so much personal attack and ridicule, becomes "an enemy," can only be an enemy.

The give and take of representative democracy, the sense of the large if imperfect unity of a people, within which viewpoints have the possibility of growth, transformation, and coalition, this is completely missing from this equation. The possibility that the country could find common purpose around encompassing, rather than winner-take-all approaches, disappears from view.

In the case of Limbaugh, who in the waning weeks of the presidential campaign made the rounds of the news-talk shows as a "legitimate" commentator, the level of disinformation and spinning through the eye lens of his clearly one-sided analysis becomes an inducement to hatred. The man may deny he is hateful; but his impact leads to positions of anger and hate.

Thus, the whole other side—the Liberals, the Democrats (the eggheads, the feminazis, the wacko environmentalists, the Indian savages)—can be lumped in one circle, which is to be attacked, attacked, attacked. In Rush's book of life, these are a whole set of people (half of voting America, by the election numbers) who are always wrong, insincere, dishonest, etc.).

The insulting, sarcastic, downright nasty example that this type of journalism sets is bad for America. It was bad enough when it sprang from a big mouth daytime talk-show host who laughs his way to the bank each day, but it is cause for high alarm when such national journalism figures as Tim Russert, Brian Williams, Chris Matthews, and Wolf Blitzer parade Limbaugh through their prime-time shows like one more reasonable analyst, further opening the door of national respectability.

We can forgive news shows that in the rush of deadlines might make a wrong call in a tight political race. That's one problem in American journalism, but it pales by comparison.

Much more dangerous, for journalism and for all of our peoples attempting positive self-government, is the slippery slope toward mean spirited, hatefully one-sided, thus bigoted, positioning.

This seems to be the American dilemma at the end of the twentieth century. Daily confrontation is required to compete for market share. No one knows this better than Limbaugh. Positive, if firm, and substantial dialogue, from which the best common opinions can surface and be gathered into action, this becomes a fantasy, a nice thought, but unattainable.

Yet, there is no other way for human beings to sustain a positive, prosperous, and progressive country. The ultimate logical consequence of the other approach is a clear and hard division of America along ideological lines.

Permission to anger and hate as a primary motivation in political discussion and practice is very dangerous. The airwaves are full of it, most of it right wing, after a decade developed into a very tightly woven ideology. Limbaugh, G. Gordon Liddy, Laura Ingraham—glib, quick, funny, and mean, very mean.

The easy disrespect for people who are actually running the country, from people who have seldom done anything but talk in front of an open mike, is pitiful. It is probably the worst element to enter national American consciousness in the past decades, itself the clearest example of the decadence about which they complain.

Wall Street Journal Loses Respect
March 7, 2002.

It will be very difficult from this day forward to have serious respect for *The Wall Street Journal*, a newspaper with which we have often disagreed but had at least appreciated for its range of writers and coverage and for its long-term existence. The appreciation vanished this week as we read *The Journal*'s March 1 editorial, entitled "Big Chief Pataki," which excoriated New York Governor George Pataki and took a pretty wide stereotypical and prejudicial swipe at American Indians.

Now, the criticism of a politician is not beyond our scope. No doubt, over the seasons, we have taken the New York governor to task ourselves on a number of issues. Most recently, however, we have seen his approach of using Indian economic-recovery options to ameliorate his state's financial woes and land claims as pragmatic and open-minded. The New York governor, we believe, is generally on the right track with Indian nations across the state. His plan to negotiate six new casino compacts with Indian nations, although still saddled with some political baggage, has opened up diplomatic channels and fostered government-to-government negotiations that could lead to real economic gains across the board.

The Wall Street Journal, in its editorial against the Pataki plan, did not rely on serious information. It chose instead to marshal innuendo and misinformation of the cheapest order and displayed a complete lack of understanding for the Indian gaming industry and its resulting economic, social, and cultural benefits.

To start, the editorial called Pataki New York State's "new Indian chief and gambling boss." The appellation of the title "chief" is familiar to every American Indian who has ever been stereotyped, in the workplace and other public situations. Being called "chief" for Indians, when delivered with the same derisive tone as *The Journal*'s editorial, is tantamount to a black man being called "boy," and is just as insulting. Perhaps the insult will give the governor an idea of what it is like to be an Indian.

Later in the editorial, *The Journal* also calls Pataki "Great White Father," another term we had thought hackneyed to death long ago. The name-calling is belittling and prejudicial and it marks the editorial down to the lowest of journalistic levels. But *The Journal* doesn't stop there. The gratuitous insults are matched in their appalling intentions by its dishonest arguments. Apparently driven by a nearly religious hostility toward Indian gaming, the editorial makes these main points:

Gaming enterprises are bad, bringing, "lowlifes and organized crime, drugs, prostitution, loan sharking and money laundering. The mob infiltrates and corruption in local government often follows … "

This is misinformation of the highest order. The FBI, the DEA, local police departments, not to mention hostile investigative reporters, have scrutinized Indian gaming and have found remarkably little evidence that either the mob or so-called "lowlifes" have infiltrated Indian gaming. A notorious *Boston Globe* series a season ago (apparently the main source for *The Journal* editorial writer) found only one case, involving mob influence on a small tribe in California, and that itself was three years old. Indian gaming is among the most regulated industries in America.

In fact, none of the dangers mentioned in the editorial have even penetrated the barriers of regulation and self-regulation, imposed and self-imposed, that surround Indian gaming enterprises. The evidence for this assertion is simply not there. This is the type of cheap accusation worthy of talk-radio demagogues, not serious journalists, and in fact it derives mainly from the dishonest exaggerations spread by Congressmen Frank Wolf, R-Va., and Christopher Shays, R-Conn., and refuted by the very GAO reports they commissioned.

Certainly, *Indian Country Today* would investigate such allegations and it would publish those findings, not to demean the Indian gaming industry but always to attempt to encourage the highest integrity possible in this most important sector for Indian revival.

Tribes are currently seeking recognition "because of the windfall that usually follows." It attacks the federal recognition process as "out of control and rife with special favors," when in fact the process is extremely slow and difficult.

The editorial mentions the Ramapough Mountain Indians on the New York–New Jersey border as perhaps one of these tribes, an especially puzzling reference since the Ramapough petition has been repeatedly turned down by the Bureau of Indian Affairs' Branch of Acknowledgement and

Research. However, the Ramapough, as with nearly every other tribe seeking state and/or federal recognition, started their process many years before
gaming became an option for Indian economies. Their story is one of racial
discrimination against the mixed-race tribal remnants in the East, in this
case of the Leni Lenape, that anthropologists treat as "tri-racial isolates."

The editorial dismisses the "economic development" argument by
pointing to Atlantic City, warning readers to consider "the mean streets
behind the glittering boardwalk." Indian gaming, it says, "promises more
than it delivers."

Although there exist no Indian casinos in Atlantic City, let's consider
the actual objectives of Indian gaming. For tribal nations seeking to recover
from centuries of dispossession of land and resources, destruction of culture, and severe economic deprivation, not to mention racism, gaming is
always intended as a means to rebuild the nation. The industry has helped
to re-empower American Indian communities and fuel the bases of social
services necessary to bring their peoples out of poverty. For tribes across
the United States, economic and cultural recovery is the primary objective
of the gaming option. Many are actively seeking diversification into other
economic bases, including a quite impressive range of tourism, manufacturing, and other business options. Perhaps *The Wall Street Journal* editors
should read this newspaper's Trade and Commerce section.

Local and regional non-Native communities have also benefited
greatly. A 1999 Lexecon, Inc., study of Indian gaming in Arizona found
that the seven tribal casinos had directly created more than 1,800 ongoing
jobs for nonmembers and contributed $128 million annually in purchases
of goods and services. The Gila River Indian Community alone used its
gaming revenues to support capital improvements generating 1,100 new
jobs and adding more than $98 million to the state's economy. These find-
ings have been replicated over and over in every region of the country.

The editorial expresses great fear of the "land into trust" swaps that
are sometimes available to tribes, which it calls, "another bit of gaming
corruption."

This bit of name-calling exposes the core of the editorial writer's ignorance. There is no corruption in this opportunity. Trust responsibility and
the designation of trust lands served this country well at various points in
history. It became the reality of land tenure for peoples who held substantial territory that even when conquered and occupied, never could quite be
cleansed of its original Native title.

The Journal's position on Indian gaming in New York State and
nationally is part and parcel of a growing national backlash against
Indians. It seeks to disparage and to castigate Indians with all the same

stereotypical images, denying the real economic base of the issue and mangling the facts.

These are stereotypes—"pow wows with Mohawks," "Big Chief," "Great White Father"—that have plagued Indians from the time of earliest contact to the present. They are the reasons why, notwithstanding the results of a recent *Sports Illustrated* survey on the topic, the so-called "mascot" issue is so vitally important. The primary stereotype is of Indians as "fleecers" of good Americans, when in fact the reality is quite the opposite. The intent is to create a wrong perception on purpose.

Strangely, a newspaper otherwise known for its business insight has not a clue about the real financial and social benefits of Indian gaming for the tribes, their neighbors, and even the states within which they are positioned. It is glaringly evident that the newspaper misrepresents the facts, even confusing the history of American Indian gaming with that of Las Vegas and Atlantic City. But we suspect the problem runs much deeper than that. The editors of *The Wall Street Journal* simply don't want to know the facts.

The editorial raises another specter. It intimates that the Seneca, Mohawk, and Oneida Indian nations are controlled by gaming interests, "the same white guys hiding behind the curtain." These tribes are perfectly capable of determining their interests and running their own business affairs—with or without partners—but *The Journal* prefers the image of Wizard of Oz characters pulling the levers of a make-believe Indian world. Nothing could be more insulting to American Indians than the subtext evoked by *The Journal*.

The Wizard was, after all, a character created by L. Frank Baum, who, ten years before he penned his famous book, published the Saturday Pioneer, a weekly newspaper in Aberdeen, south Dakota. Before and after the Wounded Knee Massacre of December 28, 1890, Baum published two editorials that called for the annihilation of the Sioux people. Following the murder of Sitting Bull, Baum published the statement on December 20, 1890, that with Sitting Bull's demise: "the nobility of the Redskin is extinguished, and what few are left are a pack of whining curs who lick the hand that smites them. The Whites, by law of conquest, by justice of civilization, are masters of the American continent, and the best safety of the frontier settlements will be secured by the total annihilation of the few remaining Indians. Why not annihilation? Their glory has fled, their spirit broken, their manhood effaced: better that they die than live the miserable wretches that they are."

After the Wounded Knee massacre, Baum's newspaper on January 3, 1891, reprised its earlier genocidal message: "The Pioneer has before

declared that our only safety depends upon the total extirmination [sic] of
the Indians. Having wronged them for centuries we had better, in order to
protect our civilization, follow it up by one more wrong and wipe these
untamed and untamable creatures from the face of the Earth. In this lies
future safety for our settlers and the soldiers who are under incompetent
commands. Otherwise, we may expect future years to be as full of trouble
with the redskins as those have been in the past." Baum was born in 1856
in Chittenango, New York.

By denigrating American Indian nations and delivering a fusillade of
misrepresentations, factual errors, and disparaging stereotypes *The Wall
Street Journal* has done little better than perpetuate the rather bleak journalistic tradition of Baum's Saturday Pioneer.

George F. Will's Homogeneous America
March 31, 2002

George F. Will is the master thinker on the conservative flank of national
pundits. His opinion in columns and television talk shows commands a
large audience. Will has a way of lining up his arguments that makes a
reader feel intelligent just for following the logic and the obscure refer-
ences; indeed, it takes an effort to fully understand the high erudition and
sheer intelligence of Will's prose. As one intends to digest it, however, the
message often brings up its own difficulty.

In a recent column, Will makes the heaviest of arguments for the view
that a unicultural America, one with a "unified" point of view, is one of
the great results of the 9-11 tragedy. He makes this sound as if this were
the return of the natural order of things, that somehow this foreshadowed
an America made up of "unified individuals again," rather than, as he
expresses it, "coagulated groups."

By "coagulated groups," columnist Will means the varieties of cultures and subcultures in American life, some organized as political entities,
from nonprofit organizations to interests groups, and, of course, potentially
including the reality of American Indian nations, perhaps the ultimate
interest groups in some minds.

The national will to unity, indeed, the "national mind," is now most
"malleable," according to George Will. This is a good thing, he reasons. It
is as things should be, as it was when America knew it was right and the
world was wrong; when America was the Good and whoever was the Evil.
Remember when Indians were disparaged as the precursor to removing
them from their lands.

Now we know the evil again, Will exults. Now, we are back to the way it was. We know who and what "evil" is. Amazingly, in Will's America, as he argues, the problem, perhaps a source of "the evil," has been "multiculturalism," which brings on, evil of evils, "cultural relativism." Yes, in Will's America, "multiculturalism" is definitely a source of "evil."

If all these evilisms induce a bit of seasickness, we apologize, but the code talking is everything among the spin-doctor pundit class. It is good for us to see the argument coming and to try to analyze it just a bit. Will's argument is troublesome because he is saying that America should not be multi, but uni. We are not many cultures, he wants to drive home, we are one culture: American. Thus, is George Will happy, loading up his particular definition of nationalism onto the "morality" of the American mission. But which America? Which American?

Will seems to argue that the return to standards of beauty and grace repudiates "multiculturalism" and toleration of "diversity." Leave aside that he cites examples from the music of Diana Krall, a Canadian who grew up in Nanaimo, British Columbia, and the world of jazz, one of the great triumphs of the American blend of cultures from alien continents. Will is muddling together two very distinct philosophies. When he attacks "multiculturalism," his real target appears to be "cultural relativism," the position that all cultures are equally valid. All "value systems" are products of their time and place; none has a claim to universal validity. Tesuche Pueblo or the Sistine Chapel, each is admirable in its way. None is to be preferred to the other, because no external, abiding standard exists by which to judge them. This sort of cultural relativism is a product of nineteenth-century European thought. Both smug and hypocritical, it assumed the superiority of the European academic who can rise above the belief of all other cultures that their way is the best.

We base one point of defense of "diversity" on an even older European principle, one expressed in medieval Europe by the great Florentine poet Dante Alighieri. Around 1312, Dante wrote a political tract De Monarchia, defending the (hypothetical) universal government of the Holy Roman Empire on the paradoxical ground that it would best allow human diversity to flourish. He argued that the end of man was to exercise his intellect in contemplating creation. But since creation's possibilities were infinite, no single human perspective or single culture could possibly appreciate it all. "And since that potentiality cannot all be reduced to actuality at the same time by one man or by any of the particular groups distinguished above, there must be a multiplicity in the human race by which precisely the whole of this potentiality may be actualized."

This is the diversity treasured by the First Nations of this continent, who universally have found a moral order in the universe. For thousands of years, individuals here have divined this order through their own unique experiences, not through books of revelation or Aristotelian three-step logic. Their practices were as diverse as the hundreds of tribes and languages that flourished here, but the end was the same. It took the European intrusion to begin the process of restricting and extinguishing this rich array of perspectives, a process that reached its peak here just as the European worldview was collapsing at home.

Will's phrase, "multiculturalism," is code-speak for the "other" peoples of America, mostly minority races, those beyond the mainstream that he speaks to and for. "Multiculturalism" is code for those that argue that America is a composite of many cultures and ethnic groups and Indian nations, each with its cultural and social and legal histories and each contemporary in its unique way. To Will, this is the thinking of some sort of internal enemy.

In the same column, Will exults in President Bush's "promiscuous use of the word "evil," which he notes is an "unselfconscious expression of his [the President's] religiosity." Religiosity, yes? But, again, what religiosity? Whose religiosity? Would it have to be Christian for Will to prefer it? In any event, just where does this "religious" international policy take us? Why does religion have to play a role in setting U.S. international policy?

Will exalts Ronald Reagan for having "remoralized foreign policy" back in the 1980s. We recognize President Reagan's accomplishments. However, to us the call to "unify" at the expense of the other cultures casts the shadow of Manifest Destiny, the great justifier of the fastest, most drastic land dispossession in history. Will is excited by the strength of his own one-mindedness, but again, he expresses it as an idea that despises distinct cultural constructs and traditional social bases. His described "unity" would apparently opt to destroy or more politely "erase" such bases to create the individualized entities that make up his sense of "individuals united"—as the concept of the American nation. Gone, presumably, would be the "coagulated groups"—who might be who, ostensibly—American Indians? Latinos? Jews? Homosexuals? African Americans? Is it in the national mission to search for and destroy the diversity of the nation-state as part of the mission to combat an evil or barbaric enemy? Will seems to be saying just that. What Will calls "multiculturalism," is this the new straw man of misinformed conservatives, a reinvented boogeyman.

Proud of his patriotism, Will would have all of us know that he is also an ardent nationalist. He defines "nationalism" as "the rejection of cultural relativism, the basis of 'multiculturalism.'" He wishes a bad week on those "diversity mongers" who think America is actually a "mere" mosaic. It certainly would seem that, according to Will, multiple points of view, particularly perspectives arising from a cultural prism, need not express themselves in American life. Perhaps he should spend some time talking with American Indian veterans, those who know all too well how to consider several social, cultural, and national prerogatives all at once. After all, they have protected and defended the freedoms and sovereignties of European nations, of the United States, and of their own governments, simultaneously, without stumbling into the same philosophical trap from which Will seems unable to extricate himself.

That is why George F. Will's argument is not acceptable. Not when in our common history American Indians have been among those determined to be "the other," the "evil ones," "anti-Christian," "devil worshipers." Remember the quote "The only good Indian is a dead Indian"? It wasn't so long ago. Most painful were the periods of long-standing denials of Native identities and spiritual beliefs by varieties of Christian institutions and Christian-led governments, right to contemporary times.

When the lands of the American Indian nations were taken by the newly arrived, who immediately invited all their relatives over, the great and complicated and perennial world that constituted the original, diverse Native America was rolled over, trampled, and damaged by those who pretended to possess the superior culture. Fortunately, however, many strong pockets of Indian culture, of family, clan, and government did survive. Multiculturalism of the highest order still lives on in Indian country, and, in fact, is evident by its incredibly diverse display among the more than 500 Indian nations still active within the United States.

A multicultural mosaic emerges just to look at Native America today—distinct languages, varieties of Creation stories, varieties of survival narratives, deep desires for self-representation. Then look at the whole of America, as the waves of migration receded, what pockets of cultures were left in the wash—a vibrant and important variety. And then incorporate the African experience in America, cultures brought and a culture re-enlivened, a dimension denied, segregated, then emergent again. Now comes the brown wave again from the South, including many indigenous people, some migrations even of whole cultures.

We all understand and fully have felt the barbaric assault upon America on September 11. That the United States had to react and pursue and punish the perpetrators of the crime was completely rational and justified, and must continue. But that horrific assault should not be used by pundits to weave arguments that can cause the diminution of the rights and freedoms and legitimate legal protections of others. We live in a multicultural society and tribal sovereignty exists and has a basis in historical fact. Multiculturalism is not a political stance, Mr. Will, it is a social demographic and long-standing reality of American Indians, Indian country, and therefore, of America.

We would like to think that the right wing, for all its faults, upheld the great virtue of tradition, that it valued the wisdom of the ages accumulated in a variety of cultures. To abandon this birthright for the homogeneous porridge of 1950s sitcoms would betray the deepest tenets of what we would like to think was the highest intellectual tradition of the conservative movement.

Manipulated Journalism Seeks to Tarnish Indian Voting
November 29, 2002

The age of manipulative journalism is certainly upon us. Remember investigative journalism, when the idea was to find out the truth? Well, it has been replaced. Manipulative journalism is becoming the norm of the times.

This is how it works. Anything about your opponent that anyone has ever criticized, no matter how spitefully or how dishonestly, is fair game for scandal mongering. Once planted anywhere, no matter by what operative or other manipulative outlet, keep spinning the rumor and exaggerate it into popular reality. Fairness be damned; accuracy be damned. Make the truth fit your particular telescope at all cost. Some call this practice "spinning," but it is really outright manipulation. It is dishonest and without scruple.

The Democrats toy with the idea but their political discourse resembles a Tower of Babel these days. It is the right wing of the Republican Party that has this practice down to a tee. The right has accomplished a communications coup of tremendous magnitude, building steam for at least ten years. There is a strongly doctrinaire approach to news and commentary that flows back and forth from *The Wall Street Journal* editorial pages to the many right-wing pundits and the hordes of talk-radio hosts—led by the ever present Rush Limbaugh—who agitate the airwaves daily and incessantly.

The latest campaign to spin a minimalist story into national truth aims to stain broad corruption onto the South Dakota Indian vote that reelected democratic U.S. Senator Tim Johnson. This was prominently and shamelessly fueled November 14, in *The Wall Street Journal*'s Review and Outlook section, under the heading, "The Oglala Sioux's Senator."

Sprinkled with phrases that would suggest fraud but without introducing any evidence whatsoever that widespread fraud had taken place, *The Wall Street Journal*'s editorial page editors once again gave indication of willing distortion and anti-Indian motivation. According to the *Journal* editorial, Senator Johnson won reelection over Republican challenger Representative John Thune, "the Chicago way."

The 2002 South Dakota senatorial race was decided in "highly suspicious, if not crooked, fashion," writes the *WSJ*, wondering out loud about the, again, "suspicious circumstances under which [Thune] lost by a mere 524 votes."

The editorial is obstinate disinformation at its best. Citing for its base a hocus-pocus statistical analysis by Michael New, billed as a postdoctoral fellow at the Harvard–MIT Data Center, it sets out to assume, against all real evidence on the ground, that fraud decided the South Dakota senatorial election. The vaunted researcher found something "fishy" in an increase of 89 percent in Indian voter turnout for Shannon County, which went overwhelmingly Democratic. New pointed out that Johnson picked up a hefty 92 percent of the votes cast by the largely Oglala Lakota voters of Shannon County. This, he exclaims, is the cause of suspicion. You want proof? Hey, this is twelve points better than Senator Tom Daschle, D-S.D., did in 1998. Definitely something fishy. That's the extent of it. This, *The Wall Street Journal* publishes as a serious fact-pattern.

The sorry editorial fails to point out, of course, that solid Democratic vote is the norm on the Pine Ridge Reservation, that in 1996 against then-senator Larry Pressler, as challenger, this same Johnson got 85 percent of the vote. Then too, in the 2000 election, 85 percent of Pine Ridge voters went for Democrat Al Gore over the Republican victor, George W. Bush. Again, it is the least of mysteries that Shannon County and the Oglala Lakota have always voted very much as a Democratic bloc. With 4,000 new Indian registered voters, turnout was up 20 percent or more in South Dakota counties neighboring reservations. Turnout skyrocketed to 44.6 percent in Shannon County (Pine Ridge Reservation), 51.8 percent in Todd County (Rosebud Reservation) and 56.7 percent in Dewey County (Cheyenne River Reservation), according to the Sioux Falls Argus Leader.

The Journal editorial brazenly implies that "Thune thinks the election was probably stolen," which Thune has not expressed directly. Given the "dubious details of how he lost," the *Journal* editorial castigated Thune for "throwing in the towel." The vanquished candidate, insisted *The Wall Street Journal*, "owed his many supporters [the demand of] a recount." It went on to claim that Thune would not because he was afraid to get "beat up by Tom Daschle's political machine."

Meanwhile, South Dakota Attorney General Mark Barnett, a Republican, denies the allegations of voter fraud, citing the miniscule examples that involved two voter-registration workers, both of whom were immediately fired. Barnett, who expects to indict one registration worker, assigned thirty agents to review the issue in every county where possible misconduct could have occurred. Even before the election, Barnett's office identified fifteen irregular absentee-ballot applications, while reviewing as many as 1,750 absentee-ballot applications. Signatures on suspect ballot applications are verified with the specific voter it belongs to. *The Wall Street Journal* claimed that "Thune's lawyers have affidavits from about fifty people attesting to voting irregularities, including from four Indians saying they were each paid $10 to vote." Barnett has asked to know the source of their information, which he labels, "rumor."

Attorney General Barnett is joined by South Dakota Secretary of State Joyce Hazeltine, also Republican, in attesting that there were no problems or improprieties during the voting. In fact, they asserted, no election-day complaints were filed with the state and there was no evidence that the highly publicized but minor incidences of fraud in any way tainted the vote. Lawyers from both parties were on hand in Shannon County on Election Day.

In typical "piling-on" fashion, other right-wing ideologues have jumped on the fraudulent Indian vote bandwagon. The conservative magazine *National Review* commented on the fraud potential of the so-called bilingual voting factor even before the election. An article titled "Lost in Translation: Bilingual voting and the South Dakota Senate race," October 22, by Jim Boulet Jr., assumes as reality a South Dakota "Indian reservation voter-registration scandal." Boulet, executive director of "English First," goes on to make a convoluted claim of potential would-be fraud by translators who assist non-English–speaking Indians.

Boulet's point is that since "many Indian languages lack written alphabets." This means their bilingual ballots are actually cast via oral translation." Translators working with non-English–speaking Indians are thus prone to conduct fraudulent voting schemes with groups of Indians. Boulet's assumption, quickly becoming an across-the-board factuality for right-wing pundits—is that the voting fraud on reservations "has happened."

Boulet writes, "Given these two facts, all anyone needs to sway this year's South Dakota Senate race is a list of fraudulently registered Indian voters, a willingness to round up a few Indians, and a bus to bring them to a polling place. The person with the registration list then claims to be translating for each person in the group and helps them cast their ballots for the candidate of his choice under the names registered earlier."

Recognizable hogwash, this kind of editorializing is grist for the scandal mill of manipulative journalism. Pile on enough innuendo through the printed media and soon there is enough for the right-wing talk-radio hosts to belabor the lie ad nauseam. The lie this time, eagerly activated and pursued by

The Wall Street Journal before, is that Indians are easily corruptible. The implied insult: Indians are too stupid to vote independently.

Now, this is truth:

The South Dakota victory of Senator Tim Johnson, obviously produced by a highly effective voter-registration campaign among Indian voters, is a grand and glorious chapter in American democracy. It marks one of those rare times when the national electoral process has actually rewarded Native participation and it should be a great source of pride for every American. The right-wing campaign now afoot to besmirch it is vindictive and un-American. That *The Wall Street Journal* editorial board has chosen to lead this manipulative, slanderous bandwagon is a point of continual shame for a newspaper that has now lost any and all credibility on American Indian issues. The man who ran the editorial page since 1972, the highly respected Robert Leroy Bartley, is now ending his active career. It's a shame that his colleagues are sending him out on such a low note.

Asked *The Wall Street Journal* editorial in increasingly recognizable bigot-baiting style, "But how many smoke signals does it take to wonder if there's also fire?" We might ask a similar question of *The Wall Street Journal*'s senior editors. How is it that every time you put ink to paper on American Indian issues you lower the discourse?

TIME Has Slanted View of Indian Country
December 13, 2002

Make no mistake Indian country, in a cyclical repeat of American history another attack on tribal rights is coming on full steam. The long, hard fight for the hearts and minds of the American public on the economic reconstruction of Indian country is not yet guaranteed—not by a long shot. Brace for it, strategize collectively, dedicate and apply significant resources, develop national campaigns to get tribal perspectives heard, get ready to fight the forthcoming media stampede to ridicule and misrepresent this new era of Indian economic recovery. Every experienced tribal leader cognizant of America's legacy of distorting Indian history and of taking Indian assets knew this day would come, again.

In the national media, once a certain tack on coverage is taken by two or more of the heavyweights, the herd instinct is to follow. *TIME* magazine, a venerable weekly, just launched the latest and most concentrated anti-Indian rights hatchet job imaginable in its December 16 cover story, "Look Who's Cashing In At Indian Casinos," billed as a "special investigation" by Donald L. Barlett and James B. Steele. The thirteen-page spread serves up a barrage of negativity about Indian gaming as an economic motor for Indian country. A thick layer of antitribal attitude permeates this salvo of a story, which is intended to prove, once and for all, that Indian peoples and their self-governance rights are unfair, corrupt, and inept. The piece gives such a negative take on tribal reality that it seems strategically intended to directly challenge the positive concept of hard-won tribal gains.

Indian country can expect this negative onslaught to build up over the next few seasons. It is set to spearhead the justification for great new federal intrusion on Indian life. Of course, Barlett and Steele are already parading through the media as the new Indian experts. Enemies of Indian country gaming under tribal sovereign rights are quickly sharpening their knives.

TIME's attack goes all out. All the current tricks of polemical journalism are evident. The main premise is that speculators and non-Indians are getting rich off Indian rights. The inside summary to the same piece reiterates the argument: "So why are the white backers of Indian gambling raking in millions while many tribes continue to struggle in poverty?" This is nonsense. The tone and inaccurate approach do not deviate throughout the whole story. There is no other possible interpretation, according to *TIME*, which here publishes a cover story shamelessly out of context and out of balance.

The article makes much of the fact that non-Native backers of tribes often make a great deal of money while getting certain tribes going in gaming. So what? Is this not what investors do throughout all business? In all cases we know of, the tribes set goals to pay off the investors and obviously many do quite well after their start-up investors are paid off.

The assumption is that the tribes are getting ripped off.

TIME complains that despite casinos, there is still Indian poverty; it irks *TIME* that some tribes are better prepared or better situated than others. But these are accidents of geographic location and also depend on a particular tribe's leadership and human resources. But it also misses the big picture. American Indian governments are sovereign entities.

TIME charges that the gaming option produces "hundreds of millions of dollars to one Indian tribe with a few dozen members—and not a penny to a tribe with hundreds of thousands of members." Again, a small tribe with few members has opportunities that tribes from more isolated areas don't have. The only tribe with hundreds of thousands of population that does not run gaming is the Navajo Nation, which, for religious and other reasons, voted not to set up tribal gaming. Again, where is the problem with that? The difference is only in geography and in the Navajos' own free, democratic choice. But the article assumes something is socially and perhaps even legally unfair in this reality. Nonsense again.

This poor rendition of journalistic sleight of hand tends to reduce the

Indian world to anecdotes that freeze-frame and greatly stereotype what is actually a far more complex, diverse, and dynamic reality.

Several anomalies in the national scene, such as the one-member tribe in California that set up a casino and still receives federal aid, get much play in the piece. The same article that bemoans the general poverty of Indian people complains, "that the tribes collect millions in aid from American taxpayers." However, it does not explain that these are the many tribes that are not in gaming-rich situations. Some Native nations, such as Oneida Nation, actually turn back federal funds no longer needed, and request these be distributed to more needful tribes. And the article completely misses a core principle of the Indian Gaming Regulatory Act, which makes Indian gaming 100 percent taxed since the earnings are mandated for tribal government services. And American Indians who receive per-capita payments from gaming revenues pay taxes on all their earnings. How could two purportedly acclaimed journalists miss those basic facts?

Whether about Indian gaming or any other context where federal law establishes specific avenues for Indian self-governance, *TIME*'s reductionist journalism in this instance will greatly reinforce an overall image—and impact—intended to diminish the Indian reality. To do this, of course, it can go and find its share of contradictory, ornery, ridiculous, and questionable Indian situations. *Indian Country Today* has reported on most all of *TIME*'s examples and many more for years. This is not difficult given there are more than 550 American Indian nations, each with its own unique social and political dynamics and, sometimes, dysfunctions. Certainly, these are out there and, certainly too, a false construct can be put together by highlighting and stringing together just a few—but such an approach only provides a distorted view of a much larger reality that intersects on culture, tribal identity, and membership, and which, for lack of experience, *TIME* ignores.

The American Indian world is an amalgam of many currents and identities; tribal nations have very specific histories and cultural imperatives. Since tribal sovereignty, an inherent political reality and assertion, became the dominant concept in tribal aspirations in the past thirty years, however, liberals and conservatives alike have seen the Indian litany of victimhood complaints turn increasingly to social-political victories in education, cultural recovery, and now economics. The opportunity to secure capital bases from which to rebuild the nations is certainly not without its pitfalls and horror stories, but it is the big story of Indian country the past ten years. We contend that it is a largely positive, very incomplete story that is yet in its early stages. A decade of economic movement is nothing compared to the history of American conquest and its severe disruptions and outright thefts of American Indian assets.

To be fair, some issues raised in *TIME*'s critique are on the mark. It is true that, "Montana, Nevada, North Dakota, Oklahoma and South Dakota account for less than three percent of all casino proceeds," yet they account for half of the Indian population. For these tribes, "[o]n average, they produce the equivalent of about $400 in revenue per Indian [person]." Then there is the reality of heavy-handedness on the part of some leadership, the usual range of corrupt politicians, (and the usual range of prosecution and clean up).

The issue of growing economic disparity in Indian country is most important. *TIME* made its points in this regard, and no doubt it needs addressing. But attempts to address this disparity are already a hot topic in Indian country. At all times and for all peoples, the natural tendency for those with new capital is to amass, to learn to compete, and to use whatever legal tools are available. As experience with capital matures, at its best, it works to establish the most adept institutions and to develop a social contract worthy of a hopeful community future. Many successful Indian governments are going in this direction, while some are not yet there. This is being accomplished through the development of American Indian financial institutions, banks, community and Aboriginal capital-development corporations, and through the creation of foundations and collective and private philanthropy. Philanthropy, in the Indian context of nation building, is not just passing out money, but is also the funding of useful and well-managed projects, some profit making, some not, that are productive for the tribal society and, when possible, for the mainstream.

This is a hugely important goal for Indian country leadership. East and West Coast Native nations with increasingly well-founded financial resources might consider setting up developmental and philanthropic program models. These might include "no tribe left behind" foundation initiatives, with programs to support projects in education (youth and colleges), economics (lands, business, international Indian trade and commerce), health (community clinics, maternal care), governance, and cultural enhancement. This tradition of sharing would go a long way in generating much-needed common goals within the national Indian currents and causes. California has one model for sharing by gaming to nongaming tribes; many tribes donate to one another. Some eastern tribes such as the Pequot, Mohegan, and Oneida have donated tens of millions to tribal and national Indian cultural institutions. When White Mountain Apaches suffered devastating fire losses, a California Mission Tribe sent them a million dollars.

But these and far more numerous on-the-ground developments that constitute the visible results of the Indian economic recovery, largely based on Indian gaming, curiously did not make it into *TIME*'s frame of reference.

Virulent antagonism such as displayed by the *TIME* cover story should serve as a wake-up call to Indian country leadership. Indian country needs to address some troubling issues, but it also needs constantly to find its bases of unity and stick to them, in the face of media willingness to manufacture perspectives to exploit internal Indian contradictions. Question always whether the intent of the journalism is to diminish the tribal base, or to help build and strengthen it.

No doubt, appreciating the positive trends of the past ten years requires a deeper understanding of the intensity of the destitution suffered by Indian peoples, how much worse things were just thirty years ago, even ten years ago. To so wantonly now attack these legally instituted financial trends in Indian country is to work to reverse important restitutional policies and processes. To do as *TIME* magazine and even some myopic Indian commentators suggest is to help break the back of the only hopeful major economic initiative to grace Indian country since the colonies and later the United States began their coast-to-coast sweep across Indian country. First our lands. Then our natural resources. Followed by successive legislative and judicial waves to destroy the powers and authorities of our Indian governments. And now our markets. It has become an all too familiar story.

However, the lesson for Indian country is clear. Unity and mutual respect is a high priority, a requirement for any collective national strategy to retain tribal powers. A trend is visible in this direction, as most tribes can and do benefit in various ways from recent economic developments. Indian leadership has become increasingly astute and is better resourced to be responsive to both the great needs that remain in tribal America and the threats that emanate from misinformation campaigns such as those generated by *TIME*.

How to improve the conditions for American Indians nationally while respecting each tribe's sovereignty is already a loud conversation in Indian country. One simply needs to hang around long enough to hear it. Apparently, *TIME's* fledgling Indian country reporters did not have enough time for that.

Robert Novak Needs to Apologize to Indian Voters
January 30, 2004

National political commentator Robert Novak is being wrongheaded even beyond his conservative partisanship. On the national level he is in hot water for "outing" a respectable U.S. intelligence professional who was required to work incognito and whose career he essentially destroyed. In that case, Novak was playing footsies with the vindictive climate at the

White House, letting himself and his profession be used to wreak vengeance on the wife of a perceived political enemy, regardless of her record of service to the country. Later, Novak would cheapen the finest of journalistic ethical arguments—the privacy of sources—to protect his handler within the administration.

Now, out of the blue, Novak resurrects a well-demolished rumor: that South Dakota Senator Tim Johnson's election to the U.S. Senate in 2002 over Republican candidate John Thune was fraudulently "stolen by stuffing ballot boxes on Indian reservations." Novak made these remarks January 6 while appearing on CNN's *Crossfire*. Novak had already made a similar remark on *Crossfire*, December 13, declaring: "The Indians, they got the phony Indian votes out there."

Returning to the subject on the January 13 edition of "The Capital Gang," Novak refused to apologize and continued to stand by his remarks, though he retreated considerably in the language used and now pretends he did not say what he in fact said. He has dropped the openly racial language, but continues to contend that, "very serious voting irregularities," took place.

Which is scurrilous nonsense. No fraud or even "serious" voting irregularities took place, and no votes were cast in the election as a result of problems with voter registration. Everyone who needs to in South Dakota knows that and many across the political spectrum, from Democrats to Republicans, including John Thune, the opponent who lost the election (Thune lost in 2000; won in 2004 against Tom Daschle. Ed.), responded negatively to Novak's accusation. Novak is besmirching Indian political participation, just as reservation voter-registration drives are attracting Indian people to vote in elections, often deciding close contests.

What happened was this: Republican John Thune lost the 2002 senatorial election by 524 votes, a margin of victory attributed by Democratic candidate Tim Johnson and most everyone else to the Indian swing vote coming from the state's nine reservations. The superlative Indian voter turnout was due in large measure to a Democratic Party registration drive strongly supported by Senator Tom Daschle, D-S.D.

Three actual incidents involving three registration workers came quickly to light. In one, a man from Rapid City farmed out voter registration to friends who worked from a phone book to fill out the required forms. In a second incident, Rebecca Red Earth-Villeda, an independent contractor to the Democratic Party, is accused of handing in applications for absentee ballots that had forged signatures on them. This all happened in the registration phase and not at election time.

South Dakota Secretary of State Chris Nelson, a Republican, confirms that no illegal votes were cast as a result of the very limited voter-registration problems. "There were no stuffed ballot boxes in South Dakota's 2002 election," Nelson told the *Rapid City Journal*. "We all know there were attempts at voter registration fraud. I am confident our county auditors and the law enforcement of this state were able to stop that and that no illegal ballots were cast."

The condemnation of Novak for resurrecting the slander was pretty universal in South Dakota. Thune's current campaign manager, Dick Wadhams, called Novak's remarks "inappropriate [and] off the mark." Republican Governor Mike Rounds said he found Novak's remarks "ignorant." Randy Frederick, South Dakota's GOP Chairman called Novak's assertions "appalling" and "insane." And to repeat, according to Republican Nelson: "No illegal ballots were cast."

To be generous, we suggest perhaps Mr. Novak hit that easy trap that propagandists big and small often stumble into, believing their own politically exaggerated sources whose sole purpose has been media spin designed to besmirch perceived enemies. The way Novak's sources worked in this instance takes a page from Al Franken's description of the derivative journalism attack methods now regularly used by operatives of the Winged Right.

On October 22, the *National Review* ran an article titled "Lost in Translation: bilingual voting and the South Dakota Senate race," by Jim Boulet Jr., which assumes as reality a South Dakota "Indian reservation voter-registration scandal." Boulet, executive director of "English First," goes on to make a convoluted claim of potential would-be fraud by translators who assist non-English-speaking Indians. It is nonsense to the charges bandied about, but it opens the gate.

November 14, *The Wall Street Journal* weighs in, in its Review and Outlook section, under the heading, "The Oglala Sioux's Senator." The *Journal* asserts that Senator Johnson won reelection over Republican challenger Representative John Thune "the Chicago way." The 2002 South Dakota senatorial race, it claims, was decided in "highly suspicious, if not crooked, fashion," noting the, "suspicious circumstances under which [Thune] lost by a mere 524 votes."

Then, on December 23, the *National Review* runs as its cover story the supposed expos of the mythical stolen election based entirely on a Republican collection of affidavits from voters, which was already discredited as fraudulent itself. The piece was replete with cited problems that convinced none of the people involved. State Attorney General Mark Barnett, himself a Republican, denounced the *National Review* story by Byron York as "shoddy, irresponsible, sensationalistic and garbage." But the right-wing media hoop had come full circle. A record of so-called fraud, well spun to sling out into media space. Novak clearly loaded his cannon from such sources.

Novak backs up his assertion of fraud, dismissed in unusual nonpartisan consensus, by blaming even the South Dakota Republican Party for not confirming his shaky misinformation. Novak claims GOP officials declined to protest the irregularities "for political purposes." Novak backtracks (like a fox) on the "stuffed ballots" statement, but shifts to blame the South Dakota Republicans for not backing him up. That they will not do so is much to their credit. They understand that fraud is not an issue and that the Indian swing vote is a reality.

Both political parties in this case actually acted quickly to quell any misinformation put out by their own overzealous or corrupted operatives. While the Democrats fielded and caught several fringe registration workers that were willing to fake voter registrations, on the other hand, as reported in an *Indian Country Today* story by David Melmer, ("Voter fraud charges in South Dakota prove fraudulent," Vol. 22 Iss. 29), "Republican attorneys fanned out across the state on Election Day November 6 to gather affidavits to show voting irregularities. Now the most serious of those affidavits have been found to be fraudulent themselves. Republican State Attorney General Mark Barnett said of the fifty affidavits the Republican operatives collected, only three alleged criminal activity, and two of those "proved to be false." The Republican group had "drawn up stock affidavits with blanks for the signature and then went looking for people to sign them."

It wasn't pretty but it was business as usual. Yet, both parties went on to clean up and safeguard their approaches. And it was, after all, a Republican Secretary of State who declared: "No illegal ballots were cast."

"Stuffed ballots" Novak still needs to be questioned and consistently on his comments about voter fraud on South Dakota Indian reservations. This kind of off-handed slap at American Indian integrity has to be challenged. If, as he claims, he "did not intend any bias against Native Americans," then why take such casual approach to insulting a whole people, calling their honest attempt to vote into question?

If you ask us, Novak really needs to clarify his statements. He needs to apologize.

Educate America or Perish Is Challenge for Indian Country
November 12, 2004

High on the reading list of the Web site of One Nation, the anti-Indian organization, is the article titled, "Schwarzenegger, Tribes on Collision," by Alan Murray of CNBC. The main thrust of the article is to cheer on the terminator-governor from California as he shakes down the tribes for all they are worth.

That's the opportunistic focus on one coast. Elsewhere in the country, United Property Owners of Redmond, Washington, has announced that they will be merging with One Nation of Oklahoma to form a new nonpartisan anti-Indian organization called One Nation United. The new organization states it will have approximately 300,000 members in all fifty states. New York will be represented on the One Nation United Advisory Board by David Vickers, president of anti-Indian organization Upstate Citizens for Equality.

The news is a reminder of the steady stirring by anti-Indian groups nationally. One Nation is the Oklahoma-based portion of the nationally fast-growing coalition of organizations intent on the destruction of tribal freedom throughout the United States. Wrapping themselves in the American flag, these groups seek to gain both a national profile and national influence. At this time in history, given the trend toward majority excesses and the tenuous support for Indian positions in federal courts, this is a movement that is poised to become seriously dangerous to Indian governments. Indian country leadership dismisses it at its own peril.

The enemy's argument against Indian tribal rights, and particularly against the sovereign jurisdictions asserted by American Indian nations, is being finely honed. The modern anti-Indian movement has been brewing for more than thirty years: from small groups of non-Indian reservation residents clamoring to start enclaves of state jurisdiction within Indian land; to the hue and cry of convenience-store operators near reservations who must compete with separate tax bases; to the toothy grins of the state governors, legislatures, and municipalities positioning in the good old American dance to secure for themselves Indian property or the jurisdiction thereof.

In America circa 2004, public metaphor is everything. One Nation and other groups that need someone to attack, joined to the politicians of various states, are now onto something: the power of the Indian image in the American mind can perhaps be damaged and reversed: from legitimate governments comprised of the first peoples and rightful property owners of this land, to greedy, special-interest casino kingpins. Say it and portray the seedy image enough times, it becomes the overriding public metaphor, one that will last a long time. The antagonist idea is to denigrate Indian jurisdiction in the public mind, paint the American Indian as getting a free ride, as conniving and thievish, and you can get a measure passed against them!

Here is how the danger grows. The anti-Indian movement is shopping for a national voice and face. Much like the National Rifle Association gained tremendously from the voice and face of Charlton Heston, so can the anti-Indian movement gain from the recognizable voice and face of someone, say, such as Arnold Schwarzenegger. This would be (perhaps already is) a huge escalation of the Indian profile problem. But this is only a tactical problem. Like the Democrats who have not been able to get ahead of the Republican game plan for two elections now, Indian tribes will progressively lose in the court of public opinion and ultimately in legislatures and Congress, unless they think ahead of this growing problem. There is still time, but as the California experience reveals, events can turn on a dime.

While Indian enemies envision the complete deconstruction of Indian sovereign bases, the fight over Congress, and by extension, over the hearts and minds of the American public, becomes paramount. Remember John Kerry's "flip-flop" image, how, true or not, it stuck. Again, that was just a tactic. The damage was done through a public relations strategy built on repeated innuendo. The same is happening to Indian issues. It is not fair and follows no logic but manipulates anger and intends to diminish any gains by Native tribes. Thus, the push is on to portray the tribes as lobbying nightmares, enclaves of values-less societies rolling in ill-gained casino dollars. This is cultural preparation for the political kill. It's the swift-boat attack of the Indian issue polemic: Indians as "rip-offs," "cheats," corrupt lobbyists as "special interests," as impediments to American unity. The only thing in the way is that pesky American Indian sovereignty and "properties" over which these phony governments exercise control.

American Indian nations beware. This is not about a fight between the rich gaming tribes and the poorer, big-land tribes. Indians fighting Indians is not, once again, the inherent contradiction (although plenty will promote such). The response to the anti-Indian movement is not in pitting one group of tribes against another. The solution is in the active defense of the overall interests of all of Indian country. The solution is in the gaming-rich tribes leading a major—hugely major—national television and print educational initiative to introduce this current moment in the history of the tribal nations to America and to educate the American people about who Indian people are, what they know, and what they mean to this land. The overall humanity of Native people needs to be emphasized and the place and role of gaming in the overall uplifting of many, but not all, Indian economies must be explained and made acceptable and understood by the American public.

Most of all, such campaigns must let America see and hear from and get to know the core personalities and values of Indian America. Always stressing that which is real, they must engage the public mind at all times, in all the major venues where the world of American Indian people can be presented. It must present the Native family and the wisdom of the most superlative of Native ways when properly applied to the building of family and community. It must present the American Indian military presence, the proud veterans, what they gave and give and what they aspire. And certainly such a campaign would be structured and launched most successfully on the foundation of a discernable American Indian philanthropy, in the context of an Indian country where the financially strong tribe is best recognized and admired who extents a helping investment to the less fortunate tribes also seeking self-sufficiency.

Such a public media campaign would gather the best of Indian talent and strategic and creative thinking and install the best of Indian communications talent in the circle of the most respected media renowned among the friends of Indian country. Such a campaign, to succeed, must be done actively and proactively, starting now, week by week, venue by venue. This is the most important task facing the collective Indian country, because the elements of active destruction are growing, they are consistently meeting, improving their rhetoric, honing their arguments, making strategic alliances, positioning themselves closest to the American flag and to the American mission. When their moment comes, they will be ready and the attack will be thunderous. The campaign to dislocate the Indian image in the public mind and relegate it to the outer edges of American consciousness—along with other "troublemakers" or anti-American elements—puts in peril the Indian generations. Indians must do that one better. We need to cover the same ground much, much better, much more consistently, with better quality, and, most importantly, with the truth.

There are positive, negative, confusing, and simply neutral media stereotypes. American Indians have suffered them all and, of all of them, the one most closely tied to reality, even when romanticized and overused, is the American Indian as "caretaker" of these lands. That national image of American Indians, particularly as captured and projected through the 1970s and 1980s, rested on a sense of spiritual integrity the public sustained about Indian cultures and particularly Indian elders. This is an important public image for any people to enjoy and to consider. It is an image that still lingers in the mind's eye of most of the American public, slowly clouded and wrapped over by the casino and high-roller image, but nevertheless still palpable. It is still based on substantial reality and remains a potential factor to revitalize—with more precise intention—to once again reach into the hearts and minds of the American public.

Indian country cannot afford to wait for this latest termination trend to walk in its front door. There are more than enough lessons in the history of the United States to teach us that these threats to our inherent and hard-preserved freedoms require the utmost vigilance and defense.

Respect Native Women—Stop Using the S-Word
February 28, 2001

Suzan Shown Harjo, *Indian Country Today*

The women's sports teams at St. Bonaventure University were once called the Brown Squaws. The men's teams at the school in upstate New York were called the Brown Indians.

"We were so proud to be Squaws," a former Bonaventure sportswoman told me, on the condition that her name would not be used. "I'm ashamed of it now, but it was part of my identity—it made us feel equal to the men.

"Then a Seneca chief and clan mothers came over from the reservation and asked us to stop using the name, because it meant vagina. We almost died of embarrassment. Of course, we stopped using it immediately."

It was in 1975 that the Seneca delegation visited the players and coaches at St. Bonaventure. It was in the same year that the school retired Brown Squaw, without fanfare or publicity, without being begged or sued. It responded to a dignified request to remove an indecency by doing so, quietly and quickly.

Since then, Native peoples have succeeded in removing the s-word from hundreds of places and things, but the dialogue is not as civil today as it was twenty-five years ago. Polite requests often are met with even more name-calling—liars and politically correct whiners are the usual ones.

I was a guest on a 1992 *Oprah Winfrey Show* on the topic of stereotypes and explained why the viewers should stop using the s-word. For years afterward, I was stopped in airports, restaurants, and other public places by people (mostly non-Native women) who thanked me for educating them about the word and said they had stopped using it and had told others to do the same.

The only negative reaction was from a Smithsonian "Indian expert" (isn't there always a government-paid "Indian expert"), who has since insisted to anyone who would listen that squaw only means young girl, in a language that no one living speaks fluently.

What do the real Indian experts say? Women and men who are fluent in the pertinent Native languages say that the s-word and variations of it are in several tribal languages of the Algonquian and Iroquoian linguistic stocks. They are descriptive words for a woman's genitalia.

The s-word was not and is not used by Native peoples to describe, address, or stand for a woman herself. In the 1600s and 1700s, European trappers began calling all women by that term. English dictionaries cleaned it up, defining it as an Indian wife or woman, or as a jocular reference for any kind of wife.

White men who married or consorted with Indian women were called squawmen by their brethren. It did not mean that the woman was the belle of the ball or that the man had married well. In American literature, movies, and cartoons, the s-word always means the dumb, dumpy, loose, old, and/or ugly thing walking ten paces behind a man. It never means that the woman in question is smart, stunning, or a sweetheart.

In 2000, as the Maine legislature was considering a law to drop the s-word from all place-names in the state, 20/20 host Barbara Walters and correspondent John Stossel derided the effort in a "Give Me A Break" segment. The bill's cosponsor, Representative Donna Loring, Penobscot, said the "name is offensive to us and we feel that, if the name is offensive and abusive, then change it."

"There is, by no means, unanimity in the Indian community about the name," claimed Stossel, who predicted that "tourists looking at maps won't find the ski resort, plus taxpayers have to pay to change all the signs." The Maine bill was passed in the legislature and signed into law less than one month after the broadcast.

Despite the sniping, Native peoples are enjoying steady success in removing the s-word. Native and non-Native women in Oregon initiated a movement in 1992 that resulted in squawfish being eliminated as an official name for the endangered pikeminnow.

A cross-cultural coalition convinced the U.S. Board on Geographic Names in 1997 to change the name of Squaw Gulch in the Klamath National Forest in California to Taritsi, which means "Indian woman" in the language of the Shasta Tribe.

Last year, after Forrest Cuch, Ute, drew attention to shot glasses that sported the s-word, their distributor not only took them off the market, he apologized for the offense. Cuch, who directs Utah's division of Indian affairs, is promoting a renaming measure for places throughout the state. Arizona's was the first legislature to see the introduction of a statewide bill, sponsored by Representative Jack Jackson, Navajo, in 1992, but it did not make it to the governor's desk.

Minnesota was the first state, in 1995, to establish a law to remove the s-word from all its sites, followed by Montana in 1999 and Oklahoma in 2000. Nebraska has changed some place-names and one in Colorado is under consideration for change.

Credit for the victory in Minnesota belongs to the Ojibwe and other students at the Cass Lake-Bena High School who started the Name Change Committee, which remains a force in activities nationwide. Montana Representative Carol Juneau, Blackfeet, spearheaded the effort in her state and Red Rock Mayor Geary Watson, Choctaw, inspired the Oklahoma law.

In Canada, the government of British Columbia announced at the end of 2000 that it would rename all places in the province that use the s-word. It had already been dropped from other Canadian geographic locations in Alberta, Prince Edward Island, Saskatchewan, and the Yukon.

Legislation to eliminate the s-word statewide is pending in Idaho and South Dakota. Prospects are good for both bills, which are supported broadly by tribal and state officials. The Idaho Senate just passed its bill with only one naysayer, who wondered aloud if the Indian tribes would compensate private businesses for any losses from the re-designations.

Words to the wise: it's best to avoid talk of making Native peoples pay for anything associated with this degradation and to get on with the business of doing the right thing. Respect Native women and drop the s-word.

Taking Back America/David Horowitz on (and on and on) Indians

May 20, 2002

Suzan Shown Harjo, *Indian Country Today*

The rallying cry for today's white movement of disparate interests, from the genteel and well-heeled white supremacists to the skinheads and crackers, is "Let's take back America!" They look down on each other, but are united by the thinking that the country is overrun by racial and ethnic minorities and needs to be reclaimed.

The clever people in the white movement do not talk about it that way. They say they want the government and everybody to stop counting, hiring, or making decisions about anyone on the basis of race (that is to say, anyone else's race).

The "take back America" crowd has shamelessly and illogically claimed the catastrophic events of 9-11 as a justification of their agenda, which they disguise in such civil-rights terms as "equal opportunity" and "level playing field." But anyone who has been on the receiving end of bigotry can detect it through the code words and secret handshakes.

The Indian item on their agenda is plain: abolish Indian treaties, tribal governments and jurisdictions, Indian status property, and federal trust laws.

One of the white movement's best politicians is author David Horowitz.

He started off the new century by lobbing incendiary devices on seventy college campuses in the form of provocative ads opposing reparations for slavery, then feigned surprise at the predictable response. In a February 21 speech at Villanova University in Pennsylvania, he called this an "experiment to see if you could address an issue which the left thinks is vital to its cause and an issue involving race, and engage in a civil dialogue about it."

One of the loudest of the 1960s Berkeley leftists, Horowitz has since denounced his former politics and friends with a level of animus more commonly seen in hotly contested divorces. Mentor to conservative soul mates, including author Ann Coulter, he makes a living taking potshots at everyone in the world, except fellow wing nuts, then squeals at the mildest backfire.

Horowitz says he is now "the subject of a national hate campaign." He says the real issue was "Do we as citizens—black, white, whatever—owe a debt to this country? After 9-11, we all have an understanding for why this matters. All America understands this, because every American who is not black can be the target of an attack like this."

It is likely that playwright Edward Albee had just such a whiner in mind when he rewrote the nursery rhyme line as, "Georgie, Porgie, Put Upon Pie."

In the body of his speech at Villanova, Native peoples were not even a footnote, merely a gratuitous swipe along the way to another point: "Black people are the oldest Americans. I mean, the oldest are probably the Indians—it's politically correct to call them Native Americans—except they don't consider themselves Americans. They think they have independent nations."

When Horowitz finished his speech, a white student asked this question: "I was talking to some University of Penn students yesterday—and I'm a big-time pro-American, I love America—and this black guy comes up to me and says, 'What about the Indians, what about the slaves?'—all these bad things America's done. But, what are some good answers I can tell him, because we did some pretty bad things to the Indians."

Horowitz interrupted the student with a diatribe about Indians: "One of the worst things we did for the Indians was setting them up in independent nations on these reservations where they, you know, live in absolute squalor and alcoholism and what not."

There it was again, Horowitz mocking tribal sovereignty and nationhood, which is inherent and recognized in U.S. law, as some foolish Indian notion or failed federal program. He continued, dismissing other factors that led to conditions of poverty and dysfunction:

> There is no nation on Earth—black, white, whatever it is—that wasn't built on a conquest. The tragedy of the American settle-

ment is one of the less embarrassing tragedies, if I can put it that way, of the founding of nations. A third of the Indians, for example, died of probably smallpox before the Pilgrims ever landed, because European sailors had landed on—and, you know, they had smallpox and the Indians got it—and they didn't have any immunity to it.

The Indians paid us back, by the way, by spreading syphilis to Europe. Are we going to blame the Indians 'cause we got syphilis because they had it first?

Where to start? The Europeans sailors and their rats and fleas lurched upon our shores with smallpox, plague, influenza, measles, mumps, tuberculosis, and syphilis. Syphilis was rampant in Europe. More than ten years ago, scientists found the oldest evidence of syphilis anywhere in the world, in Greece, a few thousand years before 1492.

The European diseases quickly spread throughout the Western Hemisphere, wiping out whole nations—500 at a minimum—and nearly obliterating hundreds more. No one knows how many Native people died from the foreign diseases or were murdered or were killed in battle.

It's a cold point Horowitz makes that, because many succumbed to disease, it was "less embarrassing" and the "tragedy of this encounter" was that Indians were "a Stone Age people." Horowitz knows better than that, but it's a point that appeals to the sense of racial superiority and Manifest Destiny in the white movement.

"I happen to have written a book about the early Indian wars, so I know what I'm talking about here," he said.

Oh, well, the white guy wrote a book and that makes him an Indian expert. In a very young child, such arrogance piled atop so much ignorance might be laughable. In a grown-up—especially in a setting where students may believe his distortions are our reality—the combination is anti-intellectual and dangerous.

Horowitz kept talking. He was a film critic, recommending the racially biased, inaccurate "Black Robe" as "wonderful." He was a medical researcher, concluding that "Indians are genetically prone to alcoholism." He opined (wrongly) on the decline of animal populations and Indian economies.

In mid-rant, he seemed to remember the question:

Where there really bad things done? You know, everybody knows the smallpox in the blankets. Were Indian treaties betrayed? Well, of course. This was an expanding civilization. The Indians had a static one. They needed huge areas of land, you know, they practically exterminated the buffalo, also, by running them off cliffs.

Ah, Indians were the ones who nearly drove the buffalo to extinction. So, those 7,500,000 buffalo that the U.S. Army estimated that white hunters killed between 1872 and 1874 alone were just part of a little herd-thinning program.

And Horowitz went on and on, still responding to the same question.

When people come at you like that, what they're doing is picking one little piece of the puzzle. You might say, you know, what have the Indians—you know, there are three million Indians, almost as many now as there were at the time of the settlement. I hate to say this, but if you want to throw something in their face, you know, what have the Indians produced in the last 300 years but casinos?

For starters, Native people have produced an extraordinary body of fine art and a literary and legal canon that is particularly impressive in light of what was going on contemporaneously. We can only imagine what might have been produced if white supremacists had not murdered some of our greatest visionaries, brainwashed and tortured generations of our children, stolen our treaty-guaranteed land and water, and destroyed our natural economies.

"If you really care about Indian people," said Horowitz, "you will want to get them off the reservation and into the American economy. ... You want them to learn how to speak good English. ... "

At long last, he wrapped it up, demonstrating his own mastery of the language:

Uh, you know, people who want—you know, uh, Indian culture—it's nice in museums, it's probably nice, you know, around the campfire, but, uh, you know, it's not—in a computer age, it's not going to bring these people into a world where they can enjoy, uh, you know, the pleasures that, from the looks of you, most of the people in this room do enjoy.

After a few more questions and shorter answers, it was over. One of the student hosts thanked Horowitz and sent the audience off with, of course, "Let's take back America!"

Chapter Six
Hemispheric Indigenous: The Americas

The memory of Columbus and the symbol of his enterprise binds and braids the Indian peoples' historical sense of the Americas. From the conferences on the indigenous at the United Nations over thirty years, many relations, congresses, and gatherings among representatives of indigenous communities, north and south, have multiplied and deepened. Maya altars of traditional prayers and Maya aspirations to increased political power within Guatemala and Mexico are comparable to tribal hopes in North America, for example among the Iroquois in the United States and Canada. Northern Indians are interested in their southern relatives and not a few North American tribes have relations, projects, and investments in Venezuela, Ecuador, Peru, and Bolivia, among other countries, where indigenous populations are flexing muscle. Conversely, the North American diaspora gathers immigrants from many Native nations, many of whom increasingly maintain their indigenous language and cultural traditions.

Columbus: The Christ-Bearing Colonizer

October 25, 2000

Given the actual (and prophetic) meaning of the name Christopher Columbus, which literally means "Christ-bearing colonizer," perhaps nothing would have made a difference.

Perhaps, as many historians claim, there was nothing Columbus or anyone could have done differently to change the course of history.

Until just a few years ago, Columbus was the epitome of heroism in the Western Hemisphere. Mariner, explorer, adventurer, settler, he cut a swath of action celebrated throughout the Americas. Countries, capitals, and counties, even spaceships were named after him. Native people, of course, have known and have experienced for generations the most negative of results of that history, but, by and large, the American republics unabashedly celebrated Columbus' memory.

That changed in 1992, when the planned 500-year celebratory party was heavily crashed by the concentrated response of the indigenous peoples of the Western Hemisphere.

By 1992, American Indians had logged fifteen years and millions of flying miles in the international circuit. Once the most removed and isolated of peoples, by virtue of kinship recognition, great persistence, and similarity of issues, Native networks had grown exponentially. But the anti-Columbus quincentennial organizing generated an explosion of Indian communication and political-action participation unequalled in hemispheric history.

Among its results have been Indian movements in Ecuador and Bolivia that have become important national factors. The International Decade of Indigenous Peoples is another result. The outreach via Indian networks employed by the Zapatista movement in Mexico that generated instantaneous response was greatly aided by the many communications projects of Native peoples.

The recent altercations in Denver, with American Indians and their supporters battling police in protests over a Columbus Day Parade, reminds us that the issue is fraught with tension. Inevitably, such protests will grow. They do not need to be violent to be effective, but no one should question that the anger is real.

How can American Indians be asked to celebrate the beginning of so much genocide?

Nevertheless, about Columbus himself, the debate sees too much misinformation all around. Columbus was not simply "lost." He was not "a horrible sailor." In fact, he has been widely recognized by many famous mariners as one of the finest if not the most keen deadfall sailor of all time.

So it simply twists reality to say that what Columbus did was easy or by sheer luck, although certainly there was luck involved. The Admiral of the Ocean Sea was clearly talented on a ship on the ocean. Moreover, he was actually a prophetic figure; as in the case of his name, his writings depict a destiny-ridden man, driven to do precisely what he did. He was no ordinary man, Columbus, but neither was Custer, neither even Adolf Hitler.

Because there was another piece of Columbus: the Christ-bearing colonizer. And this other piece was rapacious, cruel (even though less so than his brother, Bartholomew, who burned Indians in groups of thirteen to recall Christ and his apostles). And Columbus was cognizant. He knew what he was doing.

It was Columbus who first in the Americas issued the *requerimiento*, where he would read to Indians that if they did not accept the Spanish King, forthwith, brutal war would commence. Since the Indians rarely even understood anything about the procedure, the "just" war certain to follow made the taking of slaves a legal enterprise.

It was Columbus himself, against the wishes of Queen Isabella, who forced the first load of Indian slaves be delivered to Spain. The Queen reprimanded him and even made him send some back.

Columbus was financed by bankers from Castile and other principalities and they expected him to make good on their substantial investment in his enterprise. He was obsessed with finding suitable commodities to sell. Having been among the earliest of the African slave traders in his youth, he knew just what to do when the opportunity to enslave Native American people offered itself.

It is true that perhaps other conquistadors were much more cruel, over more time, than Columbus. Others would express more outright racism and much less wonderment about the Native peoples and their ways than he did in his journals and letters.

Again, he was a complex man, and if we are to understand history, we should take the broader view. But the treatment of Indians and the definition of their standing before law and court, that was his decision. He set the pattern. Columbus and his brothers were a decisive factor in the early relations with Caribbean Native nations. The tragedy that followed had roots in the way they acted and thought.

For those who say that Columbus' decisions are excusable because of the historical period in which he lived, we refer all to the work and opinions of contemporaries such as Father Las Casas and other great liberals of

Spain during that time who denounced the actions of the conquistadors, even as they were taking place.

For Columbus, there was even a crucial moment of truth. Chroniclers of the time tell of a day in 1496, when Guarionex, a Taino cacique, came to Columbus with a thousand of his people, ready to plant. They had yucca (manioc), corn, beans, calabash, and many other Indian agricultural wonders. The Taino chief offered Columbus and his brothers the fruits of "a plantation 80 leagues by 30 leagues," perhaps thousands of acres, to feed the Spanish, "here and even back in Castilla."

This had always been their way, to feed their visitors and even their occasional enemy visitors, so as to pacify them. In return for the offer to equalize with the bounty of the land, the Taino wanted Columbus to let them off the doctrine of gold tribute, imposed on their people by Columbus' men, who cut and killed Taino people at will if they did not turn up just so much gold every month.

The Columbus brothers turned Guarionex down. They laughed at the idea that people could live in peace by sharing food and being friendly neighbors and human beings. By those very men, war and slavery, rather than mutually beneficial trade and commerce, were established ad infinitum and ad nauseam.

Columbus had a choice. The Taino offered him peace. He decided to enslave, exploit, and sell them. It was the beginning of the original American sin; the beginning of racism in the Western Hemisphere.

Yanomami Challenge Anthropology, Demand Blood Samples Back
April 22, 2002

Three Yanomami leaders were in Indian country in early April, at Cornell University in Ithaca, New York, for a parley with highly placed academics and human-rights researchers. Two Yanomami from Brazil and one from Venezuela actually met together for the first time after several generations of enforced separation by an international border.

The cream of pro-Indian activist anthropology, including Professor Dr. David Maybury-Lewis of Cultural Survival and other important players of the movement, such as Terence Turner and Leslie Sponsel, heard the admonitions and premonitions of the three Yanomami leaders. Author Patrick Tierney, whose revealing investigatory book, *Darkness at El Dorado*, blew the lid on horrendous treatment of the Yanomami by anthropologists, also attended. They all addressed the reason for the meeting: the objectionable behavior of controversial anthropologist Napoleon Chagnon, who ushered into the Amazonian territory a blood-sampling campaign that extracted thousands of vials of Yanomami blood and other tissues later deposited in universities and other institutional collections in the United States.

The Yanomami want their blood back. In their tradition, the blood of dead relatives "should be properly destroyed." The ones from Brazil are ready with a ceremony for such a return; the Venezuelan villages have yet to meet, but will, on the issue of what to do with the blood and other biological samples taken over the past thirty years. At least one collection, held at Penn State, is available for return. The curators at Penn State understand serious violations took place in the gathering of the material. The Yanomami were seen in the 1960s and right up to the 1990s as exploitable subjects. It was as if those types of researchers felt that a deep forest people could never emerge into their own countries or even out of their countries to challenge their treatment.

The three leaders spoke of Chagnon and other blood takers as very bad memories. They were given machetes and pots for their blood and told it would be analyzed for "little animals that are hurting your health." It was a lie. No application that had any health impact came out of any of it. The worse of it was the vilification of their culture and people, they said. Chagnon "writes about us as the fierce people," said Davi Kopenawa Yanomami, a shaman and leader from Brazil. Kopenawa and his companion, Toto Yanomami, spoke lengthily in their own Yanomami language and later translated to Portuguese and English.

"But we are not fierce people," the Yanomami emphasized. The Yanomami leaders delivered a message of guardianship and harmony with the forest and the Earth. "How are you going to eat, if you destroy the Earth?" Toto asked, "If you cut down the forest, where will you get your medicines?" Said Davi Kopenawa: "Mostly we like to laugh and to feel good and feel happy. Chagnon only saw one thing, what he wanted. Chagnon is the fierce one, he is."

Chagnon is the poster boy for poor research ethics, the one whose tactics all good anthropologists should want to question and censure. Tierney documents the bulk of it in his controversial book, which has American anthropology upside down. It was Chagnon who bargained under bad pretenses for blood and forbidden information around dead peoples' names; the one who seemed to introduce diseases wherever he traveled; who manufactured a movie that led to hostilities between villages. Not a few Yanomami chiefs and warriors have promised to apprehend Chagnon if he ever enters their territory again.

The image of fierceness created by Chagnon's widely used work "Yanomamö: the Fierce People" has cost the Yanomami dearly. Meeting

Chagnon was in many ways like meeting a new man, a twentieth-century Columbus. Later, as Yanomami leaders began to act on their own behalf in political affairs, Chagnon attacked them as puppets of the anthropologists and of Indian support groups. He accused the support groups of being "communists," insisting that there was no helping the Yanomami. Thankfully, the Yanomami have gathered some good allies, in Brazil, Venezuela, Europe, and the United States. They have won some victories; lost a few.

Their world has changed a great deal already. They are still facing epidemics that can be greatly helped with more serious assistance. (A ten-year fund for Yanomami health, from a group of resource-wealthy American Indian nations, would be great to see.) They have begun to educate a few dozen of their young people. They are now traveling and representing themselves. They are looking for help in designing a good way to interact with "the white people." Contemptuous researchers and scholars such as Chagnon really do disservice to their professions. It is good to see the Yanomami, deep-forest Indians, be able to throw on a coat and hat and fly to the United States to represent themselves.

These are obviously serious people. They were honest about their priorities. The "blood issue" was uncomfortable for them. It reminds them of a bad time, when many of their people died. As Davi said, "The blood we should take care of so we can go on to other things that concern our villages." All three leaders spoke concern for the whole of their peoples. Their main issues are the day to day health problems of the present Yanomami population. They are a strong population who want to get well again, Davi said.

Once, Chagnon and his type of academic researcher may have thought that their Indian subjects would never be able to travel and enter their world and be able to recount and reveal the record of their behavior in distant lands. This is no longer true. Proper treatment, relations, and covenants with communities are necessary prerequisites for cultural and social exchange to take place.

Guatemala Maya Futures Deserve Real Thinking
June 25, 2002

Terrorism has been going on for a very long time and in many forms. The terrorism that kills Indian leaders kills other people too.

Just a few weeks ago, Guillermo Ovalle, an associate of Nobel Peace Prize winner and Quiche' Indian leader Rigoberta Menchu Tum, was assassinated by unknown gunmen in Guatemala. Recently, a death threat was faxed to several of Guatemala's most prominent human rights organizations.

Early reports attribute the high-tech death threat, which targeted about a dozen human rights activists and journalists as *enemigos a la patria* (enemies of the state), to a clandestine organization allegedly linked to the army high command.

Things are not going well in Guatemala. The Guatemalan case is doubly troubling. It is a country of great social injustice that is, at the same time, a solid agricultural producer with a potentially strong economy. Among the great producing class in Guatemala are the millions of Indian campesino, artisan, and business people who constitute a very hard-working population and hold up whole sectors of the country's economy.

After thirty years of very brutal war, Guatemala suffers the consequences. A wave of violent crime has become the permanent reality. Perhaps it is the large numbers of orphaned children of war-torn families, many who are now tormented young adults. More likely it is the result of having a huge number of trained excombatants, left and right, in a country of high unemployment and many available weapons. Bandits roam. Assaults are common. Violence is for hire, quite openly, quite with impunity, if the contractor gets the right people to do the job. Assassination for hire can be a fact of life.

It is not an easy place for a Native culture to survive. But there are a lot of Maya in Guatemala, perhaps as many as 6 million. We hope all the pressures the Maya population is facing will not become points of violence that could be aggravated into another genocidal campaign against their communities.

The history is ugly enough. Enough mass graves are dug up every week to feed the narrative of massacre and brutality that were the 1980s for this beleaguered country. This history is alive in the psyche of the people, who do hunger for justice or retribution for their horrible suffering of twenty years ago, but not as much as they hunger today for want of food security and basic necessities. Among the most pressing need is for equitable access to lands by the agricultural producers among the Maya population. This huge need and social disparity is refueling old tensions. The hunger for land turns increasingly into the battle cry, "Land or death."

In the midst of the harsh reality, Guatemala's Indian country is flexing its muscle intellectually, politically, and economically. At the same time, movements are afoot, including outright invasions of private farms, that are dangerously reminiscent of the time just before the years of intense massacre. These movements can easily reignite the military madness that resulted in the torture and massacre of tens of thousands of Indians.

The recent brutal revelation of the shadowy hand of the Death Squads in a spate of assassinations going back to the 1980s also augurs badly. In Guatemala and other such dictatorship-to-democracy "successes," recurring periods of intense repression and killing are all too often the norm. These intensify when the United States is in a militaristic mood; they lessen when economic visions fuel the world and promise appears possible.

We urge the United States, Canada, and Mexico to request restraint on the part of the military in Guatemala. Their repression might be focused on the criminal element and not the social sector. When the tension of criminal violence fuels political instability, military force can sometimes impose its own justification, often with disastrous results for Native peoples.

Somehow, in the midst of its current war footing, we encourage the United States to also project and support peace and security issues that give hope of good life to good people. The world, including countries such as Guatemala, cannot just be driven by the fear of retribution, which is the strategy of targeting broadly all countries perceived to be critical or oppositional to U.S. international policies and interests.

Maya Indians, who like to hold their community lands in common with collective titles owned by extended families called matrilineages and patrilineages and that form communities, might be perceived as exotic potential enemies in this context. Or they might be seen as a source of hope and stability if properly supported toward their own cultural approach to economic productivity and prosperity.

In Guatemala, the horror of mass-institutionalized terrorism remains fresh in the memory and is a historical cycle that could again become a lived reality. New models that include old, proven incentives are much needed at this time in history.

Fujimori's Genocide Frames Peruvian Politics
August 7, 2002

Peru, the most populous Indian nation in South America, now under Quechua president Alejandro Toledo, just admitted that it forcefully sterilized more than 200,000 Indian women between 1996 and 2000 during the regime of former president Alberto Fujimori.

This terrible news, in the form of an actual apology by the Peruvian Health Ministry, confirms occasional reports of the past few years. What is perhaps less expected is the huge number of women subjected to the practice. From all indications, the campaign was directed at Indian women from traditional villages in the Andean Mountains. It has caused a radical demographic drop.

Peru was seriously ransacked in the 1990s during the regime of Alberto Fujimori, a Japanese-Peruvian who ruled the country through military repression. During the Fujimori years, with the consistent backing of the U.S. government, Peruvians endured dozens of massacres and thousands of individual killings. A lot of it happened at the command of Fujimori's secret police and military squads. Fujimori is now in exile in Japan.

The sterilizations of Indian women occurred under the worst of conditions. Illegal as a birth-control method in this largely Catholic country of 26 million people, sterilization for contraceptive purposes was legalized by Fujimori's government in 1995. With substantial assistance from the U.S. Agency for International Development (AID), teams of doctors and nurses scoured the highlands, targeting Quechua and Aymara communities. Officials threatened, bribed, or misled women to submit to the operation. Health workers, trained by U.S. personnel, were under obligation to meet quotas. They "sometimes visited individual women several times as the hard sell for sterilization became steadily more aggressive," according to an early report on the Peruvian sterilization controversy that appeared in *Native Americas* magazine (summer 2000).

The same report noted that sometimes twenty to thirty tubal ligations per day were performed by doctors and nurses who were paid bonuses of $10 to $30 per surgery. The use of force was reported in many cases. The program increased the number of tubal ligations in the country from 10,000 in 1996 to roughly 110,000 in 1997, with Peru becoming U.S. AID's largest program of population control in Latin America. According to a UPI report, some 55 percent of the women, some 110,000, endured the operations without any anesthesia. Aftercare was not available. Infections and other complications are common among the women victims of this horrible crime. There are at least seven deaths to be fully investigated.

This imposed terror on Andean women and men (16,547 vasectomies were also performed) has caused a serious drop in population among highland Indian traditional communities. There is a shortage of young families and some communities are demographically disappearing. Peruvian traditional indigenous women have families with an average of seven children. Thus, perhaps as many as 1.5 million Peruvian Indians were sterilized out of existence. These numbers are in-line with results anticipated by a 1974 report prompted by Henry Kissinger for the National Security Council. That report argued the case for population control as a means to reduce smoldering unrest in Third World countries experiencing rapid increases among their rural populations.

Good thoughts are expressed at Peru's beleaguered Indian President, Alejandro Toledo. His historic election gave Peru an Indian president for the first time ever and put an end to the Fujimori dictatorship, but it has turned to political quagmire within a year. The idealistic and highly trained

Toledo went in with a free-market approach to economic stimulation for Peru, but found out that the common people, certainly the Quechua and Aymara, who participate mostly in local and regional economies, largely have different ideas.

An attempt to privatize the electricity service in the country's second largest provincial city resulted in major strikes, barricades, police and military attacks, and two deaths. Peruvians are highly impatient, after so many years of dictatorship, to improve the widespread conditions of deep impoverishment. The globalization policies begun by Toledo, who graduated from Stanford University and worked at the World Bank, are largely not the stuff of Indian dreams in Peru. Toledo has tried to mediate and play the two sides of the argument, but it is backfiring and his popularity has dropped from 55 percent to a low of 18 percent. The fact that he is defending against a highly public out-of-wedlock paternity suit has not helped.

Toledo is dealing with long-entrenched problems and is caught between the free-market reforms, which call for stern measures and privatization of government services, and political leaders at the local and community levels, who complain that the globalization approach only increases their misery by extracting profits and jobs and hiking rates of every type.

The apology under Toledo's administration for the destruction of so many Indian families by the Peruvian government is welcome, though belated, as a sign that such policies will never again be instituted. The incredibly brutal callousness of this imposed "ethnic cleansing" of Indian people in one of this hemisphere's most indigenous countries is appalling. That is happened in this day and age with the participation of the U.S. government makes it virtually incomprehensible. The call is out for severe punishment for the architects and managers of the program. Peru is a tough country. It should mete out swift and heavy justice against those who prescribed such a revolting idea. We urge that it be so. Compensation to the many victims, particularly in the way of ongoing medical attention to the many women continuing to suffer from the operations, is certainly in order.

The United States has a major responsibility in the horror that was imposed. Indian country must take note and make its collective outrage heard on this horror that befell its sisters and brothers within Peru. Let us hope that the family of world nations is also watching.

Latin American Indian Hunger

December 23, 2002

Confrontation with Iraq dominates U.S. foreign policy agenda. This is Washington's singular preoccupation and, of course, the media focus is on this international issue almost exclusively. As a result of this American policy and media myopia, for long periods of time, goings-on and trends in other parts of the world are largely ignored. This is a mistake—and a troublesome media lapse—because even a titanic superpower is limited in the full global context.

Just before September 11, 2001, Congressman Gary Condit and his missing intern were the media frenzy. It was like nothing else was happening in the whole world. Who would have thought of Afghanistan, Pakistan, Azerbaijan? Well, there's a big world of change happening—burgeoning populations, diminishing resources, and increasing disparities between rich and poor. The opportunity to make a decent living is rare now in many countries, even for the well educated.

This is certainly true for Latin America. Almost out of public view, the southern nations of the Western Hemisphere are experiencing a political sea change, based on a decade of very bleak economics, with massively growing poverty. The poorest of the poor, of course, are the indigenous peoples. As other more-numerous populations suffer from destitution, they tend to move farther into the Indian regions, taking over and often destroying Indian habitats. The economic situation is dismal all over.

Argentina is in disarray. Prices, even for bread, have doubled in the past year and unemployment is rampant. Well-dressed middle-class citizens are seen looting stores, as hunger of children and adults drives even the most law-abiding to extreme measures.

Throughout Latin America, the much-touted open-market policies of globalization are universally regarded as failures. A severe and sustained drop in income throughout South America and Central America place the whole region at risk of following the pattern in Africa, where disease and famine are becoming commonplace. As columnist Nicholas D. Kristof noted in a recent *New York Times* column, "South and Central America are quietly falling apart." Per-capita income in Argentina, for example, is less than it was a century ago, its economy shrinking by 10 percent a year.

Paraguay, Uruguay, and Bolivia, as Kristoff points out, are all considering default on their international debt. Brazil, which just elected a socialist president, is not far behind in considering default on its $260 billion foreign debt, a move that could trigger international economic upheaval. Colombia is mired in a forty-year-old war, into which the United States is stepping deeper and deeper, while neighboring Venezuela is experiencing political turmoil that could easily lead to open conflict. In Peru and Ecuador, alliances of Indians and labor unions are growing, while the economics of both countries worsen. The most radical elements of both are becoming dominant.

In Central America, Guatemala, Honduras, Nicaragua, and El Salvador are experiencing massive hunger and starvation is increasingly in evidence. Political upheaval threatens Mexico as well, where early hopes for resolving immigration issues have faded in the wake of the September attacks and the U.S. fixation on international terrorism. The destruction of the Indian *ejido* or common-lands farming communities is leading to mass migration.

A U.S. policy that vacillates between negative interference and neglect is largely to blame for Latin America's neither-here-nor-there economic process. The interference has been in the form of military and war-driven aid, while drastic reductions in economic aid reflect a growing neglect of social and political problems. The direction has been to move countries away from their own agricultural production for local-regional consumption. Mass-marketing of specialty mono-crops for international consumption leave local people without locally priced foods.

As always, the indigenous people of the region are suffering most, while the strong Native cultural sense of community offers some relief and potential hope. In this the stress is on local and regional solutions to specific problems. Indigeneity—that is, the opportunity to coalesce around indigenous bases of identity, territory, and other commonalties—is one important response. This has its national manifestations, where ethnic group rights are defended and debated, and, even more importantly, express local and eco-regional reflections.

Village and barrio community is still very much alive in Latin America. The state is distrusted, disdained, and, when possible, avoided. Families are still big, and crucial in the maintenance of community. For many, the productivity of local community is the avenue to possible solutions. However, this is a prescription that is assailed by the technocratic planners of global markets and by the economics-by-conglomerate crowd, but it is the oldest and safest approach to survival. To damage local agriculture is to destroy people's ability to stay in their aboriginal areas. The result is to force poverty upon the people and to stimulate mass migration. The huge potential then is for political instability, with inevitable and increasing violence. These self-serving U.S. policies threaten to haunt North America for years to come.

Indigenous Latino and the Consciousness of the Native Americas

February 4, 2003

Borders between Indian peoples—as psychological as language and as legalistic as those of national frontiers—are coming down. A sense of relations, all our relations, is increasingly apparent in the communications between Indians throughout North America, Central America, the Caribbean, and South America. It is a refreshing trend that we encourage.

We note the recent repatriation of Taino human remains from the United States' Smithsonian Institution's National Museum of the American Indian to a small Indian enclave in Cuba's eastern mountains, the community of Caridad de los Indios. Navajo, Mohawk, Algonquin, Kaw, Paiute, Chicano, and other peoples, including scholars and participants from several countries, witnessed the unique ceremony, which coalesced the forces of many people to guarantee its success.

The reinterment gave evidence, too, of the survival of Native traditional culture and peoples in the most remote and unpredictable places in the Americas. For the small enclave of Taino descendents at Caridad de los Indios, high up in the mountains of Guantanamo, Cuba, to make themselves known and respected at an international level after nearly 500 years of supposed extinction is a marvel in itself. That a repatriation could be conducted between two countries still in the throes of political hostility gives evidence of the growing level of cooperation going on among Indian peoples of the countries of Latin America and North America.

Jose Mart, the Cuban national hero, was quoted by elders at the repatriation in Caridad de los Indios. Mart is one poetic voice from the anti-Spain liberation movements that has become an integral part of the Cuban spirit. The prophetic Mart, who is respected throughout Latin America, declared to the world more than 100 years ago: "The American intelligence is to be found in an Indian head dress." He also wrote, "America will not walk until the Indian walks."

The American Indian is walking today. There is nothing crestfallen about this moment for the peoples of Indian country and the Native Americas. The Indian peoples of the Americas are relatives to each other and constitute the primary cultural and sometimes-human foundation of the modern American republics. This is a large idea, but a true one, and we believe a desirable one for all Native peoples to ponder with an open mind. Throughout North America, Indian peoples are advancing their interests.

In Canada, the Aboriginal population surged over the past century, increasing by some 22 percent in the past five years alone. Aboriginal Canada has developed a great national presence in the midst of significant

challenges and is now projecting an awareness of indigenous affairs internationally. As one example, The Canadian International Development
Agency (CIDA) recently launched the Indigenous Peoples Partnership
Program (IPPP), a $10 million four-year pilot initiative to support develop-
ment partnerships between indigenous peoples in Canada and indigenous
peoples around the world, while focusing on the Americas.

In the United States, an economic base of muscle-flexing proportions—upheld by legal rights based on Indian jurisdictions and the reality
of government-to-government relations—has begun to emerge. All of this is
quite different and the result of much self-determined efforts over the past
thirty years. These are trends that usher in a new era of possibility for
Native nations.

The Indian presence in Latin America is particularly strong. Lowest
estimates are 40 million, but in fact, it is much more than that. Indigenous-
ness is the reality of an identity that has many dimensions. There are core
Native populations in some countries, such as Ecuador, Bolivia, Guatemala,
and Mexico, that are huge. Then, too, it could be argued that Latin
American cultures are more fused and layered than in Anglo America;
Canadian or U.S. indigenous beliefs are much more interwoven into many
of Latin America's national cultures. And indigenous Latin America is
migrating north in bigger waves.

In many places in North America, Native tribal sectors are taking hold.
The Maya community of Central Florida, for example, sustains its own
Native population (tens of thousands), languages, ceremonial fiestas, even a
midwifery project, all signaling a permanence as Native people coalescing
from a modern yet already mythical migration. Mexican Miztecas and
Zapotecas have ethnic and linguistic communities coming together in parts
of California and the Northwest. Garifuna from Belize and Honduras number around 60,000 just in the New York metropolitan area. The Boricua-
Taino identity is resounding in Puerto Rico and the diaspora. In the arts,
people such as Carlos Santana, who has mystically wandered the landscape
of spirituality, is deepening into his own indigenous Mexicano roots.

There is a very large and potent underbelly and undercurrent to the
American indigenous world. It is transforming itself with its great surge of
activity and it just may help change the world's perception of itself. Of the
approximately 40 million Hispanics (or Latinos) counted by the U.S. Census,
a large proportion has indigenous American roots. This is an identity in the
very throes of revitalization and actively searching, and often finding, its
own indigenous legacy. This is a phenomenon whose time is here.

For long-standing, federally recognized North American Indian peoples,
the growing relations with southern Native peoples are best seen for their

positive potential. Rather than offering a competing agenda, the alliances and collaborations of communities based in Native legacies can have substantial cultural, political, and economic benefits for all Indian peoples.

It is true enough that some of the relationship brings tension. A case in point is the Mexican border, where Native Mexicans cross American Indian lands, sometimes heightening lawlessness. However, the search for common roots, for what makes us similar rather than what makes us different, usually furnishes the greatest rewards. Indigenous initiatives at the United Nations, for example, which have provided valuable contacts and effective advocacy for indigenous rights, have generally grown out of strategic sharing and cooperative lobbying in that international body.

The Indian Americas, by seeking and sharing fundamental human values and recognizing the common objectives of all tribal and kinship communities, is indeed beginning to get into a good stride. We celebrate indigenous intelligence in setting the direction and destination of that steady pace. Nothing will be easy, but at the turn of a challenging century, Indian peoples of the Americas are continuing to provide a unique yet practical set of answers to the serious problems facing their communities and humankind. And bound together on that journey, the consciousness among American Indians and many Hispanics is inexorably linked.

Surviving Columbus in Puerto Rico: the Myth of Extinction
October 6, 2003

The story this week of a new major DNA study showing considerable American Indian ancestry in the population of Puerto Rico is intriguing and revealing. Of course, there has been for more than two decades considerable agitation by Taino people of Puerto Rican nationality on the island and in the diaspora. But now Dr. Juan Martinez Cruzado has shown that as high as 61 percent of Puerto Ricans carry American Indian mitochondrial DNA from their maternal lines.

The level of Native genetic ancestry is impressive and, once more, evidence that the legacy of American indigenous peoples, across the Western Hemisphere, has been all too easily diminished or denied. The claim that all Native Caribbeans succumbed to war, slavery, and disease, that they in fact became "extinct" as peoples and cultures by the 1600s, has been asserted as truth by governments and academics for more than a hundred years. However, in Puerto Rico, as elsewhere in the Caribbean, actual, surviving Native communities and numerous families and people of Native ancestry have increasingly revealed themselves. The Nacion Taina de las Antillas and various networks and individual personalities have emerged to give representation and leadership to this growing movement in Caribbean life.

This revitalization is happening among the Taino-guajiro of Cuba, the Taino-jibaro of Borinquen (Puerto Rico), and the Taino-Indio families of the Dominican Republic. Dr. Martinez Cruzado recounts as part of his study that in Puerto Rico, "there are many people who use medicinal plants and farming methods that come directly from the Tainos. This is especially true of the areas once known as Indieras, or "Indian Zones." Again, this agricultural way of life is equally evident in Cuba and Dominican Republic, and to a lesser degree, also in Haiti and Jamaica. Direct work with the Earth remains a major repository of Native culture and belief.

In Cuba, in the same area where resides the most recognized Native community in the Greater Antilles, the enclave of la Rancheria at Caridad de los Indios, in Guantanamo, a *guajiro* farmer recently found a living mammal thought lost to extinction, the insect-eating almiqui. News of the little possumlike creature's return from extinction went around the world. So it is with the resilient people of Native ancestry in the eastern region of the island. Because they have not been visible to academics (who have hardly looked), nor quantifiable by governments (who have sought their invisibility), it does not mean that their existence can be denied. The same is true in other parts of the Caribbean. In Puerto Rico, we find a Taino movement and now these history-busting new DNA studies by Dr. Martinez Cruzado; in Cuba, in 2003, dozens of North Americans witnessed the repatriation of Taino remains from the Smithsonian Institution to the "community of relatives," in the Guantanamo mountains; at Dominica, St. Vincent, and Trinidad, Carib communities still farm and fish and sustain many of the same customs found in the bigger islands; while on the coastal rim of the Caribbean Sea, Garifuna, Carib, and Arawak, Miskito, Wuayu (Guajiro), Kuna, and many other Caribbean indigenous relatives interact and are beginning once again to hold regular conferences and tribal gatherings across the whole region.

Christopher Columbus, who will be celebrated and denigrated next week, did not finish the job of genocide with which he is charged, not quite and perhaps not by far. This is not to say that the great mariner did not try to completely enslave the Caribbean's indigenous peoples. No doubt Columbus was one of the best "dead-reckoning" sailors who ever lived; equally without doubt is that he was a cold and calculating colonizer who singularly forced the idea of *encomienda*, slavery, and servitude, when a more respectful trade and commerce would have been possible, as was even desired by Queen Isabella of Spain herself.

In the core and heart of the Native Americas Hemisphere, the Caribbean basin, the assumed extinction of Native peoples is being revisited. Old customs around the use of herbal medicines (ceremonial relationship with nature), around the planting of many crops by the phases of the moon, are widespread among farmers and are clearly of indigenous Taino origins. There is also much evidence of respect and prayer with and to the identity of sacred places. Among some folk, orations, certain massages (called *sobabo*), ceremonies that burn tobacco and intone the Four Directions and the various gifts of the Mother Earth, are still conducted; there are many indigenous elements among the countryside people, the *campesino* or *guajiro* communities in particular. There are also many families where the inheritance and legacy of Taino ancestors is still present.

The denial of existence, however, has been brutal. No one was meant to survive the conquest, with its terroristic impositions, diseases, and the overwhelming quest to own everything that rightly belonged to the Indian peoples. If survival of customs has been documentable, the idea of genetic and or familial extinction was posited as complete. It was a dictum of the Spanish Empire that to declare the Indian race extinguished was the quickest way to clear title to lands that might be contested in time. Still, many Indian-descendent families hold land and retain social and spiritual culture that sustain and transform directly from very early contact times. With the advent of DNA studies, lo and behold, these same general populations who maintain these indigenous customs are seen to be actually—genetically—of direct Indian ancestry, specifically matrilineally, that is, through their mothers. Again, the tree can be cut, the branches loped off, the trunk pulverized, but the roots remain, and over time the shoots of new generations emerge to claim their indigenous place.

A presentation by the distinguished scholar Dr. Helen Tanner recently at the University of Wisconsin at Madison gives concreteness to the idea of Caribbean indigenous survival. Dr. Tanner, a witness to the repatriation in Cuba earlier this year, spoke exactingly on the survival and continuity of indigenous people and their place in the Caribbean universe. Numerous teachers and professors heard her lecture. Thus, the actual and corrected information moves into curricula and to a new generation of students.

Indeed, American Indian peoples and open-minded academics are rolling Columbus back. In fact, the reindigenization of the Americas is in process. It was inevitable. Truth is power, and on this widespread and necessary effort to educate the Americas, truth is on our side.

The Reality of a Sordid History
August 13, 2004

When Democratic elections in foreign countries don't go the way of U.S. policy makers, all too often, particularly during the Cold War, intervention, assassination, or coup d'etat followed.

This is not to depress anyone, nor to demean America as a whole. We freely here express our appreciation for the central pillars of the American secular republic—which, hopefully, can guarantee room for all discussion, as long as sovereignty, peace, and freedom are respected. We just don't much care for what the hidden hand of our national government has represented to many parts of the world, too often shielded from the public eye. There is a lot of history glossed over but the reality of unleashed violence has not been erased or forgotten, particularly in Latin America.

From the bully days of Theodore Roosevelt, American superpower politics has had its hidden but also notorious dark side: in Latin America, the history is of all-too-numerous bloody and highly unpopular interventions. Often, it was to impose terms of trade, terms of property holding, and acquisition by American firms. This is the overwhelming view in the Latin American street, where the outstanding example is Chile in 1973, featuring the violent overthrow of the democratically elected government of President Salvador Allende, who was bombed and strafed to death by his own military, encouraged and guided by the likes of Henry Kissinger, then–U.S. foreign policy architect. To remember those days more generally: in Vietnam, a widespread program of policy-driven assassination is not forgotten; in Cuba, where Castro has counted into the fifties the number of attempts on his life, there are whole museums dedicated to such histories. We don't have to like these governments to understand that they are expressions of sovereign peoples, whatever their choice of system.

Consider Venezuela, where America's assigned nemesis these days is President Hugo Chavez, a no-nonsense populist who has carried on a tumultuous social revolution within the confines of legitimate presidential elections. Chavez, facing a U.S.–supported referendum and consistent hostility from current U.S. policy, suddenly pulls out in front of his opposition with a 60 percent support rate, according to even U.S. pollsters. And, wouldn't you know it, talk of assassination has begun.

Hemispheric Affairs, a Washington think tank on Latin America, reports that "the opposition is increasingly desperate and will resort to illegal means to tear the results."

Carlos Andres Perez, former president and campaign manager for the referendum, has stated: "We Venezuelans have to liquidate Chavez through violence, because there is no other way." Later, he was quoted by *El Nacional* newspaper in Miami: "Unfortunately the referendum has proven to be a failure—It will fail." The U.S. ally added: "Chavez must be killed like a dog, he deserves it—no offense intended against all good animals." (*La Jornada*, Mexico).

Chavez is not everybody's hero—as neither is Bush nor was Clinton—but in fact, he won the presidency by a landslide in 1998 and again in 2000 (56 percent of the vote). His were reputable elections in a country with serious social polarization, which in Latin America is usually between very few rich people and increasingly poor and marginalized populations. Venezuela, being oil rich for generations, still has not resolved its social problems. Being oil rich, of course, it gets a lot of attention from the United States, which is not happy that Chavez is pursuing a radical social-change agenda that taxes the oil industry to create expensive and popular programs to feed and educate the poor.

Chavez has spawned much fear and some chaos. His move to change the Constitution of Venezuela was highly controversial as are his *turbas*, or directed street protests, which have engaged in violent aggression, some-times in defense of government institutions. At the same time, an international Miami-based opposition movement has wreaked havoc on much of industry and civil life in Venezuela. At times, it has deployed sharpshooters to cut down pro-government demonstrators.

It is no great secret that the United States wants Chavez gone. A coup d'etat against his government in April of 2002 had traceable involvement by the United States and Spanish embassies in Caracas. The short-lived new government was immediately acknowledged by the United States, which refused to condemn the coup. But the coup ultimately failed, as Chavez was reinstated by popular demand in Venezuela's streets, and the eyes of the region watch intently to gauge the ongoing conflict with the United States.

Foretelling the California Recall Initiative, the Venezuelan opposition moved to force a referendum before the end of Chavez's term. Funded in part by Washington, the August 15 referendum vote now decides the future of Venezuela.

We hope the United States will keep its hands out of anything like Mr. Perez suggests in Venezuela. Latin America is changing and is not likely to play lapdog to external interests forever. Popular movements are coming back with much passion and Venezuela is just the beginning—yet it is democratic.

For way too long, American dictates south of the Mexican border to Tierra del Fuego demanded a "with us or against us" stand that has caused the death of hundreds of thousands. A lot of killing took place in Latin America during the 1970s and 1980s that American television largely ignored while it happened and now conveniently forgets.

It is best not to forget, lest a major superpower with the greatest potential for peace and freedom in the world blunder into outright negativity again.

PERSPECTIVE

Bolivia's Indians Confront Globalization
August 20, 2004

John Mohawk, *Indian Country Today*

In 1781, Andean Indians laid siege to La Paz, the capital of Bolivia, for 109 days. The white people were reduced, it is said, to eating shoe leather and rats. A Spanish army rescued the colonists and captured the leader, Tupak Kateri. His was a gruesome execution (tied to four horses, drawn, and quartered), but he left his tormentors with a prophecy: "I will return," he said, "and I will be millions." It is a prophecy that is echoing in the mountains these days and it has the attention of the United States. Bolivia is the poorest country in South America and the Indians are the poorest people in Bolivia. For three years, there has been political turmoil there (some call it insurrection, a term that has a connotation that agitation for political change lacks legitimacy), and the movement has frustrated multinational corporations, challenged the American behemoth's designs for globalization, and nearly elected an openly Indian president. Had it been successful in the latter endeavor, it would have been the first Indian president of any country in the Western Hemisphere since Benito Juarez in Mexico in 1858.

The current movement began with the Zapatistas in 1994 (also directed against globalization) and was echoed in movements in Ecuador, Guatemala, and especially in Bolivia. Bolivia is special. About 1.5 million Indians live in autonomous villages—places over which the government has little or no control. Their movement is evolving in an unusual way. Most movements for change idealize a past and try to rebuild a version of it. Many see their movement as postmodern, where modernity is defined as the arrival of Columbus, the conquest, the subjugation, slavery, racism, and all the negatives that define Indian life since 1492. They speak of going past all that to a new day, and in Bolivia, Indians lead the anticorporate, antiglobalism effort. In 2002, Indians led a revolt against privatization, a key piece of globalization policy, when the Bechtel Corporation tried to gain a monopoly over all the water in Cochabamba, Bolivia's third largest city. Bechtel tried to charge so much for the water that it threatened to bankrupt the people of the city. Demonstrators forced Bechtel out and reinstated the public ownership of the water system.

In 2003, following U.S. desires, the Bolivian government sold rights to natural gas, which was then headed to the market for Mexican and U.S. consumers. On October 12, the 511-year anniversary of the landing of Columbus, Bolivian soldiers attacked Indian peasants in the Andean city of El Alto, the largest Indian city in Latin America. Hundreds were wounded and sixty-five died, but it sparked a nationwide movement of peasants, Indians, and workers that culminated in the siege of La Paz and forced President Gonzales Sanchez de Lozado to flee to Miami. (The President had impeccable globalization credentials: a mining executive trained at the University of Chicago in free-market economics.)

Indian movements have shaken the status quo in Latin America. The Mapuche Indians are part of a major political resistance to timber companies in southern Chile, and in Ecuador, Indian demonstrations against oppressive prices toppled the government in 2000. Critics of the Indian movements such as *The Wall Street Journal* speak with alarm about an Indian movement that wants to do away with the nation-state of Bolivia and return to the days when Indian nations ruled the land under traditional laws. Proponents of that way of thinking say that in those times, there were no rich or poor and no acquiescence to exploitation. Bolivia is a mountain country with cities in very cold areas. It also has enormous natural gas resources. American companies see the problem as how to get the gas out of Bolivia to someplace friendlier, such as Chile, where it could be liquefied and sent to markets in the North. They would like to accomplish this with as little interference from Bolivia's Indians as possible.

The way the advocates of globalization see it, the Indian movement would discourage investment and the country will become even poorer. The Indians in opposition to globalization are called radicals and other names because of their opposition. They point out that they benefit little from privatization of their natural resources and suffer much from the imposition of economic policies from the North. Since then, the new president, Carlos Mesa, has promised to hold a referendum on how the gas can be developed. Plans are being made for a new constitutional convention that may give Indians more political power.

The most extreme advocates of unrestrained globalization believe in the privatization of everything, and they are intent on exporting this idea to the world. Such people believe there should be no public ownership of anything. Under their plans, postal services, social services, prisons, public transportation, parks, roads, utilities, water works, and everything governments have been known to own should be sold off in the name of "efficiency." At Cochabamba, Bechtel laid claim even to the water that ran off peoples' roofs. Needless to say, "efficiency" means providing services at the absolutely lowest cost possible and has resulted in prisons that are seriously understaffed and would threaten service in remote areas, including telephone, postal and even electricity, because corporations would cease functioning whenever they were not making money. In the United States, corporations long ago acquired the status of "persons" under the law, but they are not people. Given the standard of behavior they exhibit, if they were persons they would be diagnosed as sociopathic because they exhibit no sense of responsibility to society. Ask Bolivians about this.

Bolivians have written letters to Iraq with stories of the struggle against Bechtel. Iraq is to be the U.S poster child for privatization and under occupation its laws were changed to permit foreigners to own practically everything. It is illegal under international law for an occupying power to transfer the assets of an occupied nation and this may be a reason for the early transfer of "sovereignty." The Baathists were a socialist political party and the government provided free food and a wide range of benefits to the population and owned a wide range of assets. Iraqi oil, when it is flowing as the Bush administration hopes, would provide a revenue stream that could pay for a whole range of corporate services, from water to transportation to electricity to education and more.

That's what was, and is, missing in poor countries such as Bolivia: a revenue stream to enrich the corporations. In Bolivia, the problem was getting blood from a stone. In Iraq, the problem is winning the hearts and minds while bleeding the people through corporate billing for everything of value while keeping them from having anything to say about it.

C. COLUMBUS

Chapter Seven
Global Tribal: The World, War, and Terrorism

American Indian delegations of chiefs, clan mothers, and other leaders have traveled the world in search of spiritual, cultural, and economic understandings. Many others have experienced the world through military service, as Native people are proportionally first in representation in the Armed Forces. Native populations suffer discrimination by national borders that cross their territories and divide their peoples; their villages often sit on contested lands, held by long inhabitation but lacking clear title. Conflicts over lands have led to widespread atrocity and war; economic displacement and migration are issues. The hope in this context is principally for peace and harmony in the world. American Indian spiritual leaders have led prayers for peace in many forums and ceremonies throughout the American hemisphere and the world. Productive commerce and diplomacy are seen as antidotes to war and violence. When religion and ideology justify war, a more pragmatic approach and deeper philosophies are called for. International recognition of indigenous peoples' issues is a strong motivator over three decades of American Indian international relations.

International Arena Is Important Work

September 13, 2000

A victory of substantial proportions was won recently when the United Nations Economic and Social Council adopted a resolution establishing a Permanent Forum for indigenous peoples within the international body. Although some wonder about the worth of international representation, it is undeniable that the effort to reach out beyond the national borders that contain them has yielded some important results for tribal peoples.

In 1977, on the occasion of the first major meeting of indigenous peoples at the United Nations in Geneva, Switzerland, few people in the world were interested in the rights of Native nations. Just five years earlier, a case in Colombia had given evidence of the level of infamy and disdain to which Indian people were being subjected. In that instance, a gang of cowboys had lured a small tribe of Indians out of the forest with the promise of a feast. As the Native guests ate, the cowboys fell upon them, killing sixteen, including women and children. The atrocious act came to public attention and the cowboys were charged with murder; however, they were acquitted of their crime. "They did not know," the cowboy's lawyer argued successfully, "that it was wrong to kill Indians."

In Brazil, Bolivia, Paraguay, Guatemala, Mexico, and every other country in the Western Hemisphere with indigenous populations, rapid depletion of forest was eradicating tribe after tribe from ancestral lands. When this type of rapacious development was opposed by tribes, severe repression followed, including massacres of whole villages.

In the United States and Canada, the scale of anti-Indian carnage was not at massacre levels, but nevertheless a major current of intolerance and racism against Indians had generated high levels of violence. In several Western states with significant Indian populations, murder of Indians by whites met with lenience in the courts all too frequently. In a policy climate still bent on dispossession of lands and other tribal resources, the Native movement exploded into Alcatraz, the Trail of Broken Treaties Caravan, the challenge at Wounded Knee, and many other confrontational events and situations that signaled the need to seek strategic alliances and proper legal forums everywhere possible.

In the late 1960s and early 1970s, indigenous "runners" from the southern countries had begun to come north. As well, northern Native nations, prominently the Iroquois and delegations of Lakota, Pueblo, Hopi, among others, were quietly traveling south. Thus, visionary leaders such as Reuben Snake of the Winnebago traveled to Mexico seeking contact with Native leaders there. Thus, meetings of Maya and Mohawk elders occurred in 1975 that became a cornerstone of a people-to-people alliance that has lasted over a generation. In Canada, a current of outreach instigated by Chief George Manuel would become known as the "Fourth World" movement. This first early dialogue with indigenous peoples immediately went beyond the international concept of a "Third World," thus declaring the very existence of a "fourth world of indigenous peoples."

Delegations from North America were large at the 1977 meeting. Prominently, the Lakota Treaty Council and the Haudenosaunee chiefs and clan mothers were represented and a medicine man from Oklahoma, Muscogee-Creek Phillip Deere, became a voice for millions when, holding high his medicine bundle, he declared in Geneva: "We, the Indigenous Peoples, are the evidence of the Western Hemisphere. No matter how small a tribal people may be, each of them has the right to be who they are."

The expressions of culture-bearing elders such as Phillip Deere, Leon Shenandoah, Art Solomon, David Monongwe; the vision of Native thinkers such as Larry Red Shirt, Dan Bomberry, Ingrid Washinawatok, and the lawyer Howard Berman (to name just some who have passed on) became basis for the language of indigenous peoples rights that has emerged in the international arena.

While it is true that no Native nation has yet to achieve status as a member nation of the United Nations, this remains a goal for many indigenous peoples. It is not, however, the only important benefit of international recognition and networking. The language that develops in these dialogues around concepts of sovereignty, nation-to-nation protocols, and codes of interaction between governments and political representatives is shared internationally by lawyers; it makes its way to academic and higher educational programs; it helps create a climate of deeper respect.

Most importantly, a "Draft Declaration on the Rights of Indigenous Peoples" has been under discussion in international circles since 1977. This very process of discussion of the Draft Declaration within the very slow, incremental approach toward adoption, which some critics use to disparage the international effort, is a victory in itself. It is precisely this ongoing and never-ending discussion that has educated thousands of international officials from dozens of countries about the existence, hopes, aspirations, and many contributions of Native peoples.

The movement sparked in 1977 has grown. Through the 1980s, as the wars in Central America evolved into slaughter campaigns against Indian communities, networking by indigenous peoples often was fortified by the forums at the United Nations. Often the ideological and political debates within the Indian international movement, as was the case of the Miskito-Sandinista War—which were as painful as they were deeply instructive. As peace dawned on the traumatized region in the early 1990s, that same movement supported and achieved the awarding of the Nobel Peace Prize for 1992 to the Maya activist and author, Rigoberta Menchu Tum. The awarding of the Nobel Prize to an indigenous woman symbolized an opening to crucial political space for Guatemala's Maya people; after horrible suffering, they would never again be invisible or voiceless.

By 1992, the Fourth World movement had expanded to represent the estimated more than 300 million indigenous people worldwide, including some 40 million in the Americas. That same year, indigenous peoples' cultural, practical knowledge of ecological factors in their traditional territories was recognized at the United Nations Conference on Environment and Development. And three years later, when the United Nations opened its program of activities for the International Decade of Indigenous Peoples (1994–2003), a main objective of the Decade was the establishment of a Permanent Forum at the United Nations. The United States, once a stumbling block to international indigenous rights, voted full support of the forum.

Proposed in 1993 at Vienna World Conference on Human Rights, the Permanent Forum will now provide indigenous peoples of the world with the opportunity to inject the unique voice of the Native peoples of the world into the global human discourse.

World's Rich Nations Need to "Get It"
August 7, 2001

The leaders of the industrialized world met again recently in Italy, amidst hellish street confrontations by tens of thousands of people that left a man shot to death and hundreds injured.

By the conference's end, commentators on television are once again trying to figure out just what the demonstrators wanted. Every time world leaders meet these days, large demonstrations are certain.

The pundits, uniformly and rightfully, decry the violent approach of the most radical and admit that economic globalization is "dislocating" some sectors around the world, but, by and large, tend to ridicule the protesters as spoiled kids led by disaffected agitators looking to create chaos.

Unfortunately, the violent few garner more attention than the peaceful majority that is also trying to bring forward important issues.

Politicians don't do much better. They express wonderment at so much outrage. In the words of President George W. Bush, the protesters "claim to represent the world's poor ... (but) ... they don't represent the poor, as far as I'm concerned." He insisted that the international leaders should be "undeterred" by the protests.

Perhaps the mostly European demonstrators who churned up the streets in Genoa, Italy (birthplace of Christopher Columbus), don't stem directly from among the world's most poor. But, interestingly, on the same day's front page of *The New York Times* that reported President Bush's dismissive remarks, a second long article, this one titled, "Farm Unrest is Roiling Mexico," provided strong evidence of just what the demonstrators are charging: that "globalization" as currently pursued is largely a corporate movement fueled by the United States to "privatize" the resources of the world.

Critics charge that the World Trade Organization, the World Bank, and their corporate power bases—as organizations spearheading globalization—are not so much about leveling the playing fields as they are about divvying them up. Dislocations of whole population sectors are severe and without specific consideration will generate huge problems of their own.

You could just about prove it by Mexico, where one early international agreement was hailed in 1994 as a great harbinger of things to come. The North American Free Trade Agreement (NAFTA), in fact, resulted in an armed rebellion in southern Mexico's state of Chiapas. The Zapatista declaration of war responded to the announced destruction of the Indian protected land systems known as *ejidos*.

NAFTA demanded deep changes in Mexican agriculture, including the privatization of Indian lands and the abridgement of the Mexican Constitution's Article 27, which provided a basis for the *ejido* system. The product of land rights won after the Mexican Revolution (1910–1919), the *ejidos* of Mexico are among some 3 million small farming communities and have represented a major avenue to continuing land tenure by Indian farmers.

NAFTA required the severe slashing of protections and subsidies to Mexican small farmers, particularly in the cropping of corn, coffee, and rice. A new measure approved by the Mexican congress in late July, the Law on Indian Rights and Culture, does not restore Indian land rights and has not satisfied the increasing unrest.

The *Times* reported, "by the tens of thousands, peasants in Mexico are abandoning the small lots they considered their birthright." As one Indian farmer expressed it, a "way of life is withering away." Millions of subsistence farmers (just 3.5 million of corn growers, perhaps as many as 15 million peasant farmers) are being displaced, and rapidly. The displaced Indian peasantry is flooding into urban areas of Mexico City and other northern industrial Mexican cities and, of course, north to the United States.

It is one impact of the free-trade compact that both Bush and Mexican President Vicente Fox are trying to address, with no visible success. This is largely the cause of millions of Mexican migrants crossing borders, legally or illegally, to the United States. And it is a consequence of globalization that is coming home to roost.

As the United States pushes for its brand of international open-trade covenants, the feeling rises in the world that the world's lone superpower is imposing itself on the rest of humanity, once more playing the role of gun-slinger negotiator.

A columnist for *The Boston Globe*, in fact, recently compared the United States' attitude to allies and adversaries alike abroad these days to colonial treaty making, when often American Indian delegates were some-times held at gunpoint and literally forced to sign documents giving away lands and resources.

Now we know that as the agreement that would become NAFTA and that would open up the Mexican farm sector to such devastating and cal-lous disaster was close to being signed, U.S. negotiators forcefully insisted on protections for its own sugar farmers.

For pundits who just might wonder just what is going on in Mexico City these past couple of weeks—those who always whine, "What could these people want?"—that is why 5,000 native Mexican sugar farmers are protesting in the central square of Mexico City. They know the contradic-tions of NAFTA, where the U.S. side got the whole cake and ate it, too.

As the free-trade agreement opened Mexico up to a flood of American products, pushing genetically modified corn, the Mexican farmers are los-ing steady ground. Growing edible corn for human consumption in Mexico is in-line with a deep cultural tradition; it is also the basis of a great deal of the Indian diet—in the traditional tortilla, and in dozens of other corn applications.

However, the corn imported from the United States is largely field corn, not compatible with the dietary needs of the population. So it goes. Mexican economists and technocrats at least recognize the problem of NAFTA's dis-locations, but largely write these off to the changing times, and perhaps "structural adjustments." But it is valid to express concern and deeply question whether such adjustments are pointed in the right direction.

One thing is certain. As globalization marches forward, combining governmental and corporate powers, these dislocations will continue and increasingly alter the lifeways of peoples around the world, affecting per-haps more than 70 percent of humanity (and 30 percent of Mexico).

The disparity between rich and poor, throughout history, has needed to maintain some proper degree of balance. It is undeniable that the growing misery of the masses in much of Latin America and the so-called Third World as contrasted with incredible and exploding opulence of the very rich (who are transnational) will continue to reverberate.

The dynamic of Mexico resonates through many nations. The problems will compound. Vigorous leadership that seeks social justice within economic prosperity, and not just bully tactics, is much in need.

World Needs America to Lead for Peace
September 20, 2002

In old stories of peacemaking among Native nations, the need to break the cycles of violence and revenge is central. Somewhere along the line, someone must make a decision to go beyond hatred and retribution. The call is for the use of reason, rather than emotion, to endeavor to prepare a field of peace. Among Iroquois, or Haudenosaunee, the Condolence ceremony is a guiding concept.

The speeches of the Condolence pay attention to the need to wipe the eyes clean of tears and other obstructions, to clear from the throat the thickness of noncommunication, to unplug the ears so good things may be heard. Thus is an aggrieved person or family, clan, or nation assisted in reaching a state of balance, from which the future good of all can be considered and peace constructed.

The concept may seem simple to some, although it is often difficult to apply, but today's world could much use its consideration—from within each culture and nation and among all nations. The world needs America to lead for peace. The world of today has the United Nations—a concept championed early by the United States—as a place to gather and discuss world peace. This is hugely important. More than ever, the world needs its only international forum and organization. The United Nations is the proper place for discussion and for resolution of issues between and among the nations of the world. Peace and conflict resolution, incipient in global affairs as full-fledged policy, must gain a foothold.

We believe in the rule of law. The sovereignty of nations is inherent in the history and culture of each people. This is the basis of all respect. It is an idea particularly important for American Indians and for all relatively small nations of the world, whether fully independent or living within larger nation-states. It is precisely the commitment to respect the rule of law that makes it possible for small nations to survive and prosper. Respect for the sovereignty of all peoples should be part of the United Nations mission.

U.S. President George W. Bush made the right move by going to the United Nations to lay out his case on Iraq. Certainly, the Iraq of Saddam Hussein is a society living in a severe state of repression. Saddam Hussein is a brutal, murderous dictator. And it is understandable that after the events of September 11, the United States would do everything in its power to strike at those it perceives as harboring the intent to do it harm. There is great danger, however, when the world's sole superpower is aroused to the point of seeking to initiate unilateral violence. The heat of human passion and the quest for even greater international power takes over at such times and can precipitate actions with unpredictable and dangerous consequences. A public angered and frustrated by senseless death and mayhem caused by an obscure enemy can be drawn into supporting actions that create their own problems.

Osama bin Laden and his al-Qaida terrorist network have done horrendous damage to the quest for world peace. With the brutal suicide attacks of little over a year ago, the terrorist mastermind not only destroyed the lives of some 3,000 people and their families, he set in motion a mentality and a pattern for an ideologically driven 'war without end,' the likes of which have not been seen before. Not even the Cold War had such potentially drastic results, as nation-states ultimately came to see mutual hostility as mutual destruction. But 'preemptive strikes' and wars of 'regime change' now become current concepts that seem to roll forward on their own. Once unleashed, they may land like thunder-bombs across a major geographic plain. We believe the task of coalition building, peace-making, slow and arduous, is the preferred route. The rule of international law should be upheld. Active peacemaking, while rooting out the specific enemy, is much advised. And should regime change in Iraq ultimately prove necessary, great consideration must be given to how a fully functional democratic society would be established.

We urge President Bush and his advisors to continue to press the war to al-Qaida, as it constitutes a ruthless, intertwined network, absolutely committed to mindless death and destruction and the organizing of a membership with no apparent instinct for self-preservation. But we also hope the United States will continue to pressure Iraq and other rogue nation-states within a United Nations context. We equally urge the United States to greatly increase its commitment to peace by actually hearing what other nations have to say, and by retooling through democratization its international-assistance program. As various regions of the world struggle with modernity, not all is a calm reflection of U.S. society, all clean and suburban, as most television images would suggest. A big ship of state, such as the United States, always leaves turbulence in its wake. Certainly this is evident today.

American Indian peoples have long known what it is like to live in the footprint of the world's greatest superpower. More pronounced in North America, and, of course, in the United States, this holds true only slightly less for the rest of the Western Hemisphere. We have witnessed the growth of the American nation since its birth. Sometimes (perhaps increasingly), we have adapted and even benefited from this reality, long layered upon Indian country lands, lives, and cultural influences. All too often, however, American Indian nations have been run over, pushed aside, attacked militarily and economically, and misunderstood culturally and spiritually. Most of us have accepted the reality of that history, one that also had global origins.

Adaptation, rather than reactive violence, has sustained our survival. Adaptation followed and increased our awareness of the new existence, what used to be called "civilization" and has now come to be known as "modernization." For American Indian people, still living upon or with access to homelands and guided, even conceptually, by traditional cultures that are intensely life enhancing, this historical and yet active pain has hardly turned to political or religiously motivated violence—and certainly not to terrorism. Protest, confrontation, public debate and awareness, quiet cooperation, and alliance-building and electoral politics have been the various and successful tools of American Indian survival and renewal. This is not true or possible in all cultures and places. Some adherents of Islam in Saudi Arabia, Egypt, Pakistan, and elsewhere, as everyone knows, have turned to preaching hatred and death as a form of worship. This too we condemn. We are the first to celebrate our distinctiveness, but always in the context of universal humanity.

Perhaps the worst piece of the turbulence has been the denial of the chance to tell our side of the story, the difficulty in getting mainstream America to listen and understand how various global and national politics can affect tribal nations and peoples. Without denying the positive in the modern world, we reassert that the process of contact and conquest and colonization—apparent precursors to modernization—can bring forth great suffering to peoples who are living on their own lands and based in traditional societies. Real understanding of this important factor is crucial to creating a more stable and prosperous world. The question: "Why does anybody hate us that much?" requires the deepest and truest answer possible. This piece of the global reality America needs to hear. It needs to know and contemplate it, to ponder and discuss it, even as it presses its military boot crushingly down on al-Qaida's neck, even as it necessarily identifies, studies, seeks, and destroys all forms of international terrorism.

Fallen Sister Soldier Is Symbol of Our Common Pain

April 11, 2003

Our strongest condolences to the family of Pfc. Lori Piestewa, twenty-three, of Tuba City, Arizona. The tragic yet heroic and honorable circumstances of Pfc. Piestewa's death in combat moved Indian country and all of America to mourn with the Piestewa family and the Hopi people. Many have followed her fate avidly and developed a great sympathy and heartfelt connection to the young and steadfast mother of two. Lori Ann Piestewa honored well a family tradition of military service to her tribal nation and her American country.

We take this opportunity to honor all warriors—American Indians—both men and women, who have held up a long tradition of military service in America. The Native tradition of military service is rooted in the commitment to serve the cause of "freedom." While this sentiment has spread to all Americans and runs full in the vein of the American soul, the call to defend "our own free country" runs particularly deep in the Native community.

Whether in agreement or disagreement on particular issues and politics, America must be proud of its Indian soldiers; it should celebrate not only their sacrifice but their living contribution to the motivation and fervor for freedom in the American people at large.

The freedom America sings about came at a high price for American Indian tribes. The turbulent colonial years saw the forced dispossession of many. It was, and in some cases continues to be, a contentious history. American Indians, who had freedom in their hand, lost a big piece of what was natural and self-determined, yet even while under duress, transferred the value and the knowledge of it to their new immigrant brethren. The freedom to council, the freedom of movement, the freedom to disagree with and even admonish or remove political leaders, the freedom of trade and commerce, the freedom of fundamental rights of religious expression—these were all present in Native America at the time of first contact with Europeans.

The very existence of Indian peoples created the political personality of what would become, "the American." It is a little-known fact that prior to U.S. independence, the proper subject for the term "American" was the Indian. The colonist became American in the footsteps of the Indian. He fought like the Indian and in many ways took on the values of the Indian—not only as a people, but deep in the psyche—which is the origin of an emerging American rectitude: that fundamental consciousness that seeks to make things right with the tribes.

While early American Indian military movements began necessarily as antagonistic to United States armies, and nearly every tribe has a heroic record of defensive warfare against the United States (or England, Spain, and France)—as Native peoples settled reservation territories and as an additional American citizenship was granted by the new nation-state that sought jurisdiction over Native ancestral lands, American Indians have consistently fought honorably for the righteous causes of the United States. Native peoples have carried their ancestral sense of obligation to defend freedom of their own peoples and lands onto their commitment to serve and fight the enemy with the U.S. military. This has full and actually mystical fusion: when America says "Freedom," primordially, it is the American Indian saying "Freedom."

Native American women have served in the military since World War I, when fourteen served as members of the Army Nurse Corps. Nearly 800 Native American women served in the military during World War II. Many Native American women saw service during the Korean War and Vietnam War; however, the exact number has not been documented. Two Native American women previously lost their lives in the armed services: Terri Ann Hagan in 1994 and Katherine Mathews in 1985. As of 1994, 1,509 Native American women were serving in the military forces of the United States.

During World War II, some 99 percent of eligible healthy American Indian males ages twenty-one to forty-four registered for the draft. Ten percent of the eligible American Indian population served during these years. As many as 70 percent of the eligible population served from some tribes. By the end of World War II, 24,521 reservation Indians and 20,000 from off-reservation had served. Six American Indian men received the Medal of Honor in World War II. The commitment and sense of "fighting for freedom" is high for American Indian veterans. (Thanks to that National Congress of American Indians for information.)

If good finally would manifest from this painful war in Iraq, it would have to be that the world will help a people emerge into a semblance of freedom. The tradition of the United States military has been to see itself as a liberating force, a force to defend and stand for the value of freedom.

There is fierce difference of opinion as to the lived reality of this ideal, but the ideal is nevertheless expressed and believed. Americans must always stand for freedom. Freedom is not an abstract concept. It is a hugely important value to commit to—even as many will certainly disagree about how that is to be accomplished in the real world.

As American Indian peoples have come to contribute their service to the United States—in the commitment to fighting for a free Indian country, for a free land, for freedom—so too we hope for America a continuing dedication to the value of freedom as it attempts to "rebuild" Iraq and lead the world.

We thank all our American Indian soldiers for their steadfastness in the face of duty and sacrifice. Iraq, situated at the crossways of the world with its politics layered in tribal complexity, is today's battleground for hearts and souls. May our intentions be clear, and on the side of good. The memory of all our loved ones who gave themselves to the cause of freedom will thus be always honored.

American Indian Development, a Time to Maximize Trade and Commerce
May 7, 2004

Almost all the Native peoples of the Southern Hemisphere and a substantial piece of the Indian country in North America are mired in poverty. This is particularly the case in Central and South America, but it is just as true in the United States, where every socio-economic indicator verifies the continuing misery on most reservations. Both internationally and nationally, there is a lot that can be done about it.

At the United Nations this week in New York City, more than a thousand indigenous delegates will gather to assess the problems and potentials of their nations, tribes, and communities. The much-touted UN International Decade of Indigenous People has come and gone. It can be argued that the Decade and the whole effort at the UN for more than two decades have brought serious attention for indigenous peoples and their cases. No doubt, the human and civil rights of individuals and occasionally of a whole sector of humanity have been better addressed because of the international networks developed at the UN. Certain covenants and declarations generated by the process can already, in modest ways, prove useful in Native rights cases, and most hopefully in the protection of indigenous territories from outright dispossession.

It can just as effectively be argued that the misery and poverty resulting from conquest, colonization, and marginalization have only worsened during this same time. On the ground, this is the harsh reality for most Latin American Indian communities. Survival movements of the 1970s have turned into autochthonous movements that in countries such as Ecuador and Bolivia have gained great political momentum in recent years. What no one has even remotely identified for improvement is the economic conditions experienced by indigenous peoples—which has been a disappointment during those very same years.

At the international level, with few excellent exceptions, the problem is that funding agencies are seldom geared to work with grassroots indigenous communities. A great deal of education and networking, in both directions, is severely needed. There have been too many mutual misconceptions. Development funds, which have steadily diminished in the past decade, tend to filter through layers of international and national agencies and intermediary NGOs. These tend to feed myriad professionally paid consultants whom too often consume resources that should have reached the community levels. Additionally, cultural cycles and kinship relations often lack logic to professional agencies, who don't easily square with the pace and interconnectedness of community processes, too often condemning to failure programs that could work well over longer extended periods. Then, too, since the international attention on terror, many donors are scared away by the possibility that some international agency and foundation of choice might turn out to have some link to a suspected terror organization. As a result, international philanthropic agencies and foundations must rededicate themselves given the increased complexities of the task at hand.

On the other side of the equation, generations of abuse and oppression clearly have caused among many Native peoples what psychologists these days identify as historical pain or "ethno-stress," serious decision-making dysfunctions that are not easily overcome with short-term gifts or facile commitments. For fruitful community development, a commitment of generations is required. Methodologies are crucial that expertly gather the best possible community, tribal, and nation leadership to guide development in culturally appropriate and nonconflictive ways.

In this context, we heartily endorse the efforts of the International Funders of Indigenous Peoples (IFIP), a highly energetic and well-envisioned new project that aims to educate international funders and directly connect them with varieties of emerging proposals (locally and regionally based) for indigenous-community development. IFIP coordinator Evelyn Arce White has developed a superbly useful guide to funding possibilities for indigenous community projects (*Indigenous Peoples Funding and Resource Guide*, Second Edition, IFIP, 2004—ifip@firstnations.org). It focuses at once on informing indigenous peoples' organizations on the best approaches for securing financial backing and on educating the foundation world on how to best support the responsive energies for community building among Native peoples.

Quite apart from most other indigenous peoples, in North America a good portion of Indian country is experiencing a tremendous explosion of financial power. It is not widely beneficial as yet, but it has good potential for manifesting the dreams of generations of Native visionaries for reestablishing cultural and commerce relations among Indian peoples throughout the Americas and among Native peoples worldwide. Close to two decades have passed since American Indian tribes launched the gaming era. In the past decade, some 200 tribes have achieved various degrees of success, with several deriving very substantial economic rewards and about a score emerging as significant financial players rivaling that of most major wealthy American businesses and families. Native tribal gaming is an upward of $17 billion annual industry.

Thus, the question now surfaces with increasing frequency: if a fifth of Indian country these days enjoys a growing capital base of such substantial proportions, what could be done, if wiser heads gathered and advocated for it, to defeat the widespread misery and poverty still besetting the families on the majority of reservations?

It is incongruous to see such huge economic disparity in Indian country. We believe and very much hope that it will soon be seen as shameful by all Indian people. Message: the time is now for the richer tribes to connect more intently and thus to do more for the rest of Indian country.

We are not suggesting giveaways. All tribes have many needs, even as they gather economic territory. The job of reconstruction and nation building is profound. While we respect those whose job it is to distribute charity, we do not focus on charity ourselves as the main avenue for positive change. Our goal is the economic prosperity of all Native peoples. And prosperity needs another engine other than charity. It needs production, both for family and community consumption—the insurance of the local indigenous economies—and in the organization and manufacture of goods and services that can be profitably sold or traded in the world.

The North American tribal nations need to seriously engender a major national initiative to buy and, when necessary, develop Indian production and services in every way possible. Stimulus of Indian family and community tribal enterprise is highly desired and must be highly valued. A serious and aggressive inter-Indian trade and commerce program is required. Throughout the Western Hemisphere, and certainly as close as Mexico and Guatemala, there is a substantial labor market, as well as a strongly productive Indian-based agriculture. Foodstuffs from the Andes, including several excellent Native-produced grains, as well as other products, are much worth exploring.

Our desire is to stimulate a serious, pragmatic discussion concerning the needs and opportunities for maximizing trade and commerce among American Indians and, indeed, all indigenous peoples. The major casino resorts need huge quantities of meats and other agricultural products, many goods and services, again,—billions of dollars in purchasing. We submit that every opportunity not spent doing business with other appropriate but less financed American Indian businesses is a dollar lost to the unified strength and growth of tribal prosperity and freedom.

We urge tribal leaders and their enterprise directors in North America to value the call to: buy Indian; support Indian; develop Indian. American Indian leaders must supply the political volition to make this happen within their complex and layered tribal enterprises. This itself might be their most daunting challenge. Business logic is rightfully demanding but tribal policy must also be set to support and strengthen American Indian business alliances—the primary sector among our peoples uniquely suited to expand Indian opportunity and to provide the political clout required to protect indigenous life and enterprise well into the future.

We believe increased business relations among tribal communities and enterprises will strengthen tribal unity. It is a necessary goal for which we will always advocate. It is time to cast off the dysfunctions that inhibit healthy community and intertribal relations. We call for the intense critique of tribal shortcomings that misapprehend this most important of survival lessons. A strong alliance of tribal peoples—north and south, east and west—is the stuff of life for all our nations; and it is good for America.

Onward Christian Soldiers ...
December 2, 2004

Pity for the decent evangelical folks, the gentle flock of Christians truly given to pious good deeds for their fellow human beings, pity their souls for they are increasingly represented by wolves wearing the pelts of sheep.

Pity the ones who can hope with the one who suffered on the Cross that one day the lamb will lay down with the lion, in peace and harmony and that communities of human beings, particularly those that believe in a Creator, will beat swords into plowshares—because the people who have politicized and polarized Christianity, we believe, are of a mind to alter the country, where America as a society becomes increasingly intolerant so much and so consistently that the character of Americans will change forever.

We have to believe that there is a different point of view in Christianity, that to be a lover of Jesus does not immediately make one a supporter of war policy as primary basis for dealing with the discontent of the world's peoples. This, too, deserves pity. Pity the longing of Jesus of Nazareth for a flock of human beings steeped in humility and exalting simplicity and modesty in all things.

We have to believe that there is a different point of view in Christianity because many in Indian country have lived it.

Pity the decent evangelical folks who want a better world and that can intuit from the message of their Savior, who is the Sacred Heart of their door to Heaven, that good deeds in this world must be multiplied and that good Christian society requires the provision of the million good deeds for the millions of people who deeply need the most rudimentary of human existence; pity the open-minded Christian who is curious about the world and not just scared or angry and who has lived through experience guided by good-hearted intelligence as central to the works of all the good people.

We have to believe that there are such Christians. Because right now, Christianity is being distorted and hijacked as rapidly as Islam was into hatred as worship.

Huge wealth is being amassed globally by a very few people while so many others are displaced and disjointed by the mighty pulls and pushes of the globally controlled trends and the decisions of its all-powerful, immensely wealthy captains. The good Christians, many of whom over the centuries have been of great assistance to Indian peoples, have to wonder about the place of the Christian faith now used as political ideology. The ethic that the transnational-corporate mentality follows is too often creating a world with little or no responsibility for place, nor for the people of a place. Where and who would be the Christians who will identify and assail the violent demagoguery representing them, while the mainstream media gapes at the wonderful sound bytes anger and verbal assault can produce?

Would those be the Christians, such as Quakers in northeastern North America, who took the time to debate their proper Christian conduct in their relations with Native peoples; or those such as Father Bartolome de las Casas, who principally sought peace and justice in the name of Christ; or, such as the present elderly Pope, who defies severe pain with spiritual integrity that calls for peace, for a better American understanding of the miserable poverty confronting most of the world's peoples?

It doesn't seem so. Biblical fundamentalism in today's America appears married to ostentatious braggadocio, loud-talking reverends with gold chains and diamonds and huge personal estates. It has at its own core perhaps even a mass of people embracing a righteous ignorance that, like it or not, invites comparison with the zealots on the other end of Abraham's family of warring religions, the Islamic fundamentalists. The political, emergent American Christianity is married to great wealth, not necessarily benign, and it is presently led by a political coalition that has excited masses of well-meaning Christians as much as it endangers them. Rigidity, conformity, anger, more self-righteous than righteous, fuels it.

There is nary a mention of any kind of social or economic justice approach to the world's problems, where so many huge masses of human beings are increasingly in such misery as to be unable to meet the most rudimentary requirements of clean water, food, and shelter for their families. There is nary a recognition of the swath of plunder that has passed over the world for too many centuries and that in large part has created the miserable conditions of Latin America, Africa, and most of Asia. That drive to appropriate American indigenous resources has now plowed over its own middle-class of workers and producers, selling the raw materials of the country, its production facilities, and now even its service sector directly to the lowest-labor bidder to be found, anywhere in the world. This is hailed as the wonder of globalization by entities called "American corporations," which have little allegiance to any country or peoples and, in fact, proudly embrace the label "trans-national." It is a market-driven trend that is so bent on profits it is willing to wreak havoc on ecosystems and peoples far and wide.

All of this needs to and could be done better. A more Christian attitude—the Christianity of St. Francis of Assisi, say, of Martin Luther King Jr., and not of the Jerry Falwell or Pat Robertson variety—from America would be of great relief to humankind. Pity the Christian who truly thinks that a society will function best that produces the broadest possible range of its own needed goods, trades sparingly on other items, and works to guarantee easy economic access to good food, healing institutions that work, and respect for living communities of peoples.

Many who know the history of U.S.–Muslim relations mark the turning point at the CIA overthrow of a legitimate government in Iran, which caused within a generation the mass overthrow of a Shah (the American-imposed king), whose armies actually reached the point of blood saturation when the soldiers finally refused to shoot at the civilian demonstrations that kept coming at them. Which is to say: there is a lot to know about these so-called religious wars of Christians against the Muslims, which recur every few decades and go back more than 1,000 years.

We gave up here long ago on the concept of divinely inspired wars. The forces of Creation in our estimation do not invest energies in supporting the mass murder of war, for whatever meager and pitiful reasons any particular group of human beings can construct with which to justify the killing of others. But human beings sure are good at justifying killing with their concept of God. True enough, America's evangelical fundamentalists are not as of this writing on the brutal path of their Islamic counterparts, who have eschewed all human empathy from the messages of their God—but then, again, the Muslim world's ayatollahs and imams were not so easily disposed to such violent preaching even two generations ago. Whereas now, violent hatred of America, always easily manipulated, dominates the region.

We continue to reject the notion that an unjustified war, a war that has the potential of becoming a war of religious civilizations, is the answer to the brutal crime of September 11, 2001. War, divinely inspired or not, Bible-interpreted or Koran-interpreted, is always war. A more pragmatic and less ideological approach, a less "religious" approach, we submit, would have achieved and will achieve clearer and more positive results.

For Christians, we believe, the question is still relevant: what would Jesus do?

PERSPECTIVES

Indigenous Peoples Have a Place on the World Stage
May 12, 2003

John Mohawk, *Indian Country Today*

When the Spanish first arrived in the Caribbean more than 500 years ago, the idea that indigenous peoples might possess rights and notions about what those rights might be was given scarce attention. The conquistadores approached many of the indigenous communities with a priest who read a document called the Requerimiento, a demand that the people come forth with their bodies and souls and all their property and offer these to the service of the Spanish crown or the Spanish would attack. It was read in Latin as prelude to an orgy of rape, plunder, and genocide. It wasn't until the middle of the sixteenth century that a bishop, Bartolomé de Las Casas, championed the idea of some rights of the Indians before the Council of the Indies. Although that body agreed with the principle that indigenous peoples should not be abused, the conquest continued unabated. With a few minor exceptions, the idea of the existence of indigenous peoples' rights remained submerged until the middle of the twentieth century.

Beginning in the early 1950s, some indigenous peoples began urging that the international community recognize their inherent rights to continue to exist as distinct peoples. The idea was given a significant boost in 1977, when the nongovernmental organizations of the United Nations organized a meeting in Geneva, Switzerland, to discuss the creation of indigenous rights under international law. The conference sought to create Principles of the Rights of Indigenous Peoples of the Western Hemisphere that, it was hoped, might lead to a Declaration of such rights for indigenous peoples around the world. In 1982, indigenous leaders and representatives were invited to Geneva to witness the development of the United Nations Working Group on Indigenous Populations. The context of this development is important because until that time, indigenous peoples were relegated to the most extreme margins of international affairs. The first time they appeared in Geneva, they were considered so exotic the city closed its schools so the children could witness their arrival.

This was an important step toward recognition as peoples whose issues matter and whose representatives are physically present at the meetings where decisions are made. Indigenous peoples had entered into treaties with European and Euro-American nation-states, and in the 1920s some—

most notably Deskaheh from the Haudenosaunee or Iroquois—had tried to approach the League of Nations, but the Working Group provided the first institutional setting within the United Nations in the modern era. Every summer since 1982, the Working Group has met to forge a Draft Declaration on the rights of indigenous peoples and these meetings have been one of the UN's most well-attended activities, with up to 1,000 people—business representatives, NGOs, government representatives, and indigenous representatives—attending the meetings.

In the beginning, the nation-states were cautious and occasionally hostile to the idea of indigenous rights and to the movement representing it. In 1999, the Organization of American States (OAS) was essentially closed to indigenous peoples, but they were presented with a mandate from the Inter-American Commission on Human Rights and indigenous peoples insisted on a presence in those proceedings. This year, indigenous representatives attend the annual meetings of the thirty-four member states of the OAS and are greeted with dignity and their issues are extended respectful attention. Those who attend report an atmosphere of open exchange characterizes the meetings. This has meant that indigenous representatives have joined the culture of the community of world policy makers.

Most of the fears of the states held that indigenous rights was a plot to dismantle these states, but that fear has largely evaporated, and the idea that states must play a role in protecting the rights of distinct peoples to exist in possession of their lands and against invasion by forces bringing disease and destroying waters, wildlife, and forests is increasingly accepted. In fact, many have now begun to incorporate the rhetoric of the rights of groups to a continued existence as distinct peoples and this movement has spread rapidly over the past fifteen years to include countries across the globe in Europe, Australia, the Pacific, Asia, and Africa.

A good example of the dramatic changes taking place is represented by Brazil. In the mid-1980s, indigenous peoples such as the Yanomami were threatened with extinction. Gold miners invaded their country and polluted the rivers with arsenic and 20 percent of their population was dying of malaria and other diseases. But in 1988, Brazil adopted a reform constitution that recognized indigenous rights. Today, most of the land is demarcated (reserved to its original owners) and tens of thousands of miners and loggers have been expelled from Yanomami country by the Brazilian government. Last year, the Yanomami celebrated a milestone: there was not a single death from malaria in all of Yanomami country. Brazil no longer hosts or abides wholesale abuses of indigenous human rights.

The fact that so much change could take place over such a short period of time is rightfully seen as miraculous. In the mid-1990s, nation-states strongly resisted the use of the term indigenous "peoples," preferring the word "populations" as conferring fewer rights to the indigenous and fewer obligations on the states. The idea was to relegate indigenous rights to a status similar to civil rights. London, England, has a "population" of individuals from India. Mexico is home to an array of indigenous groups who share a common language, history, and identity and who are, in every sense of the word, peoples. In 2001, in the United Nations conversation about indigenous peoples, the word "populations" was relegated to the dustbin of history when the Working Group overwhelmingly adopted the word "peoples."

The rapid evolution of growing recognition of indigenous rights has taken place since the Cold War. Today, there are young Indian lawyers in Brazil, in Honduras, in Nicaragua, working on protecting indigenous peoples under principles that only a few short years ago were unimaginable. The OAS, the World Bank, the IMF (International Monetary Fund) and all international institutions are being challenged, and all now have policies to protect indigenous peoples. There is good news here, but, of course, everything is not perfect. The United States recently announced it would refuse to comply with an OAS decision in the case of the Dann family in the Shoshone country of Nevada, and U.S. deportment on indigenous rights has definitely been a mixed bag. Much needs to be done but there is also a good foundation for optimism.

Faith-Based War Coverage
August 18, 2003

John Mohawk, *Indian Country Today*

It's midsummer, Qusay and Uday Hussein are dead, and the American occupation of Iraq has settled into a low-intensity guerrilla war with no announced exit strategy. The national affliction, Adult Attention Deficit Disorder (AADD), is in such full force around the topic of the war that the American people don't seem to remember how things came to be the way they are.

To recap: Saddam and Iraq were widely viewed as among the world's worst headaches because of past acts of international aggression, internal genocide, and political repression, murder, torture, and weapons mongering. Beginning with the 9-11 attack by a separate, unrelated group, al-Qaida, a Bush doctrine emerged that emulated what until then had been a neocon foreign-policy fantasy focused on four points: marginalize the UN, avoid nation building, avoid peace keeping, and avoid military action for humanitarian purposes. Failure to follow these principles were among what neocons thought to be the sins of President Clinton, who they thought was a Liberal.

The Bush administration's agitation for war was, in substantial ways, disingenuous. The UN agreed Saddam was in breach of the conditions that brought an alleged end to Gulf War and they seemed poised to go beyond sanctions to military intervention similar to the last war. But they wanted to exhaust all other remedies first. The United States insisted that Saddam was so close to being able to mobilize weapons of mass destruction (within forty-five minutes he could launch a chemical attack) that he had to be stopped immediately, with or without the UN. So United States and its only real ally, Tony Blair, raced to war with solemn statements about how everybody will see that there are WMD all over Iraq when American and Blair forces capture them.

Once the war was under way, there were two primary activities undertaken by the administration and its allies: find WMD and keep criticism about the commitment to nation building and peace keeping and even the rationalizations for war under control until the WMD are found.

The administration's best ally is the notorious previously mentioned AADD. For example, few outside of academia will remember the 2003 Iraq war for the credibility meltdown of the American media. Even the stalwart *New York Times* would suffer a scandal when one of its reporters was found to be filing inaccurate and sometimes-fictitious reports, but a far more serious problem was the *Times* joined the other press "poodles" as disseminators of Pentagon spin stories as fact, especially on the issue of the potential for WMD in Iraq.

Nothing better illustrates what a media enterprise with a glaring lack of interest in responsible reporting can be than Rupert Murdock's Fox Network's coverage of the war. This wasn't a matter of getting the facts wrong, but of reporting that was willfully wrong. It was enough to urge passage of a Truth in Media Reform Act (TMRA), which would require, under penalty of law, that reporters check their sources and that networks such as Fox be required to include comments from a public interest (nonprofit) media commentator to provide balance.

Here is how the scenario might have looked:

On March 14, Fox Network reports Saddam Hussein has plans to blow up dams causing floods and drowning "coalition" forces. TMRA watchdog Francis Counterpoint interjects on the air: "Dare I mention there's not a single confirmed source for this armchair speculation?" Fox heatedly repeats the prediction.

On March 23, Fox reports that a facility at An Najaf produces chemical weapons. Counterpoint replies: "Didn't the UN weapons inspectors check this out? What did they say?" Within a day, a former UN inspector says they knew about the site and no weapons were ever produced there. But Fox keeps repeating the story a full day after it had been debunked. Counterpoint added: "Gees, don't you guys get embarrassed blathering nonsense?" Apparently not.

The next day, Fox carried a story by Oliver North reporting that the French, who resisted joining the war effort because they were not persuaded by the Bush administration's bogus information campaign about the danger of imminent attack, were shredding documents in their embassy. Counterpoint: "North? His credibility was shredded years ago. How many felons are reporters here, anyway?"

On April 7, Fox breathlessly reports missiles were found near Baghdad containing poison gas. "Got any proof," asks Counterpoint. "Pictures? Affidavits? Eyewitnesses?" Fox quietly abandons this un-story. Turns out there were no missiles. There was no retraction either.

On April 9, Fox joins other news agencies showing images of a crowd toppling Saddam's statue in Baghdad. At last, the grateful crowd of Iraqis cheering American liberators—a favorite prewar neocon prediction—had materialized. Or did it? Counterpoint: "Could we get a better shot of the crowd? Looks small." Small indeed.

The next day Fox reports finding a bioweapons lab. Counterpoint: "How do we know it's a lab?" From Fox, no answer.

The next day, to illustrate that Saddam and the French are "embedded," Fox is airing news clips of a trip by Saddam to Paris in 1975. (That's not a typo.) There were no news clips of a March 24, 1984, trip by Rumsfeld to Iraq. It was the same day that Saddam's guys used mustard gas and nerve agents against Iranian soldiers. WMD, war crimes, and Rumsfeld. That kind of footage might just confuse people.

By April 15, Fox reporter Mansoor Ijaz tells us the top fifty-five (remember the deck of cards?) in Saddam's regime have fled Iraq and are holed up in Latakia, Syria. Counterpoint: "The Nixon White House had an insurmountable credibility problem, but you should stamp your reporting 'Inoperable at Birth.'" As a matter of fact, no evidence has ever emerged that even one member of the Iraqi regime went to Syria. In time, most of them are captured or killed. On April 22, Bill O'Reilly (of the *O'Reilly Factor*) warns that if no WMD are found within a month, this could spell big trouble for Bush.

By May 20, the news is full of a scandal involving the details around the rescue of Private Jessica Lynch. The *Los Angeles Times* and the BBC have reported that the story of a daring and dramatic rescue including gunfire was a fraud. Fox's *O'Reilly* turns to military "analyst" Colonel David Hunt, who assures us the Army would never lie. Hunt: "They're the best soldiers in the world. Why would they make this up?" Counterpoint: "Is it that hard to find an 'analyst' who knows that sometimes people in the Army make up stories. HELLO! Earth to Fox! Anybody there?"

By August 12, the only WMD in sight go to the Fox Network as a prize: Worst Media for Dummies.

*With thanks to Dale Steinreich, "Fibbing it Up at Fox" on www.LewRockwell.com, from which information about Fox's reporting was gleaned.

On the Words 'Tribe' and 'Nation'
December 3, 2004

Steven Newcomb, Indigenous Law Institute

At the conclusion of the War of 1812, during talks leading to the 1814 Treaty of Ghent, American and British treaty commissioners engaged in a heated and lengthy political debate over the status of American Indians. The British commissioners wanted an Indian buffer state to exist between the United States and Canada. The American commissioners were very much opposed to such a plan.

Bilateral political talks are discussions involving power and power relations. They are talks in which both sides use words and ideas to maneuver and jockey for a position of power in relation to one another. In keeping with their political perspective and their desire to establish an American Indian buffer state, the British commissioners used the expression "Indian nations" because they considered this phrase to be the most politically powerful use of the English language. The British commissioners consciously rejected the phrase "Indian tribes," thus pointing out that the distinction between nations and tribes is extremely important.

The American treaty commissioners, on the other hand, steadfastly refused to use the term "nations" in reference to the Indians, and were careful to never deviate from the phrase "Indian tribes." The American commissioners didn't want Indians to be dignified with the more politically powerful term "nations."

The sharp difference between "nations" and "tribes" in the debate between Great Britain and the United States in the early part of the nineteenth century is instructional for us as American Indians in the early part of the twenty-first century.

It is almost impossible for any attorney to write in a typical manner about federal Indian law without referring to "Indian tribes." Charles F. Wilkinson, for example, wrote: "Indian tribes are the basic unit in Indian law." However, the refusal by British treaty commissioners to use the term "tribe" in a political dispute raises the question, "Is 'tribe' the most politically powerful term to use in reference to our respective nations and peoples?"

The word "tribe" is derived from the Latin language and refers to the three (from the prefix "tri," meaning "three") main divisions of the Roman people representing the Latin, Sabine, and Etruscan settlements. Tribe refers to, "any group of people united by ties of common descent from a common ancestor, community of customs and traditions, adherence to the same leaders." Another meaning is, "a local division of an Aboriginal people." A tribe is also defined as, "a class or type of animals, plants, articles, or the like." Tribe is also a term of stockbreeding, "a group of animals, esp. cattle, descended through the female line from a common female ancestor."

The word "nation" refers to "a body of people, associated with a particular territory, that is sufficiently conscious of its unity to seek or to possess a government peculiarly its own." Also, "the territory or country itself." Synonyms include: "State, commonwealth, kingdom, realm." Another meaning is, "a member tribe of a confederation," which is a kind of state. The word national means, "or, pertaining to, or maintained by a nation as an organized whole or independent political unit," and, "peculiar or common to the whole people of a country."

The contrast between the two terms is striking. The concept of nation is inclusive of such terms as, "government, territory, realm, confederacy, independent political unit," etc., which are not necessarily or generally associated with the term "tribe."

The title of the book *Indian Tribes as Sovereign Governments* put out by Charles Wilkinson and the American Indian Resources Institute (2004) is an interesting example of the effort that must be made to link "sovereignty" and "tribes." Because "sovereignty" is not found in the etymological history of the word "tribe," federal Indian law commentators have to make a special effort to link the two concepts together. By contrast, the concept of "sovereignty" is naturally embedded in the word "nation."

A book titled "Indian Nations as Sovereign Governments" would be considered redundant because it would state the obvious: nations are sovereign. It would be sort of like a title: "Roses as flowers." Based on the word's etymology, "tribe" does not obviously mean "sovereign," or self-governing, thus the need to specify the idea of "Indian Tribes as Sovereign Governments," with the added caveat of the subjugating federal Indian law paradigm: "subject to federal supervision," or "subject to the plenary power of Congress."

If you were in a conversation with a representative of a member state of the United Nations, and referred to that country, nation, or state as a "tribe" (for example, the "tribe" of Canada), your remark would spark an immediate and sharp response. No nation-state representative would allow his or her country to be referred to as a "tribe." In fact, that representative would feel highly insulted because the Western mind immediately associates the word "tribe" with "primitive," "uncivilized," "backward," and "inferior."

Our indigenous sisters and brothers to the north saw through this semantic dilemma at least a decade ago, and began to politically demand that the dominant Canadian society refer to them as "First Nations."

The word "treaty" refers to "a formal agreement between two or more states in reference to peace, alliance, commerce, or other international relations." Not one mention of "tribe" or "tribes" is found in this definition because such demeaning terminology is outside of formal international diplomatic relations. We talk about the treaties that so many of our respective nations have made with the United States, but we allow ourselves to be demeaned with the words "tribe" and "tribal."

Mental habits are extremely difficult to break because we become emotionally committed to them whether those habits promote our interests or not. A mental habit occurs unconsciously, without thinking. When we call attention to something so customary, so taken for granted as the use of the words "tribe" and "tribal," we bring these concepts up to the level of conscious awareness and begin to ask specific questions about them. Once we have taken the time to engage in conscious and critical assessment of these terms, we can make a conscious decision to shift our language usage and our ideas toward more politically powerful terms.

As far as I'm concerned, it's time to stop denigrating ourselves with the terms "tribe" and "tribal." We downgrade ourselves, and our status, as nations and peoples when we fail to choose the most powerful terms in English to express our political identity.

"Already, the Kay Report identified dozens of weapons of mass destruction-related program activities ..."

State of the Union Address, January 2004

Prisoner
abuse

REBUILDING IRAQ

...And whatever you do don't sign a treaty with that guy!

Chapter Eight
Living on Mother Earth

Western scholars and many journalists (and even conservationists) too often go out of their way to misunderstand or disregard Native ethical motivations. While academics debate whether Indigenous American cultures actually have ecological underpinnings, in fact, throughout Indian country tribal peoples sustain nature-intensive ceremonial rituals. Furthermore, many tribes are applying newly developed environmental technologies, such as in solar- and wind-energy projects. Beyond the coincidental or gimmicky, beyond the stereotype of the "ecological Indian," Native peoples are consciously building on some superlative ancient approaches, working to protect seed varieties and natural practices of herbal medicines and food production, and retention of women's medicines and reproductive rights. These are not strange connections for eco-systemic cultures shaped by languages and cosmologies at one with earth, sky, climate, and nature.

The Sun Can Provide
April 2, 2000

Solar energy, often dismissed as too high-maintenance and expensive, is finding a niche in Indian country, at least among Southwestern tribes. Indians are among the major advocates of a better energy policy. At a time when the global energy grid threatens to affect even the very weather patterns of the Earth, it is refreshing to see Native communities and advocates moving ahead with creative solutions based on their own homegrown cultural values.

In the Hopi and Navajo reservations, projects aimed at providing energy through solar-power units have proliferated in the past decade. At Hopi Nation, a program has been established called NativeSun, responsible for hundreds of solar systems with panels dotting the skyline of Hopi villages. We are thankful to Native journalist Peggy Berryhill for her article "Hopi Potskwaniat," detailing the history and philosophy of this positive effort by the Hopi Foundation. The application of new, soft technologies in remote areas not only makes sense economically, but culturally as well. It does not replace "traditional" technology but, in fact, it usually replaces a dangerous, smelly, earlier Western technology: kerosene burners. Village elders of Hotevila and Kykotsmovi, on the Hopi Reservation, accepted the new solar panels on the rooftops of their stone houses as a step in sync with their own cultural perspectives.

As in a growing number of Native communities, this project at Hopi is made possible by the positive collaboration between college graduates and skilled tradespeople from the community, returning to the reservation, working with their elders and other tribal authorities. The Hopi Foundation, a main rotor of this movement to find collaborative working relations between traditional culture and the professional skills and attitudes of their formally trained people, deserves special recognition. The foundation's motto: *Lomasum'nangwtukwsiwmani*, means, "the furthering unity of aspiration blossoming into full maturity over time." The Native Sun team of both Hopi and Navajo technicians have worked together to install more than 300 solar systems and provide an excellent example of collaboration between sometimes-conflicted tribes.

At Navajo Nation, with 37,000 public and private structures spread out over 4.8 million acres, stringing power lines at $30,000 per mile is financially prohibitive in many areas. A new program recently funded by the feds, Native American Photovoltaics (NAPV), promises to install twenty new solar-generating systems at $10,000 each. The solar generators can fuel refrigerator, lights, water pump, computer, and television for an average family. NAPV's program involves ongoing maintenance, which has been a cause of poor performance in earlier attempts at solar power on the reservation.

A Cherokee attorney in Washington, D.C., is one of the strongest voices for solar power. Dean Suagee argues that tribes could lead in the matter of energy efficiency simply by instituting building codes that use solar-design principles. With less than .1 of 1 percent of new houses nationally using solar principles in design, this is an idea whose time is way overdue. Suagee advocates using the "lawmaking powers of our legislative bodies" to mandate changes in the way new homes are constructed. He urges tribes to move beyond the demonstration projects and make all new housing solar designed and energy efficient.

At a moment when tribes are negotiating regulatory matters with the U.S. Department of Housing and Urban Development (HUD), it is appropriate to take a strong look at energy efficiency. To institute principles of solar design at the building level is cheaper in the long run; it enhances self-sufficiency; and it is in-line with the increasing need to find solutions to the trend to destroy natural systems in the quest for energy. HUD and tribal planners might all at least look at the possibility of incorporating solar design in their new planning codes. Simple design principles such as orienting the thermal mass of new buildings and the long axis so that a "long south-facing wall is available for windows, sun spaces, and other devices for capturing solar energy," are proven to work in practice. The technology of sun power is improving. Sun- and wind-generated energy systems are expected to be a growth industry in the years ahead.

Indian planners might request that HUD release widely to tribal leadership and the Indian press its excellent 1994 booklet, "Our Home: Buildings of the Land: Energy Efficiency Guide for Indian Housing." This largely unknown resource lists, among other things, a software program called Builder-Guide, which guides designers in evaluating energy efficiency, heat needs, and seasonal, geographic adaptations of new buildings. A good piece of information, "Our Home" is highly recommended to the HUD-Tribal dialogue on housing in Indian country.

We find it encouraging that tribes are moving toward innovative, energy-efficient systems. Solar-power principles in building design is an idea whose adoption is completely feasible. And solar-power technology, which copies in glass panels the structure of a tree leaf in order to extract the energy of the sun, is in every way compatible with the idea of helping

Mother Earth endure her many abuses. Hopefully, it will not be long before solar design is adapted by more tribes and solar power becomes possible, in economic terms, in all parts of the Indian country.

Elders' Concern Is a True Sentiment
May 10, 2000

From the Indian country, a report again last week of a group of elders gathering to pray about the current condition affecting Mother Earth.

Elders from several northern Minnesota Ojibwe reservations report changes in the weather that appear drastic to them. Gene Goodsky, who convened the group, has had dreams of droughts and strange seasons, fires, and floods for more than a decade. He is a spiritual leader from Bois Forte Reservation. He joins Native traditional people from other parts of the Americas in being alarmed by the warmer weather. Sugar mapling now takes place a full month before the traditional "sugar moon" of April, he says. "The weather is abnormal."

A severe storm last July blew down millions of trees in the northern Minnesota region. "It's a wake-up call," the elders said. The Great Spirit, they say, is warning Indian people to lead simpler, more spiritual lives. The Chippewa elders' message from last week will not likely be news in Washington, D.C., but it resonates with *Indian Country Today*'s position that drastic changes are intensifying in the Earth's environment as a result of human activity. The views of Indian elders, particularly on the conduct of humans toward Mother Earth, are always received here as a trustworthy source.

We note that international agencies and federal departments have increasingly turned to Native community people with questions about current environmental problems. These include the National Aeronautic and Space Administration, many research universities, the International Agency for Environment and Development, the United Nations Development Programme, and others.

In the field of medicinal research in plants and animals, major corporations have given intense attention to the knowledge of Native shamans and medicine people.

Some writers and other would-be pundits these days are trying to cast aspersions on even the existence of an American Indian spiritual thinking or value of respect for Mother Earth. The attempt to discredit Indian natural world philosophies appears to be in vogue in magazines such as *The New Yorker*, where some months ago a book reviewer went way out of his way to "debunk" the very notion that Indian peoples and cultures might have any values or philosophies that could be interpreted as "ecological."

That writer is Nicholas Lemann and he was reviewing a book by Shepard Krech III, called *The Ecological Indian: Myth and History*, an attempt at just such debunking. It is in vogue among some intellectuals these days to put down all positive notions of Indian life and culture, particularly the idea that principles and practices of Native societies could serve as models for modern-day afflictions.

They cite all sorts of pseudoscience from disputed archaeological records and work to turn accepted history on its head. Thus, the claim is made that because a few Indians engaged in hunting buffalo during the era of the great slaughter in the Plains, Indians were culprits, too. So much for American Indian reverence for the buffalo, goes the argument, implying that Indians were somehow responsible for the slaughter of tens of millions of buffalo that took place in the 1870s and 1880s. But we know that this is simply untrue, that in fact the U.S. Army supplied much of the ammunition to hunters to wipe out the herds, in large part, as explicitly dictated by General Phillip Sheridan, to destroy the fighting tribes' food supply.

Ostensibly, according to Krech (and this is something that Lemann seems to relish), female infanticide and mismanagement of resources actually caused more death among tribes than the introduction of European diseases. Both dismiss the idea out of hand that Indians were ever intentionally infected. Yet, this happened during the campaign by English troops against Pontiac's people in the mid-eighteenth century.

The careful reciprocity with nature, and particularly the animal that is hunted, expressed in the traditional practice of hundreds of Native hunting peoples is glossed over in this recent article, which Lemann titled, "Buffaloed: Was the Native American Always Nature's Friend?" Expressions of obvious respect for a kinship relation with nature, such as the Iroquois "Thanksgiving Address" and the Lakota "Mitakuye Oyasin," documented hundreds of times, are completely ignored. Instead, this author pens theories by another academic as truth: that Native religion demanded hunters kill lots of animals, as "the Great Spirit would reward you by creating more of them." The few instances of Native mass killing, such as the buffalo cliff hunting found in some places in the Plains, are cited as some sort of "proof" that Indians were indiscriminate killers and destroyers of nature.

Krech, and Lemann by extension, seem intent on denying the legitimacy of positive values of Indian culture and history. The posture is to glibly dismiss any notion that there exists a Native American environmentalism. It is "romantic" to think that Indians had a consciousness about the care of the Earth, these folks argue. Indian culture as encompassing positive ways of life is not an acceptable opinion.

This kind of anti-Indian chic operates in an intellectual vacuum. The reality that natural knowledge found in Native cultures, amply documented, is used by much of science, including ecology, agronomy, biology, botany, and others, is not explored. Driven either by a political doctrine of the imperial kind or simply by a lazy or political approach to science and to the written record and the lived experience of many traditional practitioners from throughout the hemisphere, these kinds of articles call into question the seriousness of a magazine such as *The New Yorker*. Watch *Indian Country Today* for ongoing reports of Native elders, from the Chippewa medicine people who gathered last week to the many who are daily conducting ceremonies and other activities to hold up a human relationship with the Mother Earth. *Indian Country Today* knows the intense and actual reality that is represented in Native America's concern for the apparent destruction of the Natural World.

Even in the midst of severe problems and obligations, from the Indian businessman to the traditional clan mother, from the medicine man to the marine biologist, all Native people, in their hearts, care about the health of Mother Earth. We know that this concern runs across the Native cultures east and west, north and south, and that it represents a spiritual sentiment that is rooted in the most ancient of Native traditions.

Confronting Diabetes with Tradition
December 20, 2000

It is difficult to refute the fact that change of diet (and lifestyle) has caused serious health problems for Native people. It shows up with a vengeance in diabetes, a killer and disabler of major proportions in Indian country. Diabetes is an enemy that must be confronted: with traditional cultural knowledge, new scientific information, with encouragement and practical programming. Spirit and body need a lot of help.

Some foods are hard on Native peoples. We may not be what we eat, but what we eat becomes us. For all peoples, modernization brings on a more sedentary lifestyle and more fatty foods. For Native people, this was mostly involuntary and has meant a history of commodity foods that included sugar, white flour, cheap cheese and lard, oily peanut butter, and other products with which the U.S. government pretended to fulfill its treaty and trust obligations.

A century later, we are more clear about the effects of these types of foods; we know their use over generations affected Native eating habits fiercely; they have greatly contributed to a decline in health.

The famous, even symbolic, Indian fry bread, whose simple recipe and creative Indian-style concoction makes for a delicious accompaniment to any meal (particularly for those yummy, greasy meat stews) is one major culprit. But then nearly all of the fast foods, soda drinks, and other processed foods, particularly those most readily available on reservations and low-income neighborhoods, have high contents of refined sugars, artificial flavoring, and other elements that are as convenient as they are nutritionally worthless.

Adult onset Type II diabetes (commonly called "sugar" because it results in high levels of glucose in the blood) affects some 70,000 Native American people in the United States. Native people have the highest rates of any group in North America, with some tribes reporting as sufferers up to one-fourth of the adult population older than twenty. Among the older generations, sometimes a third or more suffer from it. Diabetes is a disorder that affects the body's metabolism, so it does not make or use enough insulin. It can result in death, severe nerve damage, blindness, kidney disease, limb amputation. Extreme sedentary lifestyles and obesity greatly add to the risk for diabetes.

The Indian Health Service reports the prevalence of diabetes among tribal groups varies by region: 12.7 percent among the Plains tribes, 10.5 percent among the southwestern tribes, 9.3 percent among the woodland tribes, and 4.5 percent among the Pacific Coastal tribes.

Diabetes affects approximately 9 percent of American Indian and Alaska Native adults.

Adult onset, or Type II, diabetes normally appears in adults and its prevalence increases with age, however, it is increasingly detected in younger and younger Native populations. Some 40 to 70 percent of American Indian adults age forty-five to seventy-four were found to have diabetes in a recent screening study in three geographic areas, the Indian Health Services reports.

It also reports that Type II diabetes is becoming increasingly common in youth. Researchers studying 5,274 Pima Indian children from 1967 to 1996 found that the prevalence of Type II diabetes in girls age ten to fourteen increased from 0.72 percent in the period 1967 to 1976 to 2.88 percent in the period 1987 to 1996. Some reports mention increasing incidence among First Nations populations in Canada. Among Pima people, the most widely studied American Indian tribal group, Type II diabetes was prevalent in approximately 50 percent among individuals age thirty to sixty-four.

As evidenced by the recent "War on Diabetes" symposium in Omaha, Nebraska, which featured the Whirling Thunder Wellness Program in Winnebago, Native tribes are aggressively combating the diabetes epidemic.

Adult onset diabetes can be managed to a reasonably good effect. Through daily exercise and careful eating habits, diabetes can be substantially controlled. In all ways, it appears, the traditional Native lifestyle, with its combination of regular physical activity and eating natural, fresh goods, lean meats, and homegrown vegetables is the best possible antidote to the bad habits that make us prone to the disease.

Interestingly, as tribes initiated programs to confront the diabetes epidemic, questions about what are the traditional foods, how are they procured and prepared, how they might be made available, have led to a generalized search for solutions.

As with many of the seemingly entrenched problems that beset Indian country over decades of federal negligence and mismanagement of tribal affairs, Native peoples are confronting the diabetes epidemic head on. Gardening initiatives, buffalo herds, exercise, and better eating programs have sprung up across the tribal landscape.

At Fort Berthold, on the Pine Ridge, at Tesuque Pueblo, Akwesasne, and among various Native college programs from the Northeast to Northwest, tribal projects with names such as "Three Sisters Gardens" and "Native America Food Systems" and the "Slim Buttes Land Use Cooperative" are visible and gaining strength. At Fort Berthold and Pine Ridge, hundreds of family gardens are put in each spring with some assistance from these projects.

Tribal buffalo herds and other wildlife and environmental restoration projects, which, hopefully, will grow and prosper, offer the opportunity to produce lean meats that were a main protein source for tribal peoples.

We celebrate these efforts by Native peoples to recover the practical and deeply meaningful rewards of the healthy lifestyles and foods developed by our ancestors over millennia. If the objective is "wellness," and not simply the combating of disease, programs that work with the land and raise gardens, particularly those that encourage the cultural-spiritual connections that those activities can engender, signal a proper and good path.

Earth Out of Balance
February 9, 2001

Vice President Al Gore and former senator Bill Bradley were debating health care in mid-January when suddenly demonstrators pushed open the door to their meeting hall and shouted: "Global warming is the issue!"

Bradley didn't comment but Gore, after disagreeing with the demonstrators' tactic, did say: "The issue is important. I've raised it, it's just nobody else wants to talk about it."

To his credit, Al Gore did raise the important issue of global warming and climate change, but it was years ago, in his book *Earth in the Balance*, which his campaign managers have timidly packed away in the nether history of their candidate. Gore is right, though: no one else even wants to talk about it.

Yet, as a current special issue of *Native Americas*, the journal of Cornell University's Akwe:kon Press, details, climate change is here and its consequences are already devastating, particularly for indigenous and disenfranchised peoples.

The basic elements are the rise in the world's mean temperatures, a factor that couples to the steady rise in carbon dioxide levels during the past century. The decade of the 1990s was the hottest ever on record. In the Arctic Circle, Inuit and other Native hunters, trappers, and fishermen despair over disappearing ice and particularly the effects of unprecedented warm temperatures on the animals they hunt and cherish. Seal pups drown or starve early as the ice floes they mature on melt months too early. Elders fear the next whole generation will be severely reduced, impacting walrus, polar bears, and other animals up and down the food chain.

In the Yukon, the caribou herds shed their winter coats during unusually long thaws, only to freeze or die of pneumonia when cold sets in again.

To the South, the northern Great Plains and the Southwest experience longer drought seasons that turn to flooding, then turn to blizzard with unheard-of fury. Farther south, witness worse: Honduras and Nicaragua in 1998, where heavy rains caused by Hurricane Mitch buried thousands of people and whole river valleys. Then witness even worse in the mud burial of tens of thousands in Venezuela in November 1999.

Caribbean storms are increasing in number and intensity, year by year, devastating countries where death tolls are aggravated by horrible poverty that forces people to live on the sides of mountains where whole towns collapse.

The difference this round pointed out in *Native Americas* is that despite the complete silence from policy makers, it is not only Native peoples, but, in fact, the vast majority of climatologists and scientists from a wide range of fields who are sounding the alarm. The special issue of *Native Americas* resulted from a collaboration with the National Aeronautical and Space Administration (NASA) scientists, whose research increasingly points out the same reality: something drastic is happening to the Earth's weather system.

Such was the report from research by the National Science Foundation, which found a distressingly high "melt rate" of the Arctic Ice Pack, a trend that, if continued, will see the pack disappear "within twenty-five years." The *Native Americas* issue, in part, reported on a unique conference held in Albuquerque in November 1998, when NASA scientists and Native traditional elders exchanged views and information on this most important concern.

Native peoples have long predicted both through prophecy and first-hand observation, that, in time, the rate of destruction of the Natural World evident in the present industrial system would have drastic consequences for human beings. The Earth, they said, would "purify" herself. Perhaps we are already in that time; perhaps it is time to heed their advice. As many elders have often said for at least two generations: "Children, be ready. Prepare to meet the conditions."

Preserving the Integrity of Indian Corn
February 8, 2002

In southern Mexico, the place where corn was born, this original gift of Indian America is now in danger of extinction. Genetically modified corn imported from the United States is rapidly blending with indigenous corn varieties. It carries high potential for destroying the local strains and threatens to obliterate the central source of food for millions of Indian agriculturalists.

The problem lies not only in Mexico. Indian farmers in the United States and organic farmers in Canada have raised the alarm on this serious problem of genetically modified plants contaminating natural varieties of local and regional farming cultures.

The contamination in Mexico appears to be in its beginning stages, but for many people, it is an aberration of nature and cause for extreme concern. In the remote mountains of the southern state of Oaxaca, transgenic strains were found in fifteen of twenty-two villages examined. Three to 10 percent of plants were contaminated in the fields tested. Scientists from the University of California at Berkeley last November used DNA testing to confirm that the plants in question were genetically modified.

Local farmers first began to notice the new "wild" corn about three years ago. The new corn, which they assert came in government trucks to be sold at community stores, would grow anywhere, even through cracks on sidewalks. The government has denied bringing in the new corn but locals can tell the difference. They say the modified corn kernels are larger and have a lighter color. The Native varieties are also sweeter.

Although it is illegal since 1998 to cultivate genetically modified corn in Mexico, the source of the contamination appears to be from U.S.

exports brought in for human consumption. Some 6 million tons of corn are imported by Mexico each year. Diconsa, the national subsidized food program, distributes corn to some 23,000 stores nationwide. Apparently, many people have unwittingly planted the genetically modified corn.

Local activists are demanding that the Mexican government stop imports of the suspect corn. They accuse Diconsa of dispersing the transgenic varieties. Officials at the national program deny it, but activists and farmers can easily identify the modified corn. Furthermore, laboratories at an agricultural research center in La Trinidad (Oaxaca) confirmed that transgenic strains are found in samples of corn sold at the Diconsa stores.

Those who planted the new corn reported good results, at first. For one thing, it yielded two or three ears per plant, compared to one ear by their own strains. It also seemed to spring up anywhere. As the plants matured and ripened, however, they showed themselves susceptible to local plagues. Local strains have been selected over generations to resist plagues and diseases found in the area. The new corn is a weak corn, tampered with for reasons not amenable to cultures that sustain and consume foodstuffs as a fundamental social value.

Corn is a central staple of the diet for Mexican village farmers. Farmers take scrupulous care in safeguarding their seeds (germ plasm), and consider corn to be an actual relative. As the Mexican scholar Arturo Warman has put it: "What the Europeans found in the Americas was not only a plant, it was a cultural invention, the product of the initiative of millions of people for thousands of years that produced a treasury of genetic knowledge." The potential contamination of their principal source of food and culture came as a surprise and has become a serious cause for worry in a region where nearly every house and even many government offices and businesses are flanked by fields of corn.

Even scientists admit they don't know the ultimate impacts of transgenics on the environment. It is still an unknown quantity. But certainly, the immediate impact of contamination of natural varieties planted and consumed by millions of indigenous and other small farmers throughout the world portends serious problems for millions of people.

Just last month, organic farmers in Saskatchewan concerned over the same problem have filed suit against the two giant biotechnology conglomerates, Monsanto and Aventis SA, whose genetically modified varieties are contaminating crops in western Canada. In their case, the complaint concerns genetically modified canola, a crop often staggered with wheat. In the lawsuit filed in January, the organic farmers charge that the genetically modified varieties are invading their fields and denying their right to the "organic" designation that provides them their primary market. The suit has kept Monsanto from commercially releasing genetically modified wheat until a decision is reached by the courts.

This week, two major events touching on the issue take place. In Montreal, hundreds of delegates from the Convention on Biological Diversity's 182 parties, other governments, indigenous and local community organizations, and various institutions are gathering to explore how indigenous and local communities' knowledge and practices can help conserve the world's highly threatened species. The use of traditional indigenous knowledge is a focus of discussion in the search for solutions. Most indigenous and local communities are located in areas where the majority of the world's plant genetic resources are found. Conference organizers recognize that the skills and techniques of indigenous peoples, as cultivators who have used biological diversity in a sustainable way for thousands of years, provide valuable information to the global community and are a useful model for biodiversity policies.

Another event, a day of awareness and prayer called "Safeguarding the Sacred," involves concerned agriculturalists from Pueblo communities. They are calling on grain exporters and the U.S. government to protect corn biodiversity and to honor the global treaty on biodiversity (the Bio-safety Protocol signed in Cartagena, Colombia, February 2000) by ending the dumping of U.S. taxpayer-subsidized genetically engineered corn in Mexico.

New Mexico writer Robin Seydel points out that the U.S. Environmental Protection Agency itself maintains that genetically engineered organisms must not be planted in regions that are home to wild relatives, where the results of genetic contamination could be disastrous. "With over 60 wild relatives of corn, including what is believed to be corn's ancient ancestor, the wild grass, teosinte, growing throughout Mexico, genetic contamination of these ancestor species could affect corn farmers and backyard gardeners here in New Mexico and nationwide." The indigenous Mexican corn varieties go back at least 10,000 years.

Last year, under the North American Free Trade Agreement, Mexico imported 6 million tons of corn from the United States, a quarter of which is genetically engineered. This corn is grown for human and animal consumption in government stores throughout the region. It is now widely believed that when people ran short of their locally produced seed, they planted it, unknowingly violating their government's ban on genetically modified cultivation.

Public outrage and international alarm has been such that the Mexican Congress, which had not yet banned the importation of genetically engineered corn for human consumption, has now called for a ban on the import of genetically modified corn.

This is a most serious problem. As with so many issues raised by globalization, it affects local, land-based, and indigenous populations. The growing infection of natural and organic varieties easily becomes a source of outrage and hostility. The wanton impact on peoples' foods and, as importantly, on the central living source of their spiritual traditions, is not easily forgotten or forgiven.

Says Clayton Brascoupé, program director for the Traditional Native American Farmers Association (Tesuque, N.M.): "Generally Indian and Hispanic communities grow open-pollinated varieties of corn. What I can see happening is our landrace varieties becoming contaminated by this genetic pollution. The contamination will sever a major tie with our culture. For us corn is not just food, it is "medicine." If it becomes contaminated, it would make the practice of our religious beliefs very difficult. It might even make it impossible."

Indigenous Geography as Discipline Arrives
March 26, 2004

There is an Indigenous Geography in the making—a new approach to land consciousness involving map reading and map making that is leading to the establishment of an encompassing, innovative, and pragmatic new discipline.

Arguably, the genius of American Indians and of indigenous peoples generally is their intense attachment to and study of their places of origin and occupancy—the homelands. Among study areas of interest, Native land researchers, scholars, and activists are finding a compatible, productive, and useful discipline in geography, in the study of their lands with all the new tools available to modern science—but with the clear intention of generating models that emerge from their own traditional knowledge branches. Numerous efforts and initiatives activated throughout the Americas reveal that the Indigenous Geography movement is well under way.

In mid-March, the International Forum on Indigenous Mapping gathered nearly 200 indigenous-community experts from dozens of Native nations in twenty-six countries. Meeting in Vancouver, Canada, they compared notes on some fascinating projects, networked their organizations, and shared their range of productions.

We were privileged to listen in on some of the most crisp, practical, and solution-oriented presentations regarding Native homelands we have heard in a long time. Native community intelligence of great depth and honesty have coupled affirmatively and confidently to complex and sophisticated scientific tools and computer-modeling programs. Surfing on the winds of the remarkably adaptable discipline of geography, the emergent Native projects base themselves on ancient oral traditional knowledge yet incorporate, as resources allow, modern cartographic technology to define and articulate their own perception of their own lands and territories. It is a terrifically inspirational, not to mention useful, combination.

Map making seems uniquely suited to the needs and perspectives of indigenous peoples. In the hands of indigenous-community planners and resource managers, it becomes an Indigenous Geography that joins leadership, educators, legal experts, and tribal members young and old in exploring traditional culture, indigenous language, and working toward the gathering of knowledge on their homeland watersheds and river systems, coasts and plains, ocean sites, etc., to create user-friendly knowledge bases.

Indigenous peoples are reluctant to forget, despite the many horrible attempts to separate the peoples from their own cultures, their homelands and customary resources. By and large, they take heart in the memory of their origin places, whether still held in the tribal territory or long lost to encroachment, removal, or perhaps outright decimation as populations. We are pleased to note that all indigenous mapping practitioners who presented expressed their respect and enthusiasm for the cultural-spiritual elements in the attachment to their lands. In the practice and in the culling of the living culture, indigenous sensibility to the natural gifts of their environs is front and center.

This was the major theme in Vancouver: the consciousness of place, the indigenous love and identity of place as being the fuel of defense, sustenance, and identity of tribal peoples.

"We are our lands," said Alvin Warren, lead coordinator for the conference from Santa Clara Pueblo in New Mexico, in his opening remarks. "We are intent in finding our places. This is a unity of purpose that we share. As we learn about our lands, we learn about ourselves."

Another major theme of Indigenous Geography is the love and conscious revitalization of the Native languages. This task and duty was endorsed universally: to capture and incorporate the traditional indigenous language as it describes place, explains natural and human phenomena, and describes spiritual concepts emerging from Creation stories and other formative narratives of Native peoples.

The Indigenous Geography genesis also finds its roots in other forums. Consultations in the late 1990s among indigenous community educators at the Smithsonian's National Museum of the American Indian led to the initiation of an Indigenous Geography research emphasis (also translated into *Geografa Indgena* for Spanish-speaking regions of the Western Hemisphere). Recognizing the essential link between Native communities and their environments, this project studied the integrative approach of an innovative Indigenous Geography—combining environment, society, economy, and culture—to produce community-focused products, including Web sites, with content derived almost entirely from local informants.

The proposed program offered clear and comprehensive portrayals of contemporary Indian life and land, focused on cultural values as lived within Native communities, and provided an invaluable resource for the production of Indigenous Geography education materials tailored to the needs of Indian students—but that would also seamlessly provide an exciting pathway for all students to learn more about Native community cultures, histories, philosophies, and environments. This project included the sustained study of languages and their cultural contexts through basic vocabulary, place-names, and stories. Understanding of contemporary indigenous issues and questions of human existence that transcended cultural and geographic boundaries was also to have been fostered. That the program was designed to be consistent with all standards and guidelines for national geographic education made it all the more impressive.

This project had the larger goal of re-creating geography education for Indian America, providing a rich introduction to the comparative study of indigenous cultures that would have assisted teachers in facilitating critical thinking among students. A similar program for indigenous Pacific Island cultures, Pacific Worlds, is already well under way, with six community Web sites, free curricular materials, and workshops being hosted for island teachers to foster indigenous understandings of space and place.

Indigenous Geography is also gaining prominence within the discipline of Geography at the national level. A growing number of Native and non-Native scholars forming the Indigenous Peoples Specialty Group of the Association of American Geographers (AAG) have been organizing conference sessions at the American Association of Geographers' annual meetings. For the past four years, these sessions have pushed harder on the acceptance of indigenous understandings, posing Western geographic approaches as but one colonially inspired way of viewing the world. *Indian Country Today*'s own Dr. Jose Barreiro served as a plenary speaker at this year's AAG conference, and a top-ranked disciplinary journal out of Sweden, *Geografiska Annaler: Series B—Human Geography*, has commissioned a special issue on Indigenous Geography. This momentum is expected to continue at next year's meeting in Denver, and beyond.

Elsewhere courses and exhibits in Indigenous Geography are offering viewers and participants a new way of understanding the world in which they live. Universal Press Syndicate columnists and University of California at Los Angeles (UCLA) Cesar Chavez Distinguished Community scholars

Roberto Rodriguez and Patrisia Gonzales offered a course in Indigenous Geography at UCLA this past spring and will teach it again at the University of Wisconsin at Madison this summer.

This course includes an examination of maps and chronicles from the 1500s–1800s that reveal Mesoamerican roots in what is today the United States. It is part of a larger collaborative and ongoing research effort that examines oral traditions from throughout the continent regarding ancient connections between peoples of North and South America and the Caribbean. Many of the maps point to several sites, purportedly associated with Aztec/Mexica peoples and their migrations, but also with older ancient Mexican, Chichimeca, and Toltec migrations, and that of Central and South American peoples as well. It challenges the popular belief that it was the romanticism of nineteenth-century U.S. archaeologists that caused them to place such place-names (Montezuma, Aztec, Anahuac, Tula, etc.) throughout the country. However, these maps (representative of hundreds more and found at most major libraries and research institutions around the world) clearly demonstrate that such sites were well established long before the existence of the United States.

Rodriguez and Gonzales, along with researchers Dr. Antonio Rios Bustamante, Dr. Juan Gomez Quininez, Dr. Reynaldo Macias, and Dr. Irene Vasquez, plus UCLA students Daniela Conde, Cynthia Gonzalez, and Rosario Luis, have also developed an exhibit that grows from their understanding of Indigenous Geography. On April 1, the UCLA Young Research Library will introduce a special and historic exhibit of sixteenth- to nineteenth-century maps that indicate an ancient Mesoamerican presence and migrations within the United States. The exhibit also includes "chronicles, codices, annals, and interviews regarding oral traditions that speak to ancient connections between peoples of the north and south." Part of the objective of the map exhibit examines how cartographers dealt with this subject from the 1500s through the 1800s. Much like their course, their exhibit research also places an emphasis on oral traditions and introduces concepts of Indian origins and migrations that are at times both complex and philosophical.

The people in attendance at the Vancouver Mapping Forum included many dedicated and strong activists of cultural and land recovery. Elders, young activists, and community practitioners, environmental professionals, academics, and lawyers talked and showed the power of maps, of an Indigenous Geography that is as respectful of the internal community needs and wishes as it is charged with the incorporation of traditional knowledge of the land and environs as well as the most advanced range of geographic tools possible.

Mapping, as we know, started with hand-drawn maps, with mental maps and star maps and even song-maps. Now indigenous peoples are accessing the tools of Western mapping, Global Information Systems, and Global Positioning Systems. The counter-mapping movement that dates from the 1970s intends to recreate the maps of our territories with our own knowledge. It is a powerful initiative that fits like a glove the pattern of knowledge of the land that is retained by elders and which is inherent in the ancient languages. From all indications, young people are receptive to this knowledge as curriculum method as it combines practical experience relative to land, tribal identity, culture, and language, and scientific currents.

The emerging linkages across networks, definitions, and methodologies now available to Indigenous Geography practitioners, as one forum participant put it, "means we are now using the master's tools to dismantle the master's house." Warren reminded the gathering of the late, much-respected geographer Barney Neitchman, who once said, "More Indian land was taken by maps than by guns." Indigenous Geography, which is increasingly gaining adherents across a wide spectrum, remains nonetheless a proactive and uniquely Indian led and conceptualized discipline that has grown from practical community-based needs.

The forum concept—the common endeavor of many people and organizations, including some excellent, forward-thinking foundations—was to work with indigenous peoples around the world who are using Indigenous Geography practices to recover traditional cultural knowledge, to assert legal rights to territories and natural resources, to negotiate comanagement agreements, and to introduce their young people to their identity in the land. We salute them all.

No Relief for Salmon in Bush Regimen
October 10, 2004

Every step of the way, it seems, the Bush administration declares itself against nature. On environmental issues, as in most everything else, the message is clear: no accommodation is wanted, or necessary.

In the Bush world of nature, no right of a fish or animal species is apparently enough to cause discomfort to any citizen holding a deed to land anywhere in America. This must be what they mean by achieving an "ownership society." The more the land is owned by individuals, the more privatized, the less there is in commons, the less we have the right to even care what happens to any of the natural wonders of Indian country's remarkable landscape.

This season the pressure is again on the Pacific salmon. The "dry out" of the salmon has begun in earnest, as the Bush administration has opted to drop protection from four-fifths of protected rivers, judged crucial to the recovery of salmon and steelhead, from southern California to the Canadian border.

Declaring that these are no longer critical for salmon and steelhead recovery, tens of thousands of miles of river have been set lose for change and exploitation in the broadest environmental-policy reversal in recent history. Down to only 27,000 miles of river, according to National Oceanic and Atmospheric Administration (NOAA) fisheries, the federal agency assigned to handle salmon recovery. "A Flip-flop on Salmon," the *Idaho Statesman* calls it.

The decision reverses what had been a crowning touch of the Clinton administration, when, in 2000, NOAA fisheries defined the comprehensive system of rivers and policy protection needed for salmon and steelhead recovery.

The approach to major change and mayhem is simply to shift the rule defining what constitutes critical habitat. Critical habitat is a legal definition to describe areas "essential" for the survival of threatened or endangered species. Eighty percent of rivers that had been considered essential to salmon and steelhead survival, according to the Endangered Species Act, now, five years later, are apparently no longer considered critical. A free-for-all of project is expected.

Federal officials speak of "carefully balancing the needs of threatened and endangered salmon against human demands for water, energy, timber, and real estate along the Northwest's cold-flowing rivers." Last week, too, the administration finalized a decision that rejects the proposal to demolish the Snake River hydropower dams, as a way to help restore salmon runs. In this equation, as with so many of the recent changes on environmental protection, the environment loses.

Who got their way? The National Association of Home Builders, which sued after the 2000 designation, spearheaded the developers' drive. A federal court agreed, and considered their economic loss more important than the needs of the fish. Now the federal agency is forced to scramble to please them—the rule change allows for exemptions for property owners in broad areas of the Northwest and California. Who lost, besides the salmon and their immediate natural relations? The American Indian tribes with treaty rights to salmon and who depend on the fishery, both traditionally and commercially. Also, many small towns along central Idaho's Salmon River. The fishing season is perhaps worth tens of millions of dollars a year for them.

While the feds argue that the change will help them focus recovery efforts where they would do the most good, natural-resource specialists warn that it will set back recovery, perhaps irreparably. To be fair, the agencies committed to expanding efforts to reduce predators that prey heavily on young salmon. They also promised to outfit the major dams with spillway weirs, which supposedly help young fish pass the dams beyond the sucking of the turbines and by transporting some 90 percent of the young salmon stocks past the dams by barge or truck.

Nevertheless, the science is clear that cleanliness, even pristineness of rivers, is critical to the salmon population's recovery, which is in itself indispensable for bears and eagles, which depend on a strong yearly salmon run. "The actions," according to *The Oregonian*, "signal far-reaching changes in federal enforcement of the Endangered Species Act." The reductions in critical habitat going into effect will impact twenty populations of Pacific salmon and steelhead. Patti Goldman, an environmental attorney in Seattle, stressed that exempting lands covered by the Northwest Forest Plan from critical habitat would be a "disaster" for salmon.

The feds under Bush have very poor record on salmon issues.

There is not much credibility left to the administration on this one. According to Bush science, genetically similar—but less hardy—hatchery fish are as valuable as wild fish in recovering salmon and steelhead. Every study says different. On the decision to not remove the Snake River dams, which many assert will greatly recover the runs, the feds claimed that "man-made dams are simply part of the natural environment young fish must learn to navigate en route to the Pacific Ocean" (*Idaho Statesman*). Most scientists disagree with these types of claims, which only diminish the climate of study and care around species survival and recovery issues.

The move to destroy the salmon rivers protection initiative is part and parcel of an alarming strategy of negating three decades of U.S. environmental protection by the newly reelected White House. One main priority is to open up the Arctic Wildlife Refuge for oil drilling. This plan was defeated in 2000, but the administration now has the votes for victory. It will propose the continuation of the nuclear power program, paralyzed by the 1979 Three Mile Island accident. A comprehensive review to limit the Clean Air Act is also promised. The Act is credited with cutting air pollution nationally by more than half over the last thirty years. The Endangered Species Act, main line of defense against the logging of the United States' remaining (and endangered) rain forest, is in the line of attack, as is the whole National Environmental Policy Act, the one that mandates environmental impact studies of major developments before they proceed.

Reelected by an American population that certainly knew the stakes,

Bush's post-environment politics claim a mandate to open the country up for grabs.

A grand movement is needed to question this direction for the country.

On the salmon and other Northwest fisheries, Indian leaders and professionals, such as Olney Patt Jr., executive director of the Columbia River Inter-Tribal Fish Commission, which represents the Nez Perce, Warm Springs, Yakama, and Umatilla tribes, see the federal government "turning its back on that [treaty] obligation." The feds are sacrificing the salmon for the sake of developers, say the tribes. The feds' plan focuses on what the tribes believe are failed techniques of salmon-barging and on new technology—removable spillway weirs—that are not yet proven for specific specie.

The Columbia River treaty-fishing tribes are denouncing the federal plan as "a step backward." It dismisses their salmon-recovery efforts, they assert, and instead provides more power to the federal Columbia River power system. "As co-managers of the salmon resource, we believe this plan falls far short of its legal, biological, and trust responsibility," Patt emphasized. "It takes the weight off the dams and hoists it firmly onto the backs of salmon-dependent communities."

Notably, two weeks ago, 250 fish biologists and other scientists petitioned President Bush to make stronger efforts to protect salmon and other fish and their habitats.

Community by community, it would appear that the fight for a livable and satisfying environment is entering a definitive phase.

Nature Conservancy Efforts Disregard Indigenous Peoples
November 24, 2004

Native and traditional peoples around the world are primary practitioners of earth-based survival lifestyles. Whether by cultural preference or by necessity in the face of industrial scarcity, the encouraged participation of Native peoples in creative ways of protecting environmental resources and of resolving their eco-systemic water and food security (self-sufficiency) problems is completely in order.

Controversy has been growing for a decade over policies by the three superlarge international conservation organizations, which tend to shun social issues of indigenous and traditional peoples and which are sometimes positioned in antagonistic roles to Native and traditional villages. This long-festering problem finds the three major professional organizations working in nature conservation, which has raised concerns over diminishing the potentials of indigenous peoples in their quest to demarcate and manage biodiversity "hot spots" around the world.

A recent article published in *World Watch* magazine by Mac Chapin (November/December 2004 *World Watch* 17, "A Challenge to Conservation-ists") lances the boil of this controversy and we find ourselves highly interested in his assessment. Chapin is somewhat controversial himself as a combative anthropologist who has long worked on behalf of Indian causes, but he is certainly a painstaking researcher and he knows the field like few others.

Chapin reports that somewhere in the mid-1980s, the budding alliance between traditional Indian and environmental movements began to dissipate. Particularly these three big ones—The Nature Conservancy, World Wildlife Fund, and Conservation International—began to shy away from the complexity of Indian social and political issues, many of which press for land demarcation and jurisdictions as part of the social justice solutions to long-term problems of obvious origins.

Retooling their shield on behalf of scientific inquiry and techno-management of large and complicated ecosystems ("hot spots"), the three major conservation organizations projected a global mission and then set out to successfully dominate the fund-raising strategy in the field. In 2002, for example, the take of the three major organizations amounted to more than half of the estimated $1.5 billion available for conservation. Impatient with the claims and often the traditional knowledge of people who resided in those areas, incidents of evictions of indigenous peoples have taken place in regions embraced by conservation projects. More often, local peoples are limited or criminalized for hunting, gathering, and other traditional and accustomed practices.

The controversy gains focus and certainly calls attention to itself as a result of the Chapin article, which comes at a moment of high intensity for the issue. In characteristic fashion, Chapin revealed his intentions to publish a sizable challenge to the big three (activists label these "bingos" short for the "big NGOs") at a session of funders of indigenous peoples coinciding with the UN Permanent Forum on Indigenous Issues in New York. He makes it true with his present article, which is a somewhat caustic call to dialogue, but whose call is worth heeding nevertheless.

The indigenous leaders at the 1977 Geneva International Indigenous Conference made the challenge, and in the Amazon it was followed by the indigenous Amazonian coalition, COICA, which sponsored the tribal conference that issued, "The Iquitos Declaration," signed by many conservationist groups and Native peoples. International organizations at major conferences, such as the UNCED–1992 (United Nations Conference on Environment and Development) followed with greater calls for research and collaboration with indigenous peoples in the concept of sustainable development. Many good projects did develop from these collaborations but a general pattern of paternalistic management, dominated always by the funding NGOs, tended to diminish the Indian role and the community-based experience. The hard work of discerning the most sound, traditional leadership in many areas was beyond the major organizations. Conversely, Native community issues through the 1990s turned increasingly militant in several major countries, including Peru, Ecuador, Bolivia, Brazil, Guatemala, and Mexico. Rather than sustain the effort to work with local populations to resolve major conservation issues, the big three, by and large, have opted to demarcate, protect, and manage away from community needs and inputs.

This is regrettable on its face, and we commit to doing everything possible to help educate the major conservation movements and organizations to the practical wisdom of working closely with local, particularly indigenous and traditional, peoples, who have cultural and customary bonds with positive links to their ecosystems. We agree this is not always easily done, but there are many great examples where it has proved an excellent approach.

In setting out to protect and propagate natural areas that can sustain eco-systemic variety of plants and animals, working with local indigenous and traditional communities of people is quite possible and advantageous. Policies antagonistic to indigenous and traditional-use communities are shortsighted, sometimes dangerously so, and obviously counterproductive in the long run. Human misery and need, if simply rejected and suppressed, will find a way forward in desperate consumption fed by lawlessness and ignorance. A front line of defense promoted precisely among those populations with the most instinctive human relationship to forest and other ecological regions is very desired and has all the potential in the world to actually address the problems of severe degradation.

While front-line natural use populations often diminish natural abundance by overuse, nonetheless many times they have natural eco-friendly methods of food and medicinal plant and animal production, grounded in the indigenous cultures and in the blend of cultures of the various regions. Rather than dismissal and antagonism against such peoples, interactive pedagogy—fully endorsing the potentials of education and the re-harnessing of traditional environmentally protective knowledge—should be a central philosophy. Partnership through environmental education that assists natural world productivity is a crucial component to successful protection of the natural world. No doubt, some special areas with maximum propagation away from human intervention are best protected by imposed isolation, but this is best done with education and local consensus rather than only the imposition of criminal or military sanction.

An appreciation to Mac Chapin for opening the dialogue between two important human communities: indigenous land movements and Western conservation movements. We urge that the dialogue now move in constructive ways, as all can benefit from the mutual analysis and common objectives. These are two sectors gravely important to lead on these most crucial of survival questions.

Safeguarding Our Healers

July 16, 2003

Katsi Cook, *Indian Country Today*

Among the various activities conducted by *Iewerokwas* (Mohawk for midwife), our midwifery and women's health program, we are most proud of our Healers in Residence project. Over the years, we have gotten to know many excellent practitioners of the ancient healing arts of the Americas.

In my own practice of midwifery, the connection to the many families has provided opportunities and experiences with elders and individuals of great knowledge and abilities. There are not too many, but there are some still who are genuinely trained from within our Native cultures and who are constant fountains of learning. The older practitioners, especially, are not prejudiced in their treatment of other human beings, while most prefer to cater to their own clans and tribal peoples. All the genuine ones are humbled by what they do at the same time that they take great care and pride in the detail and sincerity of their ceremonies and healing ways.

A common thread in indigenous healing practice is the work with dreams. The sharing of a dream is central to the relationship of trust between those who seek healing and those who themselves have experienced healing through dreams. In the same way that traditional healers and midwives maintain their own spiritual disciplines through dream practice, those seeking support in their own healing journey naturally dream.

For example, expectant mothers "in the family way" may have a significant dream or series of dreams that yield information that can inform a midwife and her helpers how to prepare for and guide a birth. Dreams can help straighten out a family discord; they can stave off deeper disharmonies. But the dream healer must be familiar with the rich imagery and language of dreams as well as that of indigenous epistemologies that guide dream interpretation.

Interpretation is everything, and those who know these ways, who are few and far between, do travel the directions with much work to do for the people. He or she must know what they are doing. It takes experience to recognize the good-minded one from the weak-minded one.

In following the trails of seeking authentic indigenous midwifery knowledge, I was lucky and gifted to gather trusted teachers from the four directions. There were my grandmother and my mother; also my father and grandfather. All were at ease with natural processes, birth included, because they trusted their common sense and practical knowledge. Then there were elders such as Joe and Hattie, who lived in the bush and with whom I spent very instructive seasons. Later, in my travels, I met healers and medicine teachers from many other relatives and nations—Lakota, Anishnawbe, Navajo, Pomo, Maya, Taino. My practice is continually enriched by these wonderfully gifted people, all of whom are important assets to their communities and who, in the presence of other healers, are mostly generous and good teachers.

Our indigenous healers are a very strong part of my universe of knowledge, at once my consultative group or "think tank" and my respected prayer leaders. In my work in family and community education and Aboriginal midwifery curriculum development, it has been very helpful to consult with these elders, to compare medicines and teachings. In common, we have shared the ceremonial and medicinal use of such medicines as tobacco, copal, peyote, ayahuasca, and many others of the family of plant life.

Similarly, the spiritual healing entities of the various traditions, through dream and ceremony, reveal intelligence and power to restore harmony. Of course, these exchanges are infrequent and require notable exertion and sometimes even risk for these elders, including long travel, going into strange surroundings, and, as seen in a recent case in Canada, facing alien legal jurisdictions where criminality over function and substance differ from what they have at home.

The news during the past year of two medicine men from Ecuador detained in Canada after a person died during their ceremony was sorrowful. The father and son are healer and helper in a ceremonial team that uses, among other practices, the herbal medicine tea known as ayahuasca. They were invited into Canada by a First Nations community, whose health program financed the trip. The unfortunate death, however, later judged to be incidental and not caused by the taking of ayahuasca nor by the ritual itself, brought forth criminal charges against the two Ecuadorian healers, who were tried in Ontario court.

Although the case was resolved with some degree of justice recently, the nearly two-year-old ordeal had grave consequences for the two healers, whose families were left behind in South America while their principal breadwinners were unable to work and were threatened and fighting a situation of long-term incarceration.

What happened? I don't need to judge. But the lesson to be extracted is important. In this age of international travel among Native peoples, let's act responsibly with our international guests.

The economic resources of the South and the North are hugely different.

Indigenous families in the South, especially, live in marginal economies, enduring political realities that hearken back to even medieval times. It is still possible to buy land in Guatemala and get the Indians that come with it! The cost of a meal or a hotel room in Canada or the United States is prohibitive to most Native people from the South. It is among our oldest traditions to think in this way about our guests—how what we are offering them can be detrimental—so we must put ourselves in their shoes.

As we saw in the Ontario case, legal jurisdictions are serious entities and we must be aware of the way international guests will be affected by them.

Since the 1992 Regulated Health Professions Act of Ontario, Aboriginal healers and midwives are exempt from any regulation by the government. This legal exemption is good news, but in its lack of specificity, it is not definitive. We may claim a degree of sovereign immunity from Canadian and American jurisdictions, but this is sometimes tenuous, and cannot often offer real protections. While Native members of local tribes and territories, bands and reserves, often can point to a protected status in matters of religion and customary practice, these don't often transfer to your Native guest from another country. You may wish it to be so, but it will not be necessarily so. The result can be catastrophic for your generous guest who graciously accepted your invitation to travel and conduct ceremonies.

It is most important for Native peoples to share knowledge of health and welfare with their relatives across the hemispheres. It can be the stuff of miracles; but it requires very refined and well-informed responsibility. With this in mind, let's protect and respect the spirit of all our ceremonies and tribal lifeways.

American Indian Religious Freedom Act at Twenty-Five
August 1, 2003

Suzan Shown Harjo, *Indian Country Today*

The American Indian Religious Freedom Act (AIRFA) turns twenty-five on August 11, and there is every reason to both celebrate it and complete its unfinished agenda.

AIRFA articulates the policy of the United States to "protect and preserve for American Indians their inherent right of freedom to believe, express, and exercise the traditional religions of the American Indian, Eskimo, Aleut, and Native Hawaiians."

After generations of traditional Native religions being federally driven underground or to extinction, it was a needed and welcome policy.

AIRFA laid the groundwork for federal museums returning Native human remains and sacred objects, and led to the repatriation laws in 1989 and 1990.

During the religious freedom law's initial implementation, the ceremonial use of peyote was recognized as a traditional Native religious practice and Congress amended AIRFA in 1993 to codify protections for its use by Native American Church members.

Over the quarter-century life of AIRFA, numerous traditional and customary areas have been returned or protected through comanagement agreements. During the same time, however, other sacred places have been damaged or destroyed, and far too many are under attack today.

Native traditional religious leaders and practitioners started the movement for the religious freedom law in 1967, after ceremonies at Bear Butte in South Dakota. As the group expanded, its annual regional meetings increased to seasonal ones held in various parts of Indian country and Hawaii.

Participants in these meetings were happy about achieving land returns, access agreements, and protections for the use of feathers and other sacred objects.

At the same time, each meeting was followed by the death of one participant. People joked about who the sacrifice person would be, but adhered ever more closely to traditional admonitions to greet and leave others as if it were the last chance to do so. Those meetings and that phenomenon would continue through the enactment of the repatriation and the peyote laws.

The Agriculture, Interior, and Justice departments in the Nixon and Ford administrations opposed religious freedom legislation. Candidate Jimmy Carter made a campaign promise to Indian leaders the week before the election that he would sign religious freedom legislation.

Among AIRFA's original cosponsors were the most conservative and most liberal senators—Barry Goldwater, Republican of Arizona, and Edward M. Kennedy, Democrat of Massachusetts. The measure moved along at a rapid clip until it hit the House floor. The Forest Service successfully lobbied Agriculture Committee Chair Thomas S. Foley, Democrat of Washington, to neuter AIRFA on sacred lands or kill it.

AIRFA's House champion, Morris K. Udall, Democrat of Arizona, had to do the dirty work and say that the bill was a fine policy statement but had no teeth to protect sacred sites. We'll go back and pick up the cause of action later, he said.

President Carter kept his word and signed AIRFA. His top political advisors said that the administration would ask Congress for the sacred sites cause of action during the second Carter term. There was no second term, of course. Foley went on to House leadership positions, the Supreme Court ruled that AIRFA carried no cause of action and Udall retired without being able to amend AIRFA to add the needed door to the courthouse.

Indian traditional and tribal leaders tried to get a legislative cause of action during the Clinton administration, but Interior politicos and natural resources lawyers in Justice and the pollsters in the White House opposed it.

Native leaders negotiated a substantive executive order on sacred sites, but it was changed unilaterally to a mere shadow of AIRFA.

Now comes a shadow of that shadow in the form of a bill in the House that purports to "codify" that executive order. Sadly, the main thing it would do is make mischief.

It would disenfranchise the traditional religious leaders and practitioners, who are the ones who hold these places sacred. It would put the tribal governments in charge with nothing to guarantee that they won't turn a sacred place into a casino or a mine.

For those Indian nations that are theocracies, it makes sense for their traditional governments to have sole standing. For the other 99 percent of the tribes that are not theocracies, it is nonsensical and backward to recognize the secular entities to the exclusion of the traditional religious entities and practitioners.

While the bill in the House includes even those tribes that have no traditional religions, it excludes those non-federally recognized tribes and Native Hawaiians who do have traditional sacred places to protect.

The House bill contains a virtually unusable cause of action. It sets the bar at the lowest possible standard—arbitrary and capricious—which means that a federal agency would have to laugh in your face and at the law, and all in writing, with witnesses, before you could take it to court.

It has a clumsy definition of sacred site that demonstrates the danger in attempting to define the sacred. It would do much harm by leaving out whole categories of sacred places and forcing proof that others are included. No other people in America have to define the sacred. Native Americans should not have to do so.

Proponents of the bill use the known sacred places that are under attack now—including Bear Butte and burial grounds and ceremonial areas along the Missouri River—to justify the need for their bill. Sadly, it would do nothing about any of those places. The bill's boosters also seem to be making it a Democrat bill, a strategy destined to fail at a time when both Houses of Congress and the White House are under Republican leadership.

What is needed is a bill with a substantive cause of action to defend sacred places in court and to serve as incentive for serious negotiations for the return, comanagement, or protected status of sacred places—one that does not try to define or limit the sacred.

Not nine months ago, traditional and tribal leaders, practitioners, and advocates who are among the most knowledgeable on these issues developed clear, concise lists of essential elements and objectionable elements for any public policy on Native sacred places.

Those lists are being turned into draft legislation that includes all segments of Native America with traditional and customary sacred places to protect, leaving out no category of sacred places and respecting traditional religious tenets and tribal law regarding nondisclosure of confidential and private information about the sacred.

Following those guidelines would not only keep faith with the people who reached consensus on these sacred-places matters last year, but would honor AIRFA and the myriad people who sacrificed to achieve it and its follow-on laws. This is a good thing to do in AIRFA's twenty-fifth-anniversary year.

Women Are the First Environment
December 23, 2003

Katsi Cook, *Indian Country Today*

In the Mohawk language, one word for midwife is *iewerokwas*. This word describes that "she's pulling the baby out of the Earth," out of the water, or a dark, wet place. It is full of ecological context. We know from our traditional teachings that the waters of the Earth and the waters of our bodies are the same water. The follicular fluid that bathes the ripening ovum on the ovary; the dew of the morning grass; the waters of the streams and rivers and the currents of the oceans—all these waters respond to the pull of our Grandmother Moon. She calls them to rise and fall in her rhythm. Mother's milk forms from the bloodstream of the woman. The waters of our bloodstream and the waters of the Earth are all the same water.

In the early years of my midwifery work at Akwesasne (St. Regis Mohawk Reservation, New York), I was confronted with one mother's question: is it safe to breast-feed? In 1983, vast contamination of our local environment with industrial organochlorines, PCBs, specifically, of which there are more than 200 congeners, was disclosed by the General Motors Corporation, the second largest employer in the United States. Earlier veterinary research in the 1970s by Dr. Lenaart Krook of Cornell University's

College of Veterinary Medicine revealed disabling fluorosis in local cattle as a result of atmospheric deposition of fluoride ash spewing from Reynolds Metals smokestacks on pasturelands on our reservation. Ensuing years would see the community's continuing struggle for remediation and restoration with an ever-expanding circle of polluters and pollution sources throughout the Great Lakes Basin.

If you look at a map of the world, you can easily see that 25 percent of the Earth's available freshwater is located in the sweet, water seas of the Great Lakes Basin. We quickly realized that Akwesasne is a veritable sink of the Great Lakes Basin, downstream and down-gradient from some of the world's most persistent and problematic pollution. On its way through the St. Lawrence River to the Atlantic Ocean, contaminated sludge and sediments bioaccumulate and biomagnify toxic contaminants in the food web of which we are all part.

In what would become the first Superfund site in the country to include human health in its environmental assessments, Akwesasne emerged a leader in environmental justice practice, engaging community members, health-care providers, and leading scientists and institutions.

Women are the first environment. We are privileged to be the doorway to life. At the breast of women the generations are nourished and sustained. From the bodies of women flow the relationship of those generations both to society and to the natural world. In this way is the Earth our mother, the old people said. In this way, we as women are Earth.

Science tells us that our nursing infants are at the top of the food chain. Industrial chemicals such PCBs, DDT, and HCBs dumped into the waters and soil move up through the food chain, through plants, fish, wildlife, and into the bodies of human beings who eat them. These contaminants resist being broken down by the body, which stores them in our fat cells. The only known way to excrete large amounts of them is through pregnancy, where they cross the placenta, and during lactation, where they are moved out of storage in our fat cells and show up in our breast milk. In this way, each succeeding generation inherits a body burden of toxic contaminants from their mothers. In this way, we, as women, are the landfill.

Realizing that mother's milk contains an alphabet soup of toxic chemicals is discouraging stuff. Every woman on the planet has PCBs in her breast milk. Even in the circumpolar region of the north, our Inuit relatives of the Ungava Bay area of Nunavik (arctic region within Quebec) have the highest documented levels of breast-milk PCBs in the world. Community leaders there state, "We will continue to do as we have always done," and consume an average nine fish meals a month, including sea mammals such as whale and seal. The essential fatty acids of this subsistence diet are highly protective of the cardiovascular system.

In a recent document from the Nunavik Regional Board of Health and Social Services to the Quebec Minister of Health and Social Services, the Inuit midwives say:

> There are few issues more fundamental to any people than birth. This intimate, integral part of our life was taken from us and replaced by a medical model that separated our families, stole the power of the birthing experience from our women, and weakened the health, strength and spirit of our communities. Over the last twenty years, however, we have developed a midwifery system that has restored birth to our culture. Birth has come back to Nunavik, and with it, a sense of meaning and identity that can serve to rebuild the health of our communities.

It is well established that the integration of valued lifeways and cultural acts such as midwifery and breast-feeding into health-care delivery systems are fundamental steps toward good health. In creating how we live, we also create how we die.

Wind Not War, Democratizing Power Production
January 12, 2004

Winona LaDuke

The United States is the wealthiest and most dominant country in the world, and we can't keep the lights on in New York City nor can we provide continuous power in a "liberated" Baghdad. Centralized power production based on fossil fuel and nuclear resources has served to centralize political power, to disconnect communities from responsibility and control over energy, and to create a vast wasteful system. We need to recover democracy. And one key element is democratizing power production.

Let's face it, we are energy junkies. The United States is the largest energy market in the world, and we consume one-third of the world's energy resources with 5 percent of the population. We are undeniably addicted—whether to an economy based on burning of fossil fuels and wasteful production systems, or to oil. Ninety-seven percent of the total world oil consumption has been in the past seventy years. We even slather oil-based fertilizers and herbicides on our food crops.

We have allowed our addictions to overtake our common sense and a good portion of our decency. We live in a country with the largest disparity of wealth between rich and poor of any industrialized country in the world. And, we live where economic power is clearly translated into political power. As Lee Raymond, chairman and CEO of ExxonMobil, remarks, "Energy is the biggest business in the world, there just isn't any other industry that begins to compare." Energy companies have immense influence in public policy and often flaunt their violations of the law and of modesty. (Just take a look at the closed-door meetings with Cheney if you need a refresher course.)

It's fourteen years after the Exxon Valdez oil spill, and only two of twenty-eight species almost obliterated by the accident are recovering. That's about it. ExxonMobil has thus far wiggled out of paying the $5 billion fine levied against the corporation for its negligence, and seeks to reduce the fine to $25 million, or $17.5 million less than Lee Raymond made in 2002. Halliburton, Dick Cheney's old corporate alma mater, is the happy recipient of a $1.7 billion no-bid contract in addition to hundreds of millions in other no-bid contracts to keep Iraqi oil flowing. And, while Enron's Kenneth Lay, who along with his colleagues was able to loot $2.1 billion from the 401K pension funds of thousands of Enron employees, might get a slap on the wrist, Martha Stewart is skewered. And then there is the Saudi Arabia example—one of our favorite oil suppliers. Although a dozen of the 9-11 hijackers held Saudi passports, we have made few comments, and, instead, invaded two countries with only marginal, at best, relationships with the 9-11 incident. Saudi Arabian officials remain welcome guests at the White House, and any Saudi human rights violations, or (their) absence of democracy, are ignored in our foreign policy.

Alternative energy represents an amazing social and political reconstruction opportunity and one that has the potential for peace, justice, equity, and some recovery of our national dignity. The Great Plains is the Saudi Arabia of wind power, representing this continent's greatest wind potential. Twenty-three Indian tribes have more than 250 gigawatts of wind-generating potential; add to that a host of farmers and ranchers. That represents more than half of present U.S. installed electrical capacity. Those tribes live in some of the poorest counties in the country and yet they are putting up wind turbines that could power America—if they had more contracts and access to power lines. The Rosebud Sioux Tribe's 750-kilowatt wind turbine is the first commercial turbine, with 30-megawatt projects planned for the Northern Cheyenne Reservation (Montana), Makah Reservation (Washington), and Rosebud in South Dakota. As well, the Assiniboine and Sioux tribes of Fort Peck (Montana) hope to bring a 660-kilowatt turbine on-line. That turbine alone will reduce the tribal electric bill by $134,000 annually, and help establish a senior citizen's kitchen to feed elders daily and to finance other programs through savings. And this is just a beginning. Solar power has similar potential. Each year, as Dennis Hayes (founder of Earth Day) notes, the sun pours more power onto America's highways than all fossil fuels used in the world.

Renewable energy makes economic sense. The Apollo Project, representing a host of environmental groups and twelve labor unions, points out that America has lost 2.7 million high-paying manufacturing jobs since 2000. Investing in alternative energy is investing in jobs since the fuel supply is from the Creator, there is no middle man. The European Union estimates 2.77 jobs in wind for every megawatt produced, 7.24 jobs/megawatt in solar, and 5.67 jobs/megawatt in geothermal. Or, in short, 1,000 megawatts of alternative-energy power averages 6,000 jobs, or sixty times more high-paying jobs than in fossil fuels and nuclear power. It is our choice. We can either create jobs and economic stability in Indian country or we can continue to line the pockets of utilities and energy companies.

Conservation and limited applications of alternative energy make huge economic sense. The Starwood Hotel group, (which includes the Sheraton and, for instance, the Gila River Wild Horse Pass Resort), recently invested in energy-smart solutions for 748 properties. The investments saved the corporation $6.1 million in one year, or the equivalent of 9,400 hotel-room bookings. And, these energy savings represented the equivalent of taking 1,800 automobiles off our roads, or planting 2,400 trees, or disconnecting 1,200 homes from the electric grid. The Mohegan Sun, the Mohegan Tribe's casino in Connecticut, is also looking at alternative energy, having purchased two PC25TM fuel-cell systems. Each cell produces 200 kilowatt-hours of electricity and 900,000 BTUs, which will be used for space heating and hot water. While traditional generating systems create as much as twenty-five pounds of pollutants to generate 1,000 kilowatt-hours of power, the same produced by fuel cells equates to less than one ounce of pollutants.

Right now, we are missing the canoe. While renewable energy is the fastest growing market in the world, the United States is dropping way back. The Rosebud Sioux had to import turbine parts from Denmark, and that's a long way away.

Some of us believe that instead of nuclear waste going to Newe Segobia (at Yucca Mountain), there should be solar panels. And we know that the wind blows endlessly on Pine Ridge, where we believe that, in the poorest county in the country, there should be wind turbines. We must be about democracy and about justice. We must put the power back into the hands of the people.

Global
Warming

MARTY TWO BULLS
© 2002

©2003 Marty Two Bulls

CHAPTER NINE
INDIAN LIFE IN THE AMERICAS

Indian life has its own internal logic. The connection to land and place is undeniable. High generosity blends with severe misery. Mastery over time provides extra perception but can make us late. Spiritual tradition and intensity sustains Indian independence and also produces the most devout of Christians. Institutional brutality, faith, hope, and charity all roll into one. Family, lineage, and legacy—source of both comfort and pain—provide the first definition. Indian life in America is about retaining identity in tribe and tradition, not letting go, regardless. Jurisdictional rights fuel new enterprises, including gaming and entertainment resorts. Returning the gift to their own people—returning "full circle" to their own people—is a common theme among Indian college students. What is sought is the opportunity to make a good effort to ensure the future of the people.

Recovering Indians: A Good Way

April 19, 2000

As harsh and difficult as life sometimes seems in the Indian country, there are as well elements of forgiveness and renewal not often found elsewhere.

Many years ago, an elder at the Minneapolis Indian Center told the story of a man we'll call Harvey. Harvey was an alcoholism counselor. He was a very good counselor and was known throughout the Indian community in the Twin Cities for his ability to bring people out of drinking. He had a way of listening and empathizing with the state of mind of down-and-out men and women that inspired confidence.

Some said it was in the depth of his eyes, the kindness with which he looked upon his people. Others credited him with the fact he had made it his duty to read about the problems of drinking and alcoholic behaviors and so he was up-to-date on the developing theories of recovery and could certainly dialogue with the range of professional probation officers, social workers, and psychiatrists that studied social pathologies.

The talking circles he conducted and his sessions with individuals grew and over time many people came to depend on him to help them through their days of crisis and hardship.

One day Harvey didn't come to work. He didn't call, and before long, he had been missing a whole week. There was a great deal of commotion until one day one of his regular clients came across Harvey in an alley behind an out-of-the-way bar. Harvey had fallen off the wagon.

Professionals around town were stunned that their golden Indian counselor had gone on a drunk. Most comments were harsh. "He must be fired," said one of the program's funders. "It's the only proper thing to do!"

Harvey was suspended from his job. It took him a few weeks, then he got control of himself again. But when he started to come around, professionals in town avoided him. "Never again," they said, "you blew your chance."

But Harvey's Indian clients thought differently. They continued to seek him out. It wasn't long before, to the chagrin of the non-Indian professionals, the Indian program hired him again. "The thing was," the elder explained, "he was still Harvey. And he was still the best alcoholism counselor we ever had. Heck, maybe he was even better after his fall."

A noted writer once said there are no second acts in American life. He meant they don't give you a second chance. The moral of the story is that often a second chance makes all the difference. Indian country is full of recovered people; sometimes they make the greatest of contributions.

Indian Country Today congratulates the Navajo Nation on its 1998 election of Kelsey Begaye, a self-described recovered alcoholic who is steering that most populous of Indian nations through difficult times. "Navajos are forgiving," Begaye said recently in an interview. In his own case, Begaye credits spiritual renewal as a source of his recovery. Most of all, he says, "My positive has outgrown my negative."

Kateri Tekahwitha and the Miracle of Prayer
May 17, 2000

Whether traditional or Christian, American Indians are spiritual people. The power of connection to spirit, the belief in life beyond the physical, and the impetus to pray are deeply held convictions throughout the Native Americas.

For sixteen years, as Patricia "Happi" White Bull lay in a coma in a New Mexico hospital, members of her Standing Rock Reservation family gathered to pray. Doctors had told the family that Mrs. White Bull, who had lost consciousness during childbirth in 1983, was unlikely to ever come out of the coma. There was nothing else that Western medicine could do for her.

Sixteen years is a long time. Many people would have given up hope. But not the White Bull family. As do many Native American Catholics, they sought the help of the Blessed Kateri Tekakwitha, the "Lily of the Mohawks." Periodically, Mrs. White Bull's mother-in-law joined some twenty other members of the Kateri Circle in Rapid City, South Dakota, to pray for Mrs. White Bull. When the stricken Native mother awakened on Christmas Eve 1999, many believers joined the opinion of New Mexico Archbishop Michael Sheehan that her case is "a good sign of miraculous intervention."

Kateri Tekakwitha is the closest thing American Indian Catholics have to a saint. Born near Auriesville, New York, in 1656, the young Kateri was baptized in 1676. She died on the Mohawk Reserve of Caughnawaga, Canada, in 1680. The daughter of a Christian Algonquin woman captured by Mohawks and married into their tribe, Kateri was a victim of smallpox early in life.

The disease left her scarred and nearly blind for life. A reserved young woman, Kateri refused marriage and, despite great hostility, became a devout Christian. Practicing her religion in the face of violent opposition, Kateri became known for her ministrations on behalf of her people and for her physical sacrifice and self-torture (mortifications of the flesh), a practice that is credited with bringing her perfect union with God in prayer. Since Kateri's death, many Indian people have manifested great devotion to her. Her grave and nearby monument on the Caughnawaga Mohawk Reserve in Quebec are considered shrines by believers and many pilgrims visit them every year to gain her intercession with the Creator. There are numerous Kateri Circles throughout North America, on reservations and in cities. Kateri Tekakwitha was declared Venerable by Pope Pius XII, January 3, 1943, and beatified by Pope John Paul II, June 22, 1980. Her feast day is celebrated on July 14. She is a candidate for sainthood in the Catholic Church.

Many Indian people, of course, reject the Christian teachings. And certainly, the instances of intolerance, outright denial, and even persecution of Native spirituality—fairly recent in some cases—make it difficult for many to look upon Christian claims with anything but disdain. However, our most fundamental teaching, as Native peoples, has always been to show respect for one another's vision.

Leaving aside for the moment the well-known and true problems between Catholicism and traditional Indian lifeways, *Indian Country Today* celebrates the good fortune, divine or not, of the White Bull family. We are particularly happy for the conscious reunification of a mother with her children, who never lost faith through sixteen years of quiet solitude.

We join with the family and with people of goodwill everywhere in wishing Patricia White Bull a continuous and full recovery. A miracle may well have occurred and Kateri Tekakwitha, the "Lily of the Mohawks," may well have been its divine intercessor. Indian Catholics everywhere will certainly rejoice in that and pray that the Church in Rome will fully note it.

Kateri's candidature for sainthood has awaited a "miracle." Perhaps it has occurred; perhaps it is time for the Church to fully rejoice in the devotions of its Indian flock: "Saint Kateri," has a good sound, and since this past Christmas, it rings true.

Forced Sterilization Is Ethnic Cleansing of Indians
June 14, 2000

More than twenty years since testimony against the practice at the United Nations, indigenous women in Mexico and other Latin American nations are still routinely sterilized without their consent. Believe it—sterilization of women is a fact of Indian life in the Americas. We have recent reports from Dr. Joy Mockbee, Tucson, of interviews last year with Indian women in the Ocosingo region of the embattled Mexican state of Chiapas.

Dr. Mockbee, a visiting physician, was frequently asked by her Native women patients about their condition. She found that a great many had been implanted with intrauterine devises (IUDs) without their consent. In many cases, the women had not even rudimentary knowledge of the procedure.

Half a world away, in Omaha, Nebraska, clinicians working with migrant Mexican populations report the same situation. Many of their Mexican Indian women patients, complaining of infertility, are finding that they have been sterilized or implanted with IUDs during previous childbirths. The clinicians report that such complete lack of "informed consent," the determinant concept in women's health care, is appalling.

The continuing intensity of sterilization as a social policy directed at rural poor, and particularly at Indians, in Latin America has all the feel of eugenic control. It may or may not have its origin in racialist ideology but it certainly appears to have turned that way. Clearly, Indian populations are most severely affected.

According to Mexican health reports, the State of Chiapas, in southern Mexico, scene of the Zapatista uprising since 1994, has sterilized more than 30,000 Native women. Chiapas is at the epicenter of the largest American Indian population north of Peru. Just the Maya of the Mesoamerican plateau (we could also mention Nahuatl, Zapoteca, Mixteca, and many others) number more than 6 million; they have an impactful population that speaks more than twenty languages. Thus, it must be regarded as significant that the government-sponsored program of tubal ligation and IUDs has accelerated there in recent years and appears vigorous.

In other countries, such as Puerto Rico and Brazil, clusters of cases of surreptitious sterilization of Native women have also surfaced. But it is in Peru, the other major epicenter of Indian population in the Western Hemisphere, where the most intense program is also reported. In Peru, tubal ligations increased from 10,000 in 1996 to 110,000 in 1997. The Andean country has the largest "population assistance" program in Latin America, provided by the U.S. Agency for International Development. The program has been so intensive that it generated a peculiar opposition alliance of Native rights groups, the Catholic Church, feminists, and conservative critics of Peruvian President Alberto Fujimori. Several tragic deaths have been caused by overzealous and overworked clinicians, who have performed as many as thirty tubal ligations in a day. Quotas and bonuses for high numbers were offered as incentive. Unsanitary conditions added to the frenzied work pace made for botched operations, as Indian women were directed to sign forms waiving the right to sue for the obvious malpractice.

For smaller tribes, the sterilization of relatively small numbers of women can have devastating, even genocidal, impacts. This is the case of several tribes in Brazil, where some villages, particularly among the Pataxuhe, in the Brazilian state of Bahia, large numbers of women have been sterilized. These jungle sterilization programs are widely and openly supported by invading colonists, who fear most of all a robust indigenous population that can challenge their illegal land occupations. There is the notorious case of Ronald Lavigne, doctor and politician, who as part of his campaign platform, offers money to Indian women if they agree to tubal ligation. It doubles his votes among the new settlers, who appreciate the scheme.

Critics of sterilization programs point to a 1974 National Security Council report issued under then-secretary of state Henry Kissinger that called for population control as a way of capping smouldering unrest and slowing natural resource consumption in the Third World. Responsibility also falls on the Rockefeller Foundation, which, among others, pushed early for population control as a model of poverty alleviation.

Whatever the original intentions, aggressive population-control programs should be abandoned. Not only are they eerily racialist and antipoor (rather than "antipoverty"), it is also true that population rates have been naturally declining around the world. Thus, the main reason for these easily misdirected programs, the specter of overpopulations exploding north from the Third World, is already a moot scenario.

What we cannot forget is this:

In the modern twentieth century, undoubtedly the most savage in history, humankind recoiled more than once from the practice of eugenics—the base for racial or ethnic cleansing—but has not entirely given up the idea. Eugenics laws passed by thirty states and Puerto Rico over the first half of the century have largely been found unconstitutional during the second half—but the original impulse is evident still, in places such as Bosnia and Rwanda and in the persistence of socially directed sterilization programs. Those early-twentieth-century laws allowed for the forced sterilization of: "the criminally insane ... parents likely to experience mental or physical or nervous disorders ... people whose children might turn out 'socially inadequate,'" etc. In the United States, African Americans, Puerto Ricans, and American Indians suffered disproportionally from these laws.

Congressional watchdogs from the subcommittee on International Operations and Human Rights have advised cutting such programs until abuses have been addressed. We would add that enough is enough. Aggressively directing women toward sterilization is a dead-end policy that results in substantial abuse. USAID needs to stop funding it.

Catholic Church's Next Step toward Respect

August 9, 2002

The same week that Pope John Paul II traveled the Americas to canonize an Indian saint and to beatify others, an unnamed Navajo medicine man, working from oral tradition, correctly identified the meanings of a buffalo-hide shield perhaps 600 years old.

Pope John Paul II is an incredible bastion of heart and spirit. Frail, bent by Parkinson's disease, he spoke to youth in Toronto, then flew over the United States to land in Mexico, where he spoke directly to huge Indian crowds and where he anointed an Indian saint. By all accounts, it was a tremendous event and perhaps the culmination of a trajectory that has seen this pope travel the globe in search of a better understanding among Christians and all peoples.

In the large measure of things, we can thank Pope John Paul II and his "Popemobile movement" for expressing outrage against both historic and present oppression of Native peoples and for recognizing the range of humanity and spiritual value that is to be found in Native populations. In Mexico on July 31 he canonized Juan Diego, who legend tells was a Chichimeca Indian to whom the Virgin of Guadalupe appeared in 1531. Always a controversial story, (many Indians say it was made up), it is the very basis of the policy of *mestizaje*, the racial and cultural integration pre-scribed by the Conquest. Juan Diego, Cuauhtlatoatzin (Talking Eagle), now a saint, and his vision of the apparition of the Virgin of Guadalupe is divinity itself for millions of Catholic Indian people not only in Mexico but throughout much of the Americas.

Clearly, the Church has come a long way from the days when Indian medicine people were hanged by their feet and burned, in groups of thir-teen, so as to commemorate Jesus Christ and the twelve apostles. It will always be remembered that the Church landed on these lands in the full vigor of its own period of Inquisition and that the torture-chamber cruel-ties that were just beginning to abate in Europe wrapped their gnarled and bloody tentacles around the most knowledgeable holy people in the Native nations of the Americas. For many centuries, right through three-fourths of the twentieth, all things Indian that dealt with spirit, with living ancestors' memory, or with the cosmological relation of humans to the Natural World were judged to be things of the Devil, to be suppressed, denied, replaced. A lot of suffering was generated by this attitude, which the Pope recognizes has not nearly disappeared.

Under John Paul II's leadership, the Catholic Church has made sweep-ing reforms in the way it approaches Native peoples and cultures of the world. In doing so, John Paul II brings back into his flock many who have strayed into the hands of Protestant evangelical churches, some perhaps even from among the many others who have quietly gone back into the Indian spiritual ways. Of this relationship, a lot remains to be understood.

While expressing respect for Catholic Indians, and while the new, more inclusive approach toward Indian customs and traditions is welcome, a question remains for the Church. What about Native peoples who do not necessarily want to believe that their cultural and spiritual roots are found in Adam and Eve, but instead believe in their own cosmology and creation stories, who enact ceremonies and practices of thanksgiving from their own cycles of Creation, and who wish to keep those practices separate from other religions, including Catholicism? Apart from its new inclusivity, which is a form of recognition desired by huge numbers of Indian Catholics, will Catholicism ever see a bona fide Indian religion or spiritual tradition as worthy of the same respect it now accords to Islam, Judaism, Hinduism, or Buddhism, among many others? More than most, Native religions (many prefer the term "lifeways;" we use "religion" as the general term for a common spiritual belief) are not based on conversion of others but are held and spread through family, clan, and tribe, or nation. But to describe these independent lifeways or religions—certainly on a par with other such spiritual systems—as mere "customs" does not do the reality justice. In fact, Native lifeways or religions are complete systems of spiritual interpretation, where worship is intently prescribed for the good of all. There is room for more recognition, not so much inclusivity "within" the Church itself, but an affirmation of existence, of intrinsic right to exist as independent spiritual systems.

Which brings us back to the Navajo medicine man. The Associated Press story that broke the news of the shields did not record his name, and this may have been his wish. He did something remarkable for his tribe by offering compelling evidence that identified the symbols and meanings on buffalo-hide shields that likely come from the time before Columbus. The medicine man came from the family that hid the shields around 1860 in the area of present-day Capitol Reef National Park. The shields were discovered in 1926 and have been held by Park officials. He convinced officials at the Park that the shields should be in possession of the Navajo Tribe. In his place of origin, he still remembered the sacred knowledge handed down through his generations.

It is this independent, residual knowledge, still at work in the contemporary world, that defines American Indian lifeways, which are not perhaps religions in the exact definition of Christian churches, but which deserve all the world's respect for being, each and every one of them, a distinct spiritual way. That resiliency of belief—local and eco-systemic—is a miracle of sustenance and the breathing spirit of most tribal peoples.

Many Native people, as is their right, are pleased to merge the various ways of belief, from Catholic and other Christian forms to Pipe and Four Directions ways and other indigenous systems. This is also traditional, to layer onto the consciousness, rather than to draw a barrier, or to reject and be decimated. This has also been a way of survival for Indian spirituality. Perhaps ultimately, in its quest to envelop Indian traditions, the Catholic Church will become more indigenized, at least within Latin America, than it now can contemplate, perhaps even more than Indians will be Catholicized.

Nevertheless, those who belong to or have experienced in any way the intricate, independent, and yet interdependent spiritual traditions of any American Indian people, anywhere in the hemisphere, will always attest to the seriousness and potency of traditional ceremonies, healing activities, and prayers. These are ways of life that are important and deserve to be respected, in their own right. They are still around, after 500 years. Given the right of tribal integrity, these traditions will survive. They have much to teach the various other traditions of humankind.

Into the Culture Wars
March 5, 2004

With all the gay marriage going on, culture-war topics are likely to dominate the political landscape for at least the next few months. We expect the political campaigns will settle on war and economy as main topics, but for the moment we are stimulated to ruminate on the morality issues.

Suddenly, as Janet Jackson's breast was being stuffed back in the fold, gay marriage exploded everywhere. In San Francisco, City Hall decided to marry same-sex couples. Ditto for Portland, Oregon, and San Bernalillo, California, and New Paltz, New York, among others. Thousands and thousands of gay couples came out of their homes. "Rosie (O'Donnell) Takes a Wife," said one headline. In Washington, with the Christian Right gearing its battle, President George W. Bush decides to support the Federal Marriage Amendment recently introduced by Collin Peterson, D-Minn., Mike McIntyre, D-N.C., Ralph Hall, D-Texas, Marilyn Musgrave, R-Colo., Jo Ann Davis, R-Va., and David Vitter, R-La.

The proposed new Federal Marriage Amendment (H.R. 56) reads: "Marriage in the United States shall consist only of the union of a man and a woman. Neither this constitution or the constitution of any state, nor state or federal law, shall be construed to require that marital status or the legal incidents thereof be conferred upon unmarried couples or groups."

Nationally, the antigay marriage fervor is at 65 percent against, although the amendment—seen by many as overreaching and motivated by the presidential campaign—faces an uphill bipartisan battle in Congress.

The gay marriage question brings to the table the legal protections and structuring that the institution provides heterosexual couples. This, despite the railings of the religious right, appears a reality whose time has come and is a right that persons perhaps cannot be denied. It is generally true that approaches to gay behavior among Native peoples has gone from the times of natural acceptance to a period of sporadic intolerance to per- haps more understanding these days, as contemporary society opens up to the reality that a percentage of people naturally bond with their same sex. It is an issue best contemplated in the context of family, where compassion can enter the picture. As a "wedge" issue in the culture "wars," it can have nothing but uninformed, negative, and destructive uses.

Regardless of how one views the marriage of same-sex couples, one thing is certain: when it comes to degradation by the media, almost all of us feel our own decency and our senses insulted and assaulted regularly. There is a sense of progressive collapse of American societal values in the media. Perhaps this is just a parallel reality, but: more children are being sexually abused more horribly and earlier than at any other time in history. And many more children do more horrible things earlier than at any other time in history.

Traditionally, good morality is predominantly taught in the family. In Native communities, by and large, the old morals were strict. The need to maintain reasonable relations among the extended families of siblings was paramount in the ways of tightly knit clans and tribes. This dictated that proper behavior govern marital and all intimate relations. Children were understood to learn best by example. Passionate disputes that emerged from destabilizing behavior on the part of a man or a woman were severely sanctioned. For most of our generations, tribes and communities and fami- lies needed to sustain good working harmony within the group or survival itself was threatened.

On the other hand, the personal and spiritual nature of each being was generally respected. Earthy commentary and humor, and tolerance for the dictates and requirements of young love, was the norm as well. Different or strange people, who perhaps did not pair off just as most people do, might be let alone, to fulfill the best roles and relationships they might engage. Tolerance for the making of necessarily difficult, or even bad, choices in life still survives as a value in most Native societies, some say to the detriment of more effective discipline among the young people.

Pundits bemoan the loss of "family values," but family life is difficult in modern times. Finding a compatible mate, bonding as a spouse, forming a family to raise children, setting goals in a long-term approach to life and happiness that sacrifices to provide a decent, perhaps even prosperous, life for others—this requires profound daily commitment. We are quite conservative in our respect for that type of commitment: what it takes for a woman and a man to marry and raise children through twenty-odd years to bring those young people to fruitful lives as adults. These days, perhaps more than ever, this is a huge and sometimes desperate task. Not nearly enough appreciation is given to those heads of family, male and female, that do this day in and day out.

Among our peoples, customary conduct varied from nation to nation, and, of course, 500 years of contact and change has altered much of that; nevertheless, the wish for good behavior in the families and good treatment for all remains the most positive goal of Native social prerogative. The love of our children remains the basis of our unity. Wherever elders have maintained their own integrity in the treatment of their families, they are recognized by their offspring for their successful lives. That part of the general Native culture—respect for the good elders—survives and still strongly informs Native family life today. It is the braid of decency that struggles against the disintegration that also plagues family life: severe and grinding poverty and alcohol abuse over generations. These have done generational damage that often calls for incisive and long-term tribal intervention, beyond the possibilities of the particular family.

Complex enough? These deep, personal issues need to be, and to achieve positive solutions require discussion far apart from the shrill of political campaigns. We dislike the definition and the approach to such personal questions as "cultural wars." Strength of family, respect for women and men of good character, vigorous support, defense and protection of children, tolerance of personal choices, and acceptance of natural inclinations among adults—these things we support. We don't like government in the bedroom. We severely dislike those who preach religion in our faces and pretend to dictate morality through political manipulation. We don't like crass behavior; vulgar language; disrespectful or angry or hateful words.

Speaking of culture: it behooves all of us to maintain a watchful eye on the media. It wantonly distorts for the sake of buzz and has become completely corporate in its pursuit of provocative material. These days, the aim is to push the envelope to the worst possible taste allowed. Western civilization is not going to crumble, whatever the president says, but the media—in its growing monopolies and its so obvious lack of ethics—does need attention. Media informs and affects our daily lives. More than ever, media dictates how people think and act. Sex and violence, and often violent sex, abound all around, as pornography becomes increasingly mainstream. In particular, young people coming up on television culture get saturated with it early. Patience, dedication, commitment to elders and the young, love of family—these are not values easily found in most profitable and popular media programming today.

September 21, 2004: A Native Universe Opens
September 21, 2004

There was a pause—an opening—in the fabric of the natural world this week as the Native nations of the Western Hemisphere took their proper place at the center of American consciousness. The prayers and good wishes of hundreds of Native nations offered sincere thanks that, for once, something positive and good has happened.

The call to consciousness came from the National Mall in Washington, D.C.—that old Piscataway country of marshes and meadows that is now home and the seat of government to the richest and most powerful country on Earth. Thousands of Indian people came to town to launch the opening of a wonderful museum and cultural project within the venerable Smithsonian Institution—the new National Museum of the American Indian (NMAI).

More than 1,000 Native nations are represented in the Western Hemisphere. Despite 500 years of denial and oppression, a great diversity of cultures, languages, identities, and histories persists. Traditional and modern alike, the Native nations emerge from a deeply connected sense of the natural world. There are American Indian peoples in every region and nation-state—from Alaska to Tierra del Fuego—and as Phillip Deere, Creek Medicine Man, used to say, "Every one of them, no matter how small, deserves the right to be who they are."

This is the philosophy of the new museum on the National Mall. For more than a decade, the NMAI has carried out the most extensive consultation with Native peoples—from traditional communities to professional circles in the highest of academic centers—ever conducted in history. Hundreds of circles of discussion with thousands of people have been held, in Washington, D.C., and just about everywhere else where the NMAI may have touched a Native culture or institution. Front and center: respect for all cultures of Native peoples, and equal treatment under the law.

Created under the National Museum of the American Indian Act of 1989, the NMAI has been a museum for, about, and largely by American

Indians. From its inception, with its hemispheric vision and its magnificent collection of more than 800,000 cultural icons and artifacts from throughout the Americas, the NMAI has maintained a clear commitment to an American Indian cultural self-representation and self-interpretation the likes of which had not been experienced since the times of first contact with the European migrations.

More than a decade in gestation, the new museum's journey parallels the International Decade of Indigenous Peoples at the United Nations, and is the result of similar and perhaps just as intensive activism. It has been no secret that the perceptions and voices of Native peoples have been missing from the world of museums and from the cannon of scientific research about Native cultures and communities. Throughout history, the bulk of research and writing on Native cultures has come from outside and with a clear dictum to observe and analyze "the other," who was thought to have no true knowledge of the world and whose testimony was incorporated as fodder for external ideas and other-cultural theses.

The NMAI process has challenged all that. It was experienced Indian activism that led to the establishment of the new museum, and the activists had an idea or two about content, about approach, and about ultimate purposes. People of established reputations as scholars and cultural interpreters, such as Suzan Shown Harjo, W. Richard West Jr., Drs. Dave Warren, Charlotte Heth, Vine Deloria Jr., among many others, had challenged the disrespect and disdain shown by museums and science in general to Native human remains, as well as to Native cultural or religious objects collected privately and publicly over the past century and a half. As the Indian case mounted, many allies in museology, politics, academics, and other fields—good people who "get it"—agreed to pressure for a change of approach. When the remains of ancestors of these same activists started turning up in Smithsonian drawers, the potential public embarrassment led to the passage of both the 1989 NMAI Act and the Native American Graves Protection and Repatriation Act of 1990.

As planning and construction activities for the new museum got under way under Director W. Richard West Jr., in partnership with venerable Smithsonian administrator Doug Evelyn, it became apparent that the new approach involved consultation with a deep and wide spectrum of Native opinion leaders—from both community and academic bases. These consultations have been numerous and are continuous. They have provided knowledge, culture, and guidance as the staff of the growing museum tackled the difficult tasks of managing and curating the extensive and valuable collection, of designing and executing relevant contexts for exhibitions, and of creating a serious outreach and networking program with Native community bases. Of core importance at the NMAI: a mutual and interactive communications and education process with Indian communities across the hemisphere. A major goal was to guarantee an Indian community-based mission, while generating an inclusive, multicultural staff. Thus, talented Native and non-Native professionals and resource people were incorporated into the vision as articulated by Native elders, scholars, artists, and community leaders.

Noteworthy among the many professional staff who approached the work with sincerity and who exhibited respect for Native peoples both within Indian communities and on staff are Jim Volkert, associate director of the Mall transition team, Donna Scott, assistant director for administration, and Terence Winch, head of publications. They have demonstrated unwavering loyalty to American Indians and helped the Indian leadership set the proper tone for the institution.

Indian country pitched in not only culturally but financially as well. Mashantucket Pequot Tribal Nation, Mohegan Nation, and the Oneida Nation of New York each contributed $10 million over ten years. This $30 million boost and other contributions from tribes, corporations, foundations, and tens of thousands of individual members have greatly strengthened the confidence and momentum of congressional supporters.

The result of such collaboration is this week completely refreshing news. In fact, it has been revitalizing news over a decade, as the turn of the century came and went, to know that the new museum was engaging serious projects: rededication of a new facility, exhibits, and public programs in New York City (The George Gustav Heye Center); new construction of a site for the huge collection, in Suitland, Maryland, near Washington, D.C.; extensive sessions, planning, breaking ground, and extensive campaigns on behalf of this substantial national project. As deadlines approached, quality sustained and more than most staffers have worked around the clock to meet them. The dedication of the staff was palpable to all who worked with the NMAI, and most people have come to respect the grueling pace that the active developers of the NMAI have endured. The journey to the opening day of September 21 has been arduous, but serious and resilient talents contributed in countless ways to carry the work forward to completion. Indian country can only welcome the lesson of good partnership the NMAI team has exemplified. Young people everywhere can now contemplate the lesson of success that is possible when people keep their "eyes on the prize."

The opening of the National Museum of the American Indian on the National Mall, September 21, 2004, is a major marker in time, noting a turning of the public mind to the tribal history, inheritance, and cultural legacy that all of America must treasure and hold dear. We congratulate the institution in holding fast to its mission, which extends the American Indian world and heightens understanding among cultures. We congratulate the many people who made this wonderful cultural achievement possible—all those who envisioned, directed, guided, managed, coordinated, produced, curated, fund-raised, protected, and projected—we hope you will now proudly enjoy the fruits of your hard work, your creation.

The time of the Indian is coming, said elders of the last generation, when the world will understand the wisdom and beauty of our cultures. Truth to power for the National Museum of the American Indian. Prophecy turns to promise fulfilled this week on the National Mall.

Enemies within Indian Country
June 9, 2002

Suzan Shown Harjo, *Indian Country Today*

In Shakespeare's "Othello"—a play about jealousy, envy, and treachery—the title character is an acclaimed military hero with a loving wife and dedicated friends. By the last scene, he has strewn the stage with loved ones killed in a fit of jealousy enflamed by lies of his false friend, Iago.

The treacherous Iago understands jealousy all too well and defines it memorably as the "green-eyed monster which doth mock the meat it feeds on."

Even though Shakespeare was English (and as smart and eloquent about jealousy and envy as anyone has ever been), these afflictions are not particular traits of the British or Europeans or white folks. From the plains of Africa and Asia to the islands of Polynesia and the Mediterranean, every culture the world over has a good-luck charm, an animal's foot, a magic potion, or some other medicine to ward off the evil eyes of envy and jealousy.

Jealousy and envy are diseases that metastasize into disloyalty and betrayal over love, land, money, talent, looks, position, fame, recognition, and mostly just stuff. They are so pronounced in Indian country that many Native people talk about them as indigenous to our hemisphere and cultures. While they are not unique to us, they are intensifying, not lessening, in their severity.

In every Indian gathering, large and small, even the most casual observer can see jealousy and envy at work:

- In the sideways glances of aging aunties at their favorite nephew's too-flaming flame
- In the pursed lips of beer-bellied uncles when fancy dancers stop right on the beat
- In the folded arms of people in a crowd who resent not being the center of attention
- In the way the begrudging clap ever so slowly when a rival is being applauded
- In the squint-eyed glares of the spiteful who covet the gifts of the talented
- In the self-sabotage of those who are afraid they might not get

the credit for a victory
  • In the clenched teeth and fists of those who suspect infidelity

The jealous, says Iago's wife Emilia, "are not ever jealous for the cause, but jealous for they are jealous: 'tis a monster begot upon itself, born on itself."

I watched a stark example of jealousy—inexplicable, illogical, and uncontrolled—some time ago at a conference gathering. A tribal leader stood in a room filled with his peers, extended his arm to point at a brilliant, hardworking Native man and thundered, "You stole my international reputation and I want it back."

The tribal leader was inconsolable when he realized that everyone understood very plainly what he really meant: if the smarter, more industrious man did not exist, the thicker, lazier one would be famous. He might as well have been Iago explaining his envy of Othello's closest aide: "He hath a daily beauty in his life that makes me ugly."

For us (and probably for all colonized peoples), jealousy and envy are tied historically to the politics of food, starvation, and hunger. This comes to us through oral history, but functions like imprinted cellular memory.

We still watch for the well-fed families among the starving people. How many "Hostiles" did these "good Indians" have to name in order to get good food when everyone else was eating rancid rations or nothing at all? Whose secrets did they sell? Whose land? Whose children?

In the "starve or sell" policy era, which was actually articulated on the floor of Congress, the goal was to get Native land and gold by any means necessary. Food was a lethal weapon in General Philip H. Sheridan's "total destruction" war game. The key to winning the West, he said, was to kill the Indian commissary (the buffalo).

When Sheridan heard that white hunters were slaughtering the great buffalo herds of New Mexico and Texas in 1873, his public reaction was, "Let them kill, skin, and sell until the buffalo is exterminated, as it is the only way to bring lasting peace and allow civilizations to advance."

Native peoples were separated from buffalo, elk, salmon, beans, corn, and other traditional foods and were made dependent on lard, white flour, sugar, and other government handouts. Penalties for Indian offenses were open-ended sentences of confinement and starvation.

Food was used as both an inducement to inform and a reward for collaborating. The betrayers justified their disloyalty as being practical and provident for their families. When they turned on their relatives, they spoke of the good of the tribe. When they betrayed their people, they spoke of throwing off the blanket and floating down the mainstream.

Here we are, more than a century and a quarter past genocide and we still are admonished from childhood to be very careful of the guests we invite to eat, lest the enmity of the envious poison the food and water. We still vie with each other for the last of the Indian agent's beef issue and carry on blood feuds over a neighbor's extra pinch of salt.

Still today, we equate the smallest measure of success or prominence in the most modest of settings with eating too well (meaning selling out the people). Even more today, our envy sits in the back of the throat and bottom of the stomach, growing with our desire for what we do not have and finishing off what the Indian wars started.

Guard against these enemies within Indian country, jealousy and envy that gnaw like hunger from the inside out and consume all in their path.

Stay loyal and true, good friends, and be generous with your admiration and compliments and compassion and kindness and love.

Or, as Shakespeare put in the mouth of Iago: "Good Heaven, the souls of all my tribe defend from jealousy."

Mission School Remembered ...
September 2, 2003

Charles Trimble, *Indian Country Today*

It was back in 1971, and several of us were sitting around a bar table, trying to out-Indian each other. The competition was who had it roughest in boarding school. National Congress of American Indians Director Leo Vocu and I held for the mission schools, a couple other guys for the Bureau of Indian Affairs schools. I don't remember the outcome—it wasn't important; but the gist of my recalling the occasion is how we viewed our boarding-school experience—as a challenge met and endured, and to be boasted about. But the horrors we recalled, even exaggerated, were not as horrible as some being described now in class action litigation against the schools.

News of the litigation has gotten many old boarding-school chums to communicating—via e-mail, telephone, and through the mail, recalling our own experiences and comparing notes.

Several years ago I heard the venerable Sioux elder, Sid Bird, very movingly tell about his introduction to boarding school when he was a child. I have heard others tell a similar story of their first day, a story of betrayal in the earliest years of a boy's life. It's an experience vivid in my memory.

My father died in 1937, leaving my mother alone to raise five boys. Although the Great Depression was on the wane, there was little money.

Two years later, with the threat of losing me to adoption as social workers were insisting, my mother decided instead to place me in a Catholic mission school, even though I was only four years old at the time.

It was to be the first time I would be away from home for an extended period and I dreaded it. My brother, slightly older, would be there with me, but that was little comfort to me. While my mother enrolled us, I stayed close to her side. But my brother lured me into the playroom to see a special toy or game. Being inside overly long—perhaps only a few minutes—I sensed that something was terribly wrong and panic hit me. Tearing back outside, I saw that my mother was gone. My brother held me fast to keep me from running after the car, and he was crying too as he held me. Thus began my school days at Holy Rosary Mission in Pine Ridge, South Dakota.

I hated my brother for his betrayal, but later realized that he did it only to spare our mother further heartbreak, added to the terrible sadness she felt over what she had to do. I forgave him.

I spent the rest of my school years at the mission, graduating in 1952. Over those years I met good people—teachers, administrators, and fellow students. Some have become lifelong friends, and I hold most with good memories.

Life would have been better if I could have stayed in Wanblee with my mother and brothers in our home, which was very poor in material goods, but rich with love and affection. Looking back now, I see Wanblee as always Christmas or summertime, for those were the only times I spent there during my growing-up years. They were wonderful times, with relatives, childhood friends, and the old people, especially. If the mission meant to kill the Indian in me—and I don't believe that was their intent—it would have been futile anyway, given the fullness and richness of my cultural world at Wanblee, even in those few months I spent at home each year.

Life in the school was often very hard, especially for the little ones. There was debilitating homesickness. Discipline was strict, and spanking was not uncommon. The food was perhaps nutritious, but seldom appetizing. In the crowded dormitories, disease, such as measles and whooping cough, spread rapidly and laid up many students at any time. But, as with children everywhere, there was also warm friendship, joy and laughter, adventure, and much mischief.

I survived bullies, who were the scourge of school life there. For protection, we little kids would pledge for a whole year our dessert or the single pat of butter we would get at each meal. But that only worked if one's hired bully was tougher than other bullies.

And life was frustrating for adolescents. The school had some 200 on the boys' side, and perhaps another 250 on the girls' side. Classes were coeducational through the fifth grade; from there on, the gender separation was complete. In junior high and high school years, of course, there was first love, albeit always from afar. Except on Sunday afternoons and at sodality dances, there was never a chance to even hold hands.

I was not a good student, nor a scholarly one by any measure. My transcript bears that out. I was a problem to most of the teachers, and was sent many times to the principal's office. A demerit system was in place, with the worst punishment being study hall instead of the movie on Saturday night. I missed many movies, and spent much time struggling to write the required 500-word compositions while listening to the laughter and clapping in the gymnasium above, where the movies were shown. On one occasion I was nearly expelled, saved only by my mother's intercession.

I learned to survive, however, and am proud of the fact that I finished school there; and other Indian boarding-school graduates have told me of their pride.

But many traumatic experiences now being described in news stories and presumably in depositions are horrors the likes of which I never witnessed or even heard rumors of during my twelve years in school; and some of them involve the same school I attended a quarter century earlier. Schoolmates I am in touch with say that they never witnessed such horrors either. I witnessed and experienced spankings, but nothing that could be described as beatings.

I remember no prohibition, written or otherwise, on speaking the Lakota language. And if there was, signals were certainly confusing, for there were prayers and songs in Lakota. Student dancers performed in full regalia before each basketball game, and there were cheers in Lakota during the games. To refine his newly acquired language, Jesuit scholastic John Bryde regaled young students with the *Aeneid*, much improvised and in Lakota.

This is not to deny the hardship that existed in the lonesomeness, strict discipline, and the constant survival struggle in the boarding schools. But by the time I graduated, conditions were much improved over what they were when I first started. Daily Mass was no longer mandatory, for example, and students were allowed to go home on weekends. A decade after I graduated, Indian studies was incorporated into the curriculum, including Lakota language. And, later, much-respected elders Matt and Nellie Two Bulls were retained to be on campus to mentor students and otherwise lend a traditional presence.

I do not mean to even try to discredit those who may rightly be seeking justice in lawsuits. The courts will decide on their veracity. But perspective is needed, and we must look to various experiences among our people in order to achieve it. My story is intended to help provide that, and there are many others with whom I am in touch who tell much the same story that I do.

My greatest motivation for toughing it out was the fact that the person who placed me in the school and kept me there was the one who loved me the most, and cared the most about my future. That, of course, was my Lakota mother. Knowing that, I was able to endure.

I have no regrets. For any measure of success I have achieved, I owe much to my education at Holy Rosary Mission, which is now the Red Cloud Indian School.

Is it "Eskimo" or "Inuit"?
February 11, 2004

Rachel Attituq Qitsualik

I answered a letter a while ago, from someone at a museum in Alaska. They wanted to know why Inuit (which I am of) dislike being called "Eskimos." After all, many Alaskans don't mind being called Eskimos, and even seem to dislike the term "Inuit" when southerners apply it them, however well-intentioned.

I am not surprised by the confusion. The ascendancy of Inuit culture, through good reportage and the establishment of Nuvavut, has conditioned southern folks to say "Inuit" instead of "Eskimo."

Southerners have complied beautifully, but at last they are running up against peoples, related to Inuit, who insist that they are Eskimos. The confusion derives from this sticky fact: Inuit are not Eskimos, and Eskimos are not Inuit.

In simple terms: the first Mongolic peoples of North America (linked by genetic heritage to the Mongols of Asia) settle in Alaska as early as 8,000 years ago. Paleoanthropologists like to call them the "Arctic Small Tool Tradition," which, frankly, is fine by me.

Millennia creak by. Some of these people move east across North America in waves. The first such Mongolic wave (I dislike the term "Mongoloid") finishes settling as far as Greenland about 4,000 years ago. Once they settle, they are dubbed the "pre-Dorset" culture, later developing into the more advanced "Dorset" culture. These are a Mongolic people from Alaska, but they live in an incredibly cold world without dogsleds and most of the technologies Inuit are used to. Their rectangular encampments are bordered by short walls of flat stone. They are obsessed with art, particularly images of human faces, which they leave everywhere around the Arctic.

Then the Earth warms up a bit. Between the period of Europe's late dark ages to its early middle ages, about 800–1200 A.D., a new Mongolic people, dubbed "Thule," sweep eastward from Alaska. They are tool-obsessed people (more than forty items in a seal-hunting kit alone), mainly following whales and walrus along newly opened channels in the ice. These are the inventive souls who bring such innovations as dogsleds, soapstone lamps, float bladders, *igluvigak* (igloo) building, waterproof stitching, and toggling harpoons with them. By the time they have completely occupied the area from the eastern edge of Alaska to Greenland, around 700 years ago, the Earth cools again. It is time to curb the nomadism.

They supplant the Dorset, and become Inuit.

Now, I have read too many interpretations of "Inuit" as meaning "Humans" or "The People," probably under the (incorrect) assumption that this is every culture's name for itself.

However, having been a translator for thirty years, I can guarantee you that "Inuit" is a specific term. It precisely means, "The Living Ones Who Are Here." It denotes a sense of place, of having arrived, a memory that Inuit knew they had kin somewhere else. It also betrays the fact that Inuit once knew they were not the original peoples of their lands. Interestingly, in this way does language act as a code to preserve heritage.

The Alaskan Eskimos are descended from the Mongolic peoples that continued to develop into diverse Western cultures. As such, they have their own preferred words for themselves, such as "Yup'ik" and "Aleut" and "Nunamiut." Nevertheless, none of us has completely left our heritage behind, and I still get a kick out of it when I understand the speech of people from Alaska, or even the Chukchi Peninsula.

There was only one culture in the Canadian Arctic and Greenland before Inuit. These, Inuit refer to as the "Tunit." These are Dorset. Inuit remember them well in their oral traditions. The Tunit were small, very strong, incredibly shy. It is said that Tunit taught Inuit about their lands, that they built the first *inuksuit* ("images of men," manlike stone structures) to herd caribou along predictable paths for hunting. Paradoxically, they were thought of as poor craftsmen.

Unfortunately, the Tunit are now extinct. Inuit, therefore, have the luxury of using "Inuit" in a wide context, since they are the only ones remaining. But even this can get politically tricky, since there are a couple of peoples adjacent to them—"Inuvialuit," for example—who do not always approve of being called Inuit. But, generally, one can get away with using "Inuit" as a kind of umbrella term for Eastern Mongolic peoples.

The umbrella term for the far west, Alaska, is "Eskimo." Alaskans do not seem to mind its usage these days, simply because it provides a handy general term. And there may be another reason not to mind it, as well. The old thinking was that it derived from Cree, derogatorily meaning, "Eaters of Raw Meat." It was thought that it was overheard by French missionaries, distorted to "Esquimaux" or "Esquimau," then Anglicized to "Eskimo." It is amazing how widespread this belief has become, so that it is cited by all but the most informed sources. Yet, while remaining a bit of a mystery, the missionary origin of "Eskimo" is pretty much discounted today, since there is some compelling evidence that the word was existent in precolonial times. Some researchers have made a good case for it coming from Montagnais vocabulary, literally meaning, "snowshoe net-weaver," but culturally being a term that indicates any craftsman of great skill. It seems to me that this makes more sense and, if true, would mean that the word is not derogatory after all.

Inuit, however, can never be Eskimos. Existent in the west or not, preferred by Alaskans or not, it was simply never part of their vocabulary. Inuit, after all, have their own name for themselves: Inuit. Today, "Eskimo" only reminds Inuit of the days when missionaries kidnapped them, dumped flea powder all over them, and assigned "Eskimo numbers" to them, instead of bothering to note the proper name for the culture or the individuals within it.

It all really boils down to choice, the right to accept or reject specific labels at will, the right to be known as one wishes to be. And is that not what liberty is all about?

Pijariiqpunga. (That is all I have to say.)

Our Vision for a Living Museum
September 18, 2004

Suzan Shown Harjo, *Indian Country Today*

Our vision for a Native museum is first, last, and always about living beings, not objects or buildings.

That may seem an odd thought to advance on the occasion of the opening of the National Museum of the American Indian's (NMAI) museum on the Mall. There, the design and construction of bricks and mortar and the arrangement of things will be in the spotlight, just the way we many parents envisioned and brought them into focus from the 1960s to this day.

I am bursting with pride over the museum, especially as I see in her stature, dignity, and strength my own family traits and those of countless other people I love. This child has great genes.

I would like for all who come to applaud the building and the objects she holds so carefully to also perceive and marvel at the life behind, around, and beyond this place, this moment.

Life will be very much in evidence on the museum grounds and on the National Mall during this opening week. Thousands of Native people are gathering to be a part of this history, more than at any time since the great Anacostia feasts centuries ago.

Prayers are being offered by Native people throughout this hemisphere— our part of Mother Earth. Journeys are under way and each person who gathers here will represent myriad generations, past and unborn.

For millennia, Native people flourished in this rich area—with its lush and bountiful rain forests, fields, and waterways—and then they did not live anywhere. They did not move away and they did not have a peaceful passage.

We parents of the museum envisioned that all visitors would think, if only for an instant, about the humanity and history of the Anacostia and other nations whose names live on in this beautiful Capitol City as place-names.

We envisioned that the museum would help educate the decision makers of today and tomorrow to reflect on the fate of the Native people whose home this once was.

We envisioned that the museum would face the Capitol and stand as a reminder to the entire policy industry to support measures that enhance Native life and to oppose those that lead in any other direction.

I am privileged to have been a part of conceptualizing the whole NMAI system and developing its legal underpinnings. That began with the coalition that formed at Bear Butte in 1967 to deal with the maltreatment of our dead and living relatives in museums, to protect our burial grounds and other sacred places, and to gain respect for Native peoples in general society.

The steady gains made by Native traditional people—from return of sacred places and enactment of the American Indian religious freedom law in the 1970s to the development of Native American repatriation policy in the 1980s—are the firm foundation for the NMAI and its new museum.

I have also been a part of the physical shaping of the museum on the Mall, starting in the 1980s, when we negotiated its square footage, secured the NMAI establishment act, and began meeting with spiritual leaders; artists; and community, museum, and technology specialists to design its indoor and outside spaces along cultural, functional, and visual lines.

In 1990, we picked the perfect first director for the NMAI, my

Cheyenne brother, W. Richard West Jr. During the past decade, we solicited architectural ideas and selected the many designers who carried out the Native consultations that we made sure were mandated by law.

It has been a pleasure to watch the museum grow bones and skin, and stand on her own. But, even though I saw this physical growth many times each week, from the groundbreaking in 1999 to this year, the museum only started to come to life for me on Father's Day.

My daughter, Adriane Shown Harjo, and I were taking an evening walk to inspect the progress on our museum. As we neared the construction site, we saw a crowd of fireflies following a large white squirrel around the trunk of a tree. Muscogees view them as beings of good fortune, and they were a good sign for the health of my dad, Freeland Douglas.

We walked around the museum and watched insects and birds feasting at the water of the newly installed pond. It was a joyous moment to see living creatures grace the building and breathe life into her. I had the same feeling in mid-August, when I heard that 1,000 ladybugs were released in the museum landscape.

I experienced that joy again the week before the opening, as I watched a Snake Doctor (a dragonfly) sitting quietly on a leaf in the pond. His wings—one set for carrying prayers and another for spirits—were at rest, and he did not move for a very long time. Spending time with this ancient repatriator brought me full circle to the purpose, context, and power of the museum.

We will gather to honor all those Native nations and people who have not survived. We will gather to represent all those who have survived and the miracle of that. We will gather to mark America's symbolic promise that we shall not return to the tumult of the past. We will gather to celebrate the achievements of our ancestors and our children.

I plan to walk from the Smithsonian Castle to the NMAI Museum with my daughter and son, Duke Ray Harjo. They, too, have sacrificed and worked toward this day. We, like all the other Native people, will walk for all our ancestors who sacrificed so we could have this good day and greet it in a good way.

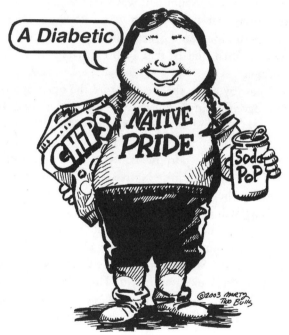

News Item: Lakota spiritual leaders agree to ban non-Indians from participating in Sun Dance ceremonies.

Together as one voice our songs will be heard...

National Museum of the American Indian

Chapter Ten
Appreciations and Remembrances

There are many heroes in Indian country, and these that follow are but a very few them. Some have passed on after a brief time on Earth, leaving significant legacies—Ingrid Washinawatok, for one, and Richard LaCourse, for another; they are brilliant examples of productive lives. Then there are older and young ones who walk amongst us yet: former senator Ben Nighthorse Campbell; Billy Frank Jr.; the Chickasaw astronaut and Navy commander John Herrington; the Olympian Naomi Lang; Ray Fadden-Tehanetorens, grand old man of the Mohawks—representations of commitment and dedication to service, to excellence, and to contributions well made. May they represent all the heroes—young and old—who do their duty by their families and nations, by their professions, and by their communities. "To honor, honors," wrote a great poet once. Indian country's heroes need recognition, for us, for them, and for the generations. They are found in every family, in every tribe, and in every nation.

Let Us Remember Ingrid, Flying Eagle Woman
March 15, 2000

Family and friends around the world recently memorialized Ingrid Washinawatok on the one-year anniversary since her tragic loss. At one event in New York City's American Indian Community House, several hundred people came out over two days. The one-year feast was held; more than a dozen spoke about Ingrid's superlative human quality.

Ingrid Washinawatok El-Issa is a true American Indian martyr. Highly loved, highly skilled, highly dedicated, she died while bravely confronting the violence of war-torn Colombia on a mission to help out a Native people. Reared in a family that was at the forefront of the Menominee Restoration movement, she had matured into a dedicated warrior for Indian sovereignty. As one of her friends said, "Ingrid walked the walk."

She was very special. She was a born activist who loved the people. She never spoke a bad word of anyone; she commanded mammoth respect and affection. She knew the issues, stood up in the trenches, cooked all day with the elderly ladies, attended international forums, leveraged funds from foundations for Indian projects, created major projects, such as the Indigenous Women's Network and the Fund for the Four Directions; Ingrid Washinawatok, in her forty-one short years upon the Mother Earth, was one superbly positioned Native activist who followed her heart while moving in bold, certain, and practical steps to create opportunities for Indian people.

Deeply rooted in tradition, Ingrid was a modern woman. She was a woman of powerful projects and of even more powerful projection. Young, gifted, incredibly energetic, and physically strong, she was influential in many quarters. People, from tribal elders to international figures from Desmond Tutu to Fidel Castro, were always immediately impressed by her. One speaker put it this way: "The personal and the political blended completely in Ingrid Washinawatok."

Ingrid never judged anyone, another speaker said. Someone else said: she was always for the People. She had a unique quality of love. All who spoke referred to Ingrid's ability to make each and every one feel special. Someone else declared: "Ingrid would have made a formidable elder."

Ingrid Washinawatok El-Issa should be remembered by all Native and non-Native people who value and love the People and Mother Earth. Not only in her own Menominee Nation, but all young people all over the world should be told about this courageous fighter for Indian rights—how she chose to live her life; what she struggled for and died for.

Ingrid is as close an example of a true martyr as we have seen in this modern era. This is not lightly stated. Many times she risked her life in human-rights missions on behalf of Native activists and community leaders throughout North and Latin America. It was reiterated at the New York memorial that through all her work, she was especially effective in being, as large numbers of people called her, a "best friend." Chiefs, ambassadors, foundation people, major movie personalities, tribal brethren, many, it turns out, were paying attention to her work. One speaker said: she threw forty pebbles in the lake, creating huge numbers of ripples. The ripples continue overlapping.

The spirit of Ingrid was strong, very big; it remains so. All who knew her felt it. A beacon of light, leadership illumination emanated from her. Suddenly, she was gone, killed by cowards. One year later, the elders announced through her nephew that the Thunderbeings have adopted her on the other side. She has helpers. She will help the Mother Earth and the People.

Ingrid Washinawatok, Menominee activist, was a superlative among superlatives. *Indian Country Today* makes special note on the year of her passing. We can see that relatives, friends, supporters in her many fields of endeavor have committed to sustaining her projects, her vision, and memory. Great good wishes for such a good idea. The Silvercloud Singers, Community House Drum, created a song for Ingrid's farewell feast. "We will miss you; Flying Eagle Woman; you will live in our hearts, forever," they sang.

With the founding of the Flying Eagle Woman Fund for Peace, Justice, and Sovereignty, Ingrid Washinawatok's flight of power flashes across the Western sky.

The Great Code Talkers, Tribute to the Warriors
November 8, 2000

It would not be proper to complete a year of editorials without formally registering a warm appreciation and heartfelt respect for the contribution of the Native American Code Talkers, starting with the Choctaw Code Talkers of World War I and celebrating the service of the Navajo and other code talkers of World War II; and by extension, of course, to all of the Native American men and women who served honorably in the United States armed forces throughout the twentieth century.

The valor exemplified by Native American warriors, who have always been proportionally among the highest numbers of Americans to fight in any war, is evidence of selflessness as a value in Native cultures. As one U.S. Marine commandant has said, American Indians are recognized for their "intense desire to serve."

Even before the Indian Citizenship Act, Indian people joined in military careers and specific engagements of the U.S. Armed Forces. American Indians were found among Theodore Roosevelt's Rough Riders in the Spanish American War. Roosevelt remarked on their daring and courage as advance troops. Some 13,000 American Indians served in World War I; and in World War II, some 44,000 out of 350,000 total population served in combat from 1942–1945.

Between World War II and the Korean War, five American Indians received the Congressional Medal of Honor. Another 40,000 Native people, including many women, left the reservations to serve in war-related industries. In some cases, as with the Passamaquoddy of Maine during World War I, some 100 men enlisted together with their chief, Peter Neptune.

Already in that war, early in the century, American Indians participated in all branches of the Army, including military intelligence, cavalry, medical corps, and military police. There were also Indian engineers.

Among the Oklahoma tribes the percentages were particularly high, with 30 to 60 percent of Indian men serving in the Army. The Sioux and the Chippewa each also contributed more 1,000 men to World War I.

This proud tradition characterized the record of the Navajo Code Talkers. In some ways, they exemplify the devotion and quality of service. Between 1942–1945, the Navajo Code Talkers fought with the Marines throughout the Pacific. In fact, they are credited with making possible the taking of Iwo Jima. Six Navajo worked around the clock for the first 100 days of the battle. They sent 800 messages using the code that had been devised for their language, recording no errors.

Nor were Navajo the only code talkers. Seventeen Comanche Code Talkers served the Army in Europe; Oneida, Chippewa, Sac and Fox, and Hopi Indians also served the Army Signal Corps, using their Native languages to develop secret codes. The code talkers' contribution was considered a valuable military asset and kept under secrecy for four decades after the end of World War II. These brave Americans waited nearly fifty years to be recognized.

They were celebrated formally at the White House on September 17, 1992.

The end of World War II and the process of the Korean conflict brought major changes to American Indian communities, but the tradition of military service was in evidence again during the Vietnam War, in which some 42,000 Natives fought with honor. Granada, Panama, Desert Storm, Somalia, the Balkans—American Indian soldiers were present in all of these subsequent missions and campaigns. The continuity of intense military service among American Indian people has generated the highest service record per capita of any ethnic group in North America.

It should be noted that in many a time of need around the world our noble men and women have fought ably to secure the freedoms of other peoples, to release other human beings from brutal tyrants and oppressive systems, and to protect the sovereignty of the nations of Europe, Asia, and elsewhere.

As evidenced so boldly by our American Indian veterans, the rights of peoples to be who they are, to practice their sovereignty, have at times been generally understood yet inconsistently applied by the world's great powers. We respect our veterans for recognizing these universal truths both at home and abroad.

At the end of the twentieth century, there are some 190,000 Native military veterans. We honor these men and women. In every way we can, we will support their just issues and causes.

American Indian Representations Shine Brightly at Olympics
February 15, 2002

The international Olympics, such as the Winter Games now in full swing in Utah, are wonderful opportunities for American Indian and indigenous peoples to come forth in the world arena.

The recent welcoming ceremony, which featured Shoshone, Ute, Paiute, and Goshute tribes, along with the Navajo, each offering greetings and goodwill in their own distinct native languages to the world's finest athletes— this was a great moment for tribal peoples the world over.

Thanks to the outstanding efforts of the Navajo Nation, Shoshone, Ute, Paiute, and Goshute nations, Indian country was able to project and sustain a dignified presence at these 2002 Winter Olympic Games. The Navajo Pavillion and the many other representations, always too small, always too limited, nevertheless gave ample evidence of continuity and dignity among tribal peoples to millions of viewers around the globe.

It is not easy; it never is. An Olympics is a huge undertaking. Tribal concerns, whether over cultural representation or commercial spaces, will be diverse and very competitive and squeezed by larger players into difficult quarters. Each culture has its perspective, each artist his unique way of presenting, which makes it hard to allot the proper time and space to each individual idea or display. While programmatic improvements could have enhanced the impact of exhibiting contemporary Indian realities, there were enough positive elements to make the program effective.

In 1980, the Mohawks nearly hosted the Winter Games at Lake Placid. Those were more protest-ridden times, but nevertheless, Indians carried the torch. From the great Sac and Fox Jim Thorpe, popularly voted the greatest athlete of all time, to the long, strong run of Oglala Billy Mills (1960), to Cathy Freeman, the Aboriginal heroine of the Sidney Summer games in 2000, and to this week's featured skater, Naomi Lang, the presence of indigenous peoples at the Olympic Games has grown.

Again, this trend is greatly welcome.

To Naomi Lang, Maheetahan, Karuk member Morning Star, we send this message: we are very proud of you, representing us all. In an America where public image—its strength and resonance—greatly impacts our people's potential for influence, there is little better audience than those attuned to the Olympics, nationally and internationally, to give a public presence to Native peoples and the reality of our present-day existence. You, by your effort and diligence and talent, are today representing us. Thank you, we wish you our best, and may the Great Spirit guide and protect you.

The same affirmation is also offered to Blair Burke, Choctaw Nation member from Oklahoma, who is a calf roper for the U.S. rodeo team, and Tom Reeves and Bud Longbrake, saddle bronc riders from the Cheyenne River Sioux. We watched and rooted for you and your teams.

Thanks also to the many Native runners who carried the torch, to the tribal leaders who had the foresight to travel to Greece in the ritual retrieval of the Olympic Torch, to the organizers who put in the long hours—your efforts certainly achieved excellent goals.

One tribal leader who went to Greece was Clifford Duncan, Northern Ute elder, who was enlivened by the fact that Native peoples were not thought "extinct," but instead were "recognized as a group of people."

The fact that 30,000 American Indian residents among Utah State's 2.3 million got so much attention might have irked some people, those still clinging to America's darker legacies. But through the opening ceremonies themselves, the inclusion of tribal greetings had seemed completely natural. The Indian presence was a hit.

The welcome to the world by the Native nations in Utah, each in their own language, sent a profound and powerful message and gave proper standing to Native peoples during such a significant international ceremony. Again, this was a source of pride for all. On NBC, the particular Native peoples represented were referred to as Indian nations—another positive sign to share with the world from the reality of our self-governing histories. The program's theme, "This is Indian Country," with various native singers and dancers, brought the point home that America puts its best foot forward when it embraces its first peoples, its first societies, cultures, and governments. American Indians have many friends in Europe, where the opening ceremonies were received very well, and again, in a world influenced by mass media, important connections and alliances are thus created.

Therefore a deep, heartfelt appreciation is due to the athletes and the Indian nation representatives who toiled and achieved this exceptional presentation of Indian country. Some core organizers worked very hard to make it happen. Congratulations are offered to them and gratitude is expressed for their displaying the resiliency of American Indian peoples, an important message for these troubled times.

Visions of a Native Science: Appreciation of Gregory Cajete
August 19, 2002

In a recently published book, Panchito Ramirez, a Taino elder from eastern Cuba, reminds us, "The Indian system is a science." Ramirez referred to the *conuco* system of agriculture still employed in his mountain village. This ancient companion-planting method of the Caribbean and much of indigenous Latin America is often called "the grocery store of the forest" for its diversity, fertility, and production capacity. Says the cacique, "Respect is essential. The Indian system started with that, and it can resolve human needs."

Everywhere in the hemisphere, Native elders, educators, and medicine people will assert this reality. Whether referring to *conuco* or the corn-beans-squash agronomic combination known as the "three sisters" or the "three sustainers" by Northeastern Indians, or to the extensive repertoire of natural medicinal knowledge, the continuing point made by Native cultural principles has signaled this basis of respect. Much of what is called "primitive" about indigenous peoples' ways of organizing human activity on this Earth was quite useful, practical, and pragmatic; it followed general principles that are increasingly ignored today by much of human enterprise. Perhaps humanity will pay a heavy price yet for turning a blind eye to its impacts on the natural world.

One Native intellectual from North America paying excellent attention to this theme is the Santa Clara Tewa professor, Gregory Cajete. In his wide-ranging and well-researched book, *Native Science: Natural Laws of Interdependence*, Cajete makes an excellent argument for the scientific basis of American Indian systems. Cajete picks up on the diversity and abundance of the Caribbean *conuco*; he also interprets existence from a Native relational concept. Among his comprehensive listing of "Tenets of Native Philosophy":

- All human knowledge is related to the creation of the world and the emergence of humans; therefore, human knowledge is based on human cosmology.
- Dynamic multidimensional harmony is a perpetual state of the universe.
- Humanity has an important role in the perpetuation of the natural processes of the world.
- There is significance to each natural place because each place reflects the whole order of nature.
- There are stages of initiation to knowledge.
- Elders are relied upon as the keepers of essential knowledge.
- Every "thing" is animate and has spirit.
- Dreams are gateways to creative possibilities if used wisely and practically.

The base of all the tenets: Native science integrates a spiritual orientation.

"Everything is in the practice," a Maya elder of our acquaintance often reminds his students. Cajete joins Vine Deloria Jr., Daniel Wildcat, and others who have challenged mainstream academia to consider a different base from which to conduct research and seek knowledge. As Cajete writes, in the Native context, objectivity is known to emerge from subjectivity. In this context, however, the subjectivity is tribally developed and is not simply an individualistic quest.

Congratulations are extended to all the many Native educators working to revitalize the use of Native traditional knowledge and languages. People such as Jeannette Armstrong, Darrell Kipp, Kalena Silva, and many others, all must be commended for breaking the ice-wall of disregard for Native knowledge represented in oral memory and cultural practices. The intimate tie to the nature of place is a constant of all Native beliefs and languages. They are saying: this is where science must start. Through participation and observation of untold generations, in their languages, Native peoples exhibit an "enormous knowledge base related to the natural characteristics and processes of their lands."

Thank you, Greg Cajete, for honing the Native argument. Indian educators and students are certainly listening. Perhaps the others will hear it as well.

From Six Nations, Uplink to Chickasaw Astronaut

December 6, 2002

An event of note this week: from a log cabin on an Indian reservation in eastern Ontario, Six Nations of the Grand River, *Indian Country Today* Executive Editor Tim Johnson (Mohawk) interviewed an American Indian astronaut circling the Earth some 250 miles up in space.

Directly networked to *Indian Country Today* via Houston, Navy commander John Herrington, a Chickasaw tribal member, NASA flight engineer on Shuttle mission STS-113, and a superbly trained pilot, waxed philosophical about the heavens, the Mother Earth, Indian spiritual sacraments, and the meaning of life.

For many of us, it was the experience of a generation—to see and hear an Indian-to-Indian uplink to the heavens. Perhaps this event, as momentous as it was, is not as pressing as are the many political and economic issues confronting tribes. But regardless of that argument, and regardless too of opinions on the merits or demerits of purposes and technologies of the space program, we felt a great honor to interview one of our own, an Indian tribal citizen, at another pinnacle of American and global scientific achievement.

To this newspaper's communications group, that such a conversation could take place signaled one of those marker-in-time moments of the first decade of the twenty-first century. Remember that in 1900, Native peoples were considered "vanishing Americans." Here, more than one hundred years later, a brave and vigorous American Indian astronaut walks in outer space. Less than half a century after the first manned space explorations, an American Indian has achieved his own dream, a transcendental vision to fly into the Skyworld. The resulting story reveals a great new hero role model for Indian and indeed all youngsters. It provides a great reality to contemplate at the start of the new millennium.

We salute John Herrington: NASA mission specialist, a master of hard sciences, a person endowed with excellent physical dexterity, Herrington has sustained his tribal identity throughout an arduous career as Navy pilot and astronaut. In his quiet demeanor often noted by his colleagues, in his superb accomplishment, and in his willingness to grasp the meaning of his Indian identity, we find a role model of the highest quality.

Herrington is modest enough not to have recognized his own unique example, but his Chickasaw Nation and all of Indian country does. It is an Indian value to recognize courage (heart) and intelligence in following a dream, in the fulfillment of one's vision. The boy who sat in a cardboard box in Black Forest, Colorado, and dreamed he was an Apollo astronaut going to the moon has now flown beyond the Earth, and he was impressed with "how insignificant we are in the great scheme of things."

It was a tremendous thing just to talk to an astronaut on the hoof, Earth to orbit, but to sustain an actual indigenous conversation, one that pondered the great mystery and gave glimpses of our common sentiments on the sacred, this was of particular magnitude. Experiencing the grandiosity of the Cosmos, said Harrington, gave a "spiritual sense" of how grand was the reality of life, of "how grand is the grand scheme of Mother Earth." Imagine that, an astronaut, engineer, and pilot speaking to the whole planet about the grandness of "Mother Earth."

Commander Herrington shared an anecdote of great interest: although he was not allowed by NASA to take sacramental tobacco out into space, he and "a very good friend," used tobacco to "smudge ... outside of crew quarters prior to flight, recognizing, using smoke for purification."

Commander Herrington flew with the feather of an eagle; he carried sweetgrass and other medicines "that represent the spiritual sense we all feel." He traveled Skyworld territory not only as an American Navy officer, but as an American Indian, as a Chickasaw. Herrington speaks in two currents: he is the modest, pragmatic astronaut (flight engineer); he is a member and representative of his tribal nation.

Editor Johnson, whose Mohawk family includes ironworkers, observed that Herrington's mission, which involved steel construction on the space station during a risky spacewalk, qualified him "the first Indian steelworker or construction worker in space." Herrington responded by citing his visit to the Akwesasne Mohawk reservation on the St. Lawrence River. He recalled a monument to Mohawk ironworkers who perished when a bridge collapsed in Kahnawake in 1907. "I thought about that as I was working up here. I am working on something that is considered high steel and in my thoughts [are] condolences to those folks that perished in that mishap."

Again, to the new Indian generation this is a wonderful example of capacity and humility. From the vanishing American Indian to Indian policy makers in Washington and Ottawa; Indians at the United Nations; Indian business leaders; Indians in the cosmos. We value the exemplary life of John Herrington as a lesson in what is possible. We celebrate what it tells about the fulfillment of vision and what it signals about this time of American Indian renewal. And we encourage our young ones to aim high. For John Herrington has taught us that our potential is unlimited.

Ben Nighthorse Campbell Retires
March 12, 2004

When Ben Nighthorse Campbell, the only American Indian in the U.S. Senate, switched from Democrat to Republican in 1995, he surprised some who criticized him severely. But seasoned Indian observers saw a silver lining. An Indian senator within earshot of the Republican congressional majority was, indeed, worth having. As the Republican Party won the majority of Congress and then the White House in 2000, the logic of this position was borne out. Senator Campbell has championed all major American Indian issues in Congress. Ironically, it was the unwillingness of the Democrats then to support the Balanced Budget Amendment, among other issues, that sent him packing to the GOP.

Now that he has announced his retirement after two terms, the maverick senator that often went the extra mile for Indian issues, sometimes against his own statewide political interests, will be sorely missed. He has become a symbol of recognition and reasonable discussion for tribal interests. We hope his exit from politics does not signal the disappearance of an era when Indians could count on such dependable legislators—when Campbell and Senator Daniel Inouye, D-Hawaii, could step in and out of the chairmanship of the Senate Committee on Indian Affairs, depending on whether Democrats or Republicans controlled the powerful body.

Campbell, seventy, leaves the Senate after "much soul-searching and reflection." A brush with prostate cancer last year and an emergency hospital stop the first week of March involving chest pains apparently signaled his decision to, "return to my ranch with my family that I love."

A recent Senate ethics investigation that involves accusations by a former staff member about bonuses intended to produce kickbacks for another staffer appears not to involve the senator and he has turned over all relevant documents.

A colorful senator who sometimes showed up in a fringed jacket riding his motorcycle, Campbell is a Northern Cheyenne tribal chief, a rancher, and a distinguished artist. He is among only eight Indians to ever serve in Congress. Elected to the Senate as a Democrat in 1992, Campbell switched parties in 1995. He won again in the 1998 election as a Republican.

Campbell served Colorado well with projects from transportation to higher education to defense and aerospace industries and gets consistent kudos from fellow Colorado legislators, although certainly the jockeying for his senatorial seat has already begun.

Of particular note for Indian country, Campbell's decision means there is not likely to be an American Indian in the Senate next term. Campbell,

Northern Cheyenne, is the only Indian in the current Senate and one of only a handful to ever serve there. He has been a thoughtful champion on virtually every Native issue of note. Most recently, as *Indian Country Today* veteran Washington reporte, Jerry Reynolds noted, Campbell "oversaw the passage of a probate reform bill through an initial 'mark-up' meeting of the Senate Committee on Indian Affairs, which he chairs." Campbell has been frontline on everything from sacred sites to energy protections to Indian health to the defense of Indian economic initiatives.

He was most involved in the past season on the energy bill, which he championed for providing more power of decision making to the tribes. Dependably, he pushed for land-into-trust availability and in confirmation of tribal sovereignty while staking out a national-level position on the issue. "Dependence on foreign energy is a dangerous game," wrote the Indian senator during that initiative. "To be dependent on foreign suppliers is to be at their mercy." (U.S. Senator Ben Nighthorse Campbell: "Unlocking the potential of Indian tribal energy," *Indian Country Today*, Vol. 21, No. 45.)

Campbell: "For too long, abundant Indian energy resources have been overlooked and undervalued. The Department of Interior estimates that only 25 percent of Indian oil reserves and less than 20 percent of Indian gas reserves have been developed. Enlisting Indian tribes in the national energy effort will simultaneously help jump-start moribund Indian economies," he wrote. Campbell held up the Southern Ute Tribe of Colorado as an example of a premier natural-gas producer within the United States.

Because of his unique position as Indian rancher, tribal chief, and U.S. senator, Campbell has also been keen on cleaning up the Fractionated Heirship policy. This has been the policy of forcing progressive subdivision of tribal family allotments every generation, lands to be shared equally by all descendants. Often disallowing wills or any reasonable family dictate, the forced "equal" inheritance ad infinitum has divided and subdivided Indian homesteads so that some eighty-acre parcels have often more than 100 owners. Consensus on land use is nearly impossible in these circumstances and the land is often taken over by the Bureau of Indian Affairs for leasing to mostly non-Indian ranchers or other interests. It was a great strategy for separating Indians from useful relations with their tribal assets. As Tex Hall, chairman of the Three Affiliated Tribes in North Dakota and president of the National Congress of American Indians, reminded the Senate at that time, "President [Theodore] Roosevelt [called] the General Allotment Act ... 'a great pulverizing engine designed to crush the Indian mass.'"

Few have been able to champion solutions to the policy's tremendously negative impacts on Indian people like Ben Nighthorse Campbell. The Indian senator worked to establish a uniform interstate probate.

Inter-tribal inheritance and inheritance by nonmembers is another important area to clarify. Midwestern tribes have addressed the fractionation problem by issuing codes that will turn small portions of inherited lands into trust land for the tribe. The writing of legally sound wills is another important value.

Senator Campbell also was extremely diligent on matters of particular concern to Indian health. This resulted in increased funds and attention to diabetes prevention and treatment technology in Indian country.

A strong supporter of "contracting and compacting," Campbell sponsored the Indian Tribal Self-Governance Amendments, enacted in 2000, that made self-governance in Indian health permanent. The Indian Health Services now contracts and compacts out to tribes and tribal organizations more than 50 percent of its $2.2 billion budget.

The Indian senator from Colorado proved a loyal soldier to the Republicans and his own self-made success story has been an example of personal responsibility, self-reliance, and self-determination. His reasoning for why tribes' best interests ultimately should be identified with the Republican Party is still the most compelling.

In 2002, an *Indian Country Today* reporter asked Campbell about what each political party offers Indian country. Campbell cited a difference in their basic philosophies toward working with tribes:

> If you're trying to improve the lives of people, one way is to give more and more things, money or whatever, the other way is to put in place an atmosphere in which they can make progress on their own. I think if you talk about real sovereignty, you can't be sovereign and depend on another nation. If you're going to be sovereign, that means taking care of yourself.
>
> Democrats tend to say we're going to help Indians by making them more dependent. Republicans want to put in place things like direct pass-through money so that tribes can actually get the money they're entitled to and yet run the thing themselves.

Still, he always reiterated that the federal government had to comply with its trust responsibilities. "That's a commitment the federal government has made to tribes as separate nations," he said. His work on behalf of American Indian communities, the senator has said, was to "put those bills in place that will enable tribes to take care of themselves."

We salute U.S. Senator Ben Nighthorse Campbell upon his retirement. His commendable goals in legislation have produced an admirable standard concept and pragmatism. His tireless efforts to educate both Indians and non-Indians about how to best understand and maneuver in the American political system for maximum advantage and benefit to their communities deserve everyone's respect. Even in retiring, his focus on the importance and strength of family is an important contribution to the public discourse. We wish him health and continued strength and courage as he closes out his distinguished service in the U.S. Senate.

An Appreciation of Ray Fadden-Tehanetorens
May 25, 2004

Ray Fadden, relative and elder of several generations of the Mohawk people and legend of the Adirondack Mountains, is settling onto the bosom of the Native nation that he so loved and defended for over three quarters of a century. The noted teacher is residing at the Iakhihsohtha Home for the Elders in Tsi Snaihne, on the Canadian side of the Akwesasne Mohawk territory. As noted in *Indian Time*, the St. Regis Mohawk reservation newspaper, family and friends of the beloved elder have requested donations to help care for him in his declining years.

Donations may be sent to: The Support Fund For Elder Ray Fadden, Onake H. Corporation, P.O. Box 103, Akwesasne, N.Y., 13655. They ask that you provide a self-addressed stamped-envelope if you need and want a tax receipt.

An April 22, 2004, tribute to Ray Fadden in *Indian Time*, described the elder's highly productive and useful life this way:

> Ray Fadden has had a multi-generational influence on Akwesasne families whereby they were encouraged to take pride in their cultural heritage as Akwesasronen, as Kanienkehakaronen, Onkwehonwe, and as members of the Haudenosaunee Confederacy.
>
> Ray Fadden is well known among the Haudenosaunee communities. Since his youth he was always deeply interested in Native history, culture and traditions. He became an educator and began teaching at the elementary school at Tuscarora in the mid-1930s around the same time that he married Christine Chubb of Akwesasne. He then taught at the Mohawk School in Hogansburg starting in 1938.
>
> He has made it his life's work to teach Native American history, culture and environmental knowledge. He taught at Akwesasne for several years, and his unorthodox style of teach-

ing saw him taking students to various historic places in North America, learning first hand about Native American history. He also started a Native youth cultural awareness organization called the Akwesasne Mohawk Counselor Organization, which was comparable to the Boy Scouts. The group's concentration was on Native American history and culture.

Ray also produced 40 educational charts and approximately 20 pamphlets concerning Native history and culture. He started the Six Nations Indian Museum in Onchiota, N.Y., in the Adirondack Mountains in 1954, and he left the St. Regis Mohawk School in 1957. Ray and his family have operated this museum for 49 years. Tens of thousands of visitors from all over the world have learned from Ray Fadden during this period. From the 1930s to end of the 1990s, Ray Fadden has dedicated his life to educating Native and non-Native people about the true history of Native North American people.

Ray Fadden has a stalwart reputation among the traditional and activist families of the Six Nations people. Anyone who came to know this exceptional elder at any time during the past sixty years, which particularly includes his wide range of former students and apprentices, has been immensely inspired by his example. The man's energy and integrity of thought have impressed tens of thousands. During times when to speak of the ancestral communal history was to be branded a "communist" or a "rebel," Ray Fadden's vocal and exacting defense of Native tribal rights and his efforts to present a true history of Native life and contributions made him many opponents and enemies. There are hundreds if not thousands of stories and testimonials about the contributions and the tremendous volition of Mr. Fadden on behalf of tribal realities. Over his many years of residence in the New York mountain enclave of Onchiota, Ray Fadden not only received, personally and with great vigor, all the thousands of visitors who walked through the door, he also became the mentor of many animals of the forest, particularly to the bear, whom he befriended in the wild more than forty years of uninterrupted commitment to the medicine animal's welfare and survival.

Over time, Ray Fadden came to personify the Adirondack Mountains for all nations of Indian people and for many extended friends from many cultures and nations. Into his nineties, Fadden raised his voice against the obvious decline of habitat for animals and fish; he painstakingly documented in his oral tradition the loss of a full cycle of creation in his beloved mountains, where the bears were starving to death because of the decline of small game and berries to eat.

To follow Ray Fadden on foot to the large table of a rock where he would spread out the bones and other butcher shop leftovers for the several bear families he could identify and converse with was the biggest of thrills.

"I love these woods," Ray Fadden said to one of our editors, in 1984, during one such visit. "They are alive to me. The woods have a life of their own. From the smallest insect to the largest moose, everything has a function. It is all here for a purpose. All of them are necessary."

In the same article, the respected elder expressed the following thoughts. From "View from the Forest: An Elder's Concern" (Indian Studies, Fall, 1984):

> Now he stops by the road, near a clump of trees.
>
> "'The old Indians' way to approach nature," he says. "There was a lot of intelligence, a lot of respect to that. So, what did the priests say? That we were pagan, that we worshipped animals and trees.
>
> "That was one lie, among many. But with just that one lie they justified killing and destroying whole tribes."
>
> He steps into the trees and strokes the bark of a white birch. "Indians didn't worship trees. They talked to trees, they respected this form of life. The Christian, the European mentality couldn't understand that. To them trees, plants, animals, even whole mountains had no significance. All of that is believed to be below the human. Boy, what craziness. I wonder where they got an idea like that. They say, too. Man was created in the image of God. Boy if I were God I would be insulted. With all the destruction they have caused. How arrogant!
>
> "These birch here, any of these plants and trees, it is my belief that they are alive. The old Indians, they knew this. When the old people would pick herbs, first they would find the leader plant in the clump. They would offer tobacco and pray to that leader plant, and ask permission to pick from among her relatives. That way, it was done. But look at now, they just bulldoze a forest, cut it all, put chemicals on it."
>
> Suddenly a bumblebee flies by. Tehanetorens sights it. The bumblebee flies, then lands on a leaf. "I am glad to see this one," he says softly. "See that little bumblebee? That one is more important to the Creation than the President of the Untied States."

As reported in *Indian Time*, "Ray Fadden is ninety-three years old and now in need of the twenty-four-hour a day medical care he deserves. A decision was made to have him brought to Akwesasne and place him in the Iakhihsohtha Seniors Nursing home in the Quebec portion of Akwesasne.

There were problems bringing him to Canada because he was not registered as a Status Mohawk Indian, therefore Canada classified him as a non-Native U.S. immigrant and not eligible for any benefits from Health Canada. Regardless, the Mohawk Council of Akwesasne forthrightly honored the widely beloved elder and admitted him.

His Social Security and retirement pension covers a portion of the bill. The time that he devoted to teaching and running the museum and campaigning on behalf of Indian causes left him very little by way of any retirement benefits. The cost for his stay is more than $3,000 a month. His pension converted to Canadian funds equals $2,000 and the difference is approximately $1,000 a month.

Friends and family from the community have committed themselves to raise the difference through fund-raising activities, which will include silent auctions, sales from arts and crafts, benefit dances, both modern and traditional, and dinners. If you are able to contribute in some manner to this worthwhile effort, please do. You will have done a good thing.

Richard V. La Course (1938–2001), Indian Journalist

March 21, 2001

Suzan Shown Harjo, *Indian Country Today*

Richard V. La Course, Yakama and Umatilla, was the gold standard for Indian journalists for more than thirty years.

A founder of the Northwest Indian News Association, he also started the *Confederated Umatilla Journal* and the Colorado River Indian Tribes' paper, the *Manataba Messenger*. He was managing editor of the *Yakama Nation Review* in 1977 and its associate editor from 1989 until his passing on March 9 at age sixty-two.

Richard was born in Nespelem, Washington, where his father worked for the Bureau of Indian Affairs (BIA) on the Colville Reservation. He died not far away, in a Seattle hospital, from a postoperative stroke. His siblings and their children were with him. He liked being near his family and spent most of his life on Yakama Nation land in Washington. Now he rests with his parents in hallowed ground on the Umatilla Reservation in Oregon.

His first job was with the *Seattle Post Intelligencer* in 1969. While many Native reporters and editors worked for tribal publications, Richard was the only Indian reporter with a mainstream newspaper and the only one who went out of his way to befriend other Indians in media.

Richard contacted me and my husband, Frank Ray Harjo, Wotko Muscogee, 1947–1982, after hearing our radio program, "Seeing Red." Frank and I were producers at WBAI-FM in New York City, the flagship of free-speech radio in the late 1960s. It was a time of firsts, and ours was the first regularly broadcast Native news program in the country.

Richard had a thousand questions for us and asked them all—the kind of questions that boil down to one: "How did you get to be that way?"

After a couple of years of a terrific telephone friendship, we met at an American Indian Press Association (AIPA) conference and became even closer pals.

For those of you who know the present-day Native American Journalists Association (NAJA), with its hundreds of members and big confabs, think smaller, much smaller. The Indian journalists in the early 1970s could have met in a motel room and still had space for everyone's boxes of tribal newspapers. The broadcasters could have fit in a shower stall.

AIPA was a news service that sent out between fifteen and thirty-five stories weekly. Richard moved to Washington, D.C., in 1971 to be its news director. That meant reporting, assigning stories to precious few stringers and interns, fact-checking, editing, typing, mimeographing,* labeling, stamping, and delivering the subscribers' envelopes to the post office. (*Ancient form of paper reproduction, using a typed plastic sheet, ink, and elbow grease.)

It was great being young with Richard. It was great chasing the stories of the day. I mean the Day, as in the standoffs at Alcatraz, Ellis Island, Route 81 and the BIA building, and the killings of Leroy Shenandoah, Raymond Yellow Thunder, and many, too many more.

Richard covered most of the 1973 occupation of Wounded Knee from the Oglala Lakota Reservation in South Dakota and from nearby Nebraska. He was torn between his close personal friends on both sides of the bunkers and feared that he would join the growing list of Indians dying in unexplained single-car accidents.

That was the first of many times I heard him say, "I hope they put on my tombstone, 'He Meant Well.'"

He called in feeds for our station's newscasts every other day of the ten-week occupation. At the end of one report, I inadvertently left the tape recorder running, capturing our good-byes, the dial tone, and a man's voice saying, "Got it?" Years later, at a 1998 NAJA conference, Richard told me he had obtained documents through a Freedom of Information Act request, confirming that the FBI was tapping both of us.

Richard lived and breathed news and Indians and the ethics of journalism. He loved impossible questions and the resulting arguments no one won: which is the best paper, *Americans Before Columbus* or *Akwesasne Notes*; *The Washington Post* or *The New York Times*? Did Americans hate the Cheyennes more than other nations or did the Cheyennes just get better press? Is it more unethical to scribe a position paper for a tribal council or a dissident faction—or is either okay, so long as you don't report on it?

Then there was the biggest question of all—"Who's doing what in Washington and how are they getting away with it?"

Richard became increasingly impatient with illusive answers and with Indian and non-Indian bureaucrats and politicians who did not see him as a "real reporter" and expected him to be their press flack. He adopted a pose, perhaps from his favorite movies of the 1930s and 1940s, of a hard-bitten, hard-drinking newspaperman, churning out lots of pedestrian stories and some excellent work, furiously speed typing and burning at least one cigarette at all times.

But, try as he might, he could not disguise his true nature—compassionate, kind, humble. He gave away most of his money and lived in spartan, austere surroundings, more befitting the priest he wanted to be in seminary than the most important Native journalist of our time.

Richard slogged his way through the tough Washington beat until 1974. He called me late one night, saying he was burned out on D.C. and would I take his job. I had burned out on New York and said yes. Even today, I consider as one of my defining characteristics that Richard was my brother and colleague, and that he chose me to replace him at AIPA.

He followed his heart out West, starting all those fine tribal papers and nurturing the present and future crops of Native journalists.

I don't know if anyone will write on his headstone, "He Meant Well." If so, they need to add that Richard La Course did very, very well, too.

Navajo Code Talkers and Other Native American Heroes
August 8, 2001

Suzan Shown Harjo, *Indian Country Today*

More than a half century after they helped win World War II, the United States has paid a proper tribute to the twenty-nine original Navajo Code Talkers who invented a code in their language that the Japanese could not break.

The twenty-nine were honored with the Congressional Gold Medal, the highest award Congress confers on civilians. It seemed that official Washington was trying to make up for the six decades of lag time between the Code Talkers' essential service and the U.S. recognition of it. The tone was respectful and dignified, uncommon in the era of photo-op diplomacy.

The July 26 ceremony was convened in the Capitol Rotunda by Speaker of the House Dennis J. Hastert, R-Ill. The medals were presented by President George W. Bush in the presence of Navajo Nation President Kelsey Begaye and Speaker Edward Begay, and other dignitaries.

"Gentlemen," said Bush, "your service inspires the respect and admiration of all Americans and our gratitude is expressed for all time in the medals it is now my honor to present."

The honor came too late for most of the original code talkers. Thirteen were killed in action and eleven died since the war. Only five lived to experience the top-level appreciation. Code Talkers John Brown Jr., Allen Dale June, Chester Nez, and Lloyd Oliver received their medals in person, while the fifth, Joe Palmer, was too ill to travel. Family members received medals for Palmer and for their deceased relatives.

Brown spoke for his fellow code talkers at the ceremony and expressed their love for their Navajo Diné language, calling it "precious and sacred" and "bestowed upon us, we the Diné Nation, by the Holy People."

The president called theirs "a story that all Americans can celebrate and every American should know." He noted that the "first people" were portrayed in the paintings in the Rotunda "in the background, as if extras in the story. Yet, their own presence here in America predates all human record. Before others arrived, the story was theirs alone.

"Above all, it is a story of young Navajos who brought honor to their nation and victory to their country. The code talkers joined 44,000 Native Americans who wore the uniform in World War II. More than 12,000 Native Americans fought in World War I. Thousands more served in Korea and Vietnam, and serve to this very day."

"Military commanders have credited code talkers with (successes) in the battles of Iwo Jima, Guadalcanal, Tarawa, Saipan, and Okinawa," said Senator Jeff Bingaman, D-N.M. It was his legislation last year that authorized the gold medals for the original twenty-nine code talkers and silver medals for some 400 who followed.

The twenty-nine Navajos developed the code under wartime pressure. Then they and hundreds of other Navajo radio operators transmitted military messages that could not be deciphered. The Navy and Marine Corps WWII Commemorative Committee found that they "took part in every assault the U.S. Marines conducted in the Pacific from 1942 to 1945."

One of the original Navajo Code Talkers was the artist Carl N. Gorman, who lived until 1998. A dozen years ago in Navajoland, he explained to me that no outsider could ever break their code because they used their language in ways known only to their small circle, kept the code in their heads, and maintained the code of silence.

Gorman recalled being stuck for a word for Italy. One of his comrades came up with the answer, saying, "I met an Italian one time and he looked this way." He said they took a phrase in their language describing a single aspect of one man's recollection of another, condensed it, and made that the code word for Italy.

"At the end of the war, these unsung heroes returned to their homes on buses, no parades, no fanfare, no special recognition for what they had truly accomplished," Bingaman said. Only after the code was declassified in 1968, "did a realization of the sacrifice and valor of these brave Native Americans begin to emerge."

The Navajo Code Talkers were not unheralded in the past. They received Certificates of Appreciation from President Richard M. Nixon in 1971. President Ronald Reagan proclaimed August 14, 1982, as National Navajo Code Talker Day and they were recognized in a 1992 ceremony at the Pentagon.

"Think of this," Senator Ben Nighthorse Campbell, R-Colo., said in his

Senate floor statement, "just seventy-seven years before (WWII), the grand-fathers of these heroes were forced at gunpoint with 9,000 other Navajos from their homeland and marched 300 miles through the burning desert. For four long years the Navajo people were interned at the Bosque Redondo.

"For these men and their comrades to rise above that injustice in American history and put their lives on the line speaks of their character and their patriotism," said Campbell, who is Cheyenne.

Bush quoted one of the code talkers as having said, "The code word for America was 'Our Mother.' 'Our Mother' stood for freedom, our religion, our ways of life, and that's why we went in."

The only misstep in the hour-long ceremony was an odd moment of failed staff work reminiscent of President Bill Clinton's erroneous claim that his 1994 meeting with American Indian leaders was a first for any White House or U.S. president.

"Twenty-four Native Americans have earned the highest military distinction of all, including Ernest Childers, who was my guest at the White House last week," Bush said.

Childers was the first Native American awarded the Medal of Honor, for heroic action in 1943 in Oliveto, Italy, with Company C of the 45th Infantry Division Thunderbirds. It certainly was appropriate for Bush to mention Childers, but he has not been the president's guest.

I called Colonel Childers through my father, who was his schoolmate at Chilocco Indian School and a fellow Company C combat veteran, to ask how it was to be a guest in the Bush White House. He's met with nearly all the presidents since the war and was happy for the invitation from this one, he said, but poor health kept him from traveling outside Oklahoma. He was glad that Bush gave out the medals.

"It's about time the Navajos were honored for their great achievement in strategy," said Childers, who is Bird Clan Muscogee and president of the Mvskoke Red Stick Society for combat veterans. He recalled how the "Company C men communicated on the walkie-talkies or out on patrol in Muscogee or Cherokee or our other languages and used our different signals and noises, horse laughs, roosters crowing for 'Be Aware' or 'I'm Coming' or 'I'm Over Here.'"

Native warriors have used their languages to help the United States win wars from the Revolutionary War onward. The first who were known as a code-talking unit were the Choctaw Code Talkers in World War I. Scholars have identified a score of other code-talking groups in wars of the 1900s, including Cherokee, Cheyenne, Chippewa, Comanche, Dakota, Hopi, Kiowa, Lakota, Menominee, Muscogee, Oneida, Osage, Pawnee, Sac and Fox, Seminole, and Yankton Sioux.

Nearly all the American Indian code talkers were forbidden to speak their Native languages when they were students in federal boarding schools. One who was beaten for speaking his Comanche language was Charles Chibitty, the last survivor of the seventeen-member Comanche Code Talkers unit of the 4th Signal Company.

The Comanche Code Talkers were recognized in 1999 with the Knowlton Award for distinction in Army intelligence. Chibitty received the honor in a ceremony in the Pentagon, where he kept repeating a question, "Why did they wait so long to recognize us?"

The code talkers, at least the Navajo ones, will be recognized by Hollywood next, in an MGM movie, "Windtalkers," set to open on November 9, during Native American Heritage Month and just before Veterans Day.

Billy Frank Jr., A Warrior with Wisdom and an Elder with Courage
January 5, 2004

Suzan Shown Harjo, *Indian Country Today*

You know you have a blessed life when your friends are among the most impressive and wonderful people you've ever met or read about or seen on TV. Billy Frank Jr. is just such a friend.

From his Pacific Northwest home to Capitol Hill and back by any route, hundreds of diverse people in ordinary and lofty places consider Billy Frank a good friend, even a best friend. No matter what clout, net worth, education, or position they may have, he treats everyone equally well, and people change into their best selves around him.

Billy Frank Jr. is being awarded *Indian Country Today*'s first Visionary Award. He deserves it.

Chair of the Northwest Indian Fisheries Commission for a quarter of a century, he is a strong advocate, an effective negotiator, and a peacemaker who has successfully turned polarized fights over resources into combined efforts to save and enhance salmon, shellfish, trees, endangered species, and entire ecosystems.

Sincere and still in ceremony and joyous and buoyant in celebration, he has dedicated his life to serving and protecting Native peoples, the land, the water, and all living beings.

"As I travel around the country, I see a lot of tribes still down, and Indians eating surplus food and selling beer bottles—we've all been there and we don't want to be there again," says Frank.

"We need to get the infrastructure up and strong for all the tribes. We're on the right course, getting more elders' housing, circulating more capital. Our gaming tribes are always on the move to expand, but we need to be buying land back, too, and our watersheds and aquifers, whole aquifers, because we don't know what they're doing to our water."

And that's Billy—for every situation, a gentle nudge or a jump-start in the direction of a plan, a big idea.

Everyone calls him Billy, even at seventy-two. His father, William Frank Sr., answered to the name Willie for all of his 104 years. Billy's youngest son, twenty-one, is named Willie Frank, too.

The Franks come from generations of Nisqually families who fished along the Nisqually River. Their fishing rights were affirmed by the United States in the 1854 Medicine Creek Treaty with the Nisqually, Puyallup, and Squaxin Island nations.

Billy's large, extended family starts with the Frank's Landing Indian Community, just outside Olympia, Washington Named after his father, the Landing is home to the WaHeLut Indian School, which is governed by Billy's sister Maiselle Bridges, the Community's beloved matriarch, and her daughters Alison Gottfriedson and Suzette Bridges (both Nisqually and Puyallup).

"Billy is great with adults, but he's even better with children," says writer Hank Adams, Assiniboine and Sioux, a community member, advisor, and strategist since the mid-1960s. "He talks to a lot of students, from preschool to college, and of all races. And for fifty years in a large family of relatives, he's missed very few celebrations of birthdays for each of their children."

"That's it," says Billy. "That's our vision, educating ourselves, making our own people strong. They're there, our Indian kids. Our little guys are talking their own language and teaching it to their parents. These younger kids are waking up and getting ready to take our place."

Frank's Landing was at the heart of the fish wars on the water and in the court. On one side were more than twenty Native nations and the federal government asserting that federal-tribal treaties provided for Indian fishing in Washington. On the other side were the states' "rights" to ignore treaties, stop Indians from fishing, and jail resisters.

Both Billy and Willie Frank were witnesses in federal Judge George H. Boldt's 1973 trial in United States vs. Washington. Willie testified about the Nisqually origin and history in their traditional homelands and waterways of the Nisqually River, where they fished for food, ceremony, and trade.

Billy testified about decades of being battered and jailed for fishing by the state's fish and game wardens. His first of more than fifty arrests was in 1945, when he was only fourteen. His oldest son, Tobin ("Sugar"), was first arrested for fishing in 1970, when he was nine.

A few months after the trial, on February 12, 1974, Judge Boldt ruled that Indian treaty fishers could take 50 percent of the allowable catch of salmon and steelhead for ceremonies, commerce, and subsistence, and could fish in their usual and accustomed fishing places, both on and off the reservations.

The state appealed the Indians' victory. The 9th Circuit Court of Appeals wrote its own decision in favor of treaty fishing, upholding the Boldt principles. The state appealed to the U.S. Supreme Court.

In the meantime, Indians were still being hunted for fishing and, in the nation's Capitol, some of the incoming was friendly fire. After oral arguments to the high court, the top natural resources official in the Justice Department tried to convince various tribal leaders to settle at 15 percent or 20 percent of the harvestable fish catch, saying they would lose and end up with 0 percent.

Billy was one of the main people who convinced the others to not run scared. On July 2, 1979, the Supreme Court affirmed the appellate decision. Washington, which had fought treaty fishing in the federal courts five times that century, was chided for its recalcitrance and told not to bring the case back to court. It was a resounding win for Indian treaty rights.

"I always thought Billy was the model for Billy Jack—the solitary guy who is everywhere protecting the people and their rights," said Vine Deloria Jr., Standing Rock Sioux, author, historian, attorney, and a longtime friend of Billy's.

"You can't begin to count the times he had been beaten and thrown in jail," said Deloria. "Yet, in the end, he has become a senior statesman of the state of Washington, respected and admired by people all over the state who once called for his scalp.

"He shows what a few people can do when they stand up for principles."

Billy says he's "really proud of what we've all done in our time. We're still the bad guys every time we walk through the door. We've still got the right-wingers telling everyone we're not here. But, we're not underground anymore and we are finally getting society's attention.

"We've just got to stay on the front lines as long as we can. There's nobody that we're afraid to sit down and negotiate with, because we have our teams of experts and lawyers, and we still have people in Congress who know what's right."

Adams says that Billy's life is a "testament to how much can be built for a society and a people from selflessness. He's drawn that from his family and he's carried it to all the Indian nations of the Northwest, whom he serves constantly—with little sleep and with regular sixteen- to twenty-hour days. He's always adding on the mileage to his 'fish wagon.' And now, with cell-phone technology, his drive time is work time, too."

Billy's mind is "steeped in a living history that goes back three centuries," says Adams. "Canoes in his life sprang from seed that long ago. In testimony for one of the Boldt trials, he told of the creation of Indian people here, when lifted from the beach by an eagle or thunderbird and emerging from the shell of a clam. He could feel Creation's lingering grains upon him while testifying, and gestured to brush some off and away into the courtroom."

Adams predicts that Billy's "personal legacy" will be that "Indian children of a century coming shall yet know a great deal about those original sands and the First People."

"Here's our vision, too," says Billy, "and a hope. We are taking our place in society, and we need time. We have to hope that society gives us time to manage our money and bring back all our animals and eagles. That will take time. If we can heal all that stuff that's between us—between tribes, Indians, and non-Indians—and keep going, we can do it all."

Our Cheyenne people say we should choose our friends as we would choose people to take into battle. I would go into battle with Billy any time. Not only is he fearless and loyal in the fight, but he can be counted on to make the peace that must follow. That is visionary.

John Herrington

COMMANDER, USN ` NASA ASTRONAUT

First Native in Space

Billy Frank Jr.
AMERICAN INDIAN VISIONARY
2 0 0 4

EPILOGUE

'It Is Complete:' Trends Four Years into the Century
December 22, 2004

One of our dear columnists, Mohawk midwife Katsi Cook, often reminds her home audiences that the Mohawk word for the number four, is also the same word and expresses a related meaning for the concept "thus, it is complete."

In that vein, the past four cycles of the grandfather and elder brother, the Sun, are coming to "completeness" with the first four years of the twenty-first century, which turns within the beginning of the third millennium after the birth of the Judeo-Christian Messiah. It is the season ...

Whether we celebrate Christmas or not, believe that Jesus Christ is the One or just one of many noteworthy and luminary figures in human history, it is proper to acknowledge Creation at this time of the year, which in the northern latitudes ushers in a season of rest (under a white blanket of snow) for Mother Earth, while in tropical latitudes the Four Winds hold back the rains and assist the Earth to purify herself through a dryness that cleanses plants and trees of many parasites.

If only human history had such predictable or orderly cycles. While nature, indeed, does all it can to consistently harmonize the existence of the multiple life and energy currents that it generates, the progression of human events upon its surface manifests little such rhyme or reason; rather, by and large, humanity's trajectory appears propelled by cultural and religious distinctions and, all too often, hatreds, and by the lower passions—mainly greed and fear—manipulated by those who seek to acquire and sustain power. In reaction, what we are witnessing around the world is the rise of the religious zealots who set out as defenders of their own perfect utopias.

Signaled initially in America by the emergence of the Christian moral majority, this is a movement that all too easily takes the reins of power with the election of George W. Bush in 2000. The ultraconservative Texas Republican began as a compassionate conservative and has ushered in an American neoconservative era in world politics. American supremacy in all matters is now seen as the primary policy goal. Since September 11, 2001, this impetus takes on a global dimension and also a nearly complete, unchallenged dominion on how and where to direct the federal budget.

For Democrats and the whole progressive wing of America, a new definition has begun, based on taking the fight to the finish line in 2004 and working in unity for the first time in a generation, yet losing by a hair once again. Vigorous "open-minded" (read liberal) dialogue is at a premium. But harping and yelping will not do. Only sound alternatives and clear positions that challenge negative trends in society will fuel this movement.

Through the closely divided American body politic squeaks in the reality of tribal existence; the Indian voting base exploded into action for the election of 2004, impacting less than predicted yet growing in campaigning skills and in the knowledge that participation in state and national political currents is supremely important at this time in history. American Indian tribal sovereignty, articulated and practiced in every possible way, remains the goal of tribal nations and their governments. This recognizable and self-identified sector of America needs to coalesce even tighter into a collective approach to their common defense. Economic gains must continue to translate into improved social conditions and political clout across the board of Indian communities.

It will be a different century as a result of these past four years, a new era is perhaps upon us, one that ushers in:

- "The Preemptive War Policy." The preemptive, and some would say perpetual, war option has substantially escalated a climate of contempt of the United States by most peoples in the world. In fact, the action of attacking a country that had nothing to do with the terrorist attacks of 9-11 quickly reversed world sympathy and alliance into world derision and opposition. Beyond the natural and expected response to the 9-11 attacks from the United States, the current policy implies a much deeper and wider (and hugely expensive) military imposition by the world's only superpower. The reaction by most of the world, including many U.S. allies, has been extremely negative. America itself now runs the risk of becoming a "pariah" nation whose mighty economic power needs to be checked. This has never been so prevalent before and it is not good news for Americans and any people associated with the American interests internationally.

- "An America in hock." America is trillions of dollars in debt, and growing, as hugely expensive devices are blown up in wars while corporate and private wealth has become exempt from social responsibility at many levels. American baby boomers from the 1940s and 1950s are concerned about their social security. Services that once could sustain an American safety net for people through tough economic times are being seriously diminished. Common citizens seem to be getting lost in the tumble.

- "Exported middle-class." Outsourcing as a concept goes from occasional practice to major international trend. As so-called American corporations increasingly look toward global workforces, American labor now must compete directly with the rest of the world's low-wage labor market. The middle-class runs the risk of shrinking as rapidly as the world's glaciers as the disparity between America's rich and poor grows ever larger. The average American family is squeezed while wealth continues to concentrate in an ever-smaller percentage of the people. American Indian businesses and major tribal enterprises are notoriously of place and in place and highly unlikely ever to migrate or relocate, once established and successful. They stand in sharp contrast to the fickle loyalties practiced by many American corporations.

- "Acute ecological devastation." Environmental consciousness and practice has been set back, attacked as retrograde and anticorporate. Maximizing profits trumps just about any environmental concern in the current vogue. The global-warming trend and its clear causes in this era of massive fossil-fuel burning is obvious to the world and most of science, but not to the political champions of industrial expansion now in power. Science be damned on this question as "more research" is called for by ideological economists.

- "Mumbo-jumbo policy making based on religious faith." Scientific methodology is under attack in many parts of America and around the world. Politicians and even religious leaders denigrate it and try to inject their ideologies into it. Admittedly, science is not perfect, but the scientific method, informed by common sense, rational, inquisitive processes, and human intellectual values, is nevertheless humanity's best common standard for human development and advancement. We say this with the highest respect for all religious philosophy and practice that value enlightenment and tolerance, but we also greatly value the scientific method for its ability to discern rote belief from determined fact.

- "Corporate media increasingly geared to affluence, power, and political persuasion." The poor and dispossessed are not in vogue but out of sight and out of mind. American Indians, always on the media margins, grow in relevance with the growth of financial means. The concept of Native tribal rights has been projected into the public discourse as tens of millions of mainstream Americans visit and spend both time and money at Native-owned casinos. American Indian tribal political power, for decades a mere concept, now asserts itself with economic clout. This is new. Indian people, the most fiercely independent of Americans because of their inherent and preexisting governmental sovereignty, are now found among the country's economic power brokers. But huge problems persist, challenges remain for the communities to overcome, in both business management and governance that could and should help tackle social misery. The story of American Indian resurgence is wonderful and uplifting if incomplete, but the tribes are being recast again as America's enemies in a manipulated, and sometimes compliant, media as despicable "rip-offs" and greedy "special interests." The battle for America's hearts and minds about Indian country must be won by the tribes. This is the key campaign of the next four years.

- "Anti-Indian organizing." Coalitions of groups opposed to American Indian governance and cultural rights surface nationally once again. This time they are more sophisticated than ever and tied in to larger political machines. In an era of constant attack against ethnic forms of social and political organization as "special interests," the concept and practice of Indian rights within American jurisprudence has many vigorous enemies. This is nothing new to any American Indian student of history, but nonetheless, ignorance fueled by hatred of American Indians is again on the march in America. Tribal leaders are warned to take this development very seriously.

- "States want Indian property, again." States of the Union pull off the surgical gloves and grasp for the butcher knife as governors come after Indian financial gains with a greed lust not seen since the Termination Era of the 1950s. New York, California, Minnesota, Wisconsin, and Oklahoma are among the states putting Indian tribes against the wall and shaking them down, often successfully pitting Indian nation against Indian nation. It is a shameless conduct by some of the world's largest economies to grovel after Indian money, considering the great need nationally by tribal communities. It is also confusing as to why some Indian governments would so willingly hand over millions, if not billions, to the states when so much of Indian country needs those resources more.

- "Tribal investment and philanthropy begins to grow." This is crucial. There needs to be a lot of it going on. The "Top 100 Club" of American Indian nations—in the context of tribal revenues—needs to float a major "no tribe left behind" national development bond—in the billions. They need to encourage and sustain the move to business and self-help initiatives among disadvantaged tribes. "Buy Indian" emerges as a must-do operational directive to all tribal establishments. This is not easily done, even by the strongest of tribal leaders. They are often reluctant to interfere in their own tribal enterprises. Proper and efficacious purchasing is a crucial part of running a profitable enterprise and is understandably guarded. Nevertheless, the "Top 100" Indian economies must reach out and build the capacity for other Indians to do business, always.

- "The Smithsonian Institution's National Museum of the American Indian (NMAI) opens to great enthusiasm." Finally, there is an Indian place on the Washington Mall. It is a place of culture that the communities can inform and that employs many superlative Indian people. An expected 4 million visitors will experience the museum every year. The NMAI opening was dampened only by some critiques of the opening exhibits and core messages, but its prominent position as a fixture of Indian experience and existence in the nation's capital, combined with its ongoing commitment to excellence, serves as a powerful symbol of a hemispheric recognition and honor long overdue.

- "The plight of Indian corn." At once symbolic and completely necessary, the survival of the open-pollinated corn varieties developed over millennia by Indian farmers, particularly those within Mexico and Mesoamerica, is seriously in jeopardy. Hybrid varieties created in North American labs are beginning to contaminate the open varieties propagated by local farmers for millennia. Here is a case of science, corporate science, going awry of the current and ultimate needs of humanity, how to live on the land with respect and spiritual balance.

In many Indian communities, concurrent with the greatest higher education initiative in the history of Native peoples, and aparallel to the explosion in tribal economics, going back to the roots of cultural tradition is still the mode for many young people, as interest in the longhouse, the Sun Dance, the Kiva, and other Native lifeways continues to grow; the effort to appreciate and build the families that make community is palpable. Intense and loving attention to the proper growth and development of the upcoming generations—this is the message of the Indian country of America on these early years of new Millennium.

CONTRIBUTORS

James R. Adams, Ph.D., is associate editor of *Indian Country Today.* Adams' career includes thirteen years on the editorial page of *The Wall Street Journal,* first as editorial and feature writer and then as member of the Editorial Board; a stint as senior editor at *Forbes Magazine*; and the publication of three books on fiscal and banking policy.

Rebecca Adamson, is the former president and founder of First Nations Development Institute and a columnist for *Indian Country Today.*

José Barreiro, Ph.D., member of the Taino Nation of the Antilles, is senior editor of *Indian Country Today.* For eighteen years, he helped forge the American Indian Program at Cornell University, where he served as associate director of Akwe:kon Press. Barreiro has edited several books on indigenous topics, and is the author of the novel *The Indian Chronicles.*

Marty Two Bulls, Oglala Lakota from Pine Ridge, is *Indian Country Today*'s editorial cartoonist. His career as a graphics illustrator and editor has included positions at several newspapers, including the *Rapid City Journal,* the *Argus Leader,* and the *Lakota Journal.*

Ben Nighthorse Campbell, Northern Cheyenne, is a former member of the U.S. Senate, U.S. House of Representatives, and Colorado State Legislature. Campbell championed legislation that supported American Indian economic, educational, energy, health, and trust reform, as well as cultural interests, during an era of remarkable advancement for Indian country. He currently serves as senior policy advisor to the law firm of Holland & Knight, LLP.

Katsi Cook, Akwesasne Mohawk, is a traditional midwife and director of the Iewerokwas Program. She is a columnist for *Indian Country Today.*

Kevin Gover, Pawnee, is a professor of law at Arizona State University's College of Law and an affiliate professor of the American Indian studies program. Gover was the former assistant secretary of the U.S. Department of the Interior, where he oversaw the operations of the Bureau of Indian Affairs and its programs. He was a columnist for *Indian Country Today*.

John Guevremont, Mashantucket Pequot, is chief operating officer of Pequot Enterprises. A lifelong Republican, he has been active in Connecticut and national politics and was a delegate to the 2000 and 2004 Republican National Conventions, where he was instrumental in providing the language for the convention's Native American platform.

Suzan Shown Harjo, Cheyenne and Hodulgee Muscogee, is president of the Morning Star Institute in Washington, D.C., and a columnist for *Indian Country Today*. Since 1975, she has been instrumental in the development of key federal Indian law, including the important national policy advances for the protection of Native American cultures and arts.

Pete Homer, Mojave/Shasta, president and CEO of the National Indian Business Association, has more than three decades of experience in economic development. He is an enrolled member of the Colorado River Indian Tribes of Arizona.

Tim Johnson, Mohawk, executive editor of *Indian Country Today*, has launched or remodeled several of the leading and most influential American Indian publications in the country including *Indian Country Today*; *American Indian*, the quarterly magazine serving the National Museum of the American Indian (NMAI); and *Native Americas*.

Winona LaDuke, an Ojibwe from the White Earth Reservation, is program director of Honor the Earth, a national Native American environmental justice program. She served as the Green Party vice presidential candidate in the 1996 and 2000 elections.

Maurice B. Lyons is tribal chairman of the Morongo Band of Mission Indians. Chairman Lyons works with both state and federal legislators on Indian issues and matters affecting tribal government and economic development.

Steven Paul McSloy is cochair of the Native American practice at Hughes Hubbard & Reed, LLP, in New York City, where he specializes in corporate and finance matters involving Indian nations. He was formerly general counsel of the Oneida Indian Nation of New York and a professor of American Indian law. The views expressed herein are the author's personal views and do not represent official positions of Hughes Hubbard & Reed, LLP, or the Oneida Indian Nation of New York.

John C. Mohawk, Ph.D., is a member of the Seneca Nation and a columnist for *Indian Country Today*. He is associate professor of American Studies and director of indigenous studies at the State University of New York at Buffalo.

Harold A. Monteau is a member of the Chippewa Cree Tribe of the Rocky Boy's Reservation and a partner with the law firm Monteau & Peebles, LLP.

Steven Newcomb, Shawnee and Lenape, is indigenous law research coordinator at Kumeyaay Community College, located on the reservation of the Sycuan Band of the Kumeyaay Nation, cofounder and codirector of the Indigenous Law Institute, and a columnist for *Indian Country Today*.

Rachel Attituq Qitsualik was born into a traditional Igloolik Inuit lifestyle. She has worked in Inuit sociopolitical issues for the last twenty-five years and witnessed the full transition of her culture into the modern world. She is a columnist for *Indian Country Today*.

Charles E. Trimble is an Oglala Lakota from the Pine Ridge Indian Reservation. He was a principal founder of the American Indian Press Association in 1970 and served as executive director of the National Congress of American Indians from 1972–1978. He is president of Red Willow Institute in Omaha, Nebraska, and a columnist for *Indian Country Today*.

Carey N. Vicenti, a member of the Jicarilla Apache Nation of northwest New Mexico, currently serves as an assistant professor of sociology at Fort Lewis College in Durango, Colorado. He sits as a judicial official for several American Indian nations and was a columnist for *Indian Country Today*.

David E. Wilkins, Lumbee, is a professor of American Indian studies at the University of Minnesota and frequently writes guest columns for *Indian Country Today*.

INDEX